Building Global Labor Solidarity

Building Global Labor Solidarity

Lessons from the Philippines, South Africa, Northwestern Europe, and the United States

Kim Scipes

LEXINGTON BOOKS
Lanham • Boulder • New York • London

Published by Lexington Books
Lexington Books is an imprint of The Rowman & Littlefield Publishing Group, Inc.
4501 Forbes Boulevard, Suite 200, Lanham, Maryland 20706
www.rowman.com

6 Tinworth Street, London SE11 5AL, United Kingdom

British Library Cataloguing in Publication Information Available

Library of Congress Cataloging-in-Publication Data Available

ISBN: 978-1-7936-3150-3 (cloth)
ISBN: 978-1-7936-3151-0 (electronic)

This book is dedicated to the late Wenilou "Weng" Pradel,
the woman who introduced me to the KMU, and inspired me
to go to the Philippines to check it out. Mabuhay, Weng!

This book is also dedicated to the memory of the late Ka Bel,
Crispin Beltran, former National Chairperson, *Kilusang Mayo Uno* (KMU)
Labor Center of the Philippines. Mabuhay, Ka Bel!

Further, it is dedicated to all the women and men around the world,
in the Philippines and everywhere else, who have struggled for
or are struggling to make real the idea of global labor solidarity!

Contents

Preface

There are a growing number of labor activists and scholars around the world who believe working people are important, and who see building global labor solidarity as an essential part of advancing the positions of workers in the struggle for a better world, as well as advancing the overall struggle. This book is intended to contribute to that process.

However, while building global labor solidarity is a necessary task, it is not sufficient: we *must* revitalize our domestic labor organizations. Yet building global labor solidarity can help domestic struggles by introducing workers in "home" countries to struggles elsewhere, to new types of trade unionism developed, and to tactics and strategies developed in "other" countries that may suggest ways forward in the home countries.

In other words, we do not separate advancing labor at home (in any country) from advancing labor abroad—they are not dichotomous categories—but we see them as connected and intertwined, meaning that sometimes one area will be prioritized while the other is seen as secondary, and at other times, the emphasis will be reversed.

Accordingly, there have been previous eras over the past 175 years or so where building labor solidarity across borders has moved to the forefront, and while we see a new round beginning in 2011–2013—with the Arab Spring and particularly with the labor struggles in Egypt (see Mason, 2012)—the previous round of building global labor solidarity began in the period 1978–80.[1]

1978–2010

The 1978–80 period saw a number of developments that would advance the struggle for international labor solidarity. These included the initiation of militant strikes by the Sao Paulo Metalworkers against multinational auto companies that were the economic bulwark of the Brazilian military dictatorship (see TIE, 1984);[2] the publication of a book by Don Thomson and Rodney Larson (1978) titled *Where Were You, Brother? An Account of Trade Union Imperialism,* which condemned the British Trade Union Congress for working against the interests of workers in the countries of the former British Empire;[3] and the initiation of NILS, the *Newsletter of International Labour Studies,* by Peter Waterman. In 1979, FOSATU (Federation of South African Trade Unions) was founded in that country (see MacShane, Plaut and Ward, 1984).[4] And on May 1, 1980, unions across the Philippines united to create the *Kilusang Mayo Uno* (KMU–May First Movement) (see Scipes, 1996), while in August of that year, Polish workers created *Solidarnosc* (MacDonald, 1981; see Garton Ash, 1983; Bernhard, 1993; and Bloom, 2014).

This era certainly continued from 1978 until 1997, which saw the publication of Kim Moody's *Workers in a Lean World: Unions in the International Economy.* For one example, see Brooks and McCallum (2017).[5] However, the era arguably continued until about 2010, as signified by the publication of Jeffrey Sluyter-Beltrão's (2010) book on new unionism in Brazil and this author's book (and subsequent article) on the AFL-CIO's foreign policy program (Scipes, 2010a, b; see also Scipes, 2016a).

This 1978–2010 era is one that is only partially known by most activists, and it is still affecting developments today, although mainly through misrepresentations and misunderstandings.

The theoretical concept that unifies this 1978–2010 era is "social movement unionism."

Researchers had discovered a new type of trade unionism being developed by the CUT in Brazil, the KMU in the Philippines, FOSATU/COSATU in South Africa, and by the newly emerging trade unions in South Korea, and Peter Waterman advanced the concept of "social movement unionism" (SMU) to refer to it (Waterman, 1988e). Trying to understand it as a different type of trade unionism, these researchers began an international discussion of how it should be understood, and in a way that would encourage workers in other countries to develop it as well.

However, based on the writings of Gay Seidman (1994)—who used the term SMU, but who was not part of the international discussion—Kim Moody (1997) later applied this term to a qualitatively different social phenomena: "new" trade union developments in the United States. This inappropriate application of the concept of social movement unionism to union developments in the US led to massive theoretical confusion that still exists today—among researchers in both developed and developing countries—undermining the importance of developments among these three labor centers.[6]

This theoretical confusion was not disentangled until 2014, when this author re-engaged with the subject and untangled it (Scipes, 2014c—see Chapter 13, herein).

However, by using writings of this one worker/labor activist/researcher/scholar, the purpose of this collection is threefold: to try to raise awareness of labor efforts and better understand this 1978–2010 era by focusing on creation and advancement of the KMU Labor Center of the Philippines, as well as FOSATU/COSATU in South Africa; to reclaim the power of the concept of social movement unionism while advancing a new "form" (or "subset") of trade unionism that will properly serve to help develop theoretically the new developments among unions in particularly North America; and to learn about KMU's conscious efforts to build international labor solidarity over the past 35+ years, a project that, as far as can be determined, is unique.

Key to this process, it is argued, is evaluating previous efforts to see what we did right and what we did wrong, so as to be able to learn from past mistakes, and then use this knowledge to advance struggles today. It is time to reexamine what happened, so we can transfer this refined knowledge to workers around the world to help advance new efforts to build global labor solidarity. We have discovered that we cannot limit our efforts to only description and analysis, but that we must develop theory to help us understand and be able to better communicate our findings.

With this volume, we have a more solidly-based foundation from which to proceed.

SINCE 2010

This is important because there appears to be a real change in building international labor solidarity; so much so that I'm going to refer to post-2010 efforts as building *global* labor solidarity instead of *international* labor solidarity (see Scipes, 2020b). As Peter Waterman (1998) has noted, much of what has passed as international labor solidarity to date has been very paternalistic; has been one-way (uni-directional), from unions in the so-called developed countries (those of Western Europe, Canada, the US, Japan, Australia and New Zealand) to unions in the developing countries (those in Africa, Asia, Latin America and the Middle East); and has been accompanied by a lot of "Northern," often Eurocentric, culture, norms, values, expectations and arrogance. Sometimes, however, this solidarity has provided resources and support that has actually helped workers in these struggles in the developing countries. Other times, particularly seen in many efforts by the US labor center, the AFL-CIO, this so-called "solidarity" has actually worked to hinder or sabotage developing countries' workers' efforts[7] (see Scipes, 2010a; see also Bass, 2012; Carew, 2018; Radosh, 1969; Sims, 1992).

Tied with this reality, though, is the fact that workers in the Global South are doing things that we workers in the Global "North" can learn from, as southern workers struggle to build another world for themselves and their loved ones. They are doing these things in circumstances much worse than we face in developed countries. They are building unions and organizations to challenge the impact of imperialism on their respective countries. They are trying to build "horizontal" links with other unions across the Global "South," some more successful than others, but they are intervening in the global labor world in new ways (see O'Brien, 2019; see also Scipes, 2019): among other things, they are demanding to be included and listened to in ways not seen previously, both within the Global Union Federations and international labor confederations. Some of this confidence is due to the fact that three of these "southern" labor centers—CUT in Brazil, KMU in the Philippines, and COSATU in South Africa—played central roles in overthrowing long-standing dictatorships in their respective country. In short, southern workers are actively working to build a new world.

This is not to glorify what is being done. There are also southern unions that have won small privileges but which have worked with governments, corporations, and other reactionary labor organizations *against* more genuine efforts. So, we cannot say that everything taking place among workers in the developing world is awesome and inspiring.

However, at the same time, there are increasing efforts within the northern countries to do things differently than were done by most of the AFL-CIO projects in the past; to listen, think, and to try to learn from workers' experiences elsewhere. In other words, there are projects in the developed countries that are designed to repudiate and/or go around established relationships. Some of these are new initiatives created by labor dissidents, while others are created by people strongly established in their unions/labor organizations but who want to do things differently, and there are people who are responding to ideas coming from unions in the Global South. There are efforts to try to gather resources that can be "given" openly, without expecting something in return. These are efforts to help, not out of charity, but of solidarity. These are efforts to seek to build equal, non-exploitative and non-oppressive relationships.

It is these more respectful types of relationships that people are trying to build that this author wants to recognize, to encourage, and to support; they are different. They are not uni-directional, they are not paternalistic, and they are respectful of all concerned.

It is these new types of relationships that I want to encourage, around the world, and that's why the term "international" has been replaced by "global."

There are several things I want to say about this collection. First, these were independent efforts, written initially with no idea of ever pulling them together. Accordingly, I have had to try to work to make them fit together; some articles have been split so as to do this, while others have been "shaved" to make a better fit. At the same time, there is some repetition, as I wanted to keep the integrity of a particular article; where there is repetition, I apologize. Also, as will be quickly noted—if not already so noted—there is extensive use of endnotes, which allows me to delve into subjects at a deeper level than I could in the body. These endnotes will probably be of most interest to labor specialists. However, it is recommended that you *not* read the endnotes the first time you read a chapter unless you specifically desire, so that you get the broader argument; in any case, you do not have to read the endnotes simply because I have used them.

And, finally, the purpose of this collection is to bring together in one location a number of articles that I have previously written. They have generally not been updated in any substantive matter, although where possible, I have commented on changes that I have found. I am hoping to stimulate others to build on and go beyond my work; my thinking is not the end all and be all on these and related topics. Yet each article examines issues not commonly examined, and it is hoped they will stimulate fresh thinking. And yes, there are many references to my own work, for which I ask the reader's indulgence—I always try to connect subjects rather that to keep them separate and isolated.

I hope you find the thinking expressed in this book to be worthy of your time and consideration.

NOTES

1. It is difficult to set a date for social developments with precision, as there are questions as to when the process began that led to such development, and whether the beginning of the process should be used as the starting date, or should things be dated when they emerged publicly. The US Civil Rights Movement used the latter approach, choosing December 1, 1955—the date Rosa Parks was arrested for refusing to give up her seat on a bus to a white man—as its beginning date, even though there had been many struggles against white supremacy before that date. For dating processes, I follow the approach of the Civil Rights Movement.

2. This ultimately led to the founding of the CUT (*Central Única dos Trabalhadores*) labor center in 1983 (see Sluyter-Beltrão, 2010).

3. Thomson later played a key role in founding the British-based journal, *International Labour Report* (see Chapter 3, herein), which launched in January 1984.

4. FOSATU, which developed into a strong, democratic labor center, later played a key role in the formation of COSATU (Congress of South African Trade Unions) in late 1985 (see Baskin, 1991).

5. Brooks and McCallum suggest this "new global studies" began in the year 2000, discarding more than twenty years of innovative research.

6. The South Korean case differs from those of the CUT in Brazil, the KMU in the Philippines, and COSATU in South Arica.

While there were important struggles in the 1970s and early 1980s in the garment and textile industries in South Korea—overwhelmingly led by militant young women workers (see especially Chun, 2003)—and which ultimately laid the groundwork for the emergence of the larger Korean labor movement, it really was not until the summer of 1987 that trade unionism exploded across the country. Along with this, leadership of the labor movement shifted from female to male workers. The independent unions that emerged tried to build a larger organizational structure, but they did not create one until January 22, 1990 when the National Congress of Trade Unions (NCTU) was launched. The NCTU included only a small number of unions, and a small number of unionized workers, and only lasted for a couple of years. It was superseded in 1995 by the establishment of the Korean Confederation of Trade Unions (KCTU). However, according to Hagen Koo, author of a wonderful 2001 study of the Korean labor movement, "the South Korean labor movement did not develop . . . what Seidman (1994) calls 'social movement unionism'" (Koo, 2001: 203).

So, while I included the South Korean labor movement in my earliest writings on social movement unionism (see Scipes, 1992a, b)—based largely on early reports of the 1987 "Great Worker Struggle"—Koo has convinced me that I was incorrect, and the South Korean unions and labor centers should not be classified as exemplars of social movement unionism.

Nonetheless, Korean workers have engaged in heroic struggles to build independent, worker-controlled unions, and while they do not meet the requirements of social movement unionism, their struggles still must be respected. For writings on these struggles, see Koo (2001) for a book on Korean workers and how they developed class consciousness, and for an excellent account of the emergence and development of the garment and textile workers' union in South Korea, which played a central role in the emergence of popular, democratic and independent (from the state) trade unionism, see Chun (2003). Although written from a more traditional industrial relations approach, see Song (2002) for an overview of developments in Korean unions. Park (2007), on the other hand, examines the KCTU experience, and argues that the KCTU experience invalidates the concept of social movement unionism. For an examination of the Korean workers and the effects of neoliberal globalization, see Gray (2008).

7. The Canadian Labour Congress has also engaged in this labor imperialism (see Nastovski, 2016b).

Acknowledgments

There have been many people over the past 37+ years who have encouraged and supported me in researching and ultimately writing the articles that comprise this book. It is my pleasure to publicly acknowledge some who have been especially crucial in this process.

Geoff Meredith (aka Geoff Yippee) was the one who first inspired me to travel to Europe in the Fall of 1983. We both had been involved in "Vandenberg III," where (along with 75 others) we physically entered the Vandenberg Air Force Base on the Central California coast during June 1983 to try to stop the launching of the MX missile, which we saw as Reagan's insane escalation of the Cold War with the then-Soviet Union—we delayed it a week. Shortly thereafter, Yippee suggested we go to Germany to protest the decision to station Cruise and Pershing missiles in "West" Germany, another escalation, and a final decision that would be made on his birthday, December 12. I readily agreed; this was a decision that changed my life. I went to England early, traveled around, and we celebrated Yippee's birthday in Müttlangen, Baden-Württemberg, Germany by joining progressive Germans and other Europeans on the anti-missile blockade.

While in England (prior to going to Germany), I met Mike Press in Coventry. We celebrated Guy Fawkes' Night there—Fawkes is said to be the only honest man to ever enter Parliament (he intended to blow it up)—and Mike introduced me to the comrades in Manchester who, with him and others, were initiating the new journal, *International Labour Reports* or ILR: Stuart Howard and Dave Spooner were the editors, and they were supported by Alice Donald. ILR was planning a conference to introduce the new journal and to develop an understanding that export processing zones were not the way for workers to go in Britain or anywhere else.

Howard and Spooner took me in, including me in conference planning activities, the conference, and ultimately asking me (in 1984) to represent ILR in North America. I accepted and promoted the journal from 1984 to 1989.

The conference sponsored by ILR had a profound impact on my life: I met Wenilou "Weng" Pradel, a labor leader from the Philippines, who had been brought to the conference to share her experiences organizing and co-leading the first general strike in any export processing zone in the world! Weng and I hit it off, and she told me about this new labor movement emerging in the Philippines, united in the *Kilusang Mayo Uno* Labor Center. This intrigued me, inspiring me to travel to the Philippines in January 1986, and this has resulted in my on-going relationship with KMU that continues today. In 1996, I published the first, and to date, only nation-wide study of the KMU, a study I hope to put on-line soon as the book is out of print and I have the publishing rights. And I plan to complete another book on the KMU in the not-too-distant future.

These different things combined when I met Peter Waterman in 1984. Peter, who was the founder and editor of NILS, the *New International Labour Studies* newsletter, was also the ILR representative on the European continent, and a Senior Lecturer at the Institute of Social Studies (ISS) in The Hague, The Netherlands. He was one of the leading scholars of labor internationalism in the world. Peter came to my apartment in Oakland while he was visiting the University of California at Berkeley, and we hit it off. We stayed in close touch, and both liked to write and analyze social developments, especially affecting workers around the world, and we actively shared our writings. As a result of my labor union activism, and especially with my research in the Philippines, he invited me to apply to the ISS for a Masters of Arts in Development Studies in the Politics of Alternative Development Strategies program in which he taught; I applied, was accepted and studied there from August 1990 to December 1991, when I obtained my MA. This had been an incredible experience, as we had students and staff from over 120 countries, all working in one building!

After graduating, however, things changed with Peter. At one time, we had been as close as two people can be without being lovers. However, over time, things changed; we disagreed over the KMU: on the basis of six research trips that covered much of the country, I claimed it was run by its members; on the basis of one, very limited trip of about a month where he stayed in Metro Manila, he claimed the KMU was controlled by the Communist Party of the Philippines. I did not mind that he disagreed with me, but I minded greatly that he refused to consider evidence that myself as well as others provided—I personally handed him a copy of my 1996 book when I visited The Netherlands in 1997, and I have seen no evidence that he ever read it—

that countered his claim; he had his mind made up and he wasn't going to let the facts get in his way. (This ideological position was very different than that regarding any other issue that I had ever seen him respond to; he was incredibly open to new things and just-met people.)

Although he posted my 1996 article on how the KMU built international labor solidarity—included herein as Chapter 12—on his personal website in 2000, that was the last time he promoted my work. He went from not referencing my work, to ignoring my work, and to eventually publicly attacking me for my KMU-related research. This caused our estrangement, to say the least. He was planning to speak at an October 2017 conference at McMaster University in Hamilton, Ontario, Canada, where I would also be speaking, and I had hoped that maybe we could work something out. Unfortunately, at age of 81, in June 2017, Peter died during surgery.

Peter Waterman was a very complex man, who was one of the most engaging people I have ever met. His inspiration had a profound impact on my life, and particularly my academic career. Because of my time with him at the ISS, I met people like Ken Post and Jan Nederveen Pieterse, each who also inspired me, and I regained my love for formal education: I followed my MA with obtaining a Ph.D., first at the University of Wisconsin at Madison and then at the University of Illinois at Chicago, where I graduated in 2003. And then I've spent the following 16 + years teaching at a regional campus of Purdue University in Indiana, eventually becoming a Professor. And I'm still researching and writing about the KMU, while still building off what I learned first from Peter. (For an excellent appreciation of Peter's life, please see Amrita Chhachhi's account at https://onlinelibrary.wiley.com/doi/full/10.1111/dech.12556?af=R.)

Peter Waterman, presente!

Besides my activist/academic side of life, there is my personal life—and most important, there are my two children, Leander and Malaya. They have left home, and it's exciting to watch them enter the world on their own. They are in The Netherlands as I write, taking advantage of the opportunity through their Dutch mother, and my former wife, Johanna "Hans" Buwalda. We had some good years together—and I thank you, Hans—but the kids have proven the most enduring part.

And finally, I want to acknowledge and thank my present partner, Virginia "Ginnie" Abramowicz. We share a profound love of the blues, and although I no longer live in Chicago, we still make it to Rosa's Lounge a couple times a month to dance to some incredible musicians like Billy Branch and the Sons of the Blues, Lil' Ed and the Blues Imperials, and Vance Kelly and the Back Street Blues Band: it don't get no better than this! Ginnie and I love to dance, and usually sit down only when the band stops. (And thanks to Tony Mangiullo, the proprietor of Rosa's, for allowing it all to happen.) But she keeps me grounded, and especially when we retreat to Starved Rock State Park in Illinois and other places we share.

Yet, finally, there are two more groups of people I want to thank for their engagement and support. First are my colleagues who work at Purdue University Northwest, and who are long-time members of our AAUP (American Association of University Professors) chapter: David Detmer, Tony Elmendorf, David Nalbone, Karen Roothaan, Rita Brusca-Vega, and our ally, Libbie Pelter. The work you each do to make this university what it should be is inspiring, and I'm honored to work with you.

And finally, there are my friends and comrades in Michigan City. We have PARC (Politics, Art, Root and Culture), a community cultural center established in Michigan City by Vincent Emanuele and Sergio Kochergin, two brother Marine Corps veterans who also turned against war and the empire: thanks for doing all that each of you do!

Along with PARC, there are all the people I work with as part of OUR MC (Organized and United Residents of Michigan City). While appreciating everyone, I am especially enjoying my developing friendship with Sarah and Rob Johnson; it's inspiring to work with a new generation of community leaders, and I'm looking forward to drinking more beer in an outside tent in the dead of winter in the future!

There are many others, in the US and around the world, but I won't go on. Some I acknowledged in past books, and some will get thanked in future books. *A luta continua:* the struggle continues!

Michigan City, Indiana, USA
March 2020

List of Abbreviations

The world of labor is one filled with abbreviations. Here is a list of organizations that are included in this book:

AMBA-BALA Bataan Alliance of Labor Associations (KMU-affilated geographical alliance-Philippines)
AFL-CIO: American Federation of Labor-Congress of Industrial Organizations
BEPZ: Bataan Export Processing Zone (Philippines)
CIA: US Central Intelligence Agency
COSATU: Congress of South African Trade Unions
CUT: *Central Única do Trabalhadores* (Brazil)
FOSATU: Federation of South African Trade Unions (a predecessor to COSATU)
ICFTU: Intercontinental Confederation of Free Trade Unions (1949–2006)
IGMC Workers' Union: (trade union in garment factory in BEPZ-Philippines)
ILR: *International Labour Reports* (UK)
ITUC: International Trade Union Confederation (founded in 2006)
KMU: *Kilusang Mayo Uno* Labor Center (Philippines)
NAFTA: North American Free Trade Agreement (US, Canada and Mexico)
NED: National Endowment for Democracy (US government-created agency)
NFSW: National Federation of Sugar Workers-Food and General Trades (a KMU-affiliated federation-Philippines
NILS: *New International Labour Studies* (edited by Peter Waterman)
SEIU: Service Employees International Union (US trade union)
SMU: Social Movement Unionism
TIE: Transnational Information Exchange (The Netherlands, then Germany)
TUCP: Trade Union Congress of the Philippines

Introduction

One of the longest lived and most profound truths of the global workers' movement historically are that workers must liberate themselves; no one else can solve their problems for them.[1] This is not to say they cannot ally with others and develop solidaristic relations with other sectors of global society; it is to say that only the oppressed can end their own oppression. And, also true, the "big boys" and "big girls"—whether in this government or that; this corporation or that; this political party or that; or even this NGO (non-governmental organization) or that—cannot and, more importantly, will not solve workers' problems for workers. And this is as true globally as it is true in any specific empire, nation-state or political community.

And the liberation of working people must be done on a global basis; workers in one country cannot be free until all are struggling to be free.[2]

The powers-that-be have divided and separated workers around the world by establishing nation-states, and telling workers in "their" nation-state that they are better, more productive *and more deserving* of their elites' benevolence than are workers in other nation-states. This has led to what is called "reactionary nationalism,"[3] where workers are taught the necessity to defend "their nation-state" at all costs, less they lose the elite benevolence and sink into the impoverished, exploited, oppressed and undeserving mass of workers as is commonly projected in scenes from the Global South.[4]

This argument has certainly had an impact on working people globally. All one has to do is see how willing working people have been willing to serve in "their" respective political community/nation-states' military and fight in its wars over the ages.

Well, the gig is up. We might not be the first to figure out the "game," but we've got it now. With the global ecological crisis upon us, we have to give up this reactionary nationalism and recognize that *we can be liberated only if we join together to work for the liberation of all.* Key to this, for workers, is to build global labor solidarity[5] (among others, see Waterman, 1998; see also Bieler and Lindberg, eds., 2011; Bieler, Lindberg and Pillay, eds., 2008; Scipes, 2014a; Scipes, 2016b, 2016c; Scipes, ed., 2014; 2016).[6] To build this global solidarity—both in and of itself, and to address the intensifying global ecological crisis (see Scipes, 2013, 2017)—requires workers to become global actors. This means that while we can take pride in where we come from, we have to reject the politics and identities of reactionary nationalism; this means we have to reject being American, Briton, Chinese, Dutch, Ethiopian, Fijian, Ghanaian, Indian or Japanese, etc., and we have to become global citizens. Now, obviously, we can and should take pride in where we come from, but we've got to quit using that pride to oppress others.

That does not mean, by the way, that we should seek to partake in work to make the global economy produce more; in fact, we must work to make it produce less, but share more (see, for example, Scipes, 1991a, 2009b; 2017).[7]

Accordingly, we have to recognize the humanity of each one of us, and to join in solidarity to make a new world, one where the planet is at the center of our imagination and thinking, not greedy capitalist "man" (or woman), profit, nor any empire. That means recognizing the interconnectedness of all things, including people across the globe as well as our connection to the planet and to other species.

To do this requires that we join together to build global labor solidarity among workers of the world—both among and between workers in both the Global South and the Global North—and this book is intended to advance this project by sharing some experiences known only by a relatively few people around the world, and by generalizing the lessons learned therefrom. In other words, it is not being argued that global labor solidarity will emerge "automatically" or that it is seen as "desirable" by all workers, but it is argued that *if* we want it—and I believe it *is* an important goal—then here are some lessons we can learn from these earlier struggles that might help us in today's struggles.

The specific purposes of this book, then, are multiple:

- to show activists that we do not have to start from scratch, that there is a lot to learn from efforts to create international labor solidarity in the period between 1978–2010;[8]
- to suggest that one of the most important things we can learn from building international labor solidarity is that there are experiences beyond our's from which we can learn; arguably, the most important are from struggles to create a new type of trade unionism, "social movement unionism" (SMU), by workers in particular labor centers—*Central Única dos Trabalhadores* (CUT), *Kilusang Mayo Uno* (KMU), and the Congress of South

African Trade Unions (COSATU)—in Brazil, the Philippines, and South Africa, respectively;[9]

- to argue that SMU transcends the weaknesses of traditional economic and political unionism, and thus would be an advance over trade unionism in particularly the more economic developed countries such as the United States;
- to present the theoretical conceptualization of SMU best-developed to date, that by the *Kilusang Mayo Uno* (KMU) Labor Center of the Philippines;
- to demonstrate that KMU is an exemplary case of SMU and, thus, to argue there is much to learn from their experiences;
- to illustrate that this conceptualization of SMU is not confined to the Philippines, but can be extended to explain the development of COSATU in South Africa, at least up to the early 1990s;
- to discuss how the KMU builds international labor solidarity; and finally,
- to show how all of this knowledge can be used to disentangle the incredible theoretical confusion among labor theorists and activists that has hobbled further theoretical and organizational development.

In short, I argue that building global labor solidarity requires the building of egalitarian, solidaristic relations with workers around the world—not seeing them as better or more advanced, but not behind anyone else, either—based on respect (see Scipes, 2014a, 2016b).

Thus, this collection is intended to show to workers around the world that, collectively, we have a tremendous number of experiences that can be shared and used to learn from each other. In other words, as long as we do not confine ourselves to just our national situation, but combine each with knowledge and information from workers around the world, we can advance workers' struggles here in the United States and across the world, and improve working people's lives as we work for a better world for each of us.

Why publish a book today that is largely based on a collection of essays written in the 1980–1990s, essays that I wrote as a labor activist, based on my experiences of events in places far away, under conditions apparently far removed from the contemporary United States? Because, as I show herein, there is a lot contemporary labor activists—in the United States and around the world can learn from that period; much that is unknown by many of today's labor activists. And with the emergence of new labor movements in a number of countries—in countries as disparate as China, Colombia, Egypt, India, Iraq, Iran, Mexico, Pakistan, Venezuela and Vietnam[10]—activists there need to have knowledge of experiences shared by earlier labor movements, much of which has been "forgotten" in public discourse.

For labor activists today, the founding of FOSATU (Federation of South African Trade Unions) in 1979—the predecessor of COSATU (Congress of South African Trade Unions) created in 1985—and the 1980 founding of the *Kilusang Mayo Uno* (KMU—May First Movement) Labor Center in the Philippines are as distant as the dinosaurs. Similarly, that's true for the CUT (*Central Única do Trabalhadores*) in Brazil, founded in 1983. And that is if they even know of the existence of these labor centers.[11]

The 1980s saw the emergence of independent, militant labor organizations in a number of countries: the crucial ones were CUT in Brazil, KMU in the Philippines, FOSATU/COSATU in South Africa, the new independent unions in South Korea, and *Solidarnosc* in Poland.[12] Interestingly, each one developed such power that they played leading roles, if not *the* leading role, in ending dictatorship in their respective country. That alone means their experiences need to be shared, learned from, and used to illuminate current and future labor struggles. Obviously, these experiences should be shared across the Global South.

Let us be clear: these labor movements were, at the time, some of the leading proponents and initiators of popular democracy and worker/member empowerment in the world.[13]

How were they able to do this? How were they able to build some of the most dynamic and powerful labor movements that the world has ever seen? And how were they able to do this when their respective countries were each ruled by a dictator?

These are some very interesting questions. And with the emergence of new labor movements in places such as China, Egypt, Iraq and Iran; new developments within labor organizations in places like Colombia, India, Mexico, Pakistan, Venezuela[14] and Vietnam; and an increasing understanding of the need to build global labor solidarity that is emerging around the world (see particularly Bieler and Lindberg, eds., 2011; Bieler, Lindberg and Pillay, eds., 2008; Munck, 1988; Scipes, 2014a, 2016b, 2016c; Scipes, ed., 2014, 2016; Waterman, 1998; Webster, Lambert and Bezuidenhout, 2008)—it seems time to revisit some of the "old" struggles to draw out lessons and experiences that may help these newer labor initiatives.

For the new labor movements in the Global South, there is considerable need for more information that is outside the parameters of "traditional" trade unionism, which appears to be the format of most information commonly available to them. Certainly the International Labor Organization (ILO), the International Trade Union Confederation (ITUC) and its affiliated labor centers and unions, and the American Federation of Labor-Congress of Industrial Organizations (AFL-CIO), especially through their Solidarity Center, are each working to advance various versions of "traditional" trade unionism.

From the options presented, this approach might best meet the needs of some of these union movements across the globe; for others, however, it will not.

However, one limitation of the traditional trade unions is that they fail to ask questions of themselves—much less answer them—that are on the minds of labor activists or are of the concerns of these newer unions. Questions like how can we build Labor's power in the workplace, how can we build power in communities, and *how can we change our respective social order?*[15] That is where the experiences of a radically different type of trade unionism are valuable: not to provide a necessary blueprint that must be followed, but to share a wide range of experiences to provide newer labor organizations with information and different perspectives, so they can decide what can be learned from the earlier experiences that might be important for the newer labor organizations. These are things that the established labor organizations never consider.

In fact, the actual experiences of the "older" (1980s–1990s) labor centers *are* different than the ones today; these today are operating in a different social context, globally as well as nationally. Globally, the Cold War, like the Soviet Union, is long gone—yes, there are political rivalries and confrontations, and the US still seeks to maintain the US Empire (see especially, McCoy, 2017)—but the US simply is not as dominant as it was between the collapse of the Soviet Empire in 1989–91 and 2003 (when George W. Bush invaded Iraq). This provides opportunities, as well as problems, not faced by the older labor centers.

Concurrently, the national situation in each country is different than it was 20 or so years ago. Without going into each situation, only a quick reflection is needed to recognize the different situation being faced in each nation—none of these countries are where they were, economically and socially development-wise, 20 years ago; some have reached a higher level of development (such as in China, Venezuela before the oil crisis), some have reached a lower level (arguably Colombia, and certainly Iraq, probably Iran), and some are perhaps in the middle (Egypt, Mexico).

Yet working people in each of these countries—to different extents, to greater or lesser degrees—are having to deal with the intensifying process of corporate and military globalization, which is, in reality, efforts to impose capitalism on their peoples and at almost any price: certainly the destruction of indigenous peoples, cultures and traditions is taking place and intensifying; certainly this is also leading to the destruction of land, natural materials and local ecologies; certainly it is destroying established economies and the jobs associated with these, leading to increased impoverishment and misery; certainly it is enhancing the need for fossil fuels to extract and process minerals and other natural resources, as well as assemble and transport goods from across the globe; and certainly, all of this is contributing to the escalating assault on the global environment and the atmosphere that surrounds the planet, that has allowed civilizations to evolve over the past 11,700 years (see Angus, 2016; Klein, 2015; Romm, 2016).

People are fighting back, whether based on their identity as worker, indigenous person, woman, peasant, young person, student, whatever, or from a combination of identities.[16] While the scope of this resistance in individual cases seems limited, this resistance is taking place around the globe (see Jaffee, 2016; Klein, 2015; Mason 2012; Moghadam, 2020; Starr, 2005). People can see the social devastation that has been imposed on their country—enabled, if not abetted, by local elites—and know that this offers no real future for them or their offspring. This resistance—slowly morphing from individual and generally isolated struggles here and there into a global movement for economic and social justice, based on values of respect for Mother Earth, and seeking to construct societies based on economically and ecologically sustainable processes—is growing. It, too, is a globalization process—it seeks to build links with people around the world—but it is based on values antithetical, opposed, to those being promoted by the corporate and military globalization project (see, among others, Jaffe, 2016; Klein, 2015; Moghadam, 2020; Scipes, 2009b; 2013; 2016b; Shiva, 2005; Starr, 2005).[17]

It is this new globalization project from below—this global movement for economic and social justice—that offers hope to the world in this time of increasing conflict, terrorism, and planetary destruction.

Ultimately, the greatest "gift" people can give across national borders—in addition to any monetary or personnel resources that can be shared—is information; information that people in one country can consider and chose from to help advance their own struggle as they see fit, and as it meets the issues that are most salient to them. There are no "models," no "21 theses," etc., that can tell people how they *should* advance their efforts; there are, however, experiences and understandings from which others can learn from and select. Hence, the argument is that by providing information and analyses from previous struggles, we can contribute to current and future struggles. In other words, cross-border sharing expresses global solidarity by knowing and being concerned about sisters and brothers in other countries, and tries to provide information and knowledge useful to these people so they can act to improve their lives and, ultimately, to work with people around the world, including like-minded people in the United States and other so-called developed countries, to create a better world.

Incidentally, this information is offered without any belief that workers' experiences are any more valuable than anyone else's, or with the belief that all should defer to labor when established. It is simply being offered in the spirit of "here are some understandings by workers in certain situations, and if they can be of use, please consider them." No more and no less.

Yet what are some of the lessons that came from the experiences of these older labor centers? My knowledge of, and experience with, the KMU is by far the most extensive, so following Dietrich Rueschemeyer's (1991: 28–34) approach to analytic induction, I use my findings from my six research trips in the Philippines to study the KMU between 1986–1994 and my resulting book (Scipes, 1996) as my referent,[18] to present what can be learned from KMU (see Scipes, 2014b).[19] Five findings come immediately to mind: a different conception of what is meant by "trade unionism"; some new organizational forms for workers (alliances); an emphasis on member, not just steward-level, education; new relationships with sectoral organizations across the social order; and an emphasis on the importance on uniting with workers and labor organizations around the world (see Scipes, 1996). A few quick comments.

By imagining and creating a different conception of trade unionism, it is argued that the KMU—along with the other aforementioned labor centers—transcended the economic-political split of established trade unionism to create an entire new type of trade unionism: social movement unionism.[20] In other words, traditional trade unionism, particularly in the West, has limited itself to primarily focusing on the economic well-being of their members—with differing amounts of considering interests of non-members, from the ignoring other workers, largely found in the form of "business unionism" that predominates in the US, to the more inclusive "social justice unionism" of Canada and Western Europe, and everything in between. On the other hand, there has been the political type of trade unionism that was seen in Russia before the Bolshevik Revolution, and in a number of labor organizations in Africa over the years, that were allies of political organizations seeking "national liberation"; after their allies successfully attained power, the union leaders largely subordinated their trade unionism to the politics of these political organizations that had attained state power.[21]

Yet both of these types of trade unionism—economic or political—were efforts to confine trade unionism to limited realms. Conservative labor leaders and elites of states of many different political persuasions did not want to have truly independent labor centers, where workers could think for themselves, where their labor centers could emerge as political actors.

The emergence of social movement unionism (SMU)—and the clearest examples to date, again, are CUT of Brazil, KMU of the Philippines, and COSATU of South Africa—is an effort to establish a new type of trade unionism. SMU establishes unions and their worker-members as actors within the socio-political-economic realms of a social order, who build democratic organizations controlled by their members, and who see conditions on the shop floor as being intimately connected with and affected by not only the national situation but the position of their country in the global political-economic networks. Accordingly, efforts to advance the interests of worker-members and their many allies requires them to seek to change not only the national situation but the global political-economic order in which their country is enmeshed. Thus, seeking *qualitative social change*—taking their efforts far beyond the parameters of established industrial relations—*is integral to this new type of trade unionism.*

Unfortunately, as we've seen most clearly in South Africa—but appears to be true in Brazil as well—there is a tremendous "gravitational pull" on social movement union leaders to tuck in their wings and to subordinate their labor organizations to the political organizations with which they had been politically allied with as equals once leaders of these political organizations have been democratically elected into governments (see Barchiesi, 2007).[22] This seems to have resulted in these labor centers transforming their conception of unionism from the social movement type of unionism to the economic type of trade unionism, and of the economic type, to the social justice *form*.[23] While this needs to be investigated in depth by labor activists and scholars—so as to understand the processes that have led to this, and countermeasures designed to reduce the chances of this in the future (see Sluyter-Beltrão, 2010)—the larger point that is of immediate interest herein is that development of social movement unionism is not a one-time permanent accomplishment; changing situations can result in reverting back to other types of trade unionism. Nonetheless, without considering it a panacea, I argue that the development of social movement unionism is an important advance, and one from which many lessons can be learned.

Another lesson that can be learned from these earlier experiences is the creation of new organizational forms to enhance organizational power, and development of new ways to develop social power from below—what I call "emancipatory power"—to struggle for one's political goals.[24] This is the result of seeing one's "trade unionism" as being intimately connected with other working people and their communities, and not separate or different. For example, the creation of *welga ng bayans* (people's strikes) that have been developed in the Philippines far exceeds the development of the mythical "general strike" in the West; in fact, a *welgang bayan* (in colloquial form) *begins* with a general strike and develops from there to include the closing of all shops, stores and offices in an area, blockading of highways, and fisherfolks refusing to put out to sea. This seems in parallel with what the South Africans call a "stay away."

Another lesson regards trade union education—with a firm recognition, throughout the entire organization, of its importance. The KMU's education program is multi-layered, and develops sophistication as one moves toward higher, more advanced, levels of understanding. Its dedication to rank-and-file education is exemplary. In fact, in January 1986, while Dictator Ferdinand Marcos was still in power, the late Serge Cherniguin, then-Secretary General of the National Sugar Workers-Food and General Trades—based primarily on the island of Negros, with a membership of some of the most malnourished, uneducated and poorest people in the world—told me that all 86,000 members had completed the one day KMU course on trade unionism. Most leaders had completed the three-day "Genuine Trade Unionism" course. This education of the rank and file members enabled NFSW-FGT to withstand extreme amounts of violence against members, albeit not without retreats or losses, but in ways that ensured survival of an organization that remains today from an organizing effort that began in 1970 (Scipes, 1996: 128–158).[25]

And finally, there is an understanding of the vulnerability of such efforts—no matter how well developed—to state violence as well as capitalist dis-investment from the country, and a recognition of the need to build international labor solidarity, not only to seek help but to share experiences with workers around the world. The KMU has developed the most sophisticated project to build international labor solidarity in the world, and has been holding an annual International Solidarity Affair around May Day since 1984, where workers, labor activists and officials have been invited to come to experience their reality in the Philippines (see Scipes, 2000a—Chapter 12, herein; 2015a).

The struggles of these labor centers, as stated above, provide information to these newer labor projects across the Global South. However, these lessons and this information are not just needed for workers across the Global South; I argue their experiences as needed as much in the Global North as well, and nowhere more specifically than in the United States of America.

Why do I make this claim? Very simply—despite the efforts of the US mass media (especially movies) to generally ignore the issue—the economic situation in the United States has been bad and it has taken a long time for working people's economic situation to improve even to the extent it has.

We can see this by examining the economic situation circa 2013. The US economy for workers was in bad shape by 2007, prior to the onset of the Great Recession (see Scipes, 2009a, for details; see also Greenhouse, 2008). Subsequently, over seven million jobs were lost since the Great Recession hit in 2007, and American median income tumbled down 8.9 percent since 1999, the peak year since World War II; and median income for men and women declined 2.5 percent from 2010 to 2011 (DeNavas-Walt, Proctor and Smith, 2012: 5).

Writing in late 2010, David Leonhardt of the *New York Times* wrote:

> Right now, the estimate is that 9.4 million jobs would need to be added immediately to get the jobless rate down to 6%, which some economists are calling "full employment." That used to be around 4%, so these are skewed estimates. Nonetheless, the estimates are this: if the economy provided 300,000 jobs a month, we wouldn't end the job shortfall until the middle of 2014. (In other words, that would get us down to 6% unemployment.) If the economy grew at 250,000 jobs a month, which was the pace of the mid-1990s during the longest expansion of the economy since World War II, we wouldn't end the job shortfall under early 2016. And if the economy provided 200,000 jobs a month, the job shortfall wouldn't end until early 2020.

How were we actually doing? The title of a front page *New York Times* article on January 8, 2011 by Michael Powell and Sewell Chan suggested the answer: "Slow Job Growth Dims Expectation of Early Revival: Unemployment rate is 9.4%—Recovery Could Require Another 4 or 5 Years, Fed's Chief Says." These reporters noted that in December 2010, only 103,000 jobs were added, unemployment was expected to remain over 8 percent throughout the rest of Obama's first term, and the so-called "real" unemployment rate—which includes workers who are discouraged and have given up looking for work, or who are working only part time when they seek full-time work—stood at 16.7 percent. Further, they quoted one analyst saying "We are seeing evidence of structural employment among those in the prime, higher-earning 35- to 44-year old demographic where unemployment actually increased in December," and they reported an estimate that it would take until 2037 to regain the number of jobs lost during the great recession, which is what they're calling this crisis since 2007 (Powell and Chan, 2011).

So far—as I wrote in mid-2013—things have worked out somewhat better than this, although not by much. Only 165,000 jobs were added in July 2013, and the unemployment rate was at 7.4 percent, only a little below the 7.8 percent level at which it had been between September and December, 2012, and the lowest it's been since 2008. A number of Americans had simply dropped out of the labor market, making things look better than they really were: "For every 100 American adults, 63 had jobs before the recession; now, only 59 do."

> The unemployment rate is falling nonetheless because it only counts people actively seeking work. And since the recession, a growing number of Americans are not even trying to find jobs. Some have given up; others appear to be avoiding the labor market by staying in school or at home (*New York Times,* 2013).

Along with the jobs situation, poverty was increasing. The national poverty rate—at a terribly insufficient level that is approximately half of what is needed for long-term survival[26]—jumped from 13.2 percent in 2008 to 15 percent in 2011, while the numbers of people increased across the same years from 39.6 million to 46.2 million, the highest since the government began gathering data in 1959 (DeNavas-Walt, Proctor and Smith, 2012: 13). It also needs to be remembered that two out of three (65 percent) of all people in poverty in the US are white.

Poverty had increased when we examined the experiences of the different racial groupings, too. Poverty among whites grew from 8.6 percent in 2008 to 9.8 percent in 2011, while the Black impoverishment rate jumped from 24.7 percent to 27.6 percent; Latino impoverishment increased from 23.2 percent to 25.3 percent in 2011; while Asian impoverishment remained approximately stable around 12.5 percent.[27]

Poverty for children under 18 also worsened: from 19 percent in 2008 to 21.9 percent in 2011 (DeNavas-Walt, Proctor and Smith, 2012: 13). This is not surprising, as a 2010 report by researchers at the National Center for Children in Poverty stated, "Children represent 25 percent of the population. Yet, they comprise 36 percent of all the people in poverty. Among children, 42 percent live in low-income families [defined as below 200 percent of the poverty line-KS], and of those, 25 percent live in poor families [below the poverty line-KS]" (Chau, Thampi and Wight, 2010). Charles M. Blow noted, "The number of children living in poverty has risen 33 percent since 2000," while the child population only increased about 3 percent during the same time. Further, he reports that, "according to a 2007 UNICEF report on child poverty, the US ranked last among 24 wealthy nations" (Blow, 2010). As Paul Krugman wrote in the *New York Times*, "neuroscientists have found that 'many children growing up in very poor families with low social status experience unhealthy levels of stress hormones, which impair their neural development.' The effect is to impair language development and memory for the rest of a child's life" (Krugman, 2008). In plain language: poverty poisons children's brains.

Tragically, of those living below the poverty line, 44 percent of all people in poverty lived at half of the official poverty line or lower; that was 6.6 percent of the national population, increasing from 17.1 million in 2008 to 20.4 million in 2011. Altogether, 34.3 percent of all Americans lived below 200 percent of the poverty threshold (DeNavas-Walt, Proctor and Smith, 2012: 17).[28]

Yet, despite the terrible and escalating assault on working people—that over a third of the entire US population being below a reality-based poverty line certainly would seem an "assault"—plus the escalating attacks on the labor movement itself in Indiana, Michigan, Ohio and Wisconsin in 2011–2012 (for Wisconsin, see Buhle and Buhle, eds., 2011; Nichols, 2012; Yates, ed., 2012, and a review of all three by this author, see Scipes, 2012b), the AFL-CIO leadership has provided no leadership beyond perhaps a few speeches here or there; their "leadership" has been so insufficient that it could be considered all-but-useless (see Scipes, 2017b). How can this be explained? Is not their reason for existence to take care of and support working people?

While this has not been directly faced by the labor movement in general or even most labor activists and scholars, there have been both direct and indirect critiques of Labor's foreign policy, as a small but growing number of activists are making the connections between Labor abroad and Labor at-home.[29]

In what is one of the most direct critiques, an in-depth study of the foreign policy program of the AFL-CIO leadership, this author charged that the AFL-CIO leadership still believes that the US *should* dominate the world (Scipes, 2010a, 2010b). I argued, *"Labor's foreign policy leadership is wedded to Empire: they believe the United States should dominate the world, that unlimited financial resources should be dedicated to ensuring this, and that all other considerations are secondary or less"* (emphasis in original) (Scipes, 2010a: 113). This understanding, as I have projected, "has prevented the AFL-CIO leadership from even attempting to address the worsening economic conditions and resulting social situation that has been developing since the early 1970s . . ." (Scipes, 2010a: 113–114).

Additionally, there have been a number of other critiques of the AFL-CIO's foreign policy program. The most potent have been the challenge to AFL-CIO support for US wars in Iraq and Afghanistan by US Labor Against War (USLAW) (see Zweig, 2005, 2014). There has also been an important, but must less robust effort by the Worker to Worker Solidarity Committee (WWSC), which has focused on breaking the ties between the AFL-CIO's Solidarity Center and the US Government's National Endowment for Democracy (NED) (see Scipes, 2010a: 96–105; 2012a: 314–316).

Yet while these projects have won numerous victories, they have yet to change the AFL-CIO foreign policy program. Interestingly, while being stymied on one front, they now seem to have shifted to going around the AFL-CIO foreign policy defenses (see Scipes, ed., 2014). We can see this specifically in the struggle to build global labor solidarity.

Most importantly has been the emergence and development since 2003 of US Labor Against War (USLAW), where a significant number of the entire AFL-CIO membership has sought a new foreign policy program, particularly in regards to Iraq. This is more than of usual import as organizational affiliation must be mandated by the rank and file, as a precondition to affiliation and, thus, is not just an action of progressive officials and/or labor activists (Zweig, 2005). Yet what is exciting is that USLAW's vision has not just been limited to stopping the war, but it has built international solidarity with unions and workers of Iraq. USLAW's vision has expanded to connecting with trade unionists in places as disparate as Venezuela, Pakistan and Iran, as well as Iraq, as well as expressing solidarity with working people in Israel and Palestine, and demanding the end to Israeli settlements in the West Bank and the siege of Gaza (Lydersen, 2009; Scipes, 2012a).

The Worker to Worker Solidarity Committee, which has been working to end AFL-CIO collaboration with the National Endowment for Democracy (Scipes, 2010a: 96–105; 2012a: 314–316), also has some of its members developing solidarity with workers and unions in Colombia (personal communication with James Jordan of Alliance for Global Justice). Further, the United Steel Workers have been engaged for years in a law suit in conjunction with Colombian workers and unions against the Coca-Cola Company, trying to make Coke responsible for the violence initiated by its bottling company contractor in Colombia (personal communication with Dan Kovalik of USW).

In short, as was discussed at the 2013 Labor and Working Class History Association meetings in June, as well as the Left Forum that same weekend—both in New York City—labor activists are both challenging the AFL-CIO foreign policy program *and* going around it, developing a new labor globalism (see Waterman, 1998; Scipes, 2014a, 2016b, 2016c).

These efforts are important in and of themselves. However, their importance could be even more so in that they have the potential to free labor activists to seriously be able to engage the worsening social conditions in this country, both affecting the labor movement and the larger society.[30] Whether this can be made real, obviously, remains to be seen.

Thus, I am addressing this book to workers anywhere in the world who are trying to build new labor movements to advance their interests, or to bypass the limitations of already existing labor movements. Again, I do not suggest there is any "prescription" that should be followed; this is simply an effort to share some of the foremost experiences by workers in the not-too-distant past. My hope is that this book will provide labor activists with new information, and that it inspires new strategies and tactics that will allow their current projects to surpass those of the past.

NOTES

1. When using the term "worker" in this book, I am using it in the broadest manner possible. I am talking about people who work—whether it is for a wage or salary, who are on "commission" of some sort, or who work without financial compensation to help maintain the well-being of their respective family, however defined—and who have relatively little power individually to shape the conditions under which one

works or the social context in which the work takes place. This is much broader than a Marxist analysis, and certainly both includes and goes beyond blue-collar work.

However, holding an "objective" position in society such as "worker"—in other words, holding a job, whether paid or unpaid—does not mean one sees herself or himself (identifies oneself) as being a worker, much less acting as a worker is "supposed" to do. That person could be someone who works so they can support themself while playing in a rock 'n' roll band or doing something else they consider more important. People have multiple roles in society, and "worker" might be one of them, and that role might be important enough to identify oneself as such, or it might not be; being an electrician or teacher might be more important than being some generalized "worker," or being a spouse might be more important than the job one does, or being a parent, or being a religious believer, or one's sexual identification, etc. Or a person might identify oneself as being a "worker" only while on the job; and it could be inconsequential elsewhere. Or one might hold a managerial position and, although meeting my definition of "worker," might see themselves as a "manager" and reject any connotation of being a "worker."

In other words, to be a "worker," one must hold both a job *and* identify oneself as a worker in any particular situation. This means an individual must *choose* that identity for oneself—or consciously accept others' imposition of that identity—and until the identity is *actively claimed* by an individual, they cannot be assumed to be coming from that position in the social order.

2. However, following the sentiment of Peter Waterman (1998), I see building global labor solidarity as one of (hopefully) many efforts to build global solidarity—such as among women, students, racial groupings, the young, peasants, the urban poor, etc.—and I hope that they eventually join and work together for the good of all. In other words, I specifically do not privilege workers over everyone else, although like Waterman, I insist workers must be involved.

3. I distinguish this from "progressive" nationalism, where one is proud of their political community/nation-state without using its power to attack others, whether symbolically, ideologically or physically.

4. "Global South" is shorthand for the less economically developed countries of Africa, Asia, Latin America and the Middle East, while "Global North" is shorthand for the more economically developed countries of Western Europe, Canada and the United States, Japan, Australia and New Zealand. This differentiation has been largely a result of "Western" imperialism—except Japan, which, while not "western," still has been imperialist—where the developed countries stole land, natural resources, raw materials and/or labor power from those lesser able to defend themselves militarily, and used these resources to develop their own, "home" country (most important among others, see Nederveen Pieterse, 1989; Scipes, 2010a, 2010b, 2016a).

Obviously, things have changed somewhat and the existing situation today is more complex, as some countries from the Global South—such as South Korea—have developed economically to the extent that they are now considered among the more economically developed countries, while others, such as Brazil, Israel, Mexico, and South Africa have moved toward that level of economic development (see Mc-Michael, 2012).

At the same time, there is growing recognition of the "Global South" existing *within* countries of the Global North—such as inner-city ghettos and barrios, agricultural areas dependent on migrant labor, and isolated rural areas such as some Native American reservations and parts of Appalachia (see Hedges and Sacco, 2012)—as in the present day United States. Nonetheless, while recognizing the simplification, the shorthand terms are used herein.

Incidentally, while TV ads for organizations such as CARE often show images of poor people in developing countries who have been victimized and need Western "help"—send money!—the situation in developing countries is much more complex. As I discuss herein, some of the most dynamic and developed labor movements in the world have been built in these countries—and these workers do not see themselves as "victims."

5. Building global labor solidarity will not, obviously, guarantee the creation of a planetary ecological consciousness: that has to be imagined and constructed together by peoples and organizations around the world. Nor is this to suggest than any of these labor centers mentioned herein has created a sufficient understanding of the ecological crisis; in fact, to my knowledge, they have not.

However, from my work challenging the foreign policy of the AFL-CIO Labor Center of the United States (Scipes, 2010a, 2010b), I have come to understand the need to challenge reactionary nationalism among the population of the US as a *precondition* to getting them involved in building global labor solidarity on a mass basis. Key to that is recognizing the humanity of working people around the world, rejecting the reactionary nationalism that we in the US, particularly but not only, have been taught. At the same time, however, once reactionary nationalism is challenged on a mass level, then developing a planetary ecological conscious becomes much more possible.

6. There are many others, as I mention throughout the text, who are working on or writing about building global labor solidarity; I only mention some of the key writings here that, in my opinion, are among the most important, while always recognizing that the field is much broader than this.

7. People who want to see this perspective developed to the greatest degree should check out the journal *Green Social Thought* (GST) at http://greensocialthought.org/, and its predecessor, *Synthesis/Regeneration* at http://www.greens.org/s-r/. I have been the economic and economics editor for GST for a number of years.

8. For an interesting discussion of the history of labor internationalism, beginning before the origin of the First International in 1864 to the late 1990s, see Waterman, 1998. He argues that labor and socialist internationalism (singular)—he sees them entwined—should be reconceptualized to be only one of multiple internationalisms (plural) today. As explicated in the Preface, I want to surpass "international" labor solidarity with "global" labor solidarity.

9. Thus I reject the under-theorized and inadequate conceptualization of "social movement unionism" as advanced by Kim Moody (1997), and argue that my earlier conceptualization is superior (Scipes, 1992a, 1992b); republished herein as Chapter 6. I later disentangle the theoretical confusion caused by Moody and those who build off his work, as well as others, in Chapter 13 herein.

10. Just in case it is not obvious, I am not confining the emergence of new labor movements to just these countries; these are simply some examples; what I address herein is workers' struggles wherever in the world they take place.

11. Labor centers, in international labor union terminology, are the "peak organizations" that join a number of unions together, and each labor center, in turn, works to further unify and strengthen the member unions. This is initially discussed in Chapter 4, and is explicated in detail in Chapter 5, both herein.

12. The experiences of *Solidarnosc* differed qualitatively from that of the other named labor centers, and much still remains unknown to English-speaking audiences. It was the only case of these five where the US Government supported the insurgency—at least through the AFL-CIO—while it opposed these radical labor centers in the other cases (Scipes, 2010a). Accordingly, *Solidarnosc* is beyond the scope of this book, and will not be considered here. Nonetheless, these women and men must be given their due, and at least mentioned before limiting our focus. For a recent, excellent account of *Solidarnosc,* see Bloom, 2014.

For my comments regarding the South Korea labor movement, see Footnote #5 in the Preface of this book.

13. Following William I. Robinson (1996), based on earlier work by Robert Dahl, it is argued there are two different types of democracy (although we are taught to think of democracy as a monolith): *popular* democracy and *polyarchal* democracy. Popular democracy is what is idealized within the United States, and is what we are told exists in reality: this is the idea of one person, one vote; that everyone has an equal say in decision-making; and that everyone who wants gets to express their opinion on any subject that potentially affects them. Polyarchal democracy, also referred to as "elite democracy" or "constrained democracy," refers to the situation where only a few, elite people get to define the situation and/or select possible candidates for an electoral position, and then "ordinary" people are allowed to choose from the possible options established for them (Scipes, 2010a: 191–192, endnote #10).

Focus here is on popular democracy.

14. It should not be necessary to make this point, but because of all the lies and distortions by the US Government about the government in Venezuela and its democratically elected late president Hugo Chavez and his successor, Nicholás Maduro, as well as the attacks by the corporate media led by the *New York Times,* the point must be made: things are changing and workers are building a new labor movement in Venezuela, with the general encouragement of President Chavez and his successors, so there is no suggestion here that the government of Venezuela is a dictatorship or working to undermine the labor movement, *unlike* the other countries where these things *are* happening. For accounts of developments in Venezuela, see especially Steve Ellner (2008) and Greg Wilpert (2007). For a discussion of places where the "radical left" is in power—and this specifically includes Chavez's regime (as well as Ecuador and Bolivia), see Ellner, 2013; Ellner, ed., 2013; Ellner, 2014; Ellner, ed., 2014. For an understanding of how social movements have driven Chavez far further than he would have gone on his own, see Ciccariello-Maher, 2013a, 2013b, 2014. For contemporary accounts in English, please see the website Venezuela Analysis at www.venezuelanalysis.com.

15. Instead of the commonplace term "society," which suggests social equality between members of any grouping, I use the term "social order"; this recognizes the inequality of *every* society in existence, with people at higher levels having more power than those below them. I argue that social order is a much more accurate and representative term than is society. The term "society" can be used for groupings of people whose relationships are basically equal.

16. People have multiple roles that they play in their lives: father, wife, daughter, worker, parent, activist, etc. When one role is used to guide one's actions, that is said to be their "identity." While some argue each person has a "master" identity, I don't accept it: I argue we each have multiple identities, and the identity chosen at any time is based on our understanding of a particular situation and what we believe is the best identity to help us address that situation.

17. Despite her subtitle, *A Guide to Movements Against Globalization,* Starr's 2005 book really is about this globalization from below movement; she was writing before this different perspective became adopted by these movements.

18. This author's focusing on the KMU, and using it as referent, is much more than personal predilection: it was seen by a number of international labor scholars—including Rob Lambert and Eddie Webster (1988), Ronaldo Munck (1988), Rob Lambert (1990) and Peter Waterman (1998: 125–136)—as an exemplar of this new type of trade unionism.

[Waterman believes—contrary to this author—that the KMU is controlled by the Communist Party of the Philippines, despite not presenting any substantial evidence to support this claim, and refusing to acknowledge the extensive evidence contrary to his position. He correctly recognizes that his interpretation "would be disputed by Kim Scipes (1996)" (Waterman, 1998: 149, endnote 14). See also Scipes, 2015b.]

There was extensive international support for, and interest in, the KMU. *International Labour* Reports (ILR) reported extensively on the KMU between 1984–1990. Further, while this author strongly disagrees with Waterman's analysis and interpretation of the KMU, nonetheless, Waterman (1998: 132–136) discusses extensive support of the KMU by activists in the US, the UK, the Netherlands, and across Western Europe, and notes, "ILR gave the Philippines and the KMU more attention than any other country or organization except South Africa and the COSATU." Waterman also notes that this support extended to a number of labor organizations, including national trade union centers in Australia, Ireland and New Zealand. Additionally, Lois West researched and did her Ph.D. dissertation while at the University of California at Berkeley on the KMU; she later published her dissertation as a monograph on the KMU (West, 1997). There has been extensive international participation every year in the KMU's International Solidarity Affair (Scipes, 2000a—reprinted herein as Chapter 12; see also Scipes, 2015a). In short, KMU was widely recognized as one of the most developed and dynamic labor centers of the 1980s–90s, although written accounts of its activities have diminished considerably since 1997.

19. The research strategy for my KMU study (Scipes, 1996)—based on the research question of "how were Filipino workers able to develop one of the most dynamic labor movements in the world while under a dictatorship?"—was based on recognition that there were multiple political economies within the Philippines,

and thus the process was to try to understand the development of four different, economically-important regional political economies (excluding Metro Manila), and the subsequent development of independent labor movements in each of them. Each of the four different political economies, crossing colonial and post-colonial production systems—capitalist agriculture in Mindanao, mineral extraction (copper mining) in Cebu, plantation sugar in Negros, and non-traditional manufacturing (electronics and garments) in a multinational export processing zone in Bataan—were placed in their historical developmental context. And then, the organizational processes of the unions that developed within each of these regional political economies were detailed.

Accordingly, labor unions were shown developing independently and differently in each of the four political economies, and that they then came together in a national, centrally-coordinated organization, the KMU Labor Center, on May 1, 1980. Once this nation-wide labor center was created, the power generated could be mobilized to advance the issues and concerns of the KMU members in the respective regions, as well as to advance common positions across the entire nation. The KMU played a central role in the overthrow of the dictator, Ferdinand Marcos.

Additionally, gender relations were considered within the KMU, not only in the nation-wide women's alliance, the KMK *(Kilusan ng Manggagawang Kababaihan),* but also in national labor federations and local unions.

Together, my historically-based study—including a multifaceted range of unions and associated organizations, developed within specific regional political economies, and which joined and interacted on a national basis—showed the development over a 14-year period (1980–94) of one of the most dynamic and developed labor movements in the world, certainly in the post-World War II era (Scipes, 1996). This study will soon be published on-line for free.

Already I have begun to work on a subsequent monograph on the KMU. I have returned to the Philippines and conducted research projects in 2015, 2016 and 2018 to update my original work, publishing some of these findings, but not many of them. This new monograph, looking at how the KMU has managed to survive over the last 40 years, despite terrible conditions and extensive violence against it—both state-sanctioned and "independent"—will hopefully be published in 2022 or 2023.

20. Again, Kim Moody (1997) has popularized the term "social movement unionism" in North America. However, this is a qualitatively weaker and much more limited version of what is being talked about in regard to CUT, KMU, and COSATU. Any references to social movement unionism herein refers to my version, and not Moody's. See Note #9, above.

21. These efforts by workers to establish different types of trade unionism is, obviously, different than efforts by some elites, acting through their respective state apparatus, who acted either to establish labor organizations to control their workers, or to support more conservative, established unions against the more independent and often more radical ones. This has taken place in a number of countries, such as China, Egypt, Mexico, and elsewhere, and were far-sighted attempts to ensure that independent labor organizations could emerge only with great difficulty, if at all. The purpose of these elite projects is social control, and containing labor is seen to be a central task.

Much of the AFL-CIO foreign policy program over the past 100 years has been to undercut independent unions that challenge the elite-dominated status quo in developing countries, especially those who are seen as being strategic to the US Empire. See the case studies—from Chile in the early 1970s, the Philippines in the mid- to late-1980s, and Venezuela in the early 2000s—that this author provided (Scipes, 2010a).

The CUT, KMU and COSATU each were able to overcome such efforts by their respective state.

22. This is in addition to all of the external pressure, particularly by "business," to get them to subordinate themselves to a democratically-elected political party.

Franco Barchiesi (2007)—in making a point that all should consider because he focuses on institutional change—argues, "While social movement unionism was highly effective in the struggle against state racism, [this] story . . . shows the limitations of such a strategy in a context of democratization and liberalization. According to various scholars, the growing rift between South Africa's trade unions and community politics reflects a decline of social movement unionism linked to organized labor's changing position in the new democratic dispensation. The possibility for trade unions to defend their members' jobs and wages through institutional channels and access to the ruling party would then marginalize rank-and-file and community activism" (Barchiesi, 2007: 65).

23. As elaborated in Chapter 13, herein, I argue there are three different *types* of trade unionism in the world—economic, political and social movement unionism—and that each can be broken into subsets or *forms* of that type. In Chapter 13, in an effort to clarify and disentangle a lot of theoretical confusion by writers around the world, I argue that economic trade unionism is comprised of two different *forms* of unionism, business unionism and social justice unionism.

Hence, I'm suggesting here that the CUT and COSATU appear to have reverted from the social movement type of trade unionism back to the economic type, but of the economic type, they have chosen the social justice *form* to guide their activities. Having returned to the Philippines in 2015, 2016 and 2018, I argue that the KMU has maintained its social movement unionism (Scipes, 2015a, 2018a, 2018b).

In any case, these labor centers—CUT and COSATU—no longer seem to be challenging the established social order in which they are located, nor the global political-economic networks in which their respective countries are enmeshed.

However, for those labor centers in authoritarian situations, I suggest the experiences of social movement unionism have things of considerable value to teach.

24. See Scipes, 2010a: 139–150, for an elaboration of the "Polyconflictual" macrosociological "model of society" on which this is based.

25. It is not clear to me whether CUT or COSATU have developed rank-and-file member education programs comparable to that of the KMU. There is no question in my mind that this education program has played a key role in helping the KMU survive the physical violence to which its members have been subjected (see Scipes, 1996).

Developing and implementing a sophisticated member education program seems essential to creating the solidarity across an organization crucial to withstanding external attacks, and to reducing if not preventing division from forces within.

26. According to the National Center for Children in Poverty, "Research suggests that, on average, *families need an income equal to about two times the Federal poverty level to meet their basic needs.* Families with income levels below this income are referred to as low income: $44,100 for a family of four" (emphasis added) (Chau, Thampi and Wight, 2010: 2). The poverty threshold set by the Federal government for the year 2013 was $23,550 (US Department of Health and Human Services, 2013).

In fact, if we utilized a *realistic* threshold for the poverty rate—and not the terribly insufficient amount provided by the government—then in 2012, 34.3 percent of *all* Americans would have been below the realistic poverty line that is 200 percent of the official poverty line (see DeNavas-Walt, Proctor and Smith, 2012: 17).

27. However, what must be remembered is that approximately two-thirds of all people in poverty in the United States at any time are white, despite whites having a lower poverty rate.

28. In early 2020, when this is being finalized, President Trump has been bragging about the good shape of the economy. Yet, "Fifty million people in the United States live in poverty, with little hope for themselves or their children," according to the international NGO, Oxfam (2020). The Bureau of Labor Statistics reported, "In 2018, the overall unemployment rate (jobless rate) for the United States was 3.9 percent; however, the rate varied across race and ethnicity groups. Among the race groups, jobless rates were higher than the national rate for American Indians and Alaska Natives (6.6 percent), Blacks or African Americans (6.5 percent), people categorized as being of Two or More Races (5.5 percent), and Native Hawaiians and Other Pacific Islanders (5.3 percent). Jobless rates were lower than the national rate for Asians (3.0 percent) and Whites (3.5 percent). The rate for people of Hispanic or Latino ethnicity, at 4.7 percent, was higher than the rate of 3.7 percent for non-Hispanics" (Bureau of Labor Statistics, 2019). The overall unemployment rate in January 2020 was reported at 3.6 percent. However, the U-6 unemployment rate—said to be the more accurate account, and which includes "discouraged workers"—was 7.7 percent (McMahon, 2020).

In any case, these low unemployment rates are arguably the result of the Federal Government running a growing deficit, projected to exceed $1 trillion in fiscal year 2020 under President Trump, with the National Debt—a measure of cumulative deficits and surpluses since the US was founded in 1789 until currently—presently exceeding $22 trillion (see Emma, 2020). I am arguing, therefore, that the low unemployment rate is more the product of deficit spending (i.e., writing "hot" checks) than is the product of solid economic growth.

29. Because Americans have been taught that our country is "exceptional," and "better," we have generally seen our country as separate from others; and the idea that people are now connecting Labor abroad with Labor-at-home is a step forward (see, for example, Zweig, 2014).

However, the reality is that the US—and earlier, since the arrival of the first Europeans on the continent—has always been a global project, and has always affected and been affected by other countries.

It might be helpful to consider an individual as being placed in the center of a ring of concentric circles, like a target, with each successive ring incorporating the previous one. Each of these rings represent different networks of power, and the scope expands as one moves away from the individual. So, the first ring might represent the power relations of the family, then of the locality, the region, the (territorial) state, the nation and, ultimately, the global social order. (And people can move between these networks of power depending on the situation at hand.)

The point here, however, is that while Americans are almost never taught about the global social order—or any limitations on the power of the United States—this global level of power has existed at least since the Crusades (Nederveen Pieterse, 1989). We are just illuminating it for Americans, so they can recognize that the global level of power relations has long existed, that we are affected by and affect it, that we should consciously understand its existence, and that incorporating this understanding is something we should have been taught about since our earliest school years. In other words, that there is no "at home" and "abroad" dichotomy, but rather there is a continuum of power relations extending globally from each individual. Thus, from the beginning, working people around the world should have been presented as brothers and sisters, not as competitors or as "the enemy."

30. Labor activists and workers have long been involved in addressing issues in their respective communities, but overwhelmingly as concerned individuals; this analysis suggests that local unions as organizations could become involved in addressing issues, both at work and in their respective communities. Obviously beyond the scope of this paper, this could be a product of transforming business unions into social justice unions (see Fletcher and Gapasin, 2008). In February 2020, I raised the question for labor activists: is it time to start discussing the possibilities of creating a new labor center in the United States? (Scipes, 2020a).

Part I

EFFORTS TO BUILD INTERNATIONAL LABOR SOLIDARITY IN THE 1980s

Lost in the passage of time are a range of projects that developed in the 1980s and 1990s to try to build international solidarity among workers. Some of these projects developed in the Global North, while others developed in the Global South. This section presents three efforts to build international labor solidarity in these years to try to give some flavor of this earlier work, recognizing that it is a very limited and partial account.

We begin with an interview of a key organizer of the Liberation Support Committee in the International Longshoremen and Warehousemen's Union (ILWU) in San Francisco, Larry Wright. ILWU Local 10 members boycotted a South African cargo being carried on a Dutch ship during November–December 1984, refusing to unload it, until a Federal Court ruled that they had to unload the cargo or face such fines that could bankrupt the Local. Wright was kind enough to give me an interview in early 1985, where he explained how they were able to successfully boycott this ship, and this was published in *International Labour Reports* in May 1985 (Scipes, 1985).[1]

Chapter 2 grew out of a trip that I took to Northwest Europe during the fall of 1985; this was prior to travelling from London to the Philippines, where I spent January and early February 1986, during what became the last days of the Marcos Dictatorship. I had been to Northwestern Europe for a shorter time in late 1983, but during late 1985, I sought to understand more about the various labor movements and what they were doing to build international labor solidarity. I found a number of interesting projects, particularly in the United Kingdom as well as in The Netherlands, Sweden and "West" Germany, and learned about their links with a number of projects around the world. This is an effort to report these efforts to build "shop floor internationalism" to particularly American workers, and was published during 1988 in a journal *Workers' Democracy,* which no longer exists (Scipes, 1988a).

The last chapter of this section is an effort to remember the British-based journal, *International Labour Reports* (ILR), which covered labor globally from 1984–1990. Unfortunately, none of the staff or editorial board has ever published anything describing or analyzing the project over time, but this was an extremely bold and adventurous project, and while I cannot give an inside account, I also do not want it forgotten. I stumbled upon ILR in November 1983 as they were preparing to hold a conference in Liverpool on free trade zones, which were Mrs. Thatcher's program for reviving the British economy.

Most importantly for me, they had brought a Filipino trade unionist, Wenilou "Weng" Pradel, to speak to the conference—Pradel had helped lead the first general strike in any of these export processing zones in the world in June 1982, at the Bataan Export Processing Zone (BEPZ) in Mariveles, Bataan. It was Pradel who introduced me to the KMU and, as stated above, I went out to see if what she said was true—it was!—in early 1986.

ILR worked consciously to build labor solidarity around the world, and was far ahead of its time. They provided extensive coverage of particularly the new unions developing in the Philippines and South Africa, but coverage was global and not just limited to these countries; they often included reports on developments in Europe and North America. However, they knew there were things that workers in the developed countries could learn from those in the developing countries, and they tried to share these understandings.

This account, which to me seems terribly insufficient, nonetheless serves to recognize an important project in which I had the honor of being asked to participate. It is a tragedy that the reactionary British libel laws brought this project to a halt.

While being all-to-limited, nonetheless, this section provides a taste of some of the important work being done in this earlier period.

NOTE

1. Peter Cole's book, *Dockworker Power: Race and Activism in Durban and the San Francisco Bay Area* (Cole, 2018), detailed this and other struggles to build global labor solidarity by the ILWU on the US West Coast, as well by workers in the port of Durban, South Africa.

Chapter One

San Francisco Longshoremen

"When that Ship Came in, We Were Ready"

When San Francisco's longshoremen boycotted [a] ship carrying South African cargo last November,[1] it was only after sustained education work in the union.[2] Kim Scipes spoke to Larry Wright of ILWU Local 10.

For eleven days during November and December of 1984, members of Local 10 of the North American International Longshoremen's and Warehousemen's Union (ILWU)[3] refused to work South African cargo that arrived on the Nedlloyd Shipping Lines ship, SS *Kimberly*, in the San Francisco Bay Area, California. This boycott was led entirely by a rank and file committee within the union. Despite legal rulings by arbitrators and pressure from the Employers' Association, these dockworkers solidly maintained their boycott. It was called off only in the face of adverse Federal Court rulings, and the threat of fines of $10,000 a day against the union local. Over 250 dockworkers had refused to work this cargo, each losing an average of $200 as a result of their action.

But this was not the first time Local 10 had taken industrial action as a form of international solidarity. Local 10 boycotted South African cargo in 1977, in response to a call by the ICFTU [International Confederation of Free Trade Unions].

Five hundred people turned up at the docks to add weight to the boycott of a single ship carrying South African cargo.[4]

EDUCATION WORK

Larry Wright, an active member of Local 10, says getting this kind of response to solidarity calls has come only after long-term educational work in the union. The Local first set up a Southern African Liberation Support

Committee in 1976, after the events in Soweto.[5] Larry, who is on the committee, is emphatic that "This was a rank and file committee of longshoremen (dockworkers) that were interested in the issues."

Over the years, the Committee has done a lot in the Local, although levels of activity have varied. In 1977, they had had gotten Local 10 and the International to pass resolutions urging their negotiating committee to include in any future contacts a ban on South African cargo. These resolutions condemned apartheid, and urged all other unions to stop all trade with South Africa.

PRACTICAL SUPPORT

Of all the education work, the most important, according to Larry, are activities involving practical support. In 1978, there was a Bay Area mobilization to give material support to the liberation struggle in Zimbabwe. Local 10 pressured employers to provide free containers and free transportation for medical supplies, clothing and books being sent via Mozambique to the liberation movements and refugee camps. This saved thousands of dollars in shipping charges. The union hall was used to sort and pack up the goods being sent. Many union members got caught up in the atmosphere of work going on. "This was real important," says Larry, "having this activity go on in and around the union hall. Everybody saw it and it was talked about quite a bit. Eventually, many workers got involved. It was real important that workers could not only talk about these things, but get involved and do something."

The Local 10 Committee has played a big role in mobilizing similar efforts in the Bay Area labor movement. They joined with other trade unionists to form the Trade Union Committee on Southern Africa (TUCSA), building connections throughout many unions in the San Francisco Bay area. TUCSA, in turn, sponsored a conference in 1978 that brought trade unionists together to discuss tactics for trade union solidarity work, such as how trade union pension funds and other investments could be withdrawn from banks and companies.

In the last few years, international work in the Local has slowed down. Yet it was still from a resolution from Local 10 that the ILWU Convention passed a policy whereby it would not handle any military goods or police weapons being shipped to El Salvador. The ILWU has not handled any military goods for Chile for a number of years.

MILITANT ROOTS

So how is it that so much international support work, unusual from an American union, has come from ILWU Local 10? Larry feels there have been several reasons. "A big factor in this," he says, "is the history of this particular union and how it got started. There was the big general strike in San Francisco in 1934, in which the union was founded. There was a strong commitment by the leaders and members to set up a very democratic union. Also, from the start, the leadership discussed the struggles of workers around the world, as part of the international class struggle. All of this contributed to the general political consciousness of the union. Another factor is the specific nature of long shoring work. Traditionally, you have a whole gang of guys together. You all must co-operate to get the job done. There's a camaraderie that builds out of this. And there's also a chance for a lot of discussion, including political discussion." But the continuing education work has been key in maintaining membership consciousness on international solidarity.

"One of the most useful things was the showing of the film *Last Grave at Dimbaze*," Larry told us. "It's a lot different to be able to show what's going on instead of just talking about it. Discussing the movie was important. Another thing was the involvement we had gotten from collecting the goods for the Material Aid Campaign at the Union hall."

As the crisis in South Africa deepens and labor protest inside the country has grown, there has been a resurgence of calls for solidarity actions. Toward the end of 1984, a motion for a boycott of South African cargo was passed unanimously by the membership of the Local.

READY

The first ship to be boycotted decided to bypass the Bay Area and get unloaded in ports elsewhere. When a second ship, the *Kimberly*, entered the Bay carrying South African cargo, the Local was well prepared. "Before that ship came in," Larry told us, "we had a number of community meetings. We tried to get the support and participation of other unions, political groups and community organizations beforehand. We set up phone trees. We planned as well as possible. When that ship came in, we were prepared: nothing happened which we didn't foresee. We were ready."

NOTES

1. This article was originally published as Scipes, 1985. Slight editing has been done on it, but it was generally left as published. As it was published in a British journal, *International Labour Reports,* I have kept spelling and organization the way it was originally published. Endnotes added are new.

2. For a much more in-depth and sophisticated account of the global solidarity work of the ILWU, see Cole, 2018.

3. After a considerable number of years of struggle, led by women members, the ILWU changed its name to International Longshore and Warehouse Union.

4. This author was involved in mobilizing community support for the boycott.

5. In early 1976, the South African Student Movement (SASM) opposed the apartheid state's effort to teach mathematics in Afrikaans—the "language of the oppressor"—in high schools instead of English. The students demonstrated on June 16th to protest a police raid that had taken place on June 13th to try to arrest the secretary of a SASM chapter in a high school. During the June 16th demonstration, the police killed 25 students, and local workers were attacked without provocation. The students responded militantly, and the struggle against apartheid qualitatively escalated afterward; June 16th was the turning point in the freedom struggle.

To have this put into the larger socio-political context, see Chapter 11, herein.

Chapter Two

Building the New Shop Floor Internationalism

Workers uniting around the world to support one another and to fight for a better world for all is a dream that has existed for over 150 years.[1] Yet slowly, almost invisibly, with steps quite small, this is becoming real.

Workers are combining in many different ways. Within a number of multinational corporations, such as General Motors, Ford, Unilever, Philips, IBM and Nestle, workers are joining across national boundaries to challenge their respective corporation's power. Some workers are connecting across company lines, as within the garment, electronics and telecommunications industries, to challenge the activities of all the corporations in each respective industry. Other workers, like those of the KMU, COSATU, and CUT labor centers within the Philippines, South Africa, and Brazil respectively, are building new, independent and "genuine" trade unions, and creating international support for their organization's challenge to their respective country's existing social situation.

Most efforts are by independent workers and/or their allies at the grassroots; others are by established unions. Most include workers from both developing—commonly referred to as Third World—and developed countries. All of these efforts are building on-going, stable organizations on the shop floor to empower workers, and most are fighting for people's liberation around the world.

Sometimes this work pays off in dramatic, inspiring actions, such as the 3M workers in a South African plant walking out in support of 3M workers in New Jersey, or the rank and file-led ILWU boycott of a ship carrying South African cargo. Usually, it's much more mundane. All of it is important; and the work continues.

WHAT IS SHOP FLOOR INTERNATIONALISM?

It might be useful to clarify what I mean by shop floor internationalism. Is it shop floor workers meeting shop floor workers from other countries for common activity? Is it union representatives meeting with other union representatives for common action? Is it shop floor workers in one country contacting government officials in other countries to support the work and health of workers in each country? Just what is it?

Shop floor internationalism is workers joining together across national boundaries to support each other through concerted action on the shop floor. This activity is not one way, as in charity, but is mutual support. It is based on building on-going connections and taking economic action on the shop floor to help workers around the world. This might include using tactics such as solidarity strikes, "hot cargoing" (refusing to handle blacklisted goods) and raising money on the shop floor for strike support. Again, it is concerted action on the shop floor.

As a shop-floor worker myself—I'm a printer[2]—I prefer that these efforts develop from the base, from workers on the shop floor. We know the situation for other workers best, and we can feel for them; I believe that common effort by shop floor workers is the most desirable and most dependable basis from which to act.

Yet, I also know that, when done well, unions can work to help other workers, and that international solidarity efforts by unions bring more people into any particular struggle and more resources, especially financial. In fact, in some European countries such as the UK and Sweden, union officials are often more aware of the need to build international solidarity than are shop floor workers.

What accounts for this? It is obviously a much different situation than that in the United States.

Probably the most important difference is the philosophy under which unions developed. In Europe, unionism is a *social justice unionism* instead of a *business unionism* that predominates in the United States.[3] Social justice unionism is marked by a willingness to challenge the existence of capitalism or at least the position of workers within it. Unions not only fight corporations when necessary, or their respective governments from the shop floor, but they also help organize to elect political parties to office. These governments are based on the unions' power and work with the unions to enact legislation that will benefit workers. Sweden's Social Democratic Party, for example, is based on the unions and has been in power something like 48 of the last 52 years!

(This is not saying I'm satisfied with or accept political parties of any stripe acting for workers; again, I prefer action by the base, by shop floor workers.

This merely notes the significant differences between European unions and the ones in the US.)

On the other hand, unionism in the US is based on business unionism. This approach accepts the domination of capitalism as defined by the ruling class, and replicates this domination within the unions. It generally disempowers the rank and file, although not always. It only considers union members' immediate needs, with basically no concern for the future, or for the working class as a whole. Also, because they accept and desire the well-being of capitalism and because the US is imperialist, business unions can choose to be imperialist, which the leadership of the AFL-CIO has almost continuously chosen to do. The AFL-CIO's foreign operations certainly substantiate this point (see Scipes, 2010a, 2010b, 2016a).

Some union members are challenging the actions of their unions and some are even confronting the philosophy of business unionism itself. Some locals have begun making international connections on their own to support workers overseas. I encourage this and would like to see these efforts intensified.[4]

Some unions and some international trade secretariats—international organizations of unions in common industries—in Western Europe are working toward and building shop floor internationalism. Among the more internationalist unions in Europe are the Transport and General Workers (T&GW) Union in the UK, the Irish Distributive and Administrative Trade Union (IADTU), and the Foodworkers Union in Sweden.

These unions actively encourage internationalism and educate their members about the issues of workers around the world. They have taken concrete action on the shop floor to support workers internationally. The T&GW has told their workers not to handle military cargo being shipped from England to South Africa on at least one occasion that I know of; they have sent delegates and supported the international networks of dockworkers being formed; and they have sent money to the KMU of the Philippines to support the KMU's educational programs. The IDATU told their members not to handle South African products and then strongly backed 18 workers at Dunnes' Stores in Dublin when they fought for over six months to get a co-worker reinstated after she had been suspended for carrying out union policy. The Foodworkers not only sent money, but also stopped all production of Coca-Cola in Sweden in support of the Coke workers' plant occupation in Guatemala during 1984.

These efforts of solidarity are important. Obviously, much more needs to be done. However, getting unions to take action on the shop floor is important and needed to be expanded, and these actions are building shop floor internationalism.

WHAT ABOUT EASTERN EUROPEAN AND SOVIET WORKERS?

Quite frankly, with the exception of the struggles of the Polish *Solidarnosc,* I know very little about workers' struggles in Eastern Europe and the USSR.[5] It is something I need to learn much more about. However, I will venture a few comments.

The official unions in Eastern Europe and the Soviet Union are part of the State apparatus. They definitely are not independent. At the same time, they argue for their members' interests within the Party and State apparatus.

From this understanding, I see two important conclusions. First of all, independent workers' efforts are important and must be supported. We need to find and connect with these workers on the shop floor. We need to build solidarity for them and for us. For example, *Solidarnosc* tried to stop the Polish Government from shipping coal to the UK during the 1984–85 Miners' Strike. This is a concrete case of Polish workers' solidarity with workers on the "Western" side of the political divide. We need to be able to reciprocate.

The second conclusion from my analysis of "Eastern"-bloc unions is that "Western" unions need to try to develop some linkage with these unions. Conversations need to take place. Certainly this does not mean accepting their domination over their members. However, especially as "Western" multinational corporations invest in the "Eastern" bloc, we must have conversations with the "Eastern" unions so we can share information regarding health and safety conditions, wages, benefits, and other information which could be of help to unions on both sides. We must not let our dissatisfaction with their domination keep us so far apart that the multinationals can play "Eastern" unions off against "Western" unions or vice-versa.

THE RISE OF SHOP FLOOR INTERNATIONALISM

Besides the almost complete betrayal by traditional trade unionism, especially by American business unions, a couple of factors have been key to the emergence of an independent international labor movement on the shop floor. The development of multinational corporations, their penetration throughout the "Third World" and the economic and political impact they have had upon these countries is the most important. Another related factor is the multinationals' growing capability to by-pass shop floor action by workers in one country through increased production of the same product by workers in a plant of another country.

The global expansion of capitalism is being challenged by the growing internationalist consciousness of workers and our allies. Two non-work related factors, both linked to the Vietnam War, supplement the consciousness raising caused by the multinationals. One factor was the War itself; many workers, especially in the United States, served in the military or had relatives in the military during the 1960s and 1970s.[6] This forced them to deal with the very real possibilities of themselves or their loved ones fighting in Southeast Asia. They were forced to see that more existed than just their private enclave in a developed country.

The other factor contributing to this internationalist consciousness was the protest movement against the War, and particularly the student-led portion of it. This protest movement was international, challenging the War and the hierarchical, oppressive societies that spawned wars and dominated people's lives. Perhaps the two greatest manifestations of this protest movement were the student-led uprising in Paris during May–June 1968 and the student strikes in the US in May 1970, although almost every developed and many developing countries had major outbreaks of student protests during the late 1960s (see Katsiaficas, 1987).

These factors have combined to help develop this international shop floor movement. The actions of the multinationals, faced with a growing global consciousness among workers and our allies, have met with organizations built on international memberships.

Since the late 1970s, a wide range of efforts have been initiated. Again, these have grown out of concrete situations and most have been started at the grassroots level. These grassroots organizations are member-controlled and democratic. They will usually work with progressive unions, but have worked hard to maintain their independence and have rejected any efforts of domination by the unions.

One of the most important efforts has been TIE (Transnationals Information Exchange). TIE was started to build unity among European workers in the auto, telecommunications and agri-chemical industries. (Initially, its name was TIE-Europe.) However, in the early 1980s, TIE expanded, developing close ties with auto workers in Brazil and agri-chemical workers in Malaysia, and with workers in the United States beginning in the mid–1980s.

TIE is a network of workers, activist organizations, some unions and progressive academics that are working in or around the selected industries. It is based in Amsterdam. It has joined campaigns, acted as a resource and information network, and organized international conferences of workers and allies to help build this shop floor internationalism. For example, TIE publishes *GM Workers' Voices* in five languages for GM workers worldwide.[7]

Other similar groups that I'm aware of are CAITS (Center for Alternative Industrial and Technological Systems), TICL (Transnational Information Centre, London) and Women Working Worldwide, all located in England. CAITS grew out of the Lucas Aerospace workers' decision to develop non-military products to replace military production by their company. They have worked with GM workers and have developed appropriate technology for developing countries.[8] TICL, perhaps more multinational-focused, has concentrated on the banking and the fast food industries as well as developing networks within Unilever and Ford.[9] Women Working Worldwide is an international women's organization that is designed to build solidarity among women in developing and developed countries. Its work is focused around women workers in the textiles, garments and electronics industries.[10]

Worker initiatives to build international networks have been quite substantial in the sugar and electronics industries. The International Commission for Coordination of Solidarity Among Sugar Workers (ICCSASW), founded in 1977, builds support for sugar workers around the world as well as develops programs for diversification of sugar crops.[11] IBM Workers United, founded in the US during 1976, has joined globally with workers and unions in an effort to organize IBM workers. IBM workers have already had three international workers' conferences, and have set up an information center in Sweden.[12]

One of the more dramatic displays of shop floor internationalism was 3M workers in South Africa walking out in solidarity with 3M workers in New Jersey. A South African woman who traveled in the United States and had met with the New Jersey workers whose plant was being closed, told their story to workers at the 3M plant near Johannesburg. The South African workers' walkout in early 1986 demonstrated that solidarity is *mutual,* and not merely developed country workers providing charity for their sisters and brothers in developing countries.[13]

Another impressive display of international solidarity was a rank and file-led boycott by American workers of a Dutch ship carrying South African cargo. Longshoremen of the ILWU (International Longshoremen and Warehousemen's Union) Local 10 in San Francisco refused to unload the ship for 11 days in November–December 1984. As a result of this successful effort, each worker sacrificed over $250 in lost wages. The boycott ended only in the face of threats by the Federal Court to fine the local union $10,000 per day for the boycott (see Scipes, 1985).[14]

The emergence of African-led, member-run, non-racial trade unions in South Africa, beginning in 1973, began a new level of workers' struggle in that country. From the founding of FOSATU (Federation of South African Trade Unions) in 1979 to the unification at a higher level of most non-racial unions into COSATU (Congress of South African Trade Unions) in 1985 until today, these unions have understood the importance of building international solidarity. Their ties, political and financial, have been strongest to British trade unions, which, along with the International Metal Federation, have given the most support (see Baskin, 1991; Friedman, 1987; Kraak, 1993; MacShane, Plaut and Ward, 1984).[15]

The Metalworkers Union in Brazil has played a key role in establishing worker-controlled unions and CUT (*Central Única dos Trabalhadores*) trade union center. Strikes in 1968 laid the groundwork for massive strikes by autoworkers in 1978 and '80, and the founding of CUT in 1983. Because the target of the '78 and '80 strikes were multinationals, the Brazilians have understood the importance of building international solidarity. They have played a key role in building the new international autoworkers' networks (TIE Reports, 1984; Slaughter, 1988; see also Beynon and Ramalho, 2000; Guidry, 2003; Sluyter-Beltrão, 2010).[16]

The *Kilusang Mayo Uno* (KMU-May First Movement) Labor Center of the Philippines has emphasized building international solidarity from its beginning in 1980. The International Department produces a monthly publication that is distributed globally. Its extensive member education program is very internationalist. Since 1984, the KMU has invited workers from around the world to celebrate International Workers' Day, May 1, in the Philippines. The KMU has built important support networks throughout Europe and North America, with considerable trade union support in Europe and Australia (Scipes, 1996; West, 1997).[17]

The Asian Workers Solidarity Link brings together workers throughout the Pacific Rim countries in Asia. The two most visible groups are in New Zealand and Malaysia.[18]

During the late 1970s–early 1980s, there was a Western European port workers' organization that extended throughout a range of ports. Besides the national Spanish port workers' organization, *La Coordinadora,* there were strong organizations in Hamburg, West Germany; Antwerp, Belgium; and Arhus, Denmark. Unfortunately, it seems only La Coordinadora has survived employer—and often, official union—attacks in any strength (see Weir, 1987; Fitz, 1988, 1990; Waterman, 1998: 79–110).[19]

A very small, independent effort in the US to educate workers to unite internationally with fellow workers and to develop an internationalist perspective is my effort called IWEB (International Workers' Education Bureau). IWEB also serves as an information resource and referral service. Besides sharing information I've learned from my travels throughout Western Europe and the Philippines, IWEB distributes *International Labour Reports* in North America.[20]

Additionally, a number of "worker support centers" have been developed in countries around the world. Originally founded to support local workers' struggles, they have linked with like-minded organizations around the world. I know of centers in England, Sweden, West Germany, Sri Lanka, Pakistan, India, the Philippines, Japan, Brazil and the US.[21]

INTERNATIONALISM AMONG THE "WESTERN" TRADE UNION MOVEMENT

Within the official trade union movement, the International Union of Food and Allied Workers' Association (IUF), a Geneva-based ITS (International Trade Secretariat), is notable for its efforts to build international solidarity among its member unions. The IUF has member unions throughout the non-Soviet dominated world that are located within the food and food processing industries. Most notably, the IUF twice organized international boycotts of Coca-Cola in support of striking Guatemalan Coke workers. They also have done considerable work within Nestle. However, they are limited by their anti-Communism and the fact they are an organization of unions, and thus are subject to all the political considerations of their member unions that can negatively affect independent workers' efforts (see International Labour Reports, 1987).

The International Metalworkers' Federation (IMF), once it was "convinced" by the African-led unions in South Africa to support their struggle—the IMF had supported the white unions until challenged successfully by the new African-led unions—has played a very positive role in supporting these unions (Webster, 1984). The IMF has helped establish formal connections between unions located in plants of the same corporation. For example, there are political and financial ties between Volkswagen workers in West Germany and South Africa, as well as between GM workers in the US and South Africa.

Unfortunately, as with the IUF, the IMF discourages links between workers in "free" trade unions with those in "Communist" trade unions.[22]

Of individual trade unions within the established labor movement, the British Transport and General Workers' Union (T&GW) is certainly one of the most internationally-focused unions. Its General Secretary, Ron Todd, is Chairman of the International Relations Committee of the British Trade Union Congress. He has supported shop floor unionism, and has stated publicly that the unions must get over this Communist/anti-Communist hang-up and find ways to work together when it is to their mutual benefit (International Labour Reports, 1986). Imagine that: a "Western" trade union leader willing to support international shop floor activities and talk with colleagues from the Soviet bloc when they face a common multinational that is willing to play workers from different sides of the political divide against each other!

COMMUNICATING INTERNATIONALISM

Not only is shop floor internationalism growing, but the efforts to communicate among individual workers and our potential allies are becoming more sophisticated and far-reaching.

One of the first efforts to communicate and theoretically develop the concept of shop floor internationalism was the establishment of NILS, *Newsletter of International Labour Studies.* Started by Peter Waterman, an Englishman who teaches at the Institute for Social Studies in The Hague, this effort preceded the establishment of FOSATU (the predecessor of COSATU), KMU, *Solidarnosc,* and CUT.

NILS, with an editorial board consisting primarily of students from developing countries who are studying at the Institute of Social Studies, has served as a communication resource and provided analyses for activists around the world. It has focused on not only workers' struggles, but also on how workers' struggles affect other social movements.[23]

Another important journal, *International Labour Reports,* has taken a more popular approach to communicating about workers' struggles. Based originally in Manchester but now in Barnsley, England, ILR carries news and information about workers and our struggles from around the world on a bimonthly basis. There truly is no comparable source of news and information in the world. Started in January 1984, ILR has covered an amazing array of subjects and struggles.[24]

An excellent journal that covers workers' struggle throughout a single region of the world is *Asian Labour Monitor.* Published in Hong Kong, it provides comprehensive coverage of workers' struggles throughout Asia.[25]

An academic journal, *LABOUR, Capital and Society,* has provided a forum for progressive academics to report their research and analysis of the changes taking place within the labor process internationally. Its focus has been primarily on workers in Africa and Latin America.[26]

South African Labour Bulletin supports the independent labor movement in South Africa. It analyzes and records the efforts of this movement.[27]

The KMU's journals, *KMU Correspondence* and *KMU International Bulletin,* are substantial efforts by a labor center to communicate news and information internationally about the struggles in which its members and their unions are engaged. News of the struggles of Filipino workers is always joined by news of workers' struggles elsewhere.[28]

A journal that began with a focus limited to the US and Canada, *Labor Notes,* now regularly carries stories about workers' struggles stories from other parts of the world. Most of their international focuses on Latin America, although they have had a number of articles on the Philippines and South Africa.[29]

Journals such as *ideas and action* and *Workers' Democracy* also carry news of workers' struggles from around the world. *Ideas and action* regularly carries international news, while *Workers' Democracy* has carried excellent articles on the occupation of a Caterpillar plant in Scotland and *La Coordinadora* in Spain (see Fitz, 1987, 1988, 1990; Weir, 1987).[30]

Coupled with these on-going efforts, there are three excellent films that are designed to communicate internationalism. The first, and still the best, is California Newsreel's *Controlling Interest;* this 1978 film was the first to delve into the world of the multinational corporations, and did it extremely well.[31]

Two films that have followed are *The Global Assembly Line* and *Bringing It All Back Home. The Global Assembly Line* focuses on workers in Mexican *maquiladoras* or "border factories"—American-owned factories in Mexico, located just across the border—and on Filipino workers in multinational corporations in their country, showing how they are fighting back.[32]

Bringing It All Back Home notes the "Third World" conditions being brought into Britain by multinational capital, and looking at the effects on British workers supporting the system that is doing that to them, while focusing on women's efforts to organize international solidarity among women workers.[33]

CONCLUSION

Activists in the United States tend to get discouraged by the lack of progressive political struggles by the labor movement. Looking at efforts around the world illuminates workers and our allies building international labor solidarity by developing international organizations at the point of production to confront the power of the multinationals and the global capitalist system. It is a process more of us need to join, participate in and expand. A solid base, rooted in the productive sphere of society, is a prerequisite for building workers' organizations to participate in larger societal political arenas, and in a world of multinational corporations, our organizations must be international as well.

Understanding that our organizations must be based on the shop floor and internationalist, they must also be egalitarian (i.e., non-hierarchical) and democratic (anti-domination). This means the members run the organization, and that none are more powerful than anyone else. In addition, education programs must be developed to raise the internationalist consciousness of our co-workers. And, of course, we must organize in our unions—those of us who belong—to repudiate business unionism, and to act in solidarity with workers around the world.

International solidarity on the shop floor: much more than a moral plea, it is the material necessity for workers everywhere. The South African workers at the 3M plant near Johannesburg, the ILWU longshoremen in San Francisco, the Filipino members of the KMU, the South African members of COSATU, the Brazilian workers in CUT, the members of the British T&GW, the Irish IDATU and the Swedish Foodworkers have shown us how: shop floor workers taking their destiny into their own hands is solidarity with workers around the world is a goal we should all seek to reach. If substantial change is going to take place in this world, class-conscious, internationalist workers, acting in concert on the shop floor, are the ones who will make it happen.

NOTES

1. This article was originally published as Scipes, 1988a, and was based on a six-month trip to Western Europe in late 1985–early 1986, prior to heading to the Philippines, where I spent most of January and early February 1986. Although minor edits have been made, and a number of additional entries have been made in the endnotes, the article remains as was originally written. In January 2020, I tried to locate web sites of these organizations and, where found, they have been added. Web sites and related information supersede the earlier information.

2. I worked in the printing trades from 1979 to 1988, working in binding and printing press departments of a number of shops, generally working on printing presses themselves, mostly in the San Francisco Bay Area. In 1981–82, I spent 18 months in the southern US, trying to organize print shops in Murfreesboro, Tennessee and Shepherdsville, Kentucky, but later returned to the Bay Area.

3. This term, *social unionism,* has been superseded, at least here in the US, by *social justice unionism,* and I have adopted the latter term herein. I believe I was the first to use this term, in my (to date) unpublished 2003 Ph.D. dissertation (Scipes, 2003), but it was independently developed and used in a book by Vanessa Tait in 2005. It became more commonly known and used with a third, still independent, effort, the 2008 book, *Solidarity Divided* by Bill Fletcher, Jr., and Fernando Gapasin.

4. For an excellent account of a "worker-to-worker" model of building global labor solidarity by Canadian workers, see Katherine Nastovski (2016a). For discussion of Canadian workers' efforts to confront apartheid in both South Africa and Israel/Palestine, see Nastovski, 2014.

5. I assume the parallels in interacting with contemporary unions in China, and perhaps elsewhere, should be obvious.

6. A book published in 2013 by Penny Lewis provides a much better understanding of the 1960s–70s anti-war protest movement in the United States than has been previously presented, and attacks the prevalent belief that workers in general strongly

supported the wars in Southeast Asia; in truth, as is well established therein, some workers supported the war, but many others did not. (See Lewis, 2013.)

7. TIE, Paulus Potterstraat 20, 1071 DA Amsterdam, The Netherlands. For an in-depth report on TIE, see Jeroen Peijnenburg (1984). In 1984, TIE and the Institute for Policy Studies in Washington, DC, sponsored a conference called "Meeting the Corporate Challenge" with activist and researchers from around the world. *TIE Reports,* Number 18/19 was based on this conference and includes the most comprehensive listing of internationally-focused workers' and allies' groups of which I know.

On January 31, 2020, I searched for TIE, and it apparently has been relocated to Frankfurt-am-Main, Germany. Its web site is http://www.tie-germany.org/who_we_are/index.html.

8. CAITS, Polytechnic of North London, Holloway Road, London N7 8DB, England. They have apparently disbanded, but an article on them can be found at http://www.tandfonline.com/doi/abs/10.1080/02697458908722745.

9. TICL, 9 Poland Street, London W1V 3DG, England. TICL has apparently gone under, as the only thing I could find of them was a 1987 report on McDonald's in England at http://www.mcspotlight.org/media/reports/trans.html.

10. Women Working Worldwide, 2/4 Oxford Road, Manchester M1 5QA, England. See Hale and Willis, 2007. On January 31, 2020, I located their web site at http://www.women-ww.org/.

11. ICCSASW, 11 Madison Avenue, Toronto, Ontario M5R 2S2, Canada. They apparently closed in 1998. A search brings up a web site for "World Sugar History Newsletter," which was given the materials from ICCSASW, and has other material on the sugar industry worldwide: http://projects.chass.utoronto.ca/wshn/number37.html.

12. IBM Workers United, P.O. Box 634, Johnson City, NY 13790, USA. See Lee Conrad, 1985. Apparently, they have disbanded. For an article on union organizing in the high-tech industry that mentions this organization, see Early and Wilson, 1986.

13. The Labor Institute, 853 Broadway, Suite 2014, New York, NY 10003, USA played a key role in coordinating this action. Its web site is http://thelaborinstitute.org/about.html. For an analysis of this action, see Rachleff (2015).

14. My 1985 article is reprinted in this collection as Chapter 1.

Professor Peter Cole (2018) published a book on international labor solidarity by dockers/longshore workers, based on workers in the San Francisco Bay Area and Durban, South Africa.

15. Labor struggles in South Africa have been documented and commented on in real time more than in any other developing country, and probably in the world. The work is generally top quality. Central to this has been the widely acclaimed *South African Labour Bulletin,* a bi-monthly journal that has been published for over 35 years. It can be found at www.southafricanlabourbulletin.org.za. For the best single listing of articles and books on South African labor struggles that I know of, see my on-line bibliography at https://www.pnw.edu/faculty/kim-scipes-ph-d/publications/contemporary-labor-issues-bibliography/. See Section 3, Workers around the World, under South Africa. See also Chapter 11, herein.

16. The leader of the Brazilian auto workers. Luiz Ignacio da Silva, popularly known as "Lula," later served as President of Brazil from January 1, 2003 to December 31, 2010.

17. Key to building support for the KMU in North America has been the Philippine Worker Support Committee's *Alert,* edited by John Witeck in Honolulu.

An account of how the KMU builds international labor solidarity is Chapter 12, herein.

KMU has a Facebook page that carries news and updates in Tagalog and English: https://www.facebook.com/kilusangmayouno/.

18. Asia Workers Solidarity Links-Aoteraroa, P.O. Box 13367, Johnsonville, Wellington 4, New Zealand and Asian Workers Solidarity Link, c/o Sahabat Alam Malaysia, 37 Lorong Birch, 10250-Palau Pinang, Malaysia. (As of May 19, 2013, there is the Australian-Asian Workers Links, P.O. Box 45, Carlton, South Victoria 3053, Australia, with an e-mail address of aawl@aawl.org.au.)

19. Dr. Katy Fox-Hodess has been doing contemporary work on dockworker networks; see Fox-Hodess (2017, 2018, 2019, 2020).

20. Unfortunately, IWEB no longer exists.

21. Coventry Workshop, 38 Binley Road, Coventry, West Midlands CV3 1JA, England; Internationella Folkhogskolan, Box 2059, 40311 Goteborg, Sweden; Express, Ludwigstrasse 33, 6050 Offenbach-am-Main 4, West Germany; Pakistan Institute for Labor Education and Research, D Block, Shershah Colony, Karachi 28, Pakistan; Union Research Group, B/31 Sun e-Sea, Verova, Bombay 400 061 India; IBON, P.O. Box SM-447, Sta Mesa, Manila, Philippines (http://iboninternational.org/); Pacific-Asia Resource Center, P.O. Box 5250, Tokyo International, Japan; IBASE, Rua Vincente Souza 29, 22251 Rio de Janeiro, Brazil; and Plant Closures Project, 433 Jefferson, Oakland, CA 94607, USA. (IBON is the only organization of which I can find current information; I know the Plant Closures Project went under in the early 1990s, and I suspect the others have ended as well.)

22. For a post-Cold War study of these Global Union Federations or GUFs—they were formerly called International Trade Secretariats—and how they operate in Latin America, see Collombat, 2011.

23. NILS was shut down in 1990. Peter Waterman continued to be extremely provocative thinker and prolific author until his death; see especially Waterman, 1998. [Peter died at the age of 81 in June 2017.]

24. Unfortunately, ILR also went under in the early 1990s, the victim of Britain's terrible libel laws. For an account of ILR, see Chapter 3, herein.

25. *Asian Labour Monitor* was founded in 1976, and its web site is at www.amrc.org.hk/link.They have a number of links to labor movements, labor-support organizations and trade unions operating particularly in Asia.

26. LC&S, Centre for Developing Area Studies—McGill University, 3715 Peel Street, Montreal, Quebec H3A 1X1, Canada. Their web site is www.lcs-tcs.com/.

27. SALB continues to publish today, and it remains of very high quality. See note 15, above.

28. The KMU's publications have gone electronic and are much more irregular than they were when this article was written. For information, contact the Philippine

Workers Support Committee, 2252 Puna St., Honolulu, HI 96817. Or you can contact the KMU directly at their email: kmu.intl@gmail.com.

For more on how the KMU works to build international labor solidarity, see Chapter 12 herein. Also, see its Facebook page, provided in Note #17, above.

29. Their web site is www.labornotes.org.

30. Unfortunately, both of these journals no longer publish. The successor to *Workers' Democracy, Green Social Thought,* can be found at http://greensocialthought.org/.

31. California Newsreel's web site is http://newsreel.org/.

When I teach my "Sociology of Developing Countries in a Globalizing World" course at Purdue University Northwest, I start by showing this film.

32. *The Global Assembly Line* is no longer available from New Day Films, whose web site is http://www.newday.com/films/The_Global_Assembly_Line.html.

33. *Bringing It All Back Home* is available through the Women Make Movies website at http://www.wmm.com/filmcatalog/pages/c188.shtml.

Chapter Three

International Labour Reports
A Personal Report and Appreciation

At a conference in Liverpool, England in late 1983, a new international journal was launched: *International Labour Reports* or ILR. ILR was consciously intended to build international labor solidarity, and was an exemplary, but little known, project that existed between 1984 and 1990.

This is an effort to at least make people aware of this innovative and globally important project before it's lost.

INTRODUCTION

Inspired by Don Thomson and Rodney Larson's classic *Where Were You, Brother? An Account of Trade Union Imperialism* (Thomson and Larson, 1978), and working with Thomson, ILR was a project that brought together a number of people from across the British left. It was spearheaded by Stuart Howard and Dave Spooner who, along with Alice Donald, were to staff the new journal. Members of the Editorial Board, mentioned in the first issue (January–February 1984), included these three folks, but also Diane Elson, Ian Hartford, Fred Hassan, Nigel Haworth, Joe Holly, John Humphrey, Pat McDougal, Martin Palmer, Sol Picciotio, Mike Press, Gerry Reardon, Roger Smith, Ian Stewart, Peter Waterman and Sue Willet.[1]

I met them on a fluke. Intending to put my body on the line to protest the Reagan Administration's decision to deploy Cruise and Pershing missiles against the Soviet Union in then-West Germany during December 1983[2]—a decision that would radically change my life—and never expecting to get to Europe again, I went over early, starting in Brighton, England, on the southern coast. Going to radical book stores in every town I spent any time in, I got addresses of progressive projects throughout the country, and headed north, visiting this group and that. Crucially, I met Mike Press in Coventry, who told me about the forthcoming conference, and he then connected me with the folks at ILR.

I arrived in Manchester, where they were based, and was invited to attend pre-conference planning meetings in Liverpool, which also meant consuming large quantities of British bitters. (Extensive field research showed I could not drink as much beer as my British comrades.) The purpose of the conference was to educate and to formally announce the pending publication of ILR, which was based on the understanding that it was necessary to build international solidarity among workers and their unions; they also felt that the unions of the "third world" could teach those of us in the developed countries about ways to successfully fight multinational corporations. To begin the process, ILR staff had organized a conference on "free trade zones," Prime Minister Margaret Thatcher's then-impending scheme to "revitalize" the British economy, and had brought in a female trade unionist from the Philippines to talk about experiences there.

Wenilou "Weng" Pradel did not meet the Western image of a labor leader or activist: she was not only female, but a small woman—no bulging muscles on her!—and a little over five feet tall. What I found out, though, was that Weng had just helped lead the first general strike in any export processing zone in the world: 26,000 workers, over 90 percent female and mostly between the ages of 16–24, had gone on strike at the Bataan Export Processing Zone from June 4–7, 1982, both to defend 54 arrested co-workers and to challenge the economic policies of the Marcos Dictatorship.

Spending some time together and getting to know her somewhat, Weng told me of this innovative labor movement being built in the Philippines, united in the KMU (*Kilusang Mayo Uno,* May First Movement) Labor Center. To say I was intrigued would be an understatement—after all, as an activist within my union, I was aware of the stunning deficiencies of the US labor movement. This meeting eventually led to me make six trips to the Philippines between 1986–94; I subsequently published a book in 1996 about the KMU, to tell others what I had learned from militant workers in the Philippines: *KMU: Building Genuine Trade Unionism in the Philippines, 1980–1994* (Scipes, 1996).

[It was also in Manchester that I met Don Thomson, co-author of the classic *Where Were You, Brother?* From Thomson, I learned about the foreign operations of the AFL-CIO for the first time. This ultimately led to decades of work against the AFL-CIO's foreign policy and operations and, in 2010, I published my book, *AFL-CIO's Secret War against Developing Country Workers: Solidarity or Sabotage?* (Scipes, 2010a, see also Scipes, 2016a).

[In 1990, with the strong encouragement of Dr. Peter Waterman—who was the continental Europe representative of ILR and whom I met during 1984, one of the foremost scholars in the world on labor internationalism—I applied to and was accepted for a Masters in Development Studies program at the Institute of Social Studies (ISS) in The Hague, The Netherlands, where Waterman taught. Working with Waterman and Dr. Jan Nederveen Pieterse (double last name, no hyphen), I received my Master's Degree in December 1991. In addition to all I learned in my studies and from my fellow students, this time at the ISS rekindled of my love for formal education, and a decision to do a Ph.D. in Sociology, which I earned from the University of Illinois at Chicago in July 2003. And then on to my career as a professional sociologist.]

To return to *International Labour Reports*. As a result of our interactions in England, and after I returned to the US in early 1984, the ILR staff asked me to become their North American representative, to which I eagerly agreed. I served in that role from 1984 to 1989.

Unfortunately, as far as I know, no one has ever published an account of the founding or on the development of ILR. I want to discuss the magazine, as it is history that apparently will be lost if I don't, but it must be recognized that this account is extremely limited: I was not an insider, and played no role in the initial or subsequent development of ILR, other than I tried to promote it in North America (with extremely limited results).[3] Further, I only published two articles in ILR: "The Reagan Toll," discussing US President Ronald Reagan's impact on labor to date in ILR #6, November–December 1984: 9–10 (Scipes, 1984b); and "San Francisco Longshoremen: 'When that ship came in, we were ready,'" discussing the ILWU #10 boycott of a Dutch ship carrying South African cargo in late 1984 in ILR #9, May–June 1985: 12–13 (Scipes, 1985), which is published as Chapter 1 in this collection.

ILR published 40 bi-monthly issues between January 1984 and August 1990, most with 28 pages, plus information, inspiring graphics, useful resources, notes on conferences, books, etc., on the inside and outside of the back cover; there were also a few larger "double issues" produced. Each issue covered news and developments of workers and their organizations from around the globe, and examined many different issues affecting workers. Most importantly in their history, they covered the launching of COSATU in South Africa, and development of the KMU in the Philippines; as Peter Waterman (1998: 133) noted, "The ILR gave the Philippines and the KMU more attention than any other country or organization except South Africa and the COSATU."

METHODOLOGY

As I have an almost complete set of issues of the journal—missing only #3 (May–June 1984) and #31 (January–February 1989)—I decided to examine one issue from each of ILR's seven years of publication. Since they followed the same publishing schedule, I thought I would select one bimonthly issue and examine the copies from the same months, year-by-year. Because of the missing issues, this precluded me from examining the January–February and May–June issues; further, I did not want to include issues which included my two articles, which excluded (again) May–June and November–December. So, that left me to choose from the March–April, July–August, and September–October issues. To allow for a random selection process among those three issues, and to preclude any bias that I might have, I had my 17-year-old son blindly pick a piece of paper out of a hat with the issues listed: he chose the March–April issues.[4] I then made sure that all of these issues were available, which they were, and these were each single issues, each with 28 pages. This allowed the most robust comparison possible.

FINDINGS

Here, I simply report the material in each March–April issue, year-by-year, from its 1984–1990 issues (seven years).[5] I begin with a full account of the second issue of the magazine in March–April 1984, with its slogan "The magazine providing unique coverage of international labour movement news" on each cover, to suggest the range of issues covered each month, but then shift only to discussing "major articles," along with relevant comments. This allows us to see the breath of ILR's coverage, and how it changed over time to keep up with changing situations in the world of labor.

1984 (ISSUE #2)

The cover is a 1982 black and white photo of French workers inside of a Peugeot-Talbot factory in Poissy, highlighting "The Battle of Peugeot-Talbot."

The inside front cover is a full-page ad by the International Labour Office (ILO) of the United Nations, listing four different publications of possible interests to ILR readers.

On the editorial page, there is again an introduction to ILR (this was issue #2), an ad for the magazine, and a restatement of "The Aims of ILR," which are:

1. To provide information about national employment and production in an international context;
2. To publicize labour conditions and trade union activity throughout the world;
3. To analyze the operations of multinational corporations and report on the struggles against them; and
4. To provide a forum for the exchange of ideas and information on international solidarity links.

There are three pages of short news items, including titles and countries/corporations/unions affected. Just a brief summary gives some idea of the scope of concerns expressed in ILR: "Communications world moves" (alliance between AT&T and Philips re Western European workers); "multinational détente" (Western multinational and Eastern—Soviet bloc—government resources); "Sell off and sell out" (Associated British Foods, ABF); "Pentagon overspends" (US corporations ripping off government through defense contracts); "Union busting bank" (Citibank caught providing an "anti-union" guide in the UK); "Insurance boycott" (South African insurance company being boycotted after firing over 100 striking workers); "'Embarrassment' for jobs" (British American Tobacco in UK); "Axe threat to yellow union" (government in Indonesia threatens to close yellow labor center for not being cooperative enough); "Full stop in Uruguay" (public transportation stopped and shops closed in the first general strike in the country in 10 years); "Tebbit laws hit Canada" (reactionary labor laws passed in British Columbia); "El Salvador" (a national strike in that country by the workers of the Institute of Urban Housing that lasted from August 30–October 10); "Walk-out on the south seas" (hotel workers in Tahiti rebel at four of its top hotels); "Hungry protest at Renault" (40 Renault workers in Belgium conduct a rolling hunger strike, seeking reinstatement of an unjustly terminated colleague); "ICEF boss retires" (Charles Levinson, the General Secretary of the International Federation of Chemical, Energy and General Workers Union—an International Trade Secretariat—announces his retirement); "Unions call for 35 hour week" (The German union, I.G. Metall, is getting ready for a major fight with employers over working time); "Caribbean delegation" (a Cuban building worker who had been in Granada was going to London to try to get trade unionists there to protest US invasion of Grenada); "Union sets picture straight" (the South African National Union of Textile Workers issues report, challenging white unions' collaboration with government against them); and "Conference urges worker unity" (report of international labor conference in October 1984 in Toronto).

Major articles include "'Kabert' Olalia—A Legend in Asia" (reporting on the December 4, 1983 death of long-time Filipino labor leader and co-founder of the KMU, Felixberto Olalia); "Sweden: The rise of the worker investors"; "Veteran Trade Union Leader Transferred to Lahore Fort" (in Pakistan); "Britain's Stake in Torture" (supplying tools of repression); "Chinese permit strikes" (new trade union constitution gives workers a limited right to strike against unsafe working conditions); "Bangladesh general strike" (three million workers go out in a one-day general strike in November 1983); "Boss proof locks!" (four Chrysler executives, including chairman Lee Iacocca, were locked in a mini-van after an executive forgot to release the child-proof lock).

Letters came from Sri Lanka and London.

There were more major stories. This began with an article on "The runaway office jobs," and was followed by a couple of articles on conditions in Brazil: "Brazil: the new militancy," and a small supplement, "Brazilian women organize." "The Battle of Peugeot-Talbot" included details of that struggle, as well as a section on "The struggle of immigrant workers." This was followed by "CDC-development and terror" (discussing the British Commonwealth Development Corporation's role in affecting third world agriculture, with a discussion of "The lost command" operating in the Philippines that is implicated in village massacres and bombings to force peasants off their lands in Mindanao, along with a picture of a severed head). Then, "Central America—the AFL-CIO's backyard?" (with the American Institute of Free Labor Development collaborating with the government and other right wing forces in El Salvador), as well as "We kidnapped the boss so the army wouldn't attack us" (print workers in El Salvador). There was a story on Nicaragua, as well as one, "Unholy Alliance in Honduras," detailing the alliance between the Unification Church and "a bizarre collection of Protestant fundamentalist groups" and members of the Honduran military in a common fanatical anti-communist crusade.

This began a new section on global labor organizations, "What is an International Trade Secretariat?" plus an example of a global labor campaign: "Striking the Flag: The ITF [International Transport Federation] 'Flags of Convenience' Campaign" (which challenges countries that allow substandard ships to register under their flag); this article included historical ads regarding the organization of the ITF in the 1890s, an account of current conditions on the ship "Venus," and a quick account of using "cheap," Third World seafarers to staff their ships.

Finally, there was a story on "Using Company Information," with listings of various resources, contacts and movement-oriented advertisements. On the back cover was an advertisement for a special issue of *TIE-Europe Reports* [Transnationals Information Exchange], on "Labour in the Eighties—An International Guide," with a free copy to all new ILR subscribers.

In short, an impressive collection of news and information about workers and their struggles literally from around the world. Some of these were mere inches in length, while others were two to three pages. It was written in a popular style, with a wide array of graphics, and a sense of humor.

For the rest of this piece, I report only on major articles and, where identified, their authors.

1985 (ISSUE #8)

This issue focused on the tragedy at Bhopal, India, where a Union Carbide plant released a chemical, methyl isocyanate (MIC), that killed over 2,500 people within a week. The front cover showed two men carrying poisoned children to help. Articles included in this section included a very critical piece, "Mass Death at Bhopal—Whose Responsibility?" by Barbara Dinham; "Questioning Development Strategy," where K.P. Kannan, a prominent environmental campaigner in India, argued that this disaster required "a rethink by the government of its whole industrial strategy"; "The Bhopal MIC Disaster—The Beginnings of a Case for Workers' Control"; and, finally, "Bhopal: Campaigns," which discusses some global campaigns organizing against hazardous industrial production. These articles were accompanied by a union graphic and a picture of bodies of victims, "stacked close to morgues. The union estimates that the death toll has reached over 8,000 and is still rising."

Other major articles in this issue include "Exporting Death" by Fred Hasson, looking at the practice of western countries moving hazardous production overseas and into the "third world."

This was followed by several articles about IBM (International Business Machines), including "Big Blue's Big Family," talking about IBM's efforts to remain "union free"; "IBM Resistors," about Americans organizing within IBM and efforts to build international labor solidarity; "The Power of IBM," with "Conclusions of the first IBM International Workers Conference, Tokyo, May 1984."

Next was a series on quality circles, which was an anti-union tactic designed to undercut existing unions: "Quality Circles" in Britain; "How Does a Quality Circle Work?" and then "The 'Quality of Life' in GM" (General Motors).

Then there was a series under the rubric of "Strategies for International Organization," which included "The ITS [International Trade Secretariat-KS] Strategy": a "Declaration" from the IMF's [International Metalworkers Federation-KS] Ford World Auto Council from their January 27, 1985 emergency meeting in Geneva; "International Workers' Links," an interview with Jeroen Peijnenburg of Transnational Information Exchange in Amsterdam who discussed the September 1984 world conference of General Motors workers, which included auto workers from the US, Australia, Brazil and Europe; and then "Charting New Ground," about a November 1984 European Trade Union Conference, intended to build international union cooperation between workers in the Dutch multinational, Philips.

1986 (ISSUE #14)

This issue has a major section on unions and the textile trade. It begins with "All Out for Protection," an article by Celia Mather who examines developing country unions' willingness to support protectionist campaigns against "third world" textile workers. This is followed by a short explanation of "The Multi-Fibre Arrangement"; "Social Clauses—Are They Enough?" (a look to see if protectionism can protect workers' rights); "Hanging by a Thread" (Bangladesh's new clothing industry); "South Korea: Fighting the 'Love the Company' Corps" (about repression of textile unions in South Korea); and then, "Not Playing It British," about the closure of a Courtauld's textile plant in the UK.

This is followed by a formal ILR interview with Ron Todd, newly elected General Secretary of the Transport and General Workers Union and Chairperson of the British TUC's [Trades Union Congress-KS] International Committee. Todd questioned the ICFTU's (International Confederation of Free Trade Union, the global "Western" peak labor organization), rule of no contact with Communist-led unions, whether in Europe or in the Soviet Union.

Then, reporting on the end of the UN's "Women's Decade," with a section on "Paper Promises Need Direct Action," Belinda Coote of the UK wrote a piece, "If They Signed It, Make Them Do It," while Vilborg Hardardottir of Iceland wrote about "Icelandic Women—Doing It for Themselves," the latter discussing women's strikes of 1975 and 1985 in that country.

After that came a section on "Supertechnology: Research and Development—For Whom?" This included articles on "'Star Wars'—Dancing to an American Tune" (where implications of US President Ronald Reagan's "Strategic Defense Initiative" were being challenged in the UK), and "Laboratory Plantations," discussing biotechnology, and especially Unilever, which pioneered the cloning of crop plants with its work on oil palms.

1987 (ISSUE #20)

This issue began with a major section on black workers and trade unions, asking "Less Equal than Others?" and then "Where's the Politics?" the latter which argues that information packets given to British workers neglect crucial political issues.

There was a major ILR Interview with Dan Gallin, General Secretary of the International Union of Food and Allied Workers' Association (IUF) titled "Not East or West but Below." Gallin, a long-time anti-communist internationalist, challenged the position of Ron Todd, which was detailed in issue #14, reported above.

Mike Press reported on a December 1986 conference of telecommunications workers, "Long Distance Solidarity," that took place in The Netherlands:

> An international conference of trade unionists and researchers held in [The Netherlands] during December examined this restructuring and discussed international union strategies to combat the accompanying attacks on jobs and union organizations. Transnational Information Exchange (TIE), the international network of labour research groups which helped organize the worldwide meetings of General Motors workers (ILR 15), brought together 26 trade unionists from 14 countries, including Japan, Nicaragua, Malaysia, Brazil, USA, the Philippines, Chile and many European countries. Participants came both from service providers, like British Telecom, and from manufacturers like the Swedish multinational, Ericson.

Following was a major section on the British multinational BTR, titled "In the Dark Ages." This included stories on BTR in South Africa—"SARMCOL Strikers Killed"—and in the UK, "Sacked En Masse." Then there was a two-page report on the corporation itself—"BTR: The Dawn Raider," along with a listing of many of BTR's subsidiaries—followed by a report on BTR in Trinidad, "Illegal Lock-Out."

Then came a report by Mike Allen on "Unions Probe IBM." This was a major initiative by three major international trade secretariats—the International Metalworkers' Federation (IMF), the International Confederation of Commercial, Clerical and Technical Employees (FIET, after its French acronym), and the Postal, Telegraph and Telephone International (PTTI), who collectively count something like 26 million workers globally as members—to try to develop unions within IBM.

Following came reports on workers in Turkey—"Fit for the EEC?"—and Spain: "No Gracias, Felipe." Then came a report on Unilever's subsidiary in India, Hindustan Lever: "Dirty Deeds in India."

And finally, Mike Allen interviewed Jack Jones, former General Secretary of Britain's Transport and General Workers Union, and ex-chair of the Trades Union Congress' International Committee, about Jones's 1986 autobiography, *Union Man.* Jones talked about his combatting fascism in Europe from Britain, then going to Spain to fight Franco's fascism, and then his time in the trade union movement after the war, into the 1970s, when he traveled to meet the new black unions in South Africa. Allen pulled out an excellent quote about internationalism from Jones's autobiography:

> Internationalism is part of the life-blood of the trade unions. . . . The strongest bond of human sympathy outside the family relationship should be one uniting all working people of all nations, tongues and kindreds. The hand of friendship, not paternalism, is what is needed . . . trade unions should see their relationship in the words of the first Labour Party leader, Keir Hardie: "They are the workers, they are our kin, we are part of them—their battle is our battle. What hurts them hurts us—their gain is our gain. Feelings of international solidarity are not easy to arouse and yet are part of the fibre of trade union principles."

1988 (ISSUE #26)

This issue featured a major section on unions in Brazil. It discussed the political changes that had developed, "From Dictatorship to Democracy: Not Different Enough." They talked about "Economic Miracle?" and had a section on deforestation of the Amazon, "Mistaken and Myopic." There was a report on "Rural Unions on the Rise," and "Your Enemy is Our Enemy," about the threat of economic development to indigenous peoples.

This is followed by reports on unions and development. First, Mike Allen writes about "Solidarity or Sympathy?" which reports that workers could make tax-free donations to organizations in the third world, and then Steve Percy examines the practices of British unions in "Short Arms, Deep Pockets" and argues they need to get more organizationally involved in supporting unions around the world. This is followed by another report by Steve Percy, "Jobs—A Double Spin?" where he looks at the role of aid in helping workers overseas and in the UK. This is followed by "Protection—For Jobs and Rights" by Lance Compa, who argues that it is the denial of foreign workers' rights which undermines US labour's bargaining power.

There are a couple of articles on South Africa. First, a report on attacks on the Transport and General Workers Union by Inkatha, a right-wing, anti-leftist organization in the province of Natal, and this is followed by "Township Terror," reporting on Inkatha's efforts in Natal's townships.

This is followed by a report on restrictions in the right to strike in Italy, and a factory occupation in Guatemala that had been taking place since June 1987.

1989 (ISSUE #32)

This issue started with a major section on workers' education worldwide, "Knowledge is Power," with photographs of workers learning in Britain, Brazil, Papua New Guinea, Sierra Leon and Britain again. In this first issue of this series, they discussed the Highlander Center in New Market, Tennessee, USA, in "To Shape Their Own Destiny." Highlander has served over the years to educate activists in the CIO (Congress of Industrial Organizations) in the 1930s and 1940s; the Civil Rights Movement in the 1950s–1970—Rosa Parks attended Highlander in 1954, a year before her refusal to give up a seat on a public bus to a white man sparked the Montgomery Bus Boycott, one of the seminal events of what became known as the Civil Rights Movement; and organizing in Appalachia against mountain top removal and other forms of environmental destruction since then.

There's a major section on Nigeria, written by Abdul Raufu Mustapha and Yahaya Hasim. This begins with "Government SAPs Unions," where falling living standards and government repression are attacking unions as part of a Structural Adjustment Program, and then is followed with "Government Intervention: Not the First Time." This is followed by a column on the OATUU (Organisation of African Trade Union Unity), a profile of Nigeria, and some information on the Nigerian Labour Congress.

More articles on Europe: "A Danger to Health?" by Hilda Palmer looks at the prospects for improved health and safety measures in the single European market; and there's a report by Kevin Bruton on a general strike in Spain on December 14, 1988, the first in over 50 years.

Then to Grenada, in the Caribbean. James Ferguson reports on the collapse of a US union-busting operation after the US invasion in October 1983.

"Moving On in '88" is a report by Ben Lowe and Keith Vendables on developments in South Africa during that year. Following a strike wave in 1987, "1988 was characterized largely by political confrontations and new alliances in the face of repressive measures by the state, not least against trade unions."

Following is a report on Peru by Javier Farje, "Unions Turn on Garcia," where unions began challenging President Alan Garcia.

And, finally, there is a report on a strike in a Japanese-owned plant in China. Luo Jianlin, who had worked in the plant during 1986, wrote this report for an Asia Monitor Resource Centre's book, *Smashing the Iron Rice Pot*, and ILR republished segments of it.

1990 (ISSUE #38)

This issue begins with a major section on immigrant workers in Europe, "Against Fortress Europe." It includes a "Migrant and Refugee Manifesto," an account of "Solidarity in Spain," a list of items for "Further Reading," and a list of "Contacts," including addresses and phone numbers of organizations in Amsterdam and London.

Joe Freeman reports from South Korea that "'Minju' [democratic-KS] Unions Unite," and have created the Korean Trade Union Congress.

There is an extensive report on the multinational corporation, William Baird, titled "Don't Wear It" by Alice Donald, Ankie Hoogvelt and Tim Bamford. Baird had a subsidiary in the Philippines named Intercontinental Garment Manufacturing Corporation (IGMC), whose workers had struggled heroically to establish and maintain its union. On September 20, 1989, Baird closed down this factory, ostensibly because of a nation-wide daily wage increase of 25 pesos (approximately $1.19) made this factory no longer commercially viable; but this does not make sense for a corporation that had made pre-tax profits in 1988 of 31.8 million British Pounds. The authors dug into William Baird's corporate history and wrote a hard-hitting story on this closure. Other articles connected to this story included "How Are We to Survive?" (from the workers' perspective), "We're Not Buying It!" (the call for an international boycott of Baird products from the Philippines), and "Nifty Footwork" (the corporate history of Baird).[6]

In the run-up to 1992, when the European Union was to become a "single market" instead of a number of independent "national" markets, there was great concern among trade unionists (as well as others) about the ramifications of this top-down, corporate-led plan with massive social implications. ILR had a number of articles in a special section on 1992 in #38, beginning with an article by Neil Kay, "Single European Market: Merger Mania."

This was followed by articles by Stuart Howard, focusing on "merger mania" among the world's airlines. In two articles, "Reach for the Skies" and "Deregulation: 'Anti-Labour,'" Howard illuminates the changes taking place in the airline industry, and especially focuses on changes taking place in Europe and the United States.

Following this, there was an examination of 1992 on the possible implications for the European auto industry. Philip Garrahan and Paul Stewart contributed "Auto Industry Unions: Sayonara?" and "Nissan Workers say, 'Nothing Special Really.'"

This was then followed by an examination of possible impacts on "West" Germany workers in "So Much to Lose?" by Oliver Suri. This is joined by another article, "Centralisation and Consultation: The German Way," with no credit given although probably also by Suri, which examined the centralized bargaining system in Germany.

And finally, Adam Novak, contributed "Reforming the Unions" in Czechoslovakia, discussing trade unions in that country after the fall of the Berlin Wall and the disintegration of the Soviet Empire in Eastern Europe.

ANALYSIS

A simple listing of the major articles carried in ILR over a seven-year period reveals this to be a major contribution to the global labor movement between 1984–1990. It should be noted that this was in the era prior to the Internet. There has been nothing like it since its demise. The range of issues covered was wide; many authors from around the world contributed to it; and the overall quality of work was excellent.

This was a magazine that was written for rank-and-file activists around the world. This was sort of like the US journal, *Labor Notes,* but on a global level and with a much more sophisticated approach, both in scope and depth. It did not deeply analyze, much less theorize, developments—a limitation that was somewhat overcome in the parallel journal edited by Peter Waterman called NILS, or *New International Labour Studies* (which ended publication in 1991)—and I know this caused some discontent between Waterman and ILR over time. Yet, ILR stayed true to its audience, and provided top-flight information, contacts and resources for those facing those and related issues.

While ILR was supported by a handful of senior-level trade unionists, especially in the UK and among a few of the International Trade Secretariats, it never gained widespread support within the labor movement, which meant it was never institutionalized nor provided a firm financial footing. Unfortunately, many of these issues addressed by ILR were ignored by the labor movement. This wasn't a result of inadequacy of the magazine, but rather—again—showed the myopia of most senior level trade union officials.

And, accordingly, when sued by William Baird in 1990, this small but vibrant publication was forced to bear this corporate assault with very little support—a situation which led to the magazine's demise.

I have to think that, had *International Labour Reports* continued since 1990 until today, the global labor movement would be much stronger today, have a much more sophisticated understanding of subsequent developments, and have a stronger base of rank-and-file activists with intensified international connections and solidarity among them and their unions.

I am honored to have been a small contributor to this global project from 1984–89.

NOTES

1. Howard and Spooner were followed by Celia Mather and Mike Allen, both whom I met when I visited the UK in 1989. According to Issue #40 (the last), they were followed by Frances Ellery, Javier Farje, and Paul Jenkins.

There had been turn-over on the editorial board over the years. As of #40, the editorial board consisted of Mike Allen, Alice Donald, Joe Holly, Carol Holt, Ankie Hoogvelt, Stuart Howard, John Humphrey, Celia Mather, Ann McCall, Dave McCall, Pat MacDougall, Ron Mendel, Guy Ohlenschlarger, Roger Smith, Dave Spooner, Ian Stewart, and Hugh Williamson. Donald, Holly, MacDougall, Howard, Humphrey, Smith, and Spooner had each been on the editorial board throughout the entire seven-year run.

2. I had gotten active in the anti-nuclear weapons movement in June 1983. I joined 75 people from across California and illegally entered Vandenberg Air Force Base on the central coast, flooding the launch site for the MX missile, and delaying its launch for a week. This was done to protest the development of the MX, which was seen as an escalation of the "Cold War" against the Soviet Union, and in solidarity with the people of the Marshall Islands, where the missile warhead was to land. I got within 20 yards of the above-ground canister that held the missile without detection and laid there for several hours.

To indicate how badly their security had been breached, I turned myself in by walking into the guard shack. Not only did I surprise the guard, but I was also surprised: they had a rent-a-cop guarding the MX instead of US Air Force security personnel. I was sentenced to 120 hours of community service for entering the base illegally.

3. I'm hoping that by publishing this article, some researcher (s) will locate Alice Donald, Stuart Howard and/or Dave Spooner, as well as Celia Mather—I assume all are in the UK—and do in-depth interviews on especially the founding but also the development of this incredibly innovative and powerful journal: my report is not enough.

4. While writing this chapter, I discovered I had written a third article for ILR, about a Labor Notes conference I had attended in November 1986; an article that I had completely forgotten (Scipes, 1987b). This was a much shorter article than the other two, and I decided that it did not invalidate my choice of comparing the March–April issues for this research.

5. Because ILR is out of print and no longer easily available, and because I identify the specific issue number and the subject, I do not include any of the listed issues in this book's bibliography.

6. ILR had developed a close connection with the IGMC Workers' Union; Wenilou "Weng" Pradel, whom I met at the 1983 Conference in Liverpool, came out of this plant. ILR had included stories on the Bataan Export Processing Zone (BEPZ) and/or IGMC Workers Union in Issues #10, #16, #20, and #27–28, in addition to the lengthy report in #38. The movie *The Global Assembly Line*—mentioned herein in Chapter 2, endnote 32—focuses on workers in Mexico and the Philippines, and specifically on BEPZ.

Because of my association with ILR, I got introduced to the IGMC Workers' Union (IGMCWU) in January 1986, when I visited BEPZ; in fact, women workers smuggled me into the Zone, where I spent the night ensconced inside a cardboard "shack" on the picket line, out of sight of the police patrols who passed regularly, and talked with numerous workers. I visited Mariveles, the town outside of BEPZ, several times over the years. I also had a fascinating interview with the President of the IGMCWU, Lucina Salao, in Manila in April 1990, before traveling to BEPZ once again, to see how the workers' strike against Baird was proceeding. This conflict ended in late 1990, when the workers got back pay and separation allowances and, in turn, they allowed the company to remove its equipment and finally close the factory. This is all detailed in my chapter on "Organization in Bataan," where I discuss the Philippines' efforts to industrialize, BEPZ, the struggle to build "genuine trade unionism" in the Zone, the IGMC Workers' Union, and then reflect on the overall situation of assembly-line workers in a global corporation (Scipes, 1996: 159–180).

This report on William Baird in ILR #38 was to have severe consequences for the journal; the company sued ILR, accused them of libel, and ILR did not have the financial resources to defend itself in court under the reactionary libel laws in England. This caused the journal to close; the last published issue was #40, dated July–August 1990.

Part II

LEARNING FROM KMU

Meeting Weng Pradel in England in late 1983 had a profound impact on my life: she introduced me to the KMU. She told me about her experiences as a trade unionist in the Philippines, and about this labor movement being built there and this, quite frankly, intrigued the hell out of me. As a rank and file member of the Graphic Communications International Union, AFL-CIO—I was working on printing presses at the time—I was all-too-aware of the deficiencies of the US labor movement, and I really wanted to find out if what she had told me was true. I resolved to visit the Philippines and the KMU at first opportunity.

In January 1986, after traveling around Northwestern Europe for approximately five months, and with the financial support of Alan Powell and with the political support of comrades from the UK and the US, I flew on, from London to Manila. Things were intense when I arrived—Marcos, in response to US pressure, had called for a "snap election" in early February 1986 to confirm his continued control, and everyone was on edge. Thus, I got introduced to the KMU at a time of great stress—the word on the street was that Marcos planned to reinstitute martial law should he be re-elected. I visited numerous picket lines and organizations across Metro Manila. I didn't just stay in Manila, however; I traveled to visit the sugar workers in Negros Oriental province, and then visited the Bataan Export Processing Zone (BEPZ) in Mariveles, Bataan (see Chapter 9). I decided I would return in the future to learn more.

When I returned in 1988, I brought a tape recorder—I wanted to use it to help me in writing articles about the KMU. However, the leaders of KMU organizations were so forthcoming, I decided that I had gathered too much information to confine my efforts to magazine articles; I realized I had to write a book to share all I had learned. After four more trips—six in total between 1986 and 1994—my book was published in 1996 (Scipes, 1996).

My experiences with the KMU in the Philippines are central to my thinking on building global labor solidarity, even while knowing comparable efforts were taking place concurrently in Brazil and South Africa. However, despite my reading everything I can find in English—obviously a serious limitation, especially regarding Brazil—and finding nothing truly comparative to how I structured my research and my findings, I still think there is a lot to be learned from the KMU (see also Scipes, 2014b). It is from these experiences that I present material in this section.

There are a number of different issues addressed here in this section. In Chapter 4, using broadly comparative methods to understand global unionism is argued a necessity, as it is not enough just to use case studies of single labor movements or even narrow comparisons: doing so, we find that a structural analysis cannot provide the level of analysis needed. We then examine in Chapter 5, both labor movement and social movement theory to see what might be applicable to this study. Following that, in Chapter 6, we discuss social movement unionism theory.

This prepares us to then consider the KMU, one of the new labor centers, as our exemplar. This requires us to understand the socio-economic context in which it operates, so we discuss Philippine economic development in Chapter 7. Once done, we specifically examine what can be learned from the KMU in general (Chapter 8). This is followed with an account of my initial trip (January–early February 1986), while Marcos was still in power, and which gives some idea of the situation on the ground (Chapter 9). This is followed by an examination of alliance building (Chapter 10). For better or worse, because the articles of Chapters 9 and 10 were each written before that of Chapter 8, there is some repetition—for which we apologize in advance—but allows each chapter to stand on its own.

The most important thing to understand is the new conceptualization of trade unionism. KMU—along with CUT and COSATU—has developed a unionism that goes beyond either the established economic or political types that are so well known by labor scholars. It certainly suggests to labor organizations elsewhere that this is a viable way to proceed, albeit with risks. But when one considers the context in which the KMU has had to operate—and direct physical repression has been commonplace throughout its years of existence—the gains so far have been so much more than probably could have even been imagined at the beginning.

Thus, in this section, we move from generality toward more specific organizations and practices. This process allows us to begin to understand one of the most dynamic and innovative labor movements in the world, and to use it to confirm the power of my definition of social movement unionism (SMU). More importantly, however, this lays the groundwork for Section 3, which allows us to then discuss whether my definition of SMU applies to another labor center (and thus confirming or falsifying—i.e., denying—the generalizability of this theory); provides groundwork to discuss how the KMU consciously works to build international labor solidarity; and then disentangles the theoretical world of "social movement unionism."

Chapter Four

Using Comparative Methods to Understand Contemporaneous Labor Movements

Rejecting a Structural-based Understanding

Militant, mass-based, nation-wide labor movements of a new type have emerged in a least three disparate countries in different parts of the world—Brazil, the Philippines and South Africa—over the past 20 years.[1] These movements have served to improve the wages and benefits of their members, have helped overthrow dictatorships and expand democracy in each country and, in general, have qualitatively expanded the ability of workers to collectively present their grievances and demands to each country's elite. At the heart of these labor movements are organizations that, in international labor terminology, are called "labor centers": CUT *(Central* Única *dos Trabalhadores)* of Brazil, KMU *(Kilusang Mayo Uno*—May First Movement*)* of the Philippines, and COSATU (Congress of South African Trade Unions) in South Africa.[2]

Using the emergence of the KMU as my exemplar, but specifically including each of these labor centers within my conceptualization, it is argued that the trade unionism that has been developed by the KMU is a new type of trade unionism, which myself and others have called "social movement unionism" (Scipes, 1992a, 1992b, 1996).[3] This particular argument will be developed in Chapter 6, herein, but the discussion in this chapter will be limited to investigating the claim made by others in the literature that the emergence of social movement unionism is due to changing structural factors in a country's social order.

In the limited literature that exists, both Frederic Deyo (1989) and Gay Seidman (1994) utilize structural arguments to account for the presence (Seidman on Brazil and South Africa) or absence (at that time—Deyo on South Korea) of effective labor movements in their respective countries.[4] Seidman, in fact, goes so far as to claim that structural factors—in particular industrialization and the change in labor process—cause social movement unionism.

As she writes—hedging her bet somewhat, despite basing her argument around it—". . . there seems to be a direct relationship between similar patterns of industrialization and a *specific form* of labor mobilization" (Seidman, 1994: 11—emphasis added). That *specific form* of labor mobilization, she argues, is social movement unionism.

In this chapter, while accepting that structural changes *can* account for changed conditions leading to the emergence of militant labor movements, I argue that structural changes *cannot* account for the emergence of any particular type of trade unionism, thus specifically cannot account for the emergence of social movement unionism. Something else is operating to cause the emergence of these particular unions, and it is not structural.[5]

To address this issue, I first discuss my methodological approach to these questions. While using a comparative approach, I go beyond general comparison and specify the particular comparative approach I use.

Afterwards, I discuss the substantive issues mentioned above. I start by comparing levels of national development in which social movement unionism has emerged, and then explicate what I mean by social movement unionism. I then focus on Seidman's case studies of the emergence of social movement unions in South Africa and Brazil, and try to identify her claims; I then critique her approach. Afterwards, I then compare the experiences of the KMU in the Philippines, which differs considerably. From that, I challenge her structural change explanation for the emergence of social movement unions, arguing that her own analysis does not explain either the emergence of social movement unionism in the Philippines (across development levels) or the lack of emergence of social movement unionism within countries at similar development levels. Thus, ultimately, I argue that we must look someplace else besides a structural explanation to explain the emergence of social movement unionism.

METHODOLOGICAL ISSUES

Before selecting an appropriate methodology, the purpose to which it is being applied must be clear: we want to compare the emergence of social movement unionism across three countries—Brazil, the Philippines and South Africa—to ascertain whether the cause of this phenomenon is change in the political economic structure in each society; accordingly, a case-oriented approach is used (see Ragin, 1987).

In a comparison such as this, across national borders, it seems clear that we must accept Terrance K. Hopkins' and Immanuel Wallerstein's point that "national societies" are more than just national societies; we must recognize that "every complex social unit exists in three forms or at three levels: it is an entity in its own right; it is a context for its constituent members; and it, in turn, is a member of larger contexts" (Hopkins and Wallerstein, 1970: 184).[6] Thus, they recognize that there can be cross-national research between similar parts of different national societies.

Melvin Kohn (1987) also recognizes the value of cross-national research—"in no other way can we be certain that what we believe to be social-structural regularities are not merely particularities, the product of some limited set of historical or cultural or political circumstances" (Kohn, 1987: 713)—and while recognizing four different types of cross-national research, he focuses on situations in which the nation is the context of study. He discusses cross-national similarities and differences, and notes the greater demands required when explaining differences: "explanation of cross-national differences requires more explicit consideration of historical, cultural, and political-economic particularities than does the . . . explanation of cross-national similarities" (Kohn, 1987: 717). Following Kohn, the national contexts—levels of development—in which the particular phenomenon of social movement unionism could emerge must be considered.

At the same time that comparison of particular "parts" of society is considered acceptable, we want to make sure to follow Charles Tilly's point to "be sure of the units we are comparing" (Tilly, 1984: 80). In this case, it is relatively easy: we are comparing labor centers that have been identified previously as being comparable.

But how to proceed? Tilly suggests four different strategies of comparative analysis, although he sees them as endpoints on continuums (if one will) rather than dichotomies (Tilly, 1984: 81). This particular study is placed on Tilly's "share of all instances" continuum, leading from individualizing to universalizing strategies of comparative research, and it is placed toward the universalizing end because we are trying to develop an analysis that will (eventually) apply to all cases of social movement unionism, rather than to just the three cases examined here (see Tilly, 1984: 97–115).

Theda Skocpol and Margaret Somers (1980) suggest that there are three major logics of sociological inquiry within comparative historical work—what they call parallel demonstration of theory, contrast of contexts, and macro-causal analysis with each having distinct purposes, characteristics, strengths and limitations. Each logic is seen as having enough individual integrity that works can be seen as primarily embracing one logic or another. And while the parallel demonstration of theory or contrast of contexts logics is not thought appropriate for trying to understanding this comparison herein, it is believed that the macro-causal analysis *is* appropriate. As the authors' point out, ". . . [this logic] has the considerable virtue of being the only way to attempt to validate (and invalidate) causal hypotheses about macro-phenomena of which there are intrinsically only limited number of cases" (Skocpol and Somers, 1980: 193).

Basing their analysis at this point on Moore's *Social Origins of Dictatorship and Democracy,* Skocpol and Somers point out that Moore primarily uses Mill's "Method of Agreement." However, they note that, at times, he uses Mill's "Method of Difference," and that of the two, they see the "Method of Difference" being "more powerful for establishing valid causal associations" (Skocpol and Somers, 1980: 183). Including the KMU into a comparison of these militant labor movements allows the Method of Difference to be used to great effect: in short, it allows one to challenge Seidman's structural change model as the explanation for the emergence of these labor movements.

Yet how this be done? Dietrich Rueschemeyer's conceptualization of "analytic induction" is the best strategy that we have considered to use for this. This starts from understanding one (or more) case in-depth, then trying to generate theoretical insights from it (them), "and then these theoretical generalizations are then tested and retested in other detailed cases studies" (Rueschemeyer, 1991: 32). Now ideally, the comparison should be across a large number of cases, so as to improve the validity of the conclusions, but this is the first step of what will hopefully be an on-going series, and it is necessary to firmly ground this initial effort. However, it should be obvious that the necessary of extending this analysis across multiple cases is recognized, so as to be able to continue to validate these findings.

CASE STUDIES

To begin this analysis of the case studies, we compare the level of development—Newly Industrializing Countries (NICs) to a "would-be" NIC—among the three countries. This is followed by a brief discussion of my conceptualization of social movement unionism (Scipes, 1992a, 1992b), so as to focus the discussion. From there, an examination of the main points of Seidman's analysis of the new labor movements in Brazil and South Africa is reported, seeking areas of comparison, and then critiquing her analysis. Following that, Seidman's points in light of my research on the KMU of the Philippines are considered.

Levels of Development across Nations

The interesting thing about this set of three countries is that, while their labor movements are at comparable levels of development, the countries themselves are not. Brazil and South Africa are at comparable levels of economic development (Seidman, 1994), but the Philippines is definitely at a lower level; while the first two are considered NICs (Newly Industrializing Countries), the Philippines is referred to in the literature as a "would-be NIC" (Broad, 1988).[7] And while Seidman recognizes the similarities of the two NICs and discusses them, her discussion does not fit the case of the Philippines. Thus, in addition to similarities, the addition of the Philippines requires that we discuss differences as well in trying to examine the role of structure as a causal factor.

This leads to two very interesting questions regarding structural arguments: if structure is a causal factor, (1) how can similar labor movements emerge in countries at different levels of industrialization and economic development? and (2) how come similar labor movements do not emerge in other countries sharing the same level of development, either at the NIC level or the "would-be" NIC level?

Social Movement Unionism

In previous works, I argued that social movement unionism is a new type of trade unionism, and distinguished it from both economic- and political-types of trade unionism (Scipes, 1992a, 1992b). While I do not want to repeat the argument here—it is explicated below, in Chapter 6—it might be helpful to repeat my conceptualization of social movement unionism:

> Social movement unionism is a type of trade unionism that differs from the traditional forms of both economic and political unionism. This type sees workers' struggles as merely one of many efforts to qualitatively change society, and not either the only site for political struggle and social change or even the primary site. Therefore, it seeks alliances with other social movements on an equal basis, and tries to join them in practice when possible, both within the country and internationally.
>
> Social movement unionism is trade unionism democratically controlled by the membership and not by any external organization, and recognizes that the struggles for control over workers' daily work life, pay and conditions are intimately connected with and cannot be separated from the national socio-political-economic situation. This requires that struggles to improve the situation of workers confront the national situation—combining struggles against exploitation and oppression in the workplace with those confronting domination both external from and internal to the larger society—as well as any dominating relations within the unions themselves. Therefore, it is autonomous from capital, the state and political parties, setting its own agenda from its own particular perspective, yet willing to consider modifying its perspective on the basis of negotiations with the social movements that it is allied with and that it has equal relations (Scipes, 1992b: 86–87).[8]

And it is under this conceptualization—not Seidman's—that all three of the labor movements are included.

Seidman's Analysis

In her very innovative book, Gay Seidman recognizes the emergence of two dynamic and very similar labor movements in the 1970s and 1980s in countries usually seen as being considerably different—Brazil and South Africa[9]—and seeks underlying reasons for this process: ". . . it is precisely because Brazil and South Africa present such different histories—different working class cultures, different patterns of social organization, different relations between workers and the state—that the emergence of the social-movement unionism of the 1980s begs comparison" (Seidman, 1994: 28).[10] She decides ultimately on a structural explanation: "Rather than focusing primarily on internal dynamics of unions, or even on alliances between unions and politicians, . . . we should begin by looking outside labor organizations, at the structural changes that shape the potential for worker mobilization and militance" (Seidman, 1994: 273).

Her argument is that as a result of state elites in both countries making the decision to industrialize, these countries began industrializing in the 1960s. Out of similar industrialization processes—any analysis of these new labor movements, she states, "must begin from structural changes during the course of rapid industrialization" (Seidman, 1994: 9–10)—workers began organizing, extending their scope of organizing to include both the factories and the workers' communities. Specifically, she suggests "that changes in the organization of work and in workers' experiences, linked to the rapid industrialization strategy . . ., laid the basis for a new kind of labor movement in both Brazil and South Africa" (Seidman, 1994: 149).

At the same time, when industrial growth slowed in the 1970s, business elites shifted from acquiescing to state development policies to demanding "greater access to state decision-making bodies" (Seidman, 1994: 10). Arguments growing out of different policy options, according to Seidman, created a "political space"

> in which labor movements could begin to demand the right to organize factory-based unions. While employers certainly did not help create emergent unions, in both cases, the timing of the appearance of "new unionism" strengthened its chances for survival, as business leaders were confronted with workers' demands at a time when dominant groups were already engaged in debates about democratization and development strategies (Seidman, 1994: 10).

Thus, as she writes, "I emphasize the ways in which state and employer interventions affected labor movements' constituencies" (Seidman, 1994: 11). In other words, she argues that a change in the "political opportunity structure" was a key factor that led to the unions' emergence (Seidman, 1994: 93).

And the key actors in her analysis are workers in heavy industry, metal workers in general and automobile workers specifically. She notes that in both countries, "semi-skilled workers predominated in shaping the labor movement: the rise of capital-intensive heavy industry increased industrial workers' capacity to challenge employers on the shop floor, and the organizations they formed reflected that experience" (Seidman, 1994: 149). She again emphasizes workers in heavy industry as she discusses comparative and historical experiences of workers (Seidman, 1994: 265).

So, to sum up her approach, she sees the emergence of social movement unionism in both Brazil and South Africa as a result of structural changes in the political-economic system, and that these new unions benefited from the changing political opportunity structures, with workers in heavy industry key to the emergence of this kind of unionism.

Critique of Seidman's Analysis

Although it is not until the next section that Seidman's structural analysis is critiqued on the basis of my field research in the Philippines, it is important to comment on her own argument. Quite frankly, while her claim that rapid industrialization led to extensive social changes in Brazil and South Africa makes sense, her argument about the importance of changes in the political opportunity structure for the emergence of the new unions does not. Placing the emphasis on changes in the political opportunity structure vastly overstates the importance of inter-elite conflict, and especially within the context of emerging social movement unionism.

Basically, she argues that the changes developing from rapid industrialization led to situations whereby militant workers, recognizing the splits that emerged during the latter part of the 1970s–early 1980s between leading sectors of business and the state over further development policies, were then able to build these new social movement unions.

There are several problems with her analysis. First, as she recognizes, ". . . as in Brazil, business acceptance [in South Africa] generally responded to, rather than enabled, the emergence of independent unions on the shop floor" (Seidman, 1994: 114). She repeats the point in a slightly different way in the chapter on the emergence of the new unions: ". . . before [established-KS] unions and employers' associations began to lobby officially for new labor relations laws, workers at specific factories were already beginning to negotiate informal arrangements with employers" (Seidman, 1994: 148). And again in her conclusion: "Until factory-based organizations disrupted production processes . . . neither states nor large employers appeared eager to extend either political rights or economic benefits to the majority of their country's populations" (Seidman, 1994: 260). In other words, it was not a changed political opportunity structure that enabled these new unions to emerge but, in reality, it was the emergence and development of these new unions that led to varied responses by sectors of business and more forward-looking members of the state, which in turn, led to increased political space that the unions could then exploit.

Second, her explanations for the emergence of social movement unionism are insufficient. Yes, social movement unions have emerged and developed in both of these countries. However, there is disagreement with her over *how* they emerged. While she claims they were caused by the industrialization process, she has shown nothing of a structural nature that would result in social movement unionism; in other words, the unions that emerged out of the industrialization process might have just been of either the economic- or political-types as social movement-type unions.

This is particularly interesting in light of her discussing the development of collective identities of workers. As she shows, these collective identities developed in such a way that made the particular type of unionism now called social movement unionism a viable undertaking. From my knowledge of the labor movement in South Africa, this seems a much more promising approach to consider.

In fact, Seidman herself uses a similar approach to understanding how struggles in communities developed in such a way as to join worker demands in challenging the state: "The answer to this puzzle seems to lie neither in the objective conditions of poverty confronting the residents of sprawling slums nor in the programs of political activists, but rather *in the way activists reinterpreted* the links between workplace and community concerns" (Seidman, 1994: 202—emphasis added).[11] It would have been good to foreground this process among workers.

And third, if the development of these new unions were due to structural causes, how could other types of trade unionism continue to exist in these new situations? For example, she shows the continued existence of the CGT (*Confedereação Geral dos Trabalhadores,* or General Workers' Confederation) in Brazil, which "tended to stress national political and economic reforms that would allow labor to participate in government alongside 'progressive' national capital" (Seidman, 1994: 168). The CGT would be an economic type of trade unionism organization. Wouldn't it make sense that if there was such a structural transformation of the society, and if this structural transformation was said to cause the new unionism, that it would affect all workers—and especially those sharing common experiences—in the same way? And although CUT is much more dominant, Seidman presents no evidence that CGT has faded into insignificance. How can she suggest a structural explanation when it is clear that different actors (in this case unions) have responded differentially to the same phenomena?[12]

Research from the Philippines

My work (Scipes, 1996) on the KMU Labor Center of the Philippines has some strengths and weaknesses in comparison to Seidman's work. My study was not a comparative study, nor was I trying specifically to generalize from it, and certainly not in any formal sociological manner. Those obviously are weaknesses. However, my study is focused on the emergence of a particular organization and is not left on a more generalized level; that is, my study is the more organizationally-focused and historically detailed.

Although this was ultimately a study of this labor organization across the nation as a whole, I recognized that the Philippines had a number of different political economies, and that each had developed (generally) independently from the other.[13] Accordingly, I chose to focus on four different political economies, two colonial production systems and two post-colonial: extractive mining and plantation sugar on one hand, and capitalist agriculture and capitalist production of light manufactured goods on the other. I also recognized that different labor movements emerged out of each respective political economic system, and then joined at a national-level to form the KMU, which, in turn, was able to strengthen and support each of the regional based labor movements. So, in short, what I lost in generalizability, I gained in depth. And, after examining the labor movements in each of these regions, I argued that the KMU exemplifies social movement unionism.

So, a problem in comparing my work with Seidman's is that my approach to the subject under consideration is radically different from hers: in comparison to my multiple region approach, Seidman approaches each of her two countries as a monolithic whole; and while recognizing differences in the country, she does not engage that reality in her analysis. In other words, because each country as a whole is seen as industrializing, she does not examine various sub-units to see if they each reflect conditions of the whole, or if one region, for example, so dominates total production that it distorts the overall picture.

Likewise, by emphasizing workers in heavy industry, Seidman does not consider whether social movement unionism exists among workers in other sectors of the economy. For example, she says nothing about workers in gold and coal mining, or in light industry such as garment manufacturing, or even in the sugar industry, much less among service workers such as those who work in department stores or education, etc.

And while she includes a brief discussion on women workers (Seidman, 1994: 246–249), Seidman does not examine the impact they have on the development of social movement unionism, nor whether it takes different forms among concentration of women workers.

These points are brought up because they have a direct impact on the subject at hand: if Seidman had looked at multiple political economies, or different industries, then she most likely would not have been quite so quick to generalize across the entire nation. In other words, had she considered situations differentially, it probably would have been obvious to her that the emergence of social movement unions could not be explained by a structural approach.

However, rather than examining her work on the basis of decisions made for someone else's, it seems more appropriate to concentrate on the way she approached her study.

Unfortunately, this does not help much. Because I used a much more rigorous and theoretically developed conceptualization of social movement unionism by which to understand the KMU (see Chapter 6, herein), it seems certain that she would have to agree that the KMU should be included under her definition. Therefore, she would have to consider the changes or lack of changes in the Philippine political economy under her structural analysis.

The plain fact is that while one could say that the Philippines has shifted its exports over the last 20 years from traditional agricultural and mineral products to non-traditional, industrial ones, there is absolutely no way someone could realistically claim that the Philippines has industrialized. In fact, the percentage of the population that is engaged in manufacturing in 1990 is lower than the comparable amount in 1960! "The share of industrial employment, particularly of manufacturing, is even lower in 1990 at 9.7 percent than it was in 1960 at 12.1 percent" (quoted in Payumo, 1994: 42).

One fact alone—that there is social movement unionism in the Philippines despite the country not industrializing—counters Seidman's claim that industrialization causes social movement unionism. But if this doesn't undermine her claim by itself, how can she explain the development of social movement unionism in regional political economies—specifically, that of plantation sugar in Negros—where there has not been no industrialization, outside of a few very old sugar centrals? Likewise, how can she explain the existence of social movement unionism among workers outside of heavy industry, which was presented in my book? And how can she explain, in a country where there is only one integrated steel mill in the entire country, why the workers in that mill have rejected social movement unionism? And why in the two sectors of the economy that can be said to be industrializing—garments and electronic assembly—is there a real mixed bag of unionization across the sectors, and why some of those that have chosen to unionize have joined social movement unions but many have not?

In short, it is obvious that Seidman's explanation for the rise of social movement unionism cannot account for the case of KMU of the Philippines. Thus, her analysis simply cannot explain the presence or absence of social movement unionism in countries at differing levels of political-economic development.

Additionally, while she cannot explain the rise of social movement unionism *across* development levels, a structural change model cannot explain the emergence or non-emergence of social movement unionism even *within* the same development level. In other words, for a structural model to be valid, it would have to explain all of the cases at a particular level of development, so as to account for either the presence or absence of social movement unionism. By adding additional countries at both the NIC level and the would-be NIC level—say India, Mexico, South Korea and Taiwan at the former, and Thailand, Zimbabwe and Peru at the latter, with none of these countries experiencing the emergence of social movement unionism—a structural change model cannot account for both the presence and the absence of social movement unions at either level. In other words, social movement unionism exists in the NICs of Brazil and South Africa, but it does not exist in India, Mexico, South Korea[14] and Taiwan; it exists in the would-be NIC of the Philippines, but it doesn't exist in Thailand, Zimbabwe or Peru. It is clear that a structural change model simply cannot withstand rigorous examination.

CONCLUSION

The development of social movement unionism by the KMU of the Philippines was compared with that of CUT in Brazil and COSATU in South Africa. This was done to test a structural change model as put forth by Gay Seidman in her study of the emergence of social movement unions in the latter two countries, which claimed that rapid industrialization caused social movement unionism.

This chapter has proceeded at both the comparative and the substantive levels. Methodologically, it moved from a broad consideration down to a narrow one. It started off with Hopkins and Wallerstein pointing out that there were different levels of each society, and this was joined with Kohn's thinking, while accepting Tilly's point on the necessity to compare across the same level. Further, the study was placed on the Tilly/Ragin case-oriented approaches continuum, locating it closer to the universalizing end of the continuum. Then Skocpol and Somer's method of macro-causal analysis was used to guide efforts to identify causal processes, and it was decided that Mill's Method of Difference was particularly useful to show the inability of structural explanations for the phenomenon, social movement unionism, that was under consideration. It was deemed that a theoretical understanding that could account for the differences should be advanced, and Rueschemeyer's method of analytical induction was chosen as the best strategy by which to try to understand this phenomenon across political-economic structures.

Substantively, the level of political-economic development across the three relevant countries was compared, as was my more theoretically-developed conceptualization of social movement unionism. Following, the main points of Seidman's analysis was examined on her own terms and then critiqued, and then further examined in light of my research in the Philippines. Using Mill's Method of Difference to guide the examination of Seidman's model, it was found that her structural change model does not hold up under close examination for her own cases, but particularly does not hold up when extended across development levels to include the Philippines, or when additional countries within the same development level are added—either at the level of the NICs or at the level of the would-be NICs.

In short, a structural change model that had been suggested to explain the emergence of social movement unionism across an innovative pair of countries was examined, but it was found that the model was not valid even for the initial cases, and that it definitely did not extend to other countries. The search for a causal factor for the emergence of the phenomenon called social movement unionism must continue.

NOTES

1. This chapter has never been published; it was written for a course on Comparative Research Methodologies presented by Professor Xiangming Chen in the Department of Sociology at the University of Illinois at Chicago in Spring 1997.

2. A "labor center" is the organization to which other unions and/or national federations (depending on the particular country) affiliate, and thus serves as the "peak organization" of those sets of unions and other affiliates. In international labor terminology, the AFL-CIO of the United States is a labor center. In some countries—like the US, Australia, China and Germany and the UK—there is only one labor center. In others—such as Brazil, France, Italy, India, Japan, Mexico, the Philippines, South Africa, South Korea, and Sweden—there are two or more.

3. Other researchers who have applied this term to these new labor movements in the third world include Rob Lambert and Eddie Webster (1988), Rob Lambert (1989, 1990), Peter Waterman (1988e, 1991b, 1993), and Gay Seidman (1994), but

their conceptualizations of it have differed from mine. In fact, my conceptualization developed out of debates with Lambert/Webster and Waterman. Seidman apparently was unaware of our debates, and her conceptualization was very under theorized. I argue that my conceptualization is the most complete and useful, and wrote my book on the KMU to show how this type of trade unionism developed in the Philippines (Scipes, 1996). This is developed further in Chapter 6, herein. Also, after discussing the intellectual goulash made by various authors writing after my articles, generally ignoring my work, I disentangled this debate in Scipes, 2014c—Chapter 13 herein.

4. Deyo examines the development process in South Korea in his book, and claims that the subjugation of labor is a key factor in Korean success. However, before he completed his book, he recognized that a new labor movement might be in the process of emergence (in the late 1980s). Nonetheless, I do not find his analysis on point, and thus concentrate only on Seidman's account and claims.

5. I suggest that this unknown factor is an ideological one, based on the concept of a particular type of trade unionism, which I have labeled as social movement unionism. As mentioned above, this will be developed in chapters following.

6. Following Jaffee (1990), I would include a fourth level, that of individuals. However, further discussion is beyond the scope of this paper. In any case, Hopkins and Wallerstein's point is well-taken.

7. Robin Broad lists seven countries as NICs, including Brazil and South Korea, but notes that definitions of NICs vary by author and the category they use; the seven countries she uses—Taiwan, South Korea, Hong Kong, Singapore, Brazil, India and Mexico—jointly accounted for over 70 percent of all less developed country industrial exports in 1978 (Broad, 1988: 4 and fn. #2, page 240). Seidman equates "late industrializers" with NICs, and includes both South Africa and Brazil. It seems clear that South Africa should also be considered a NIC; and it's just as clear that the Philippines should not. For a discussion of Philippine development across a 37-year period 1962 1999—with a specific focus on the impact of neo-liberal economic policies on this development, see Scipes, 1999; republished herein as Chapter 7.

8. This is a much more theoretically-developed definition of social movement unionism than that used by Seidman: "Theoretically, social-movement unionism is perhaps best defined as an effort to raise the living standards of the working class as a whole, rather than to protect individually defined interests of union members" (Seidman, 1994: 2).

9. To suggest the broader applicability of her findings from Brazil and South Africa, Seidman briefly compares the situation in South Korea, arguing that it supports her larger argument (Seidman, 1994: 264–272). I accept the extension of her argument to include South Korea, but because her analysis is much less detailed, I focus my comments on the more in-depth analysis that she did in Brazil and South Africa.

The above was written in the original version of this paper. However, after reading Koo's (2001) excellent study of Korean workers, where he notes specifically, ". . . the South Korean labor movement did *not* develop as what Seidman (1994) calls 'social movement unionism'" (emphasis added) (Koo, 2001: 203), I have accepted Koo's reasoned analysis, and removed the Korean example from consideration. Doing so, however, does not affect my argument.

10. Although not explicitly stated, her approach is similar to that of Mill's "Method of Agreement."

11. Seidman generally implies that community members and workers comprise two different groups, rather than recognizing their substantial overlap. This overlap is particularly obvious for women workers, which Seidman recognizes: ". . . to women workers, who bore much of the responsibility for family maintenance, the relationship between workplace and community-related demands must have been unmistakable" (Seidman, 1994: 222).

12. Seidman also briefly discusses efforts to build a Union of Workers in South Africa (UWUSA) based on a Zulu tribal identity (Seidman, 1994: 183). Again, the same question as asked about Brazil in the text arises.

13. While this might sound unusual, it is due to the particular processes by which the different regional economies of the country had been integrated into the global political-economic network. See McCoy and de Jesus, eds., 1982.

14. Koo's (2001: 203) finding of "no social movement unionism" in Korea hurts Seidman's argument even more (see Endnote #9, above), as she extended her argument to South Korea, which she recognized was a Newly Industrializing Country.

Chapter Five

Understanding Worker Mobilization Theoretically

What Can Labor and Social Movement Theories Tell Us?

How can we theoretically understand labor movements and worker mobilization?[1] We saw in the preceding chapter that structural approaches to understanding worker mobilization simply are incorrect. However, if they are incorrect, how can we correctly understand them?

This chapter is intended to begin to lay the theoretical groundwork for understanding worker mobilization. Accordingly, we take two major steps in this chapter. First, instead of treating labor movements as a given, we problematize (question) the very concept: what is a labor movement and how can we understand them? Are they all the same—or are there some fundamental differences? To answer these questions, we discuss labor movement theory, conceptualize labor movements, present how labor movements are developed, argue there are three different types of trade unionism globally, and end by discussing the organizational consolidation of leadership. In short, this first section on labor movement theory challenges much of the work by labor scholars regarding established understandings of labor movements.

And is any labor movement the same over his entire life course, or is there something special—and different—about a labor movement during the period of emergence, *before* it is accepted as a legitimate social actor? We present a conceptualization of a labor movement. Further, we argue the centrality of worker activists, identify what we mean by "labor movement," and recognize that there can be multiple labor movements existing at any time in a country.

Recognizing that the type of trade unionism advanced effects the labor movement discussed, we discuss types of trade unionism, and identify three different types of trade unionism: economic, political and social movement unionism.[2] We discuss organizational consolidation and leadership. Following the discussion of labor movements, we argue that during the period when they emerge, labor movements are a particular type of social movement;

therefore, relevant social movement theory is discussed. Together, they allow us to answer the question advanced in this chapter's title.

LABOR MOVEMENT THEORY: DIFFERENT APPROACHES TO LABOR MOVEMENTS

There are different ways of looking at labor movements, and Simeon Larson and Bruce Nissen (1987) discuss how labor theorists have done so. First, they note that there is not just one theory of the labor movement, but there are a number of theories. Along with that, they note that theorists have concerned themselves with different questions—some with the origin of the labor movement, some with the role of unions in an industrial society, some with ideological direction of labor organizations, and some with their ultimate goals, etc. Accordingly, Larson and Nissen write that "not only are there sharp differences over the function and content of labor movement theory, but it is virtually impossible to integrate the various theories into one overall theory of the labor movement." They suggest that it makes more sense to develop a typology of labor theories, and they briefly discuss Mark Perlman's fivefold classification of Protestant Christian Socialist and the Roman Catholic Social Movements; the Marxian Socialist Movements; the environmental psychology discipline; neoclassical economics discipline; and the legal or jurisprudential history discipline (Larson and Nissen, 1987: 3). However, for their purposes, "we have found it more useful to group the theories according to the *overall social role* each [theorist] assigns the labor movement" (emphasis is original) (Larson and Nissen, 1987: 3–4). They see seven different social roles that theorists have given the labor movement:

> (1) an agent of revolution, (2) a business institution for economic protection of its members, (3) an agent for extending industrial democracy, (4) an instrument for achieving the psychological aims of groupings of workers, (5) an agent for moral and spiritual reform; (6) an antisocial, destructive monopoly, or (7) a subordinate mechanism with "special interest" functions in a pluralist industrial society (Larson and Nissen: 4).

However, following Bonnell (1983) and others such as Marian Golden (1988), it makes more sense to me to try to understand how the *workers*—particularly activist workers—have looked at labor movements rather than how the *theorists* have looked at them.[3] In other words, rather than placing a labor movement into a theoretical straitjacket according to the ideological presuppositions and analysis of a particular theorist, it is argued that workers see trade unions and labor movements as having multiple purposes,[4] and that theorists must recognize this multiplicity.

Modifying the above list somewhat, it is suggested herein that workers can see labor movements as being (1) agents of social change; (2) means to improve their economic situation; (3) initiators of industrial democracy; (4) forces that improve the psychological well-being of workers; and (5) vehicles of moral and spiritual reform.[5] Further, any particular worker can see a labor movement serving one or more purposes at any one time and, of these purposes, this worker might prioritize the importance of one or more at any particular time. Thus, recognizing this multiplicity of approaches that are common among workers, it is argued that it is necessary to take a worker-centered approach to the study of labor movements.

At the same time that we recognize the multiplicity of purposes of labor movements as seen by workers, we must also recognize that there is not just one common group interest that exists simply by workers participating in the social relations of production, distribution or exchange; that is, there is not an automatic workers' group interest nor consciousness that exists. A collective consciousness, identity and collective interests must be created—they cannot be assumed (Melucci, 1989, cf. Marx and Engels, 1848).[6]

Labor Movement: A Conceptualization

So far, however, common agreement about what is a "labor movement" has been assumed—it is now time to develop my conceptualization before going further. Accepting McAdam and Snow's definition of a social movement as "a collectivity acting with some degree of organization and continuity outside of institutional channels for the purpose of promoting or resisting change in the group, society or world order of which it is a part" (McAdam and Snow, 1997: xxiii), it is argued that a labor movement is one type of social movement—at least during its initial period of emergence and challenge to the established social order—and what makes it particularly important is its social location: a labor movement's primary organizational manifestation is located *within* the production, distribution and exchange sphere of society. Thus, a labor movement has something no other social group has: the ability to stop operations from inside the production-distribution-exchange process (Aronowitz, 1973). It is this social power that makes labor movements important.

Organizationally, the heart of a labor movement are trade unions and conglomerations of trade unions that are joined by a labor center that, in turn, works to further unify and strengthen the unions. Around these labor organizations are located supportive intellectuals, individuals, and other organizations; and these organizations include both those that serve the labor movement directly—such as educational institutions designed to provide labor education for labor center members—and those that choose to ally with the labor movement, indirectly strengthening the social power of the labor movement; progressive churches are an example of this. It is this combination of labor center and supporters, mobilized into a mutually-reinforcing social network, that comprise a labor movement. Accordingly, labor movements are not simply collections of workers—labor movements simply cannot survive without the support of a larger social community, however it might be constructed.[7]

At the same time, there is a range of involvement and interest in a labor center[8] or in a labor movement as a whole among members: we certainly do not want to argue that each member has a high degree of interest and involvement, no matter how much it were wished. Accordingly, labor movement members can be placed into one of three categories: activists, participants, and bystanders. "Activists" are those with high involvement and interest, and who play a leadership role. These leadership efforts can be formal, such as serving as an officer of a union or of a supporting community-based organization; they can be informal, such as volunteers—and they can support or oppose the formal leadership; or they can act as "bridges" (see Robnett, 1996) between the leaders and members, or between labor centers and allied organizations. "Participants" are those members who can be mobilized to participate around particular issues or campaigns, but generally do not initiate self-involvement. And "bystanders" generally have low interest and low involvement—they are generally the ones who Mancur Olson (1965) calls "free-riders"—although they can be mobilized at particular times and around particular interests should an effort be made to do so. And members can change their level of involvement at any time: these are not static categories.

Understanding the Development of Labor Movements

Accordingly, it is suggested—following Golden (1988)—that researchers can best understand the development of a labor movement by focusing primary attention on activists. Activists play key roles because they are the ones that do the conceptualizing and thinking for the movement and, through the framing process (Snow et al., 1997/1986), are the ones who interpret the situation, both to members and to the outside public. Therefore, activists—both inside the labor center and throughout the supporting network—are central to the development of the labor movement as a whole, serving specifically to mobilize their members while attempting to neutralize and/or counter movement opponents.

However, we cannot collapse our understanding of a labor movement to the activists. No matter how good or how innovative activists are, unless a substantial number of the members respond affirmatively to their efforts, there is not a labor movement but simply a collection of activists and/or organizations—and these are not the same! As Gay Seidman perceptively writes, ". . . while individual activists and clandestine groupings may help shape the discourse of an organization, they can hardly determine how that discourse is received or acted upon" (Seidman, 1994: 41). Thus, activists must present a program sufficient to motivate the activation and mobilization of rank and file (i.e., non-activist) workers, including both participants and by-standers.

Concurrently, however, formal leaders—most, especially in the early days of an organization, who come out of the pool of activists engaged in the project—also have an important role to play in the development of the organization/movement. And that particularly concerns their changed relationships to the activists once they assume formal positions of leadership: are they (the formal leaders) going to encourage the activists (informal leaders), or are they going to hinder their activities?[9] This can be a real help or impediment to the activists in their efforts.

Labor movements derive their power from their ability to mobilize large numbers of people as a unified force to disrupt production, distribution and/or exchange, and to withstand counterattacks from capital and/or the state. Accordingly, labor movements at all times are potentially at risk of state repression and/or countermovements that can challenge the interpretations of activists and weaken or destroy connections (and mobilization networks) between activists and members of the movement (see Meyer and Staggenborg, 1996).[10]

Concurrently, despite a general tendency to use the term labor "movement" almost unconsciously to refer to any collectivity of labor organizations, this is unsupportable: not all collectivities of labor organizations are *labor movements*. A labor movement is qualitatively different than a collection of labor organizations: *a labor movement is the combination of a labor center, its affiliated organizations and their supporters mobilized into a mutually-reinforcing social network, based on solidarity, that is focused on supporting the interests and achieving the goals of the workers and their unions as developed through an interactive process within the movement itself and in the context of external adversaries.*

And there can be more than one labor movement in any single country. There can be considerable differentiation among the ideologies of the specific labor centers, even within the same country, and this can result in a range of labor organization conceptualizations from institution to movement.[11]

Types of Trade Unionism

Key to understanding labor movements is to recognize the type of trade unionism practiced by the labor organizations at the heart of each movement.

Three radically different approaches to understanding this are offered by the works of Selig Perlman, Victoria Bonnell, and myself. These three authors are chosen because their approaches to trade unionism exemplify the three types of trade unionism—economic, political, and social movement unionism—that were delineated in a previous article (Scipes, 1992a: 124–134).[12]

Selig Perlman (1968/1928), in his comparative study of labor movements in Germany, Britain, the US and Russia during the nineteenth and early twentieth centuries, argued that activists in the US chose a conservative ideology in the face of particular structural conditions and in response against radical intellectual intervention in their movement. He conceptualized unionism in the US as an economic institution, based on "job consciousness" that limits itself to "wage and job control" (Perlman, 1968/1928: 169). Perlman saw its vision limited to survival in a terribly hostile social-political environment, and one in which maintaining organizational survival was extremely difficult (Perlman, 1968/1928: 160–169). Key to its survival, in his opinion, was in rejecting radical intellectuals and their various projects, including a labor party. Success in this project meant the institutionalization of labor.

Perlman's analysis, although he might not agree with the entire conceptualization, is of a trade unionism labeled "economic unionism":

> I define "economic" unionism as being unionism that accommodates itself to, and is absorbed by, the industrial relations system of its particular country; that engages in political activities within the dominant political system for the well-being of its members and its institutional self but generally limits itself to immediate interests . . . (Scipes, 1992a: 124; 1992b: 86).

Perlman's analysis is implicitly challenged by Victoria Bonnell's (1983) study of workers in St. Petersburg and Moscow between 1900–1914. Bonnell has argued that activists chose a radical ideology in the face of particular structural conditions and in support of radical intellectual intervention in their movement. When trying to identify how Russian workers could develop "revolutionary consciousness," she identified "endogenous" and "exogenous" understandings within social theory:

> But how do workers arrive at this rejection of the prevailing arrangements, and how do they develop an alternative vision? These issues are often conflated, but from an analytic point of view they represent distinct if interrelated problems. It is conventional in the literature to draw a distinction between two basic approaches to these issues: theories that focus primarily on revolutionizing circumstances external to the workers themselves and their milieu, and those that locate the roots of rebellion in the workers' own experiences acquired at the workplace, in the community, or in society. For the sake of brevity, I will call

> them exogenous and endogenous, respectively. They are not mutually exclusive, and elements of both can be found in some studies (Bonnell, 1983: 7).

She points out that "Exogenous theories share a common assumption that workers cannot develop revolutionary consciousness on their own," but require outside intervention by forces such as a political party or radical intellectuals. Endogenous theories, on the other hand, argue that workers are revolutionized by their own experiences, without the intervention of an outside agency (Bonnell, 1983: 8).

Bonnell's study, in fact, was designed to resolve the dispute: she concluded that workers organized themselves through creating a new understanding of their collective identity and then, from that collective identity, evaluated interactions with capital and the state and interpretations of these interactions by radical intellectuals. And, then, seeking a radical change to their situation, they decided to subordinate themselves to the intellectuals' organization with the program that they felt best met their needs. Success of the intellectuals' project in Russia also resulted in the institutionalization of labor, albeit under a more friendly, but ultimately controlling, regime.

Bonnell's analysis, although she might not agree with all of the conceptualization, is of a trade unionism labeled "political unionism":

> I define "political" unionism as unionism that is dominated by or subordinated to a political party or state, to which the leaders give primary loyalty—and this includes both the Leninist and "radical nationalist" versions. This results in generally but not totally neglecting workplace issues for "larger" political issues (Scipes, 1992a: 127; 1992b: 86).

And in explicit distinction from either Perlman or Bonnell, my study (Scipes, 1996) of the radical wing of the Philippine labor movement delineates still another type of trade unionism, social movement unionism. In this study of the *Kilusang Mayo Uno* (KMU) Labor Center, it was argued that activists chose to develop a different type of trade unionism, wherein they are ultimately masters of their own fate, rather than relying on intellectuals and/or intellectuals' organizations of either the right or the left. In other words, Filipino activists in the KMU have been willing to consider various approaches to their particular social conditions and then have decided, on the basis of their own understandings, their course of collective action. Thus, activists created a type of trade unionism that recognized their particular situation, but did not strait-jacket their efforts by limiting their conceptualization to either an economic or a political conceptualization, nor did they act only in response to intellectuals. Thus, this type of trade unionism—social movement unionism—differs from Perlman's economic conceptualization or (ultimately) Bonnell's political conceptualization:

> Social movement unionism is a type of trade unionism that differs from the traditional forms of both economic and political unionism. This type sees workers' struggles as merely one of many efforts to qualitatively change society, and not either the only site for political struggle and social change or even the primary site. Therefore, it seeks alliances with other social movements on an equal basis, and tries to join them in practice when possible, both within the country and internationally.
>
> Social movement unionism is trade unionism democratically controlled by the membership and not by any external organization, and recognizes that the struggles for control over workers' daily work life, pay and conditions are intimately connected with and cannot be separated from the national socio-political-economic situation. This requires that struggles to improve the situation of workers confront the national situation—combining struggles against exploitation and oppression in the workplace with those confronting domination both external from and internal to the larger society—as well as any dominating relations within the unions themselves. Therefore, it is autonomous from capital, the state and political parties, setting its own agenda from its own particular perspective, yet willing to consider modifying its perspective on the basis of negotiations with the social movements that it is allied with and that it has equal relations (Scipes, 1992a: 133; 1992b: 86–87).

It must be noted that, however, in each case referred to here, workers are considered active subjects and are not merely determined by the situation that they confront. Accordingly, it is possible for workers to decide on one type of unionism at one time, and then choose another type at another time: these are not immutable categories, established once and for all, but rather "living" creations that need to be periodically re-nourished.[13]

But in any case, it is the ideological conceptualization of trade unionism by activists who mobilize workers to unite and form labor collectivities that plays a central role, if not the central role, in determining whether any particular labor collectivity will act as an institution or as a movement.[14] In other words, while it may be changes in structural conditions and how this is understood that cause workers to decide to act collectively to create and/or join labor collectivities, it is the ideological conceptualization of trade unionism by activists within the collectivities, and their abilities to convince co-workers and supporters of the superiority of their approach, that determine the direction of each collectivity. Thus, the type of trade unionism chosen will shape the direction and possibilities of the labor movement in how it interacts with its larger environment (see Scipes, 2003).

Organizational Consolidation and Leadership

There is one more issue that must be addressed before moving on: organizational consolidation and leadership. Actually, this issue must be considered along with the conceptualization of trade unionism, so the two issues are enmeshed, not separate, and they should be considered simultaneously, not sequentially.

Key to developing an organization that hopes to exist over any period of time is the development of a decision-making process that is based on the values of the organizing group. A group wants to have a decision-making process that is efficient, allows everyone's voice to be heard, and yet allows work to be done and progress be made toward reaching the group's chosen goals—and sitting in endless meetings is rarely anyone's goal!

A process developed with a veterans' group in San Francisco of which I was a member in the 1980s—the Veterans Speakers Alliance—came up with a process that works quite well. First, we decided that all decisions could be categorized as either "action" issues (such as do we issue a statement on this issue, when's our next meeting, do we participate in a demonstration?) or "organizational" issues, which could have long-term ramifications that could affect the continued existence of the organization. And, accordingly, we set different decision-making criteria for each. While we always sought consensus, but when we could not reach it, we would then vote, with a 50 percent + 1 level required to adopt a position on action items. For organizational issues, we always required a "supermajority" of two-thirds or greater, so that substantive change always required greater support, and support at a level that would preclude organizational "splitting" if one side or another lost a vote. And I am happy to say these anti-war US military veterans are still working together 35 years later!

Tied with establishing a popular-democratic decision-making process, however, is the issue of leadership. Many organizations conceive of leadership as just being the roles and duties of those who attain formal offices within an organizational structure—and that is a very limited conceptualization.

A better one, I believe, is one that recognizes that anyone who helps the organization advance its goals and values is a leader, whether they hold formal office or not. These people are usually organizational activists and can play an important role in further advancing the organization's program.

However, adopting this approach of recognizing that anyone who helps the organization advance its goals and values is a leader—requires us to take a more sophisticated approach to understanding how an organization actually operates. Rather than adopting the dichotomous "leader vs. rank-and-file" understanding, which has long been common in regard to labor organizations, we have to understand that there are actually three groups involved: formal leaders, informal leaders (aka "activists"), and rank-and-file members. Once a person moves from activist to formal leader, they have a different role to play than other activists, and usually have a constitutional duty to do so. Yet, the activists (informal leaders) can agree or disagree with formal leaders, and that can enhance or oppose efforts by the formal leaders. So we have to recognize the in-between role of organizational activists, who operate between formal leaders and rank-and-file members.

Synopsis

From this overview of labor theory, it has been argued that it is necessary to recognize how workers have understood labor movements. Further, labor movements during the period of emergence are presented as one type of social movement; that labor movements are organizational manifestations of both labor centers and supporters; that involvement varies within labor movements; that labor movements can best be understood by focusing primary—but not exclusive—attention on activists; that not all collectivities of labor organizations are movements; that different labor collectivities can have different ideologies and practices—extending across a continuum from labor institutions to labor movements; and that it is ideological conceptualization by activists inside labor collectivities that are key to determining the direction of each labor collectivity. Further, it is desirable to advance an agreed-on decision-making process early in an organization's development, and to recognize a broader conceptualization of leadership for the organization.

Nonetheless, it is the ideological conceptualization of trade unionism by activists who mobilize workers to unite and form labor collectivities that plays the central role in determining the type of trade unionism that will guide particular labor movements. In other words, while it may be changes in material conditions and changed understandings that motivate some workers to rebel or even to act collectively to create and/or join labor collectivities, *it is the ideological conceptualization of trade unionism by activists within the collectivities, and their abilities to convince co-workers and supporters of the superiority of their approach, that determine the direction of each collectivity.* Thus, the type of trade unionism chosen will shape the direction and possibilities of the labor movement in how it interacts with its larger environment.

The argument here is that ideological factors are primary in the development of the type of trade unionism, with material conditions being secondary, and this obviously challenges those who argue the primacy of material conditions. I argue that if material factors determined the type of mobilization, then in a country that has multiple labor movements, the types of trade unionism and the accompanying behaviors would be the same across all of these movements. However, different types of labor movements exist in a number of countries, including Brazil, the Philippines and South Africa. Within South Africa, and particularly within the province of KwaZulu-Natal, there has been extensive conflict between the United Workers Union of South Africa (UWUSA), a center based upon political unionism, and COSATU (Congress of South African Trade Unions), which I classify as a labor center based on a social movement type of unionism. Material conditions cannot explain the differences between the two labor groupings, nor the extensive conflict (see Baskin, 1991).

But labor movement theory assumes that workers are already in motion—it does not tell us how they get active. Accordingly, I discuss social movement theory to understand how social movements emerge in general.

SOCIAL MOVEMENT THEORY

Within the literature on social movement emergence, there is material directly relevant to how labor movements emerge, and this knowledge needs to be incorporated into our understandings of labor movements. Two general approaches are structural explanations and cultural explanations (see McAdam, 1994).

The literature explaining why social movements emerge traditionally focuses on structural changes in the society, and "the emergence of popular uprisings reflects profound changes in the larger society" (Piven and Cloward, 1979: 7). Focusing on "protest movements" among the poor stratum of the working class, Piven and Cloward divide theories into those that see pressures on people forcing eruptions on the one hand, and those that see breakdowns in regulatory control of society, allowing eruptions to occur, on the other. However, they see these two factors as being connected. Focusing on the impact of sharp economic change, they point out that

> Ordinary life for most people is regulated by the rules of work and the rewards of work which pattern each day and week and season. Once cast out of that routine, people are cast out of the regulatory framework that it imposes. Work and the rewards of work underpin the stability of other social institutions as well. When men cannot earn enough to support families, they may desert their wives and children, or fail to marry the women with whom they mate. The loss of work and the disintegration of communities [means] the loss of regulating activities, resources, and relationships on which the structure of everyday life depends, and thus the erosion of the structures that [binds] people to existing social arrangements (Piven and Cloward, 1979: 11–12).

But even if sharp economic changes or the breaking down of daily life do explain *why* at least some social movements emerge, this does not tell us *how* movements emerge.[15]

However, even Piven and Cloward do not see structural explanations as sufficient in and of themselves; they add cultural ones as well to their approach. Sharp economic changes generally do not result in the rise of protest movements; *there must be changes in how people understand their respective situations:* "For a protest movement to arise out of these traumas of daily life, people have to perceive the deprivation and disorganization they experience as both wrong, and subject to redress" (Piven and Cloward, 1979: 12). In any case though, Piven and Cloward see these changed meanings as products of external, structural factors: large scale social distress (muting "the sense of self-blame, predisposing men and women to view their plight as a collective one" and blaming their rulers "for the destitution and disorganization they experience"); failures of dominant institutional arrangements; and/or splits within elite groups (Piven and Cloward, 1979: 12–13). However, and unfortunately, they have no suggestions as to the processes by which individuals come to recognize these situations as "wrong," and the processes that lead them to act to make them "right."[16]

The problem with Piven and Cloward's approach is that, even when recognizing the importance of a cultural approach, they subsume it under their structural approach; they see culture as a product of structure and not as an independent factor in and of itself. Yet this constrains, limits and ultimately defangs the power of a cultural approach. I suggest that a cultural approach that is not so constrained provides us with the tools to understand societal phenomena much more accurately and completely. I now turn to such an approach, starting with the work of Alberto Melucci, whose work from such a perspective has been pathbreaking.

Melucci (1989, 1995) questions the very basis of much social movement research, arguing that a major weakness of this research is that movements have been generally treated as empirical realities, as though they already exist. He believes researchers need to recognize the *constitutive processes* by which they are constructed; that is, that if we want to understand the emergence and development of social movements, we should not treat a movement as a given, but rather focus on the process of how it has been built.

Melucci uses cultural explanations to do this. Two concepts central to this thinking on how movements emerge are (1) the creation of a collective identity by a group, and (2) then the group's choosing to engage in collective action. And while these two concepts are not necessarily distinct empirically, it helps to disaggregate them for analytical purposes.

Social movements emerge, Melucci argues, as people recognize the need to think about society and their social experiences differently than they have in the past [see also Mueller (1994)]. Further, individual activity is crucial to the creation of collective identity, and he argues that creation of a collective identity is a precursor for consciously collective action.

Melucci defines collective identity as "an interactive and shared definition produced by several individuals (or groups at a more complex level) and concerned with the orientations of action and the field of opportunities and constraints" in which the proposed action is to possibly take place (Melucci, 1995: 44). He sees this as a process that includes a "notion of unity, which establishes the limit of a subject and distinguishes it from all others. . ." but he also recognizes that "a certain degree of emotional investment" is required in creating collective identity, which means that participation in collective identity can never be totally negotiable. He continues: "The notion of identity always refers to these three features: the continuity of a subject over and beyond variations in time and its adaptations to the environment; the delimitation of this subject with respect to others; the ability to recognize and be recognized" (Melucci, 1995: 45).

The process of creating a collective identity, an on-going process, is important: success allows potential actors to act together in ways that enable them to be in control of their own actions, and that is why it is important to understand on a theoretical level:

> . . . one cannot treat collective activity as a "thing," as the monolithic unity of a subject; one must instead conceive it as a system of relations and representations. Collective identity takes the form of a field containing a system of vectors in tension. These vectors constantly seek to establish an equilibrium between the various axes of collective action and between identification that an actor declares and the identification given by the rest of the society (adversaries, allies, third parties).
>
> Collective identity in its concrete form depends on how this set of relations is held together. This system is never a definitive datum; it is instead a laborious process in which unity and equilibrium are reestablished in reaction to shifts and changes in the elements internal and external to the field (Melucci, 1995: 50).

In other words, Melucci recognizes the interactive process between individuals that leads to collective identity and then, through on-going negotiation and renegotiation, the process that can lead to collective action once the group decides to act. Melucci sees movements not as entities with "unity of goals" but rather as "action systems": "They are systems of action, complex networks among the different levels or meaning of social action" (Melucci, 1995: 53). This means that any social movement should not be seen as a monolithic whole, but rather should be seen as having a multiplicity of politics, interpretations, possibly ideologies, etc., out of which a common politics is negotiated and from which action is constructed. But he also recognizes the interactional process that occurs between conflicting groups, and then the negotiation and renegotiation within each group as a result of that conflict (Melucci, 1989).

Hank Johnston, Enrique Laraña and Joseph Gusfield take this understanding of collective identity and focus on its interactions between individual identity and public identity (Johnston, Laraña and Gusfield, 1994). But they don't limit themselves to describing this; they go beyond this to try to connect ideology, grievances and collective identity. They admit that grievances and collective identities are not the same, but they claim that their relationship is close because "how social movement adherents think about themselves is structured in important ways by how shared wrongs are experienced, interpreted, and reworked in the context of group interaction" (Johnston, Laraña and Gusfield, 1994: 22).

Anthony Marx's 1992 study of the internal opposition within South Africa develops a parallel argument, and then takes it further. He focuses on different ideologies and how they developed over time, and shows how particular ideologies were surpassed as the organizations that had mobilized around them failed to resolve particular problems facing the movement based on that particular ideology. In his view, ideology is important because ". . . it is a way of experiencing reality, a form of 'practical consciousness,' based on a combination of culture and individual and historical processes" (Marx, 1992: 236).

Ideology helps one to understand, order and operate in her/his world: "Ideology is of central importance in understanding social movements and other political formations . . ." (Oliver and Johnston, 2000: 38).[17] If one accepts that whites are racially superior to blacks, then that person's behavior, consciousness and general approach to life—especially in relation to the "other"—will qualitatively differ from one who accepts that all people are equal as human beings. Or, if one accepts "free enterprise" capitalism as being desirable, then that person will respond differently to strong unions and strikes than one who has some form of socialism as her or his goal. Likewise, the choice of a particular type of trade unionism—economic, political or social movement unionism—will effect how one acts as a trade unionist (and, when consciously chosen for a union, how a particular union will act) regarding issues such as racial oppression in the union, workplace and community (see Scipes, 2003). Ideology can join with grievances to help create a collective identity, and the choice can effect individual and organizational behavior and development.

The connection between the creation of collective identity and grievances has also been mediated by the social psychological dynamics of collective attribution and social construction, what David Snow and colleagues have labeled "framing alignment processes" (Snow et al., 1997/1986). They argue that "grievances or discontents are subject to differential interpretation" and thus, it is not the particular problem that is so important, but rather how it is interpreted by potential actors. And adding to the complexity of the issue, they recognize that interpretations can vary "across individuals, social movement organizations, and time" (Snow et al., 1997/1986: 236). And although they refer to social movement organizations (SMOs) instead of broader social movements, as is done in this chapter, their point is quite clear as to the importance of understanding and dealing with these processes: "The ways in which SMOs manage and control these frame vulnerabilities, as well as interpretive resources in general, thus seem as crucial to the temporal viability and success of an SMO as the acquisition and deployment of more tangible resources . . ." (Snow et al., 1997/1986: 250).

Building on the different understandings of framing processes and the social construction of collective identities, Hunt, Benford and Snow try to address how they interact. They examine the way that "frame alignment processes can be conceived as rhetorical strategies to affect the alignment of collective and personal identities" (Hunt, Benford and Snow, 1994: 191). They point out that there are three basic "identity fields" of actors—"protagonists" or advocates of movement causes; "antagonists" or opponents of these causes; and "audiences" who are the uncommitted for which the protagonists and antagonists compete in the battle to win support and generate political power in furtherance of their cause—and that they each interact so as to help develop individual and collective identities which, they claim, is important "to understand the emergence of particular expressions of collective action" (Hunt, Benford and Snow, 1994: 192–204).

But it is Carol Mueller who ties these concepts of collective identity and framing together. In an analysis of Melucci's work through examining the origins of the women's liberation movement, she notes that Melucci's focus is on "submerged networks" of "small, separate groups engaging in cultural experimentation," and that

> In these cultural laboratories, new collective identities are constructed from the expressive interactions of individuals experimenting with new cultural codes, forms of relationships, and alternative perceptions of the world (Mueller, 1994: 237).

Further, she notes, "the status quo must be challenged at the cultural level in terms of its claims to legitimacy before mass collective action is feasible" (Mueller, 1994: 239).

Mueller, building off Bert Klandermanns's conception of levels of social construction, suggests four levels of analysis: "public discourse, persuasive communication initiated by movement organizations, 'consciousness raising' from participation in episodes of collective action, and the creation of collective identities in submerged networks" (Mueller, 1994: 258).[18] Obviously the processes of social construction will move back and forth, largely depending on the situation examined, but what her analysis suggests is that the creation of collective identities is crucial, and out of this, people engage in collective action from which they further learn, and these understandings are communicated to other organizations and then, ultimately, the public.

Melucci describes the overall process by which groups produce collective action:

> Collective action is rather the product of purposeful orientations developed within a field of opportunities and constraints. Individuals acting collectively *construct* their action by defining in cognitive terms these possibilities and limits, while at the same time interacting with others in order to "organize" (i.e., to make sense of) their common behavior. When actors produce their collective action they define both themselves and their environment (other actors, available resources, opportunities and obstacles). Such definitions . . . are produced by interaction, negotiation and conflict.
>
> Collective actors continually negotiate and renegotiate each of these dimensions ["the goals of their action, the means to be utilized, and the environment within which their action takes place" p. 26]. Leadership patterns and organizational forms represent attempts to give a more durable and predictable order to these negotiations. Collective action constantly requires this "social construction"—the failure or breakdown of which renders collective action impossible (Melucci, 1989: 25–26, 27).

In other words, Melucci recognizes the interactional process between individuals that leads to collective identity and then, through on-going negotiation and renegotiation, the process that can lead to collective action once the group decides to act. But he also recognizes the interactional process that occurs between conflicting groups, and then the negotiation and renegotiation within each group as a result of that conflict.

If we couple Johnston et al.; Anthony Marx; Snow et al.; and Hunt et al.'s understandings with Melucci's and Mueller's, we see that *social movements develop through cultural processes.*[19] These cultural processes begin with the creation of groups, and then creating a collective identity for each group. These groups, through a process of interaction, negotiation and conflict, then take collective action and frame the situation so as to legitimate their activities. As they act, and learn from taking such action, these groups further frame their efforts in a way so as to legitimate their actions to themselves (i.e., their members), other organizations and the public at large. They attempt to do so in a way that builds additional support for their actions among the larger public, while limiting or negating efforts by opponents that seek to counter these collective actions.[20]

APPLICATION OF THESE SOCIAL MOVEMENT THEORIES TO THE LABOR MOVEMENT

While the importance of sharp economic changes recognized by Piven and Cloward obviously can be related to the rise of labor movements, the work on collective identities is more difficult to relate. The main reason is because the theorist who is key to understanding collective identities, Alberto Melucci, argues that "this process of constructing collective identities is a unique characteristic of highly complex societies" (Mueller, 1994: 238). A reading of Melucci leaves no doubt that he is talking about contemporary, post-industrial capitalist societies when he uses the term "complex" (Melucci, 1989).

However, Carol Mueller suggests that Melucci

> may also underestimate how universal the process of cultural transformation has been as a prelude to previous periods of mass mobilization. The development of a collective identity centered on class consciousness among the working class in England (1780–1830), France (1830–1833) and Russia (1900–1914) point to a similar combination of social analysis contained within a new collective identity and institution building within submerged networks as prelude to collective action . . . (Mueller, 1994: 238).

This author agrees with Mueller: we cannot understand the process by which labor movements have risen without understanding how the development of new collective identities and organizational conceptualization and consolidation has affected this process.

However, we also have to recognize, especially in labor struggles, that collective identity is not solely created through conscious, rational, cognitive processes—it can also be created through partaking in collective action, which can be emotional but is, in many cases, non-rational when measured by the traditional standard of self-interest.[21] Rick Fantasia (1988) uses a wildcat strike in a factory to suggest how "cultures of solidarity"—"more or less bounded groupings that may or may not develop a clear organizational identity and structure, but represent the active expression of workers' solidarity within an industrial system and a society hostile to it"—can develop among a group of workers.

This can be clearly seen in his analysis of one stage of the wildcat strike:

> At this stage [after the men had taunted managers who had threatened to call the police-KS], the workers had defied company authority at its highest level and a strong sense of solidarity had emerged. . . . Solidarity among the workers was not an *a priori* "fact," but grew out of this interactive process of negotiation between workers in their confrontation with authority (Fantasia, 1988: 88).

The point here being that while collective identity is crucial to the rise of labor movements, it is not always created through a deliberative process.[22] Workers are confined within certain contexts during their working time, and situations can develop, as Fantasia has shown, where workers are forced to respond simply out of their gut: will they stand in solidarity with co-workers against management, risking their jobs, or will they side with management? No one knows beforehand which way people will jump. But when workers respond solidaristically, this leads to creation of collective identity among those that stood together. They then can decide if they want to go further or not—and develop a more conscious collective identity, and possibly even engage in collective action—or they can choose not to do so but, for workers, deliberation is not always a choice in the initial mobilization process.[23]

SYNOPSIS

We can see that social movement theory can help us understand the development of any labor organization. We have to understand that it is not changed (structural) conditions that lead to the emergence of a social movement, but a change in how individuals perceive the current structure or changes within.

Key to any such emergence is the development of a collective identity, where people share similar understandings and emotionally commit to each other to try to change things over a set period of time; at the end of such time, each can re-commit for a longer period or they can drop out without any recriminations from the others. Thus, this is a process by which people can move from "complaining" to actively trying to do something about it. To put it another way, it allows us to move from despair to action; from recognizing "You can't fight city hall" to "You can't fight city hall *alone!*"

Once a group identify is created, then members can move to engage in collective action. But any collective action must be "framed" with the values and the goals of the group; collective action can be framed in multiple ways, so any group engaging in such always wants to do everything they can to ensure that their meanings are the ones by which their actions are interpreted and valued—they never want others to frame their action for them because that will almost always result in their action and intentions being undercut.[24]

The importance of this can be seen by recognizing how uninvolved people, the "audience," will respond: 10 percent of an audience will automatically accept your efforts as valuable and worthy of support; 10 percent will automatically oppose them; and 80 percent will simply not care. The job of any "organizer"—whether individual, group or formal organization—is to get the 80 percent to join her side. Once people join, then the group collective identity must be recreated to incorporate the new members, and then you have to work out decision-making processes by which each member feels she or he has been heard, and which is run according to the negotiated values of the group. And then planning for the next collective action resumes.

CONCLUSION

In short, the combination of labor and social movement theories provides considerable theoretical mileage for a project such as this. It allows us to understand both how workers and their supporters can respond to particular material conditions in ways that lead to the emergence and development of a social movement, and how workers could choose a type of trade unionism that confronts oppression, within the social order and within the global political-economic networks in which this particular social order is enmeshed. At the same time, however, it suggests as well, albeit implicitly, why social movements may not emerge, or why workers would choose an alternative type of trade unionism.

From this general approach to trade unionism, we now shift to a specific examination of social movement unionism theory. This begins with an understanding of conditions facing trade unionists in developing countries, and how some unionists in three countries—Brazil, the Philippines and South Africa—chose to respond, creating what is now known as "social movement unionism." While repeating some of this chapter in the next, we learn how the concept was developed over time until it has reached the point to where it sits today.

NOTES

1. This chapter has never been published. It was written as a Directed Individual Study project for Professor John Walsh in Spring 1997 at the University of Illinois at Chicago, although it has been updated in a few places. In this collection, the original paper has been split, and now comprises Chapters 5 and 11.

2. Identified here, these concepts will be developed in Chapter 6.

3. I have worked from this perspective—focusing primary attention on activists—in my previous studies of labor movements: on the KMU (Scipes, 1996); in my comparison between the United Packinghouse Workers of America (UPWA) and the United Steelworkers of America (USWA) in Chicago (Scipes, 2003); in efforts to challenge AFL-CIO foreign policy (Scipes, 2010a: 69–82); and in efforts to build global labor solidarity (Scipes, ed., 2016).

4. Richard Freeman and James L. Medoff (1984) examine the effects on US society in an empirical study to evaluate the social benefits of American trade unions. They see unions having two different "faces": a monopoly face, which restricts competition and seeks gains for their members above any and all considerations, and a "voice/response" face, which allows workers through their unions to "dialog" with management and both resolve grievances and increase productive practices in their workplace. Thus, even this institutional analysis of what trade unions do—a much more limited and conservative approach than taken in this chapter—recognizes at least dual purposes for labor organizations.

At the same time, Rick Fantasia (1988: 15) notes the "complex structuring" of male working class cultures. David Halle's (1984) work is especially salient here, as Halle points out the three different "consciousnesses" combined within individual working class men: as workers, at home in their communities, and as "Americans." [We must be careful, as Halle requests, in generalizing from Halle's study. As he reports, the men in his study are "almost all white, they are all male" and "they live in the Northeast, not the South or West" (Halle, 1984: 292). In a recent study on working class responses to the Vietnam War, Penny Lewis reminds us that the "working class" is not confined to white, male workers—further discussion is beyond the scope of this issue—but see Lewis, 2013).]

In short, even when focusing on working class male "consciousnesses," it has been conclusively demonstrated to include a multiplicity of consciousnesses, and so it makes logical sense that individual workers would attribute multiple purposes to labor movements and trade unions.

5. It should be obvious that this approach looks at labor movements from the inside, that is, from the perspective of members of labor movements, and thus could be looked at differently by workers outside of them. For example, while particular workers inside a labor movement could recognize that their power comes from their ability to monopolize skills, it is doubtful that any of them would describe this monopoly as being anti-social or destructive; workers outside, however, could see this as such, especially if they were denied entrance to a monopolized craft, such as African American and/or women workers denied entry into the building trades because of their race and/or gender. And opponents of labor movements are particularly willing to use this terminology as part of their ideological and material crusades against labor.

Likewise, most workers would not consider a labor movement as "a subordinate mechanism with 'special interest' functions in a pluralist industrial society"! Besides not talking like this, they would probably argue that, while labor has certain "interests," labor's interests are more general than the narrow interests of the traditional special interest group. They are also unlikely to see labor's interests as subordinate: at least not by choice.

6. Randy Hodson (1991) looks at workers and how they deal with work, seeing these activities as multidimensional and not easily reducible to any single dimension—the prerogatives of autonomy are crucial to understanding worker behavior. He also points out that "Worker behavior also includes a tremendous amount of activity directed against other workers" (72). (My experiences in a number of print shops in the San Francisco Bay Area, Murfreesboro, TN and Shepherdsville, KY over nine years as a printing press worker confirm this.) This view also supports my statement that collective consciousness and collective interests must be constructed.

Johanna Brenner (1998), bringing women workers into our understanding, discusses how different factors—specifically including gender—affects the culture of workers and how they construct their "class" consciousness.

However, the most powerful argument against any claim of a common worker interest are findings from studies of the relationship between white and black workers in the United States, or to put it another way, the relationship between class and race. There is now an impressive body of historical research on these relationships: good overviews include work by Bruce Nelson (2001) and Eric Arnesen (1998). See also Ruth Needleman's (2003) book on five African American steelworkers, and the accounts of extensive struggles against white supremacy in the union (as well as the larger society) in Northwest Indiana. It should be obvious that the material interests of white and black workers differ, and that a common consciousness does not automatically exist. Where that common consciousness has existed, it has been created (see, for example, Halpern, 1997; Horowitz, 1997; and Halpern and Horowitz, eds., 1999).

For an excellent study of the creation of class consciousness by Korean workers, see Koo (2001).

7. As events in Indiana and Michigan in 2012 regarding "right to work" legislation have shown.

8. Hereafter, when I talk specifically about workers' organizations in general, I use the term "labor center." However, at all times, I recognize that trade unions and/or conglomerations of unions (in the US, "national or international unions") are the basic building block of labor centers, and thus any reference to a labor center will include the unions organizationally connected to the center unless specifically excluded. I do this to hopefully simplify communication.

9. In my comparative study of the development of the steelworkers and packinghouse workers' unions in Chicago, this was a very important factor in their different organizational developments (Scipes, 2003).

10. In his study of the New Unionism in Brazil, Sluyter-Beltrão (2010) specifically includes the media as being an important force that can attack and/or support labor organizations. I agree with this, and accept his "friendly amendment."

11. These are not dichotomies but merely a continuum across a range, with these being respective endpoints. The characterization of labor in these various "positions" is a *primacy* among the organizations, and not an exclusiveness; one can generally find the range of positions within each respective collectivity of labor organizations.

12. This article is republished herein as Chapter 6.

13. Sluyter-Beltrão (2010) recognizes changes in the New Unionism in Brazil over the ten years after the return to democracy, and consciously designed his study to understand these changes so that future efforts could avoid these problems.

Philip Hirschsohn (1998) and myself (Scipes, 2001) had each recognized some changes in COSATU between 1990–1994, so we recognized that types of unionism were never "settled" once and for all, but might change; nonetheless, Sluyter-Beltrão's study goes much further, focusing on these changes.

14. Again, these are the endpoints of a continuum. For purposes of this chapter, however, I describe labor collectivities with one or the other labels according to the predominance of their practices as I understand them.

15. Alberto Melucci (1989) focuses on the importance of individual needs as to why social movements emerge, and particularly the need to challenge the cultural "codes" that shape knowledge and understanding in contemporary societies, as people recognize the need to think about society and their social experiences differently than has been done in the past. Obviously, discussing this is beyond the scope of this chapter, but see Mueller (1994) for a detailed discussion of this. I include this point so to maintain the space theoretically for non-economic explanations for why social movements emerge.

16. Doug McAdam (1982) advances a "political process" model to explain social movement emergence and development that is a more elaborate and sophisticated effort than is Piven and Cloward's, but remains, at heart, a structural explanation, with its attendant weaknesses. Goodwin, Jasper and Polletta (2001: 24, FN #1) independently attribute a "structural bias" to political process theory. It is not necessary to elaborate further.

McAdam (1994) appeared to be moving away from a more structural explanation toward a cultural one. Nonetheless, in the collection that he later edited with John McCarthy and Mayer Zald (1996), the three editors highlight "political opportunity structures" (POS) as one of three main trends of social movement research, and refer to McAdam's 1982 work as being one of the early projects that that led to development of this concept. McAdam (1996) tries to overcome problems with the POS concept, but I am unconvinced. My comments above apply to political process theory as well as to Piven and Cloward's work.

17. An issue of *Mobilization* (Spring 2000) features two separate symposia on the need to re-include ideology into the study of social movements. See particularly Oliver and Johnston (2000) and Zald (2000), and then particular comments by respondents, and replies.

18. Klandermanns, according to Mueller, does not include the development of collective identities in his conceptualization (Mueller, 1994: 256–257).

19. For an interesting set of essays in a book that never got the attention I thought appropriate, see Darnovsky, Epstein and Flacks, eds. (1995).

20. Although not mentioned here, Hunt, Benford and Snow discuss how movements can frame "'outsiders' identity imputations" in efforts to negate attacks by opponents (Hunt, Benford, Snow, 1994: 201–203). For a discussion of movements and counter-movements, see Meyer and Staggenborg, 1996.

21. Much of the cultural approach to social movements has been confined to cognitive processes, but Jeff Goodwin, James M. Jasper, and Francesca Polletta (2001) make a strong argument that this is insufficient; that we must include emotions in our understandings of mobilization processes. Melucci and Mueller—in their work cited above—do this to some extent, although both are stronger on the cognitive end. I agree with Goodwin, Jasper and Polletta on this point, but because I draw off literature rather than first-hand research for this chapter, this is addressed here only to a limited extent. It is clear that the creation of collective identity is enveloped with emotions as well as with cognitive processes.

22. I also demonstrate this in my discussion of the development of a movement inside the AFL-CIO against its labor imperialist foreign policy (Scipes, 2012: 317).

23. For a detailed discussion of how workers organize themselves on the job, see Weir, 2004.

24. Another way to think of this framing process is as creation of a narrative supportive of collective action; see Reinsborough and Canning (2010).

Chapter Six

Social Movement Unionism

A New Type of Trade Unionism

Trade unionism in the less economically developed countries[1] (LEDCs)[2] is in crisis: low rates of industrialization, state opposition and/or cooptation, incompetent and/or self-serving leadership, and poor membership participation dog most trade unions.[3] Meanwhile, countries are manipulated by multinational corporations into competing for a limited amount of investment,[4] the International Monetary Fund (IMF) and the Word Bank (WB) are restructuring economies for the purpose of increasing exploitation and powerlessness, capital is making high rates of profit, workers are exploited, and the living standard for all who must sell their labor to survive and their families continues to decrease.

In many LEDCs, the trade union movement is limited to a small proportion of the work force. Workers who are lucky enough to get employment in a unionized workplace are often seen by the nonunionized as being some sort of "working class elite" or "aristocracy," and thus separate and above the large masses of people. This is not to claim that these unionized workers are overpaid, or that their higher rates of pay have made them passive, but that their interests are seen as differing from those of the large majority of workers and peasants. As a result, rather than uniting the poor and dispossessed, quite often the trade unions are seen as separating their members from the rest of the working people.[5]

At the same time, trade union members are often quite unhappy with their leaders. Unions are traditionally organized in a hierarchical manner, with decision-making confined to those at the highest levels, the most removed from the day-to-day life of the workplace. Accordingly, the interests of the leaders and the members usually differ considerably. And while some leaders are able to increase their members' rates of pay, they are almost never able to resolve the problems of oppression and alienation among workers, which are inherent whenever those who do the work do not control production.

However, trade unionism does not have to be this way. In countries as disparate as Brazil, the Philippines and South Africa,[6] labor centers have emerged that have taken a qualitatively different approach to the problems of the poor and dispossessed in their respective societies: they are creating autonomous, militant, class conscious unionism that sees the situation of the unionized workers as being intimately connected with the situation of working people throughout the country. Accordingly, they have been using their power within the production-distribution-exchange process to both fight to improve the wages and working conditions of their members *and* to fight for the improvement of the situation of all working people in the society, which means they are fighting for improvement of conditions for the majority of people in the society. However, this extends beyond issues of wages, working conditions, and employment security—traditionally considered "economic" issues—to include engaging in "political" struggles for democracy and human rights, and against "class," racial and national minority, and gender oppression. These new unions are organized democratically, with the leadership responsible and responsible to the membership. At the same time, these new unions have also developed a larger perspective pertaining to their country and its relations to other countries within the world economy. Thus the conditions in the workplace are seen as being intimately connected with the national situation; therefore, in order to change the conditions at the workplace, the society's relationship with the worlds' political-economic system must be changed.

How do we understand this new type of trade unionism? Peter Waterman and Rob Lambert have been engaged in a "discussion" over the past three or so years, trying to conceptualize this unionism which Waterman calls "social movement" unionism. I have found their thinking stimulating yet insufficient: I do not think they have it right yet. It is the purpose of this chapter formally to join in the discussion, and try to develop the conceptualization of social movement unionism to a higher degree, and to argue that this new conceptualization is the basis for a new type of trade unionism.[7]

TYPES OF UNIONISM

In this chapter, after discussing traditional conceptualizations of trade unions, I review and discuss the positions of Waterman and Lambert, and then advance my own thinking based on my experiences as a shop floor militant trade unionist, labor organizer, and researcher in the United States over a

15-year period. In Chapter 8—following a chapter on Philippine economic development that I wrote to provide an understanding of the larger social context of the Philippines in which the KMU operates—I then present a case study of the *Kilusang Mayo Uno* (KMU-May First Movement) Labor Center of the Philippines, which provides strong evidence for the power of this new conceptualization. Accordingly, I conclude that not only is social movement unionism a new type of trade unionism but that, to date, it offers the best way forward, albeit with considerable risks, for unions in the LEDCs.

Traditional Types of Trade Unions

Before discussing the concept of social movement unionism, it is important to present at least some basic understanding of traditional trade unionism. Because I am arguing that social movement unionism is a different type, I must compare it to the traditional type in order to have some understanding of how it differs.

Based on Clegg's 1976 book, *Trade Unionism Under Collective Bargaining,* Cella and Treu (1987: 197) report that there is no systematic theory of trade unionism or of national labor movements. With a fairly good survey of labor movements, particularly in the more economically developed countries, they put forth a typology of five different trade union models, which they call "opposition, business (or domestic), competitive, participation, state-sponsored" (221). They conclude that:

> short of establishing precise, cause-effect relationships, it can be said that the most decisive variables affecting models of unionism are union density, work-place organization, relations with political parties and with the political context of industrial relations (Cella and Treu, 1987: 223).[8]

However, this typology is insufficient. Each of these types of trade unionism, including "oppositional unionism" as I understand their conception, is based on acceptance of the status quo in their respective society, regardless of how the union movement chooses to relate to and influence that. There is no conception of a unionism—whether Leninist, nationalist, or any other—that challenges the status quo. Nor any that addresses the international activities of at least some of the labor movements in the more economically developed countries (MEDCs)—for example, the US based AFL-CIO, the British TUC, the German DGB—that have opposed "challenging" types of trade unionism,[9] nor any that addresses the international activities of the unions in state socialist social systems.[10]

Lambert and Webster's Conceptualization

Lambert and Webster (1988), after briefly mentioning Richard Hyman's conception of "optimistic" and "pessimistic" traditions of trade unionism, and obviously generalizing from South Africa, discuss three types of trade unionism: "orthodox," "populist," and "political, or social movement" unionism. They define "orthodox" as:

> a form of trade unionism that concentrates almost exclusively on workplace issues; fails to link production issues to wider political issues; and finally encourages its members to become politically involved without necessarily engaging itself in the wider political arena, believing that this is best left to other organizations more suited to the task. The political content of such trade unionism varies widely, but in each instance, what is common to this orientation is an accommodation and absorption into industrial relations systems, which not only institutionalizes conflict, but also serves to reinforce the division between economic and political forms of struggle so essential to the maintenance of capitalist relations of production, in the community and in the state (Lambert and Webster, 1988: 20–21).

They define "populist" unionism as:

> unionism in which trade unionism and struggles in the factory are downplayed. The latter is a tendency that neglects struggles over wages, supervision, managerial controls at the workplace and job evaluation. It places in its stead a political engagement that only serves to dissipate shop floor struggles (Lambert and Webster, 1988: 21).

And "political, or social movement unionism" as

> attempts to link production to wider political issues. It is a form of union organization that facilitates an active engagement in factory-based, production politics *and* in community and state power issues. . . . it does not negate the role of a political party, but rather asserts the need for a coordinating political body that is democratic in its practices and therefore able to relate to political unionism in a non-instrumental manner (Lambert and Webster, 1988: 21).

Lambert and Webster's conceptualizations, although based on the situation in South Africa, are much more useful for understanding different approaches to trade unionism than are Cella and Treu's because they include "challenging" types of unionism in their typology; however, like Cella and Treu, they do not address international activities of the unions in their models.

However, I have several differences with Lambert and Webster. I disagree with their "orthodox" model when they say that this type of unionism does not necessarily engage itself in the wider political arena—this certainly is not true of the British TUC nor, for that matter, is it true of the AFL-CIO (and probably not true of any trade union movement in the world in one way or the other). Both labor centers are actively engaged in electoral politics, while accommodating to and being absorbed within their respective industrial relations systems. I generally agree with Lambert and Webster's "populist" model, although I would suggest that these unions are controlled by or subordinate themselves to political parties or to a particular state, and to which they give primary loyalty instead of to the immediate interests of their members. And in cases where these unions exist within a state socialist social system,[11] they can and sometimes engage in international labor operations that are designed to support unions affiliated with political parties or states that are allied with their dominant party/state. And I will discuss my conception of social movement unionism below.

In response to Lambert and Webster's models, I suggest that there are three general types of trade unionism, although I would call them "economic," "political," and "social movement"—and I use these terms differently than do Lambert and Webster.

I would define "economic" unionism as

> unionism that accommodates itself to, and is absorbed by, the industrial relations system of its particular country; that engages in political activities within the dominant political system for the well-being of its members and its institutional self but generally limits itself to immediate interests; and which can and sometimes engages in international labor activities which are largely but not totally designed to help maintain the well-being of its country's current economic system, ostensibly for the well-being of its members, and these international activities are usually opposed to any type of system-challenging trade unionism.

I would define "political" unionism as

> unionism that is dominated by or subordinated to a political party or state, to which the leaders give primary loyalty—this includes both the Leninist and "radical nationalist" versions. This results in generally but not totally neglecting workplace issues for "larger" political issues. These unions can and sometimes engage in international labor operations that are designed to support unions affiliated with political parties/states that are affiliated with their party/state.

And, again, I will leave my discussion of social movement unionism to below.

But the key aspect to recognize in both economic and political unionism is that they do not link production issues with issues of political power.

REFLECTIONS ON THE DEBATE OVER "SOCIAL MOVEMENT UNIONISM"

In response to a request from people involved in labor studies and struggles in the Philippines, Peter Waterman (1988e) tried to develop the conceptualization of social movement unionism as an effort to assist their understanding of labor struggles in their country. Acknowledging the use of the conceptualization in the works of Webster (1987), Lambert (1988), Lambert and Webster (1988), and Munck (1988), Waterman particularly focused on Lambert and Webster's use of the term "social movement unionism," in which he wondered if this term was nothing more than a substitute for the earlier term "political unionism."

Waterman wanted to ensure that this concept was theoretically developed so that it would be much more than a substitute:

> I am concerned that the term be defined in such a way that it provides both a new theoretical tool and suggests and new political norm. In other words, that it is distinguished from traditional terminologies and from traditional practices (Waterman, 1988e: 1).

In his paper, Waterman stated the necessity of relating this social movement unionism to social movements, and then discussed the development of what he calls "movementist," or social movement, theory.

Comparing social movement unionism to the old concept of political unionism, Waterman notes, "We are not talking simply of a different union model but a different understanding of the role of the working class and its typical organization in the transformation of society." He points out that this new concept is a product of the newly emerging social movements and a new type of unionism (Waterman, 1988e: 6–7).

It was within this orientation that this discussion has taken place.

Waterman's Conceptualization

Peter Waterman has been able to develop this conceptualization more than Rob Lambert. However, this does not necessarily make it clearer.

I think there are three main points to Waterman's 1991a[12] conceptualization: one, he sees social movement unionism as being not only a different type of trade unionism but based on a different understanding of the working class and its organization in the struggle to transform society; two, he thinks this type is—and must be—radically different from the Leninist conceptualization of trade unionism; and three, he sees social movement unionism as necessarily being linked with other social movements. These three points must be addressed.

I think the first point is the clearest. It is based on the theory coming from Laclau and Mouffe, 1981, based on their understanding of and surpassing of Gramsci.[13] The concept of social movement unionism understands workers' struggles as being just one site of political struggle, and not the only or even primary one.

Therefore, social movement unions use their strategic position within society's production-distribution-exchange system to fight for the "dispossessed" and "powerless" of society—all workers, the poor, women, students, children, ecologists, peace activists, etc.—in alliance with and in conjunction with both these people organized in their own organizations and those who are not.[14] The important factor is being ready to join together on an equal basis with those who are struggling for power to change the world and particularly their respective society, and joining them when the opportunity presents itself.

Because of this different approach, it follows that this new understanding does not confine workers' struggles only to the workplace nor does it limit workers' struggles to those carried out by industrial workers. In fact, it does not even confine its definition of "worker" to those in the formal sector, to those who are waged, or even to those who are employed. Therefore, this type is a qualitatively different understanding of the working class and its organization in the struggle to transform society.

Waterman's second point—that the concept of social movement unionism is and must be different from the Leninist conceptualization of trade unionism —is supported by this different understanding of the working class and its organization to transform society.

However, the key point to be faced when differentiating social movement unionism from other conceptualizations, which Waterman is not clear on, is the relationship between economic and political struggles.[15] In contrast to Waterman, we must anticipate Rob Lambert's conceptualization and refer to his thinking because Lambert is quite clear about the issue of the relationship between economics and politics:

> the primary task of social movement unionism is the transcendence of the bourgeois separation of politics and economics that needs to be understood in the light of the relationships between economy, civil society and the state. The greater the containment of unionism within the collective bargaining system, the greater the social stability of capitalism. This is why new forms of workplace organization and practice that transcend the divide and lock into civil society and the state in new ways pose a threat to capitalist dominance . . . (Lambert, 1989: 6).

In other words, in opposition to both "bourgeois separation" and to Lenin's conceptualization of trade unions,[16] social movement unionism transcends the artificial economics-politics separation.[17] It is this issue, perhaps more than any other, that distinguishes social movement unionism from Leninism.

The third point of Waterman is that social movement unionism must be linked with other social movements. I think there are three levels to this: conceptual, ideological, and empirical. Conceptually, I do not think there is any problem, since the very understanding that workers' struggles are just one of many engaged in efforts to qualitatively change society at least suggests, if it does not demand, that workers' struggles be joined with other struggles. Ideologically, anyone who is fighting against domination and oppression would be the ally of those are fighting domination and oppression.[18] But empirically, there is a potential problem: while desiring to ally with other social movements, what happens if there are none developed or are not yet ready to ally with the workers' movement? Does that mean that a unionism built on this new understanding and which challenges the artificial separation between economics and politics, and which desires to ally with other social movements, does not fit into the category of social movement unionism? Does lacking on this one feature so radically change its complexion that it must be reconceptualized? I do not think so—and here I think that until Waterman separates the issue into different levels, he is engaged in conceptual overdeterminism.

Lambert's Conception

Rob Lambert also picked three areas that he felt were critical in the definition of social movement unionism: organizationally transcending the traditional political-economic divide; attempting to form structured alliances with social movements, and third, engaging in national campaigns of resistance against the state.

As stated above in considering Waterman's conception of social movement unionism, Lambert considers that transcending the political-economic divide to be the key aspect of social movement unionism. I think this is crucial. However, I do not think Lambert goes far enough in his understanding.[19]

I think Lambert's understanding is limited by his traditional conception of the working class. I think he uncritically adopts a Marxist conceptualization and while he tries to surpass its Leninist revision, he does this without challenging the original conceptualization, which I think is a critical flaw. This is evident in two ways.

One, although he and Webster recognize the development of alliance politics in South Africa (Lambert and Webster, 1988: 26–39), they do not suggest any change in their conceptualization of the "working class" because of that. Lambert continues to use the traditional conception of the working class in his papers discussing social movement unionism. Lambert's working class exists overwhelmingly at the workplace or when there is a community-located conception, it is only in regard to consumption issues. Yet without re-conceptualizing "working class," a politics based on alliance merely becomes a case of "adding" two subjects rather than merging both into a higher level of understanding and action.

Two, Lambert ignores thinking about how working people identify themselves. Amrita Chhachhi and Renee Pittin, writing about their research with women workers in India and Nigeria respectively, point out that women and men possess multiple identities and that "these identities have a basis in certain objective structures of class, caste, ethnic or racial group, gender, region, etc." They continue with a description of how this affects behavior with an example of how a female Indian worker in an electronics factory might confront problems in the workplace:

> Identities are selectively mobilized in response to economic, social, political and cultural processes. For instance, capital attempts to mobilize the "feminine" qualities of women workers in world market factories to ensure a docile, dexterous and cheap labor force. Identities are therefore constantly shifting, not only historically, but also at a given point in time. Faced with North Indian racism, a woman from Kerala asserts her identity as a Malayalee; in the next moment, faced with male chauvinism, she asserts her identity as a woman; and in the next hour, confronted with managerial discipline, she assets her identity as a working class woman. She possesses all of these identities and yet he is not reducible to any one of them (Chhachhi and Pittin, 1991: 24–25).[20]

By ignoring the understanding of multiple identities, Lambert limits struggles of working people to the workplace and around issues of distribution and consumption issues, prohibiting, if you will, any further possible political involvement by working people.

But from looking at Lambert's understanding of the need to transcend the economic-political separation, we must look at his second point: the need to develop structured relations with social movements. I disagree with Lambert on this point. Again, just as I criticized Waterman's formulation on this relationship, I think Lambert is overemphasizing the role of the relationship between the unions and the social movements. I can understand the logic so as to why he does this: he thinks it is necessary for trade unions to reconceptualize their factory orientation, ideological input, and the nature of collective action. He feels this is only possible within a structured alliance with the social movements, and that "spontaneously generated, non-permanent links" with social movements do not necessarily result in fundamental organizational and ideological change that he thinks is necessary.

While he does not specifically say that this organizational and ideological change is impossible without a structured alliance with the social movements, he comes very close. He strongly implies it is because of this relationship that the unions make these fundamental changes. Again, I do not think this is true—and my research from the Philippines contradicts this claim (see Scipes, 1996).

The third point, engaging in national campaigns of mass-based resistance against the state, follows very much the second. It implies the unions cannot be transformed into social movement unions without this national struggle. First of all, I do not think this is true. Second of all, it ignores the various power relationships, and does not ascertain if the unions (and other social movements) have the power to struggle against the state in a nationwide campaign and to be able to withstand any repression that might logically result, or not. If the unions cannot take on that level of struggle at a particular time, but are moving toward being able to do so, are they not social movement unions? If it is a matter of power, and they do not have it at a particular stage of development, does this mean we have to reconceptualize their existence? And again, I do not think so.

Having presented the main points of the discussion, and discussed each of them, I will now put forth my conceptualization of social movement unionism. And in Chapter 8, I present a case study of the KMU Labor Center of the Philippines that will provide empirical evidence of the power of this conceptualization.

NEW CONCEPTUALIZATION OF SOCIAL MOVEMENT UNIONISM: SCIPES

My conceptualization of social movement unionism incorporates the strengths of both Waterman's and Lambert's conceptions and goes beyond them, both in instrumental form as well as in theoretical basis:

> Social movement unionism is a type of trade unionism that differs from the traditional forms of both economic and political unionism. Social movement unionism specifically rejects the artificial separation between politics and economics that is accepted by the other types of trade unionism. Social movement unionism sees workers' struggles as merely one of many efforts to qualitatively change society, and not either the only site for political struggle and social change, or even the primary site. Therefore, social movement unionism seeks

> alliances with other social movements on an equal basis, and tries to join them in practice when possible, both within the country and internationally.
>
> Social movement unionism is trade unionism based in the workplace and is democratically controlled by the membership and not by any external organization, and recognizes that the struggle for control over workers' daily work life, pay and conditions is intimately connected with and cannot be separated from the national socio-political-economic situation. This requires that struggles to improve the situation of workers confront the national situation—combining struggles against exploitation and oppression in the workplace with those confronting domination both external from and internal to the larger society—as well as any dominating relations within the unions themselves. Therefore, social movement unionism is autonomous from capital, the state, and political parties, setting its own agenda from its own particular perspective, yet willing to consider modifying its perspective on the basis of negotiations with the social movements and/or political parties with which it is allied and with which it has equal relations.

This conceptualization recognizes social movement unionism as being not only a different type of trade unionism, but is based on a different understanding of the working class and its organization in the struggle to transform society. This type transcends the traditional economic-political divide of society, which is common to both the bourgeois and the Leninist conceptions. This type is based on democratic control by the membership within the unions, and on rejecting any external control. Further, SMU challenges the social order in which it is located, and challenges the larger global political-economic networks in which their country is enmeshed. And social movement unions are willing to ally with social movements and/or political parties on the basis of equal relations, and even consider modifying its particular perspective through negotiations. Additionally, social movement unionism's conception of internationalism is built on solidarity relations, supporting those challenging dominative power at work and throughout every society.[21]

RAMIFICATIONS OF THIS NEW CONCEPTUALIZATION

Conceptualizing trade unionism in this manner has several ramifications. First, it consciously conceives of workers' struggles as being directed against dominative power, and consciously joins workers with all other people in the struggle for emancipation.[22] Second, it sees workers' struggles as integrated with all other struggles against dominative power—thus, the separation of labor from other social movements is ended. And third, it does not limit this model of trade unionism to workers in the LEDCs; it is one that allows workers anywhere to adopt it.

The last point, in turn, gives an entire new thrust to labor internationalism. Any challenge to dominative power has the opportunity to concretely support struggles for emancipation around the world.[23] Thus, building a new labor movement on the model of social movement unionism would be a major contribution to emancipatory struggles wherever they might take place.

And now that I have discussed the debate, put forth my conceptualization, and argue that it provides a better type of trade unionism than we currently have, we shift to discussing the socio-economic context of the Philippines—using a case study of the impact of 37 years (1962–99) of neo-liberal economic policy on that country—the socio-economic context in which the unions that eventually formed the KMU had to operate.

NOTES

1. This chapter and Chapter 8 were originally published together as "Social Movement Unionism and the *Kilusang Mayo Uno"* (Scipes, 1992a), and my conceptualization of SMU was developed as a result of my research on the KMU. It makes more sense for this project to break them apart and to present as separate chapters. I would again like to thank Amrita Chhachhi, Rob Lambert, E.A. Ramaswamy, Freek Schiphorst, and Peter Waterman for their informed comments, criticisms, and suggestions of earlier drafts of the original article, while taking full responsibility for what is included.

2. Like many others, I am frustrated with the terms developed to date which are used to distinguish the more economically developed countries—often referred to as "First World" or "industrialized" countries—from less economically developed countries, which are often referred to as "Third World" countries. (I am ignoring at this point the so-called "communist" or "formerly-communist" countries.) Unfortunately, I have not come up with an alternative conceptualization with which I am satisfied.

However, I reject the term "less developed countries" (LDCs) because it specifically incorporates levels of economic development as being representative of historical or cultural development as well, which is very "Western"-centric (and here I am caught by terminology again because I include Japan), if not racist. One shudders to think of anyone considering the United States, for example, as being more historically or culturally developed than the societies of China, Egypt, Persia (Iran), or those of the Aztecs or Mayas of Latin America. But because there is a difference in economic development—obviously a product of imperialism (see Nederveen Pieterse, 1989; Scipes, 2010b: 467–469)—I will use the terms "more economically developed countries" (MEDCs) and "less economically developed countries" (LEDCs).

3. Many of these problems—although more of de-industrialization rather than lack of industrialization—also dog the unions in the MEDCs, and in the United States in

particular. While not downplaying or ignoring these problems in the MEDCs, I am limiting this article to focusing on conditions in the LEDCs.

4. Although some of those countries that are successful in competing, such as China, receive extensive foreign investment. [In the original article—written in 1991— I used Indonesia as an example, but times have changed.]

5. I use the term "working people" to signify a much more inclusive conceptualization than "working class," which is an inadequate concept as far as I am concerned. I include in my conceptualization all people who must sell their labor power to survive and who are relatively powerless as individuals as far as the overall operation of their respective workplaces and societies are concerned. Thus, I specifically include those who work in the home, with or without payment.

6. I served for five years (1984–89) as the North American representative for the British-based journal, *International Labour Reports*—see Chapter 3, herein. During this time, from reading the articles published in the journal as well as other materials—particularly Transnational Information Exchange (1984), MacShane, Plaut and Ward (1984), and Munck (1988)—and from my experiences with the KMU in the Philippines, I saw that new labor centers were emerging in these countries that were obviously different from traditional unions. The specific labor centers in these countries that I refer to—CUT (*Central Única do Trabalhadores)* in Brazil, KMU (*Kilusang Mayo Uno)* in the Philippines and COSATU (Congress of South African Trade Unions) in South Africa—are ones that, as I argue in this chapter, should be conceptualized differently from traditional trade unions. These experiences, I suggest, provide the basis for the development of "social movement unionism" (SMU) and serve as a model to rejuvenate unionism in particularly the LEDCs. And despite being beyond the scope of this chapter, I think social movement unionism—this version; NOT that advanced by Kim Moody (1997), which is discussed in Chapter 13—is a model for workers in the MEDCs as well; hence, I suggest it is an international and not just a "Third World" model.

However, I do not confine the possible development of SMU to just the countries mentioned here; it is the experiences of these labor centers, however, that are the clearest and thus the strongest bases for any new model. Certainly, the experiences of *Solidarnosc* in Poland should be considered, and *Solidarnosc* probably fits this conception at least during 1980–81—Lambert and Webster include *Solidarnosc* in their conceptualization of SMU, although in general and not limited to any particular time period (Lambert and Webster, 1988: 39, FN #3). However, I am not so sure what happened during the martial law period, and evidence I have seen is contradictory—obviously, much more research needs to be done. [For the latest on *Solidarnosc,* see Bloom, 2014.] Munck (1988: 121–122) writes of some local forms of SMU in India. Personal reports on the UNTS in El Salvador suggest it might be another social movement unionism-type labor center, but more detailed information needs to be acquired. I have heard some interesting reports on new unions in Mexico. I assume there are other experiences along these lines taking place in other countries, although they have not yet been reported. In short, I believe this concept of social movement unionism fits a range of unions beyond those to which I specifically refer.

7. Although this paper was published initially in 1992, and all of the principals addressed within have known about it, none have ever addressed my conceptualization. No one else has done so either, even when they've known about this article or a "sister" article published in *Critical Sociology* (Scipes, 1992b), or have read my book (Scipes, 1996), which was an empirically-based historical and sociological study of the KMU, and which was intended to show the validity of my conceptualization. Whether writers have known about my efforts or not, there has been a tremendous amount of confusion and unclarity about what is meant by "social movement unionism," so people use the term in many different ways without understanding what they are doing. This chapter presents the theoretical aspect of my initial article, while Chapter 8 presents the empirical base for my argument. In Chapter 13, after discussing numerous authors' works and the way the concept has been used, I try to disentangle the confusion, returning "social movement unionism" to a viable and useful concept.

8. Marian Golden, in her study of union responses to austerity programs in Italy in the late 1970s to the early 1980s, took a different approach. She tried to explain different policy orientations of organized labor, using political, sociological, economic-industrial, and organizational typologies. She found each of these insufficient, if not "patently inaccurate." She argued that "a more adequate account of union policy orientations should instead be actor-centered, focused on union officials, themselves conscious agents who evaluate situations and issues according to their goals and preferences, and on that basis, respond to structural constraints—business conditions, the extent of organizational centralization, the pressures from friendly or unfriendly political parties and governments (Golden, 1988: 5–6). And although this does not solve the problem of a lack of theory of trade unionism or of national labor movements, to me it suggests a much more interesting approach than does that suggested by Cella and Treu.

9. The best single source on international activities of the British TUC remains Thomson and Larson, 1978. For a report on the German political foundations, see Pinto-Duschinsky, 1991. The German labor center, the DGB, operates through the Friedrich Ebert Stiftung (foundation).

There have been extensive reporting and discussion of AFL-CIO activities over the years, of which the most comprehensive listing is in Scipes, 1989. For a recent overview of the AFL-CIO's foreign operations, see Sims, 1992. However, most of the analysis, in my opinion, is incorrect, blaming factors and organizations *external* to it, rather than looking for factors *internal* to the AFL-CIO, for its imperialist foreign policy. For a detailed look at the roots of AFL-CIO foreign policy, focusing on internal factors, see Scipes, 1989. [Superseded by Scipes, 2010a, 2010b, 2016a.] For the best listing of books and articles on the AFL-CIO foreign policy program—updated every time we get more information—see my "Contemporary Labor Issues" bibliography, and especially https://www.pnw.edu/faculty/kim-scipes-ph-d/publications/contemporary-labor-issues-bibliography/. See Section 1, Changes to the US Labor Movement, under AFL-CIO Foreign Operations.

10. There is one written report that I have been able to find on the international activities of the "East Bloc" World Federation of Trade Unions (WFTU), and that

is Waterman, 1986. Nonetheless, this report demonstrates that the communist trade unions function in many ways similarly to the "Western" ones, although with a lot less money.

11. Although it may seem contradictory, I think this "populist" type also fits the situation in state socialist countries, despite its name. In the typology I advance, see below, I refer to this type as "political."

12. That I referred to Waterman's 1988e piece in the section above while jumping to his 1991a piece in this section might cause some confusion among readers. Waterman set of the parameters of the discussion in his earlier piece, although his 1991 piece is considerably more developed. Therefore, while wanting to situate the debate, I also wanted to use the strongest development of his argument; hence, the shift in articles referred to.

13. Because I disagree with the theoretical basis for Laclau and Mouffe's position, although I agree with the position itself, I felt it necessary to develop my own conceptualization of this point, which I have developed in my MA Thesis (Scipes, 1991a). However, this is beyond the scope of the present chapter.

14. The way Waterman formulated the debate has confused some readers. Social movement unionism does *not* mean ignoring struggles for wages, benefits and working conditions in the workplace and only fighting for "larger" issues outside; social movement unionism *includes* fighting for wages, benefits, and conditions in the workplace *and* using workers' power inside society's production-distribution-exchange system to join with others to fight for "larger" issues.

In the latest version of his thinking, Waterman [1993] recognizes the imbalance and focuses more on workplace issues. However, since this version still does not address the key issue I see in understanding the concept, I do not review this paper.

15. Although Waterman does not accept the theoretical separation between the economy and political realms of society, as he suggests Lenin and Lambert do, the fact of the matter is that the other types of trade unionism *do* accept this separation. Therefore, Waterman specifically needs to confront this situation, which he does not do in his writings.

16. Lenin separates economic and political struggles in his conceptualization. In his classic "What Is To Be Done?" in which the communist theory of trade unionism in the period preceding seizure of state power is most developed, Lenin's argument is that trade unions cannot develop beyond the economic aspect of the struggle; to go farther, workers must join in revolutionary organization (Lenin, 1953—see particularly Chapter 3, "Trade-Union Politics and Social Democratic [Communist] Politics," 259–308). [For a quick discussion of the Marxist and Leninist approaches to trade unionism, see Scipes, 1992b: 82–83.]

17. As Amrita Chhachhi reminds me, the real issue is not the separation of the economic and political in the workplace—because workers' struggles against dominative power are immanently political—but the separation between the workplace and the rest of the workers' life-spaces.

18. This raises the crucial point of democracy in movements, and it seems very critical in trying to consider the relationship between communist vanguard parties and other social movements. Ideologically, communist parties are allies in fighting

capitalist domination and oppression; in reality, they are merely trying to replace the capitalists with their members and/or supporters. And with a system that is based on hierarchy and authoritarianism—democratic centralism—any "post-revolutionary" system of power in which the communists are dominant would itself be dominating and oppressive, and thus opposed to the social movements.

This suggests a strategy, since most people would agree that the domination and oppression of the existing system is of more immediate concern than the possible domination and oppression of a future system, although future possibilities cannot be ignored: that while the communists are challenging the current system, they should not be conceived of as enemies, but that social movements work with them only when chosen by the social movements, and only when and as long as the communists are willing to work with the social movements on the basis of equality and mutual respect. Social movements should also be working to establish structures and processes within each social movement that challenge domination and oppression within the social movement itself—and perhaps the main form of these would be against bureaucratization, although I would not limit it only to this. At the same time, the social movements should publicly put forth their values and ideology, and argue that their conception of the future is much superior to any based on domination and oppression. Thus while challenging the present domination and oppression, the social movements would also be fighting any potential domination and oppression of a "post-revolutionary" system.

And while the above comments were written from the perspective of my understanding of communist practice internationally, they may not be appropriate for local forms of communist practice. While I remain skeptical of communist practice, I recognize that ultimately it is the people in each respective area who must make their own analysis of their specific situation. Nonetheless, I believe the issues of democracy, and the relationships between communists and the social movements (and especially with social movement unions) are crucial issues that must be specifically addressed in every situation.

19. This point was suggested by Peter Waterman in response to an earlier draft of this chapter.

20. Chhachhi and Pittin do not limit identities to just the workplace. They note, "The separation of private and public, of factory and home, of personal and political creates misleading dichotomies," and then quote Donna Haraway:

> If it were possible ideologically to characterize women's lives by the distinction of public and private domains—suggested by images of the division of working class life into factory and home, and of gender existence into personal and political realms—it is now a totally misleading ideology, even to show how both terms of these dichotomies construct each other in practice and theory. I prefer a network ideological image, suggesting the profusion of spaces and identities, and the permeability of boundaries in the personal body and the body politic (Haraway, 1990: 212, quoted in Chhachhi and Pittin: 25).

21. One very clear example whereby labor internationalism is being carried out on the larger level is the struggle by the KMU to rid the Philippines of the US military bases. [They and their allies were ultimately successful in 1992, when the Philippines

refused to extend the leases on the bases, causing the US to withdraw.] While this is obviously in their own interest, they see it as an international contribution to the well-being of the world's people. They know that every time the US has intervened in Asia, it has used the Philippine bases to project its power. For a more elaborate discussion of how the KMU builds international labor solidarity, see Chapter 12.

22. Without getting into a long discussion: in a new model of society that I have proposed to better represent social reality—Polyconflictualism—I specifically develop the concept of dominative and emancipatory power: and this dual-pronged version of "power," in my opinion, supersedes the singular concept of power, based on the work of Max Weber, that sociology has long embraced. I find this traditional conception of power insufficient since it does not allow sociologists to theoretically explain the development of power from the "bottom" of society, such as by social movements and social movement unions, a problem my conceptualization overcomes. My polyconflictual model has yet to be published in a peer-reviewed journal, so this should be considered only as my "best thinking." For the fullest published explanation of Polyconflictualism to date, see Scipes, 2010a: 130–151.

23. An example of this that shows the potential of this labor internationalism, even though it was carried out by economic type trade unions, is that of national and international unions in North America organizing under the banner of the National Labor Committee for Human Rights and Democracy in El Salvador. They were able to successfully challenge the international policy of the AFL-CIO on Nicaragua in the mid-1980s [see Battista, 2002]. I believe that had the AFL-CIO been able to carry out its traditional foreign policy unopposed, it would have emboldened the Reagan Administration to invade Nicaragua. Thus, the National Labor Committee's contribution to the prevention of a US invasion of Nicaragua, in my opinion, was significant. [See Scipes, 2010a; 2012, for the most in-depth examination of the AFL-CIO foreign policy program, and how labor activists in the United States have mobilized to transform AFL-CIO foreign policy.]

Chapter Seven

Philippine Economic Development

Now that we have discussed the development of the theoretical conceptualization, "social movement unionism," and as part of our shift from general understandings to specifics, we shift to discussing the socio-economic context of the Philippines—using a case study of the impact of 37 years (1962–99) of neo-liberal economic policy on that country; the socio-economic context in which the unions that eventually formed the KMU had to operate.[1]

The Philippines is, in some ways, a special case: while its economic development program has been based on neoliberal principles promoted by the IMF and the World Bank, it did not begin as a response to the "Asian" economic crisis of the late 1990s as might be thought: the Philippines has been carrying out a neoliberal development program since 1962. And while not wanting to excuse the Philippine elite for their role in this, this chapter focuses on what a neoliberal program has meant to a country that has been following its prescriptions for the past 37 years (1962–99), to help lay the groundwork for the understanding of the emergence of a radical labor movement, the KMU.

PHILIPPINE ECONOMIC DEVELOPMENT FROM INDEPENDENCE TO DEREGULATION, 1946–1962

Like any country that was colonized, the Philippine social order was organized to benefit people in the colonizing country and not Filipinos. An extractive agricultural economy (sugar, tobacco, hemp, coconuts) and a political system dominated by members of the various regional elites were the product of 381 years of Spanish, and then US, colonization.

When the Philippines was granted "independence" by the US in 1946, it had been devastated by the Second World War: the United States used this to set up a neocolonial relationship with the now-ruling elites. Economic relief was made dependent on political and economic concessions to US investors, establishment of US military bases across the country, and a currency whose value in relationship to the US dollar could not be changed without the explicit permission of the US President.[2] These impositions, in addition to the extractive economy and corrupt political system, were all "grants" to the newly freed nation (Shalom, 1981).

An economic crisis in the late 1940s, when luxury imports by the elites threatened to bankrupt the country (in addition to a peasant revolt in Central Luzon and a newly emerging radical labor movement), forced the ruling elites to try a new economic program, with US permission. Unwilling to implement a genuine land reform program, the elites tried industrializing as a way of restoring the economy, pacifying the peasants and workers, and maintaining their land-based power. Although not ignoring the repression directed against peasants and workers (or the direct involvement of the CIA)—see Kerkvliet, 1977, for peasants; Smith, 1981, for CIA—focus here is limited to the economic policies implemented.

To implement their new industrialization program, the Philippine government initiated foreign exchange and import controls. The controls provided multiple economic benefits to the state: they limited both general imports (such as consumer goods for the rich) and repatriation of capital outside the country, and allowed the state to select imports to assist the industrialization process and to protect industry established in the country (Payer 1974: 54–55). This import substitution industrialization (ISI) program was a serious effort to industrialize.

While this program did not benefit the majority of the population at the time, it was a success as an industrialization program by 1960. A moderate industrial base had been established: the country had food, wood, pharmaceutical, cement, flour, textile, paint, pulp, paper, glass, chemical, fertilizer, telecommunications, appliance, electronic, plastic, refined fuel, intermediate steel, shipbuilding, motor vehicle, machine parts, engineering, and other industries. From 3 percent in 1949, almost 18 percent of the total national income was derived from manufacturing in 1960. And it was largely built by Filipinos: from 1949–1961, Filipinos had invested 1,400 million *pesos* in new activities as compared to 425 million by the Chinese (mostly Chinese-Filipinos) and only 31 million by US investors (Payer, 1974: 56). The Philippines was then considered to be the next Japan of Asia.

But this industrial progress came at a cost: the state maintained the *peso* at the incredibly overvalued rate of 2 *pesos* to the US dollar (established by the US Government before "independence"), and this made it increasingly difficult for agricultural exporters to find markets for their products though it aided the industrialization program. (To make it easier to follow below, one dollar would buy 2 *pesos,* or US $1: P2.) Since the agricultural elites were funding much of the industrialization program, they were in the driver's seat when they pressed the state to agree to end controls and effectively devalue the *peso.* Ultimately, in 1959, an agreement was made that the foreign exchange and export controls would be ended in 1964, and it had been these controls that had kept the *peso* so strong. This five-year interval was intended to make the transition less painful than an immediate termination of controls.[3]

IMPLEMENTING DEREGULATION

However, Diosdado Macapagal was elected President of the country, and one of his first acts after assuming the presidency in January 1962 was to terminate all controls immediately. This was supported by US President Kennedy, who arranged for the Philippines to immediately receive a $300 million loan from the IMF to cover the repatriation of $300 million of US corporate profits (Payer, 1974: 66–67). This was the beginning of the Philippines' debt dependence.

Ending these controls—deregulation in today's terminology and a major component of the neoliberal program—devastated the Philippine economy. The *peso* began weakening immediately, and was formally devalued from US $1: P 2 to US $1: P 3.9 in 1965. (A simple example: if you borrowed one million dollars at the old rate, you had to repay it with two million *pesos* before devaluation, and 3.9 million *pesos* at the new rate.) This resulted in the bankruptcy and collapse of many businesses. The balance of payments situation worsened: imports increased 68 percent between 1963 and 1967, while exports only increased 7 percent. The foreign debt doubled from $275 million in 1962 to approximately $600 million in 1965. And the manufacturing share of Gross National Product (GNP) decreased from 17.9 percent in 1962 to 7.1 percent in 1965.

TO THE RESCUE: AN EXPORT-INDUSTRIALIZATION STRATEGY

So, by the mid-1960s, the economy that looked so promising going into the decade was a shambles. Different forces with a belief in neoliberal economics—including Filipino economists like Gerardo Sicat, and the IMF and

World Bank—encouraged the government to launch an export-oriented industrialization program to solve the crisis, which was caused by neoliberal deregulation in the first place. Their argument was that by using low Filipino wage rates to attract foreign capital, and then basing manufacturing operations on cheap and controlled labor, the Philippines could export enough manufactured products (such as garments and electronic components) into the world economy to improve its balance of payments and employment opportunities. Consequently, poverty and income inequality would be reduced, ultimately enabling the state to "modernize" Philippine society.

Ferdinand Marcos, who was elected to the presidency as a "reformer" in 1965, decided to begin focusing the economy along such lines. Marcos was able to lay some important groundwork in that direction in the late 1960s but because of substantial opposition—both within Congress and larger society—he was unable to operationalize it at that time.

MARTIAL LAW

It was only when Marcos declared Martial Law on September 21, 1972 that the export-oriented industrialization strategy (EOI) could be implemented. Key to the EOI strategy was the establishment of the export processing zone at Mariveles, Bataan. Two months after the implementation of Martial Law, Marcos issued Presidential Decree 66 (PD 66) to facilitate the development of the Bataan Export Processing Zone (BEPZ), providing incentives specifically for export production. According to Walden Bello, David Kinley and Elaine Elinson, PD 66 gave firms that exported at least 70 percent of their products "permission for 100 percent foreign ownership; permission to impose a lower minimum wage than in Manila; tax exemption privileges, including tax credits on domestic capital equipment, tax exemptions on imported raw materials and equipment, exemption from the export tax and from municipal and provincial taxes; priority to Central Bank foreign exchange allocations for exports; low rents for land and water; government financing of infrastructure and factory buildings, which could then be rented out or purchased by companies at a low price; and accelerated depreciation of fixed assets." The incentives worked: "By 1980, the Bataan EPZ had attracted 57 enterprises, the great majority foreign owned, employing some 28,000 workers" (Bello, Kinley and Elinson, 1982: 140–141).

By the early 1970s, the World Bank's role in the industrialization strategy had become crucial. While it had provided the Philippines with only $326 million in loans between 1950 and 1972, it gave the Philippines more than $2.6 billion between 1973 and 1981. In addition to the money provided, the

Bank legitimized the country's economic plan to international financial institutions. Not coincidentally, the Marcos government decided to follow Bank strategy for development, focusing on "industrializing efforts emphasizing the manufacture of labor-intensive exports with the strong participation of foreign capital," again according to Bello, Kinley and Elinson (1982: 16–39).[4]

Export production in BEPZ grew steadily for the first 10 years, but then significantly declined throughout the rest of the dictatorship. Researcher Peter Warr presents data that shows huge increases in non-traditional exports: from US $.4 million in 1972 to $73.1 million in 1978 to $159.6 million in 1982. However, exports from BEPZ decreased after 1982, falling to a low point of $57.6 million dollars in 1986, according to a 1994 report from the International Labor Organization.

But are there other indicators of the EOI program's success or failure? James Boyce provides considerable data that covers the years 1962 to 1986—the period after controls were ended until the end of the Marcos dictatorship. During this period, Philippine external debt grew from $360 million in 1962 to $28.3 billion in 1986 (Boyce, 1993: 10). At the end of 1986, the country had a debt-to-GNP ratio of .90, and a debt per capita of $485 (Boyce, 1993: 4, Table 1.2).

The impact on wages for urban workers for the period 1962 to 1986 was disastrous. Boyce computed the impact of changes in wages in Metro Manila over this period: "In real (1986) U.S. dollars, the daily wage of an unskilled worker fell from $4.37 in 1962 to $1.12 in 1986, while that of a skilled worker fell from $6.18 to $1.72." In other words, daily wage rates for an unskilled worker in 1986 were 74.3 percent less than in 1962, while daily wages rates for a skilled worker in 1986 were 72.2 percent less! In fact, in 1986, the daily wage of an unskilled urban worker was substantially below that of an agricultural worker. Boyce concludes: "wage laborers in metropolitan Manila experienced a collapse in real wages in the 1970s and 1980s on a magnitude with few precedents in modern economic history" (Boyce, 1993: 27–29).

A key to this deterioration of workers' salaries was the drastic cheapening of the Philippine *peso.* In January 1962, before foreign exchange and import controls were lifted, one US dollar bought two *pesos;* in February 1986, just before Marcos was driven out of the country, one dollar could buy 19 *pesos.* Thus, imported goods—and especially oil, which is sold internationally in dollars, and which is used for everything from powering automobiles to transporting rice, the staple food—became much more expensive to Filipino consumers.

There is another indicator that can be used to evaluate Philippine development: GNP per capita, one of the World Bank's favorite comparative statistics. In 1962, the Philippines GNP per capita (measured in 1986 US dollars) was $495, and the only country with a higher GNP per capita in Southeast Asia that year was Malaysia ($820). By 1986, Philippine GNP per capita was $540—barely above Indonesia ($490), and falling increasingly behind the other economically significant countries in the region. The gap in GDP per capita gap between the Philippines and Japan had widened from $2,005 in 1962 to $16,200 in 1986. In fact, between 1962 and 1986, the annual average growth rate of Philippine GNP (of 3.1 percent) and the GNP per capita (.4 percent) were each behind those of China, Indonesia, Japan, South Korea, Malaysia, Singapore, Taiwan and Thailand.

To give one more specific example: South Korea had a GNP per capita of $330 in 1962, which was $165 dollars per person *behind* the Philippines; by 1986, South Korea had a GNP per capita of $2,345, or $1,805 per person *ahead* of the Philippines! (Boyce, 1993: 2, Table 1.1). The neoliberal program of the Philippines compared poorly to state-led industrial development of South Korea (and both countries were ruled by dictators over most of this period).

POST-MARCOS

But what has happened since the overthrow of the dictator? Marcos' successors—Corazon Aquino (1986–1992), Fidel Ramos (1992–1998), and Joseph Estrada (1998–2004)—have continued to follow an EOI strategy. Aquino committed her government to repaying all foreign debts, including the ones that only benefited Marcos and/or his "cronies," and Ramos and Estrada have followed suit.

One Filipino researcher, Pedro Salgado, put the debt into perspective early in Aquino's administration. He pointed out the $28.2 billion debt in 1987 was equal to about P564 billion, 4.4 times the national budget (or 81 percent of the projected GNP for the entire year). He then goes on to say, "If a person were to drop a P100 bill into a pit every second, it will take 179 years to drop P564 billion worth of bills into the pit!" (Salgado, 1987: 158).

Researchers have detailed how the recent presidents have gone along with the World Bank and the IMF machinations in exchange for loans. This was true under Marcos, and it has remained true since. Why? I think Temario Rivera is correct when he suggests that there is a larger reason: the ability to obtain foreign loans, no matter how bad for the country, allows political "leaders" to ignore the key issue in the country—political power based on land ownership (Rivera, 1994). And, courtesy of the World Bank and the IMF, foreign loans have been available. Philippine national debt (which was $275 million in 1962 and was approximately $27.2 billion in 1986) was $35.5

billion in 1993, and $45.5 billion in 1997, according to data from the Central Bank of the Philippines.[5]

At the same time, the shift from traditional agricultural exports to non-traditional, labor-intensive manufacturing exports, particularly in garments and electronics, has continued. By the early 1990s, over 70 percent of total exports were in these non-traditional manufacturers. However, despite this shift (supposedly the key to Philippine economic development), the balance of trade worsened between 1987 and 1996. The trade balance in goods was -$1.017 billion in 1987, -$8.160 billion in November 1995, and -$11.342 billion at the end of 1996. Note that these figures are all from before the crisis.

The GNP of the country has generally grown, albeit unevenly: it grew 5.9 percent in 1987, 6.6 percent in 1988, 5.7 percent in 1989, and 3.0 percent in 1990. It declined .05 percent in 1991. The GNP increased 1.56 percent in 1992, 2.02 percent in 1993, 5.1 percent in 1994, 5.7 percent in 1995, 5.8 percent in 1996, and 5.2 percent in 1997.

The neoliberal economic program has made things worse for the large majority of Filipinos. By November 1992, while evaluating President Ramos' first 100 days in office, IBON Databank, a Non-Governmental Organization (NGO) that focuses on the economy, estimated that the number of Filipinos living under the Filipino poverty line had increased from 70 percent to 75 percent, and noted that a *peso* in 1992 "could only buy 60 centavos of what it could have bought in 1988." The numbers in poverty are likely to have been somewhat reduced between 1994 and 1997, when the GNP of the country grew over 5 percent each year.

Roger Daenekindt (1996), using Department of Labor and Employment figures from September 1995, reported that 62 percent of the 29.2 million-member labor force was either unemployed or underemployed. Further, only 10 percent of the labor force received at least the minimum wage, but even this was insufficient as the minimum wage itself resulted in income below the poverty line. In 1994, according to the government, the daily cost of living was P 237.57 (approximately US $9.50), while the mandated daily minimum wage was only P 145 (approximately $5.80). Additionally, while nominal wages increased by more than 200 percent between 1983 and 1993, real wages for all workers (based on 1978 prices) actually decreased by 14 percent, and despite nominal wages increasing 32 percent between 1990 and 1993, real wages fell 4 percent.

Daenekindt (1996) further noted definite changes in the workplace, toward a more flexible labor regime. And "flexibility" of the labor market means that workers have even fewer chances for regular employment, as workers are forced to compete at an even greater rate than previously for the relatively small number of regular jobs that are available. This also makes it much more difficult to organize and maintain unions, meaning that workers will have even less power in workplaces where they do obtain employment, and that their working conditions will get worse. And that is for those lucky enough to have regular jobs!

At the same time that the economy is not providing a sufficient number of jobs for people, and their wages are already horribly insufficient, inflation is eating at the value of the money they do get. As mentioned above, the real value of wages for urban workers decreased by about 75 percent between 1962 and 1986. But between 1988 and 1994, the purchasing power of the *peso* declined another 49 percent. The inflation rate was 7.6 percent in 1993, and 9.0 percent in 1994.

But the Philippine State has never failed to keep coming up with grand plans designed to solve all of the country's problems in one fell swoop: the latest, initiated under President Fidel Ramos, was "Philippines 2000." Key to Ramos's vision was the Medium Term Development Plan for 1993 to 1998. Ramos stated his goals for the end of his presidency in June 1998: to raise per capita income to US $1000; for the economy to grow by at least 6 to 8 percent; and for the poverty rate to decline to at least 50 percent. He missed all three.

Ramos' larger goal was to make the Philippines a Newly Industrializing Country (NIC) by the year 2000. And how was this to be accomplished? In January 1995, at President Ramos' urging, the Philippines joined the World Trade Organization (WTO), which meant it had to open its borders to even more international trade. Roger Daenekindt commented: "We are . . . told to be outward-looking and accept liberalization. But . . . in the case of textile and garments, we enter in a stiff world of competition of cheap labor. Chinese labor is at 25 cents an hour, Vietnamese at 15 cents an hour, Philippines [at] 90 cents an hour, and there are still the countries like India, Bangladesh, Pakistan, etc." Additionally, according to former president Ramos, "Export orientation shall 'enlarge the pie'" (Daenekindt, 1996: 24–26).

And then the global economic crisis hit.

CRISIS

The Philippines was hit by the global crisis, becoming one of the Asian Development Bank's "Crisis-Affected Countries." Philippine GDP, which grew 5.2 percent in 1997, fell 0.5 percent in 1998, according to the IMF. The *peso,* which had been trading at approximately US $1: P 25 throughout most of the 1990s, lost over 40 percent of its value, falling to a rate of $1: P45, although by the spring of 1999, had recovered somewhat to trade around $1: P40.

IBON Databank reports that official unemployment jumped from 10.4 percent in April 1997 to 13.3 percent in April 1998—and yet these figures severely undercount real unemployment and don't mention underemployment. However, a 1995 government report from the Department of Labor and Employment said that unemployment and underemployment affected 62 percent of the workforce, and this was when the economy was growing strongly. But IBON also reports that there was 128 percent increase in firms closing between January and May 1998, as compared to a year earlier, and an 88 percent increase in the number of workers being affected by these difficulties.

And yet, the Philippines was hurt much less than Indonesia, Malaysia, South Korea or Thailand. Stanley Fischer, first Deputy Director of the IMF, claimed in a June 1999 speech that, of the countries at the heart of the crisis, "the Philippines' economy performed exceptionally." He suggests that this was because the country was in an IMF program at the beginning of the crisis, and that the IMF increased financing for the country once trouble hit, enabling it to avoid the worst of the crisis.

However, if it is realized that the country has been in a crisis since it began following a neoliberal program in 1962, it is clear that the global crisis has, for the Philippines, been simply a continuation of "business as usual." Since 1962, the Philippines never achieved the advances won by these other countries, and so it was spared the intensity of the drastic fall that the others suffered. And yet, it still suffered more than a 40 percent fall in its currency exchange rates.

But while Fischer suggests that Philippine performance was not as bad as the rest because of IMF advice and money, he inadvertently let the cat out of the bag, especially when we remember the overall performance of the US economy during this time: "The country benefited from the composition of its trade, which is more heavily weighted towards the United States than of the more severely affected countries." The Philippines has done as well as it has not because of the IMF, but because its' major trading partner has kept the door open to its further-devalued products despite a drastic reduction in the Philippine market for US exports.

NO REAL SOLUTION

An Export-oriented Industrialization (EOI) program was begun in the late 1960s, designed to save a financial deregulation program that had devastated the economy. The EOI strategy was implemented in 1972 after the declaration of martial law by Ferdinand Marcos; it continues today.

Because billions of dollars of economic and military aid have been provided to the Philippines by the US Government, the World Bank and IMF, and commercial banks from around the world, the agrarian system and its accompanying political system has survived. In return, the Philippines has had its industry incorporated into global capitalist political-economic networks.

The neoliberal program has been a failure on its own terms, even before the onset of the global economic crisis. The *peso's* value fell from $1: P2 in 1962 to approximately $1: P25 in the mid-1990s. Although exports shifted from traditional ones to non-traditional manufacturers, the balance of trade had deteriorated to -$11.3 billion at the end of 1996. GNP has generally increased, albeit very erratically. However, foreign debt has exploded: from a national debt of $275 million in 1962, it ballooned to $45.5 billion in 1997.[6] In short, this program has failed to provide any type of sustainable economic development for the country.

The cost to the broad masses of the people of the Philippines has been astronomical. Fourteen years of dictatorship was only the beginning. Neoliberalism has led to a social situation where approximately 75 percent of the population lived below the poverty line in the early 1990s and, while somewhat reduced since then, it is not known by how much. Urban workers had lost almost 75 percent of their 1962 wages by 1986, and things have only gotten worse since then. Conditions among the peasantry and agricultural workers have also deteriorated, to the extent that they have joined and maintained a revolutionary army for over 30 years (albeit considerably weakened since 1986—and particularly since 1993—by internal problems). Accordingly, this type of development, when viewed from the perspective of the large majority of the population, deserves to be called "detrimental development."

It is within this larger context of detrimental development—maintained at all times by armed force and a determination to use it to defeat any challenges—that Philippine economic development since 1962 has been evaluated.

A neoliberal approach to development, as advocated by the World Bank and the IMF, has only benefited the global capitalist political-economic networks (including certain Filipino partners), and the Philippine state; and these benefits all come at the direct cost of the large majority of Filipinos. This program has failed on its own terms and has been a social disaster as well.

NOTES

1. This article was originally published as Scipes, 1999, although without references or endnotes. This article was subsequently published in South Africa as "Detrimental Development: The Global Economic Crisis and the Philippines." *Indicator South Africa: The Barometer of Social Trends,* Vol. 17, No. 1, March 2000: 87–90.

2. The economic terms were established by the Philippine Trade Act of 1946, also known as the Bell Trade Act. For a summary of the Act, see Schirmer and Shalom, eds., 1987: 88–90. For commentary on that Act by an oppositionist Filipino legislator at the time, see Diokno, 1946/1987. For an overview of the Laurel-Langley Agreement of 1955, which ended some of the more extreme conditions of the Bell Trade Act (such as the need to get permission from the US President to modify the pegged value of the Philippine Peso to the US Dollar), see Schirmer and Shalom, eds., 1987: 94–96. The explicit military relationship was established by the Military Bases Agreement of March 14, 1947. See Schirmer and Shalom, eds., 1987: 96–100.

3. Instead of giving a blow-by-blow account of the development of the Philippine economy, I'll point out significant resources; these include Bello, Kinley and Elinson, 1982; Boyce, 1993; Broad, 1988; and Shalom, 1981.

4. The data on World Bank lending to the Philippines is on p. 24.

5. According to the Bangko Sentral ng Philippines, as of June 14, 2019, the external debt of the country totaled $80.4 billion. On-line at http://www.bsp.gov.ph/publications/media.asp?id=5039&yr=2019.

6. On August 6, 2013, I found a report from *The Philippine Star* newspaper: at the end of February 2013, the national government debt was $129.2 billion. Of that, $45.6 billion was due to foreign investors, and this had declined from $50.6 billion at the end of 2012. The exchange rate was $1: P43.5 (*Phil Star*, 2013). As stated above, as of mid-2019, the Philippines' foreign debt was $80.4 billion.

Chapter Eight

The *Kilusang Mayo Uno* (KMU-May First Movement)

The KMU is only one of five different labor centers in the Philippines, each with a different set of politics.[1] In addition to these, there are independent unions arrayed across the political spectrum. And while political designations are often collapsed into the categories of "genuine" and "yellow" by the KMU—the former progressive and the latter reactionary—the different formations will sometimes unite tactically on different issues, particularly regarding economic wage demands, while remaining politically opposed to each other.

Why did the KMU develop? What were the conditions that caused workers to create it? What has enabled it to survive and grow?

There were three reasons to found the KMU. First, workplace conditions were terrible, with management domination so strong that workers were almost completely at the mercy of their bosses. Second, the traditional unions had sold out workers. And third, there was a clear need for a workers' organization that would organize against foreign domination; as long as the country remained subservient to foreign interests, it would be unable to develop and confront the problems that faced its people.

KMU (*KILUSANG MAYO UNO*-MAY FIRST MOVEMENT) LABOR CENTER

KMU was founded on May 1, 1980, during the dark days of the Marcos Dictatorship. The seven founding union organizations had 35,000 members under collective bargaining agreements (CBAs) at the time, with an additional 15,000 as members but without CBAs.[2] After 10 years, there were 350,000 members under CBAs, and another 400,000 workers that were under the KMU but without CBAs.[3]

But there is obviously more to the KMU than just size or even membership growth. How did the KMU survive the repression of a dictator—including the arrest and detention of its chairperson, general secretary and almost 100 top leaders? How could the organization continue after the assassination of its subsequent chairperson, facing massive human rights violations and almost total opposition from the military and the ruling class? Where did the KMU find the strength to be able to lead and win its second national general workers' strike within nine years of its founding?

Part of the KMU's power to endure is related to its basic principles of being genuine, militant and nationalist. A top leader interviewed in 1986, who did not want his name used, explained what these principles mean to members of the KMU:

> By "genuine," we mean that the KMU is run by its members. The members are given all information and decide the policies that run the organization. By "militant," we mean that the KMU will never betray the interest of the working class, even at the risk of our own lives. The KMU believes workers become aware of their own human dignity through collective mass action. By "nationalist," we believe the wealth of the Philippines belongs to the Filipino people and that national sovereignty must never be compromised. The KMU is against the presence of the U.S. bases (quoted in Scipes, 1987b: 12).

In other words, the KMU is class conscious, believes that workers learn more from mass struggles than from leaders cutting back room deals, and is determined that Filipinos should control the Philippines.

The statement about never betraying the interests of the working class, even at risk of KMU leaders' own lives, is not hyperbole; many KMU organizers, leaders and members have been arrested and/or killed. The assassination of KMU Chairperson Rolando Olalia in November 1986 (see Jackson, 1987) demonstrated the risks involved in being a genuine trade unionist, even for those highest in the organization.

Another key aspect to the KMU's survival and growth is the organization's political concept of "genuine trade unionism." Genuine trade unionism (GTU) extends the scope of trade unionism beyond mere relations in the workplace; it also includes struggles over the political economy of the nation and its internal social relations. KMU-affiliated unions have developed this concept to the greatest extent in the Philippines, although it is not limited to them.

Genuine trade unionism opposes domination from without; it is against imperialist interference in the Philippines from particular nations such as the US or Japan, as well as from institutions such as the International Monetary Fund, the World Bank and the AFL-CIO.[4]

It is this involvement in the debate over the future direction and shape of the nation—together with the KMU's increasing ability to interfere with economic production due to its position in the nation's workplaces—that makes the KMU such an important subject for examination and understanding.

Further organizational strengths are to be found in the internal processes within KMU-affiliated organizations: the KMU is committed to union democracy and accountability of its membership. It requires sacrifices from leaders and fights internal corruption. The KMU is controlled by its membership and not by any other organization from the left or the right.

Along with being genuine, militant and nationalist, developing genuine trade unionism and being democratically controlled, the KMU has developed because of three other factors: an organizational structure that combines vertical and horizontal connections, an extensive educational program, and its relations with other sectoral (peasants', women's) organizations.[5]

Organizational Structure

The first factor has to do with the particular structure in which the KMU is organized. The KMU is organized both "vertically" with centralized national federations, and "horizontally," by workers' alliances: this organizational grid overlays the entire organization.

Eleven national federations—similar to national or international unions in North America—are affiliated with the KMU. These are hierarchical organizations, with decision-making at a higher level superseding those made at lower levels. Each federation contains at least 10 local unions.

These federations have a general membership; they organize any workers they can, although most federations concentrate on one or two particular "industries." The National Federation of Sugar Workers-Food and General Trades (NFSW-FGT) concentrates on sugar workers. *Ilaw at Buklod ng Manggagawa* (IBM: Light and Unity of the Workers) is concentrated among employees of the San Miguel Corporation, a giant beer and food conglomerate. The Genuine Labor Organization of Workers in the Hotel, Restaurant and Allied Industries (GLOWHRAIN) focuses on workers in hotels and restaurants. The Drug and Food Alliance of the Philippines (DFA) is in pharmaceuticals. The Alliance of Nationalist and Genuine Labor Organizations (ANGLO) emphasizes garments and textiles, while the United Workers of the Philippines (UWP) and the Association of Democratic Labor Organizations (ADLO) are in garments and shoes. The Southern Philippines Federation of Labor (SPFL) focuses on mining and the wood industry, while the National Federation of Labor Unions (NAFLU) is in mining and longshoring. The National Federation of Labor (NFL) concentrates on the service industry and banana plantations, and the Organized Labor Association in Line Industries and Agriculture (OLALIA) is concentrated among agricultural workers. The situation results in some duplication, but it also gives local unions a choice of federations to affiliate with, ensuring more responsive leadership.

Each federation provides legal assistance, orientation, directions for education, and plans of action—in coordination with the KMU—to their local union affiliates. In particular, federations give crucial assistance in workers' struggles to form local unions. They also help to gain recognition through winning certification elections and successfully completing collective bargaining agreements.

Local unions can affiliate with a federation by one of two different ways. A previously-organized local union may join a federation "indirectly." A group of workers seeking help in organizing may join "directly." George Aguilon, secretary general of NAMAHMIN, explained that: "In reality, there is no big difference. The only difference is that if you have indirectly affiliated, you can [leave the federation] at any time; if you are directly affiliated, you must wait until the CBA [collective bargaining agreement] expires before you can disaffiliate."[6]

The large majority of local unions are directly affiliated, meaning they must remain with their chosen federation throughout the life of the contract. Since the passage of the Herrera Law (RA 6715) in March 1989, this is a five-year period.

Besides additional membership, status and, therefore, power, affiliation beings in dues for the federation. For example, before it disaffiliated from the United Lumber and General Workers of the Philippine (ULGWP), the union at Greenfields was the ULGWP's largest local union. Greenfields is a garment factory in Metro Manila, with 2,500 union members and another 500 workers paying agency dues for the union's representation of them with management. At Greenfields, workers were paying monthly dues of 10 pesos, three of which went to the local and seven to the federation. In addition to these dues, the federation won a P10,000 a month education fee in the contract, which the company paid to the federation. From this one factory, the federation was receiving P31,000 a month, over one million pesos over a three-year period.[7]

However, despite the hierarchical organization of these federations, they are decentralized as much as possible. Federations are broken into island-wide and region-wide groupings, with the power to make decisions delegated to the lowest possible level of the organization.

The decentralized structure diffuses power throughout the organization. Immobilizing the top leaders will not stop the organization. Marcos' effort in 1982 to cripple the KMU by arresting 69 key leaders, including the chairperson and the secretary general, failed because of the KMU's decentralized organization.

Additionally, there is also an organization of women workers, the *Kilusang Manggagawang Kababaihan* (KMK: Women Workers' Movement), which is affiliated with KMU and is another type of alliance, this one based on gender. The KMK has 20,000 members. It has specifically been challenging women's oppression within the workplace, society, and the unions. In 1989, its program focused on winning greater maternity leave benefits for all women, establishing day care facilities in workplaces, ending sexual harassment, and solving health problems of women workers in the factories.[8]

Besides the hierarchically-structured federations and the KMK, there are the alliances. Alliances are "horizontal" coalitions of workers from different workplaces and unions, and are organized on the basis of geography, industry, or company ownership. The goal of each alliance is to unite workers for economic gain; provide self-defense from military harassment; win political demands outside the workplace; and give GTU (genuine trade unionism) education to all members.

Alliances are a totally new development in Filipino trade unionism, having just been established in 1982. The first alliance, AMBA-BALA, was created by the overwhelming female workforce in the Bataan Export Processing Zone (BEPZ) in response to military repression against strikers at the Inter-Asia Company during June 1982. Flor Collantes of AMBA-BALA described events that led to the creation of that KMU provincial alliance:

> The workers had gone on strike to protest intensification of their work; previously each worker operated four machines in the textile plant; management increased this to six. The military intervened against the strikers, using fire trucks, truncheons, and mass arrests in an effort to break the strike.
>
> Although strikes in the zone were illegal, other workers realized that if they allowed the military to break the strike, then the military could break any strike. Further, they realized that BEPZ was a key component of the IMF/WB/Marcos development strategy for the country, and thus union organization would have a much greater importance than in less strategic areas.
>
> The women organized clandestinely on the job, in the company-provided dormitories, and in the community. Workers in every factory in the zone were mobilized. On June 4, 1982, 26,000 workers walked out in support of the nine union organizers that had been fired by Inter-Asia and the 54 arrested picketers.
>
> This was the first general strike in any export processing zone in the world and it was successful: the strike was won, the union organizers reinstated, the people in jail released, and the first alliance, AMBA-BALA (literally meaning "AIM-BULLET"), was born (quoted from Scipes, 1988b).[9]

Each type of alliance organizes differently. Geographical alliances combine unions on the basis of locality and are the most powerful; these alliances can be formed on national, island, regional, province, city, or even district levels. Industrial alliances unite unions located in the same industry, such as health care, transportation, or mining. Conglomerate alliances join unions in multi-site workplaces owned by the same company. The industrial and conglomerate alliances focus more on workplace issues, while geographical alliances tend to focus on larger political issues—but transportation alliances have always been very involved on the political levels as well. Additionally, while most alliances are affiliated with the KMU, each alliance often includes unions from outside the KMU.

Education

In conjunction with an innovative organizational structure that reinforces its member unions, the KMU has a very developed trade union education program. It serves as perhaps the key component in leadership development. And not only is the program extensive, but the leadership of all KMU organizations strongly stresses the education process.

Known by the general name of "genuine trade unionism," the KMU education program is composed of three different courses: PAMA, GTU, and KPD.

PAMA is a one-day introductory course, which is short enough that organizers can give basic educational training even on picket lines. In this course, workers are taught not only trade union rights and responsibilities, but political economy as well. Surplus value is explained in a way all workers can understand. The term "imperialism" is demystified and shown to be a key explanation for the economic degradation and poverty of their country. Gaining national sovereignty is clearly shown to be an important part of the workers' struggle for liberation.

The three-day GTU course goes into greater detail. Workers discuss the problems of labor. They examine and analyze the differences between genuine trade unionism on one hand, and "yellow" unionism—whether of the "bread and butter/rice and fish" version or its more collaborationist form—on the other. They focus on the history of the Filipino labor movement and previous efforts to develop genuine trade unions. And workers discuss the struggle for national and working class liberation.

The third course, KPD, propagates the national democratic program. Originally part of the GTU course, KPD has been further developed on its own. This focuses attention on the struggle for national democracy, which includes joining with different political forces fighting for national sovereignty. The goal of national democracy is the establishment of a truly independent country and a national democratic coalition government, based on the various sectors of society, such as peasants, workers, fisherfolk, women, urban poor, students, etc.

Though these courses were formally developed in Metro Manila at the Ecumenical Institute for Labor Education and Research (EILER), a church-based organization, they were created in response to the high priority placed on member education at the KMU's founding congress in 1980. These courses were developed in the field—on picket lines and at union meetings—and brought back to Manila for integration and development by EILER. They were then taken back into the field, tested, and then further modified when necessary.

Education centers have been established throughout the country. Each KMU federation has an education department, as do most KMU geographic alliances. Making information available and accessible to workers is their goal.

This information is not just for KMU members. In Bataan, workers demanded that all members of the provincial alliance—even unions affiliated with other labor centers—be given genuine trade union education. This seems to be the case in most alliances. Also, in some areas, independent educational programs have been established, such as the Visayas Institute for Research and Trade Union Education in Cebu, which serves any union in the Visayas region.

This education process is one of the main differences between KMU organizations and those controlled by other labor groupings. The KMU tries to develop workers' understanding in order to get them involved in confronting their problems and the problems of the country. It uses every opportunity to educate workers, whether trying to win certification elections during respective "freedom periods" or helping workers take control over their own union to make it militant.

Key to this education process is the way it is run. Rather than just telling workers what they should think or do, KMU educators have developed curricula that enable workers to share their thoughts on various issues and discuss alternatives. It is through open discussion and input from the instructors that workers educate themselves and each other.[10]

The importance of this education simply cannot be exaggerated. It brings workers together, away from the worksite. It allows them to think about and discuss what they want and how they can best achieve their goals. It also allows them to interact with each other, building solidarity within the organization.

The most important result is the general empowerment of workers. Once workers have been through an education course, they get a real sense of themselves and what they are doing. While this sounds abstract, it comes through concretely in their determination in their particular struggles; maintaining a 24-hour picket line for over a year during a strike is common.

These courses also encourage workers to develop their own courses. For example, the IGMC Workers' Union in BEPZ developed a course for their members on the capitalist relations of production in their firm. Why is production arranged in the manner it is? What is the company trying to do? How are they able to do it? What can the union do to strengthen itself? Those are some of the questions that the course is focused on. The union had put all of its 700-plus members through the course by early 1986.

Relations with Other Sectoral Organizations

In the Philippines, national democrats within each sector of society—such as workers, peasants, fisherfolk, women, urban poor, and students—have developed organizations to meet their specific needs. These are known as sectoral organizations.

Joining with sectoral organizations to fight for demands that would benefit the entire population of the Philippines, and refusing to limit KMU's interests only to workers and their problems, is another key factor in the KMU's development. Benefiting from this cross-sectoral unity, the people of the Philippines have been able to develop a tactic called a *welga ng bayan*, or "people's strike," that is even more powerful than the almost-mythic "general strike" in industrialized countries.

A *welgang bayan* (colloquial) includes a general workers' strike, but it is much more. In addition, all public transportation is stopped, all shops and stores are closed, and community members set up barricades to stop still-operating private vehicles or they join workers on their picket lines.

The first *welgang bayan* took place in Davao City on Mindanao in 1984. The concerted actions of the people paralyzed most significant economic activity in response to increased military operations and brutality on the island. Two more island-wide people's strikes were launched during 1985, again protesting the militarization of the island. The third people's strike was so successful that when the island's military commander asked the leaders to call it off after one day, they refused. "We'll call it off when we reach our objectives," a leader told him.[11] The *welga ng bayan* lasted three days.

How did this tactic develop? Erasto "Nonoy" Librado, Secretary General of KMU-Mindanao, explained that leaders from different sectoral organizations had noticed very little response to their efforts to win their particular demands; and they began talking to see if together they could all be more successful.[12] Their efforts paid off with a tactic that, while difficult to mobilize properly, was incredibly powerful when launched.

In May 1985, the various sectoral organizations, including the KMU, organized into a national alliance called the *Bagong Alyansang Makabayan*

(BAYAN: New Patriotic Alliance). BAYAN, which means "people" or "country," is organized on a national level and it has local chapters in most major urban areas throughout the country.

The next significant people's strike took place in Bataan Province against the Westinghouse-built Bataan Nuclear Power Plant in 1985. This power plant, built on the side of a volcano in an active earthquake zone, was intended to supply electricity to the US military bases, Clark and Subic, and to the export processing zone in Mariveles. The *welgang bayan* was described:

> Several major protests have been launched against the plant. The largest was the three-day province-wide strike in June 1985. Eight towns were brought to a standstill. All banks, shops, schools, public transport, private businesses and government offices shut down. Even fishing boats in the local port refused to put out to sea. Workers from the industrial free trade zone, where the factories of the multinationals are located, marched for two days to join the protests. Workers blocked all roads to the nuclear power plant and grappled with armoured cars sent to clear a way through (Watts and Jackson, 1986).

The first nationwide *welgang bayan* was launched in August 1987 in response to an oil price hike by the government. Although called off early in response to a military coup attempt, the effort had immobilized 95 percent of the country's economically-central cities beforehand. Interestingly, the next military coup attempt took place after plans for another nationwide people's strike had been announced but before it could be launched in December 1989. Another nationwide *welgang bayan* was carried out in October 1990.

Welgang bayans prove that progressive Filipinos can gain much more together than they can alone. *Welgang bayans* also show KMU's recognition that labor must be involved in national issues that affect other sectors because these issues also affect workers as well.[13]

CRITICISM OF THE KMU[14]

The KMU's success has not been universally applauded. It has been variously labeled as a "communist front," and as being "strike happy" and disruptive. And while most of this criticism has been limited to words, the rise of the vigilante (death squads) movement throughout the country in 1987 escalated the battle—and the union representation battle at Atlas Mines in Cebu[15] saw numerous shootings and killings of KMU leaders and activists, as well as some of their closest relatives. Employer violence against KMU unions has been widespread throughout the country, both before and after the struggle at Atlas.

There have been repeated claims that the KMU is controlled by the illegal Communist Party of the Philippines. After extensive investigation during six trips to the country, extensive travel throughout the country, and interviews with KMU leaders and activists, allies, and church activists, as well as opponents of the KMU and independent foreign journalists, I wrote:

> I have concluded that the KMU is controlled by its membership and not by any outside organization, whether of the left or the right. The positions it takes are a result of political struggle within the organization, not from the outside; the strengths and weaknesses of the KMU should be attributed to the organization itself and not to outside forces (Scipes, 1996: 187).[16]

The KMU has been repeatedly charged with being "strike happy" and disruptive. It has long had the highest total number of strikes, and its members have also been willing to leave work to protest attacks on its top leadership, to fight for a higher national minimum wage, and to challenge oil price hikes that affect the poor so heavily. But it has been charged that KMU tactics have resulted in multinational corporations, such as Mattel, leaving the Philippines, thereby taking away those precious jobs. However, I think the larger issue is one that confronts militant unions around the world: do unions stand up for their members and fight the employers, in the long run risking workers' livelihoods, or do unions back down so as to preserve the jobs, risking their very usefulness as unions, whenever the employers threaten relocation in response to militancy? KMU unions have generally, but not always, chosen to fight—but, it must be remembered, only after winning support of their members to do so. The decision to strike—which almost always brings hardship and suffering, and always risks physical violence against strikers and their supporters—is never taken lightly or made reflexively.

But the charges against KMU cannot be considered in a vacuum. Its efforts and those of its allies threaten the existing power structure and social order in the Philippines. Therefore, it must always be asked in whose interest these charges are being made: are they being made by those threatened—and quite frankly, this includes a number of people in the larger labor movement—or are they being made by those challenging the status quo? Without asking and answering this question, criticisms of the KMU are considered equally legitimate. This confuses the issue, equating valid and necessary criticism of the KMU with destructive attacks. It is important for supporters to critique KMU weaknesses, while rejecting the attacks of their enemies.[17]

CONCLUSION

The men and women of the KMU have built a strong and powerful organization. The labor center is based on a philosophy of being genuine, militant and nationalist and, from that philosophy, have developed the concept of genuine trade unionism. Coupled with this has been a democratic decision-making process, a structure of federations and alliances that is mutually reinforcing, an elaborate and emphasized education program, and alliances with other sectoral organizations.

The KMU has unified organizations at a number of different levels into a national labor center. And it has survived for over 14 years, something to previous radical labor center has accomplished in the Philippines.[18]

As a result, in its first 10 years, the KMU has led two nation-wide general workers' strikes and constituted a major force in a nationwide *welgang bayan,* while continuing regional and provincial efforts. These national efforts have been a combination of KMU unions, unions from other labor groupings, and sectoral organizations.

The KMU, along with its allies, has built itself into a power economic and political force in the Philippines.

NOTES

1. This Chapter is largely drawn from Scipes, 1996: 9–21, although most of this material had initially appeared in Scipes, 1992a: 135–144. [My book is an in-depth, inductively-developed empirical study of this labor movement, and although I specifically stated that it is not an academic book (Scipes, 1996: xix), subsequent experience has shown me that I was being too modest at the time: although not responding to a specific issue raised in the academic literature, this book has, in fact, the rigor of a carefully developed academic study.] However, it must be remembered this chapter is an overall summary of the KMU: the entire monograph is over 300 pages. See also West, 1997.

Unless I can find more current information, I've left everything as it was originally written in the early 1990s.

Although I examine the KMU in this chapter, and suggest it provides evidence for this model of social movement unionism, this is a theoretical conceptualization I am using to understand the KMU, and not a term KMU has adopted to describe itself. Therefore, I bear all responsibility for any application of this conceptualization to the KMU. However, Rob Lambert has also used the KMU as an example of social movement unionism (Lambert, 1990).

2. Interview with KMU Chairperson Crispin Beltran, May 2, 1990 in Manila. All interviews referred to herein were conducted by me in the course of my research on the KMU.

3. Interview with a member of KMU's International Department on April 16, 1990 in Manila.

KMU's numerical size, while the largest labor center in the country, is still quite small in proportion to the number of workers in the society. In 1987, 40.76 percent of the labor force of 15.58 million workers—9.06 million—were employed as wage/salary workers. "Of the wage/salary earners, 2.1 million or 23% were organized into unions, of which only 346 thousand worked under a collective bargaining agreement" (EILER, 1988: 2). Nonetheless, KMU's location in strategic parts of the economy and its alliances with other social movements give it a power considerably beyond its numerical size.

[In 1993, the KMU suffered splits on two different dimensions within the National Capital Region, which covers Metro Manila. While substantially weakened in this region, the rest of the national organization remained intact and was able to act, along with remaining organizations in the National Capital Region, both in regard to local and national political issues (see Scipes, 1996: 227–245). These splits, however, do not detract from the argument herein.

[In an interview in Manila in 2016, a staffmember from EILER (Ecumenical Institute for Labor Education and Research) told me that while the splits initially appeared quite ominous for KMU, in reality, over time, they did not prove such—the organization, especially outside of Manila, remained overwhelmingly intact, and they remained generally united, even in Manila.]

4. For details on how the largest union of the Trade Union Congress of the Philippines—a competing labor center established by the Marcos Dictatorship, and supported with millions of dollars through the AFL-CIO's regional organization, Asian American Free Labor Institute (AAFLI)—challenged a KMU-affiliated local union for control over the workers at Atlas Mines in Cebu, which included integral collaboration with a death squad (no exaggeration), see Scipes, 1996: 116–125; a less detailed report is in Scipes, 2010a: 52–55.

5. For a discussion of how the organizational features could be beneficially utilized in North America, see Scipes, 1988b (and see Chapter 10, herein).

6. Interview with George Aguilon, April 12, 1988 in Davao City. NAMAHMIN is a geographical alliance covering Davao City, and Davao del Sur and North Cotabato provinces, all on the big southern island of Mindanao.

7. Interview with Lucena Flores and Beda Villanueva, president and general secretary, respectively, of the United Workers of the Philippines, June 21, 1989 in Manila. Villanueva was also the president of the Greenfields Workers' Union. [For an account of the interview, of which these quotations were only a part, see Scipes, 1996: 84–87.]

The leadership of the ULGWP had unilaterally and illegally disaffiliated from the KMU, without the permission of the National Executive Council. The majority of local unions then left the ULGWP, re-united into the United Workers of the Philippines, and re-affiliated with the KMU in early 1989.

8. For an interview with Cleofe Zapanta, secretary general of KMK, see Scipes, 1990b. [For a discussion of KMK, see Scipes, 1996: 75–84; Lois West also has considerable material on KMK—see West, 1997.]

9. This was the strike that Wenilou Pradel had helped lead, and she reported about this in the 1983 conference in Liverpool, England.

10. This approach built off the work of the great Brazilian popular educator Paulo Freire (1984).

11. Interview in Manila in January 1986 with a person who requested that I not use his name.

12. Interview with the late Erasto "Nonoy" Librado, April 30, 1990 in Davao City.

13. For more complete details on the development of the KMU, see Scipes, 1996. Another feature not included in this selection, but an important part of the book, are the chapters on women leaders and workers, both in their own women workers' organization, and within local unions and a national federation.

14. This section, except where specifically referenced, and the conclusion come from Scipes, 1996: 19–21.

15. The struggle at Atlas Mines is detailed in Chapter 5 of Scipes, 1996: 116–125.

16. I spend several pages discussing the KMU and its' ideology (Scipes, 1996: 183–192) to try to fully address this issue.

17. I critically addressed a number of issues—including KMU's ideology, the position of women within KMU, bureaucracy within KMU, and KMU's national coalition work—as well as briefly discussed KMU's international solidarity work in a chapter tilted "Overview of the KMU" (Scipes, 1996: 183–201). Further, I critically report and analyze the splits in the KMU, as well as subsequent developments (as of April 1994) in Scipes, 1996: 219–247. Much of the material on ideology, women and bureaucracy had been earlier published in Scipes, 1992a: 147–158.

There are a couple of comments in this chapter concerning the splits in the Communist Party of the Philippines (CPP) that took place in 1992–1993. Because the CPP was arguably the leader of the National Democratic (ND) movement—and certainly an important force within it—and has members throughout many of the ND organizations, these splits threatened to a greater or lesser extent many of these organizations; for our purposes, this includes the KMU unions. But based on my visit to KMU in April 1994, I then wrote:

> In Scipes (1996: 219–233) I give an extensive and careful analysis of the splits within the KMU, placing them within the larger crisis of the Philippine left. To do this, I interviewed leaders of all three of the different factions [that had emerged out of the resulting turmoil-KS]. To my knowledge, no one else has provided such a detailed examination of what happened within KMU. Further, I examine the impact of the splits on the KMU within the women's alliance (KMK), as well as impacts on the regional organizations of Bataan, Mindanao and Negros, and then give KMU's analysis of the post-split national labor (Scipes, 2018b: 365, FN #12).

Basically, the KMU leadership was confident that the organization would survive and overcome these problems. Their subsequent history shows them to have been correct.

In a 2016 interview with a staff member of EILER (Ecumenical Institute for Labor Education and Research, he told me that the turmoil within KMU had little lasting effects, and he discounted its importance. (This was the same interview referred to in endnote #3, above.]

18. May 1, 2020 was the 40th anniversary of the founding of the KMU.

Chapter Nine

A Look at KMU in 1986–1987

The Philippines is a country whose economy and political system is controlled by the United States.[1] Over 53 percent of all foreign investment is by US-based multinational corporations. The US-dominated International Monetary Fund and World Bank control the overall economy, dictating development strategies in exchange for investments and loans. These institutions have forced the Philippines to develop in ways that benefit multinational corporations and the global capitalist system against the needs of the Filipino people.

Without extensive US military and political support and aid, Ferdinand Marcos would have been unable to maintain his dictatorship and his system of "crony" capitalism, whereby he and his supporters used the government to get filthy rich. And when the Reagan Administration finally pulled the plug on US support for him, Marcos was forced to abdicate.

Like many Third World countries, the Philippines does not have just one economic system; it has two. Both of these are shaped by the global capitalist system, yet they are very different and require different responses to them from workers and their unions.

The first economic system is the "traditional" one, developed with all its faults, over the past 400 years. It includes raw materials (coconuts, sugar, forest products, etc.) and natural mineral extraction. It also includes industries such as construction, transportation, finance, telecommunications, shipping, public utilities, government services, etc.

The other economic system is one that has only recently developed. Since 1970, development of the non-traditional export economy—that tied into the multinational corporations, as determined by the World Bank and the International Monetary Fund—has soared. Made up primarily of electronics and garments, non-traditional exports have grown from US $54 million in value in 1970 to US $2.1 billion in 1983![2]

The different economic systems must be approached differently. The ability of traditional industries to relocate is extremely limited. Opposition to trade union organization in the economic system has been extensive. For example, on Negros Island, the ruling elites have fought ferociously against unionizing of workers in the sugar industry. They have continuously used the CHDF (Civilian Home Defense Force), which is little more than government-sanctioned armies of private thugs, to terrorize or kill sugar workers. Most of the workers in the traditional economy are men.

On the other hand, the corporations based in the non-traditional export economy can be very mobile. These companies can—and have—closed their operations, moved to other locations within the Philippines, and moved to other countries such as Malaysia and Indonesia. These plant closings can be "caused" by union organizing or just further greed to get workers at a lower wage rate.

Further, most workers in these industries are young, single women who have moved to the job site from their homes in the countryside. When a plant closes, the women are forced to relocate to urban areas or back to their family's land. Loss of this income can severely hurt the entire family, since most workers send portions of their wages home.[3]

In addition to these different situations, while most Filipinos are employed, their wages are extremely low. Approximately 80 percent of the entire population lives below the Philippine government-defined poverty line. As of June 1985, the government estimated the minimum daily cost of living for a family of six in Metro Manila to be approximately US $5.57. The government-legislated minimum wage for the area was only $2.85. A 1978 survey of over 2,500 firms by the Ministry of Labor and Employment found that less than 10 percent of the firms paid the minimum wage.

Things are even worse on Negros, an island in the middle of the archipelago. The legal minimum daily wage for agricultural work is approximately $1.60. Sugar cane workers—sugar is the dominant industry on the island—do not even get the minimum wage because they work in a piece-rate system. A young man in good shape—few women cut cane—and who is a good worker can cut about 1 ½ tons of cane a day. For that, he will be paid between P 10–15 or $ .50-$ .75. I talked with workers getting P 7 a day.

The workers' response to these conditions has been to organize. The Filipino working class has a militant and proud history of organizing itself for improving the standards of living for all people and fighting for national liberation (see Eiler, 1988). Without going into detail about this history, merely noting it is not a recent development, a look must be taken at current forms of labor organization.

There are four labor "centers" in the Philippines. (The AFL-CIO is a labor "center" in international labor terminology.) The two most important are the

Trade Union Congress of the Philippines (TUCP) and the *Kilusang Mayo Uno* (May First Movement or the KMU).[4] While simplifying the situation somewhat, limiting attention to these two centers focuses the issue much more clearly: these two centers exemplify class collaborationist, "yellow" unionism on the one hand (TUCP) and class conscious, class struggle unionism on the other (KMU).

The TUCP was created by the Marcos government in 1975, during the martial law period, in order to centralize and control the labor movement. It was spared the repression of the other labor centers. Subservience to the government was assured when the President of the TUCP, Democrito Mendoza, was made head of the government's Social Security Agency while he was working for the TUCP.

The TUCP works very closely with the AFL-CIO's Asian-American Free Labor Institute (AAFLI). During 1984, AAFLI gave the TUCP over US $3 million to help bribe labor leaders away from the KMU.[5]

The *Philippine Labor Alert* (1986c) states that "the TUCP has long supported the basic goals of foreign capital in the Philippines: the ensuring of cheap, docile labor market for multinational corporations, securing for them the maximum rate of profit." The *Labor Alert* details a number of the TUCP's activities which include supporting changes in the labor code to coincide with World Bank "recommendations," helping legitimize martial law through working for constitutional amendments and participating in rigged elections and plebiscites to legitimize Marcos' rule.[6] There public statements often seem more appropriately issued by an employer organization than by a union.

On the other end of the trade union spectrum sits the KMU. The KMU is founded upon the principles of being "genuine, militant and nationalist."[7]

The KMU, founded in May 1980, has grown from 50,000 to over 600,000 members in six years.

The KMU has eight federations—similar to national or international unions in North America—that are affiliated. Only one, the National Federation of Sugar Workers, is an industry-wide organization. The other seven federations organize any workers they can, in any industry or sector, except for government workers, who are prohibited from joining unions. While this results in duplication, it gives workers a choice of federations to join, which ensures much more responsive leadership.

Additionally, the KMU is building union alliances.[8] KMU-affiliated unions have taken the lead in setting up alliances with all unions in particular geographical areas, even when those other unions are often in competing federations and often in competing union centers.

These alliances can be on the island, region, province, city or even district level. These alliances build support for all workers on each level, heling to win economic demands and, more importantly, protecting each other from military harassment and repression.

How has the KMU been able to grow in the face of direct repression? There seem to be three key factors. From the beginning, the KMU has understood the importance of decentralizing power. Centralization confines power at the top and it means the entire organization can be stopped if the leadership is ever eliminated, arrested, bought-off or co-opted. Decentralization, on the other hand, diffuses power throughout the organization. Immobilizing the top leaders will not stop the organization. The effort by Marcos to cripple the KMU by arresting key leaders during 1982 failed because of the KMU's decentralized organization.

The key to decentralization is trusting the members. Unless the members are trusted, power cannot be decentralized. Few trade union leaders are confident enough to trust their members to this extent.

Another major factor is the very sophisticated and elaborate education program the KMU has developed and implemented. It has put over 300,000 of its 600,000 members through a one-day introductory course called PAMA. Of these, 150,000 have gone on to complete the three-day advanced course on Genuine Trade Unionism (GTU).

In these courses, workers are taught not only trade union rights and responsibilities, but political economics. Surplus value is explained in a way all workers can understand. The term "imperialism" is demystified, and shown to be a key explanation for the economic degradation and poverty of their country. National liberation is clearly shown as an important part of their struggle for liberation.

The GTU course, because it is considerably longer, goes into greater detail. They discuss the differences between genuine trade unionism on one hand, and bread and butter unionism—in the Filipino context, "rice and fish"—and yellow, class collaborationist unionism on the other. The marks of the genuine unions are a trust in their members, with members controlling the organization, and struggling for liberation. Time is spent discussing political economics and the future of the Philippines. What kind of economic system do workers want? How will it be set up? How will things be run? Questions not part of traditional union education.

More important than content, however, is the educational process, that is, the way the material is taught. KMU educators reject the traditional teaching method regularly used in US schools, whereby the teacher is the "expert" and shares her or his wisdom with the students, expecting it to be memorized and regurgitated upon demand. Instead, they present material that when combined with the students' experiences forms a potent combination that the student then sees as her own. This process is one which empowers students and encourages them to act collectively to make necessary changes in society.

There is a network of education centers throughout the country. These centers can be based in particular union federations such as the National Federation of Sugar Workers, or they can be based on geographic-wide alliances such as that in Valenzuela, a district in Manila. The key is making the information available and accessible to the members.

This is no mere slogan. Activists are helped by the general high degree of literacy of the Filipinos. (US colonialism differed from the British in that the Americans developed extensive education programs, albeit to teach Filipinos "the American way.")

However, even where the literacy is low, such as among the rural sugar workers, education has still taken place. Serge Cherniguin, General Secretary of the National Federation of Sugar Workers, told me that all 86,000 NFSW members have completed at least the PAMA introductory course.

The third important factor in ensuring KMU survival has been uniting with community-based groups. The KMU is a key member of BAYAN, a coalition of nationalist, cause-oriented groups, including anti-nuclear groups, groups fighting for women's rights, organizations of the urban poor, etc. BAYAN, which means "people" or "country," has a membership of 2.3 million.

This coalition of workers and community groups has resulted in a political organization that is very powerful. The best example of this is the tactic called a *welgang bayan* or people's strike.

A *welgang bayan* is called for a specific location. It results in a general strike by workers, complete stoppage of public transportation, closing of all local shops and stores, and people in the community setting up street barricades to stop any moving private vehicles, and encouraging people to join workers' picket lines. During 1985, there were three island-wide *welgang bayans* on the southern island of Mindanao, each 85–90 percent effective, according to one of their key organizers.

Earlier, the two different sectors of the economy were discussed. It's important that the KMU's approach to each be examined.

Looking at a concrete situation gives one a better idea of how things are put into practice. The situation I know best is on the island of Negros. Negros is the heart of the sugar industry.

The situation on Negros is very grim. There is widespread unemployment, hunger and poverty. On an island where the soil is as rich as any I have ever seen, there are children suffering from third degree malnutrition. They look as though they are among the starving in Africa. A local doctor told me there is no hope when children reach this stage.

Bacolod City, the capital of Negros Occidental province and the largest city on the island, has a population of 300,000. Of these, 100,000 are squatters. They live in shacks with no sanitation facilities such as toilets and running water.

And like was said before, employment on a sugar hacienda does not improve things dramatically. Most sugar workers earn between 50 and 75 cents a day.

Usually, there is only six months of work a year. The rest is "dead time." Traditionally, the planters will advance rice to help workers' families get through dead time. The rice must be paid for when work resumes.

During 1986, because of crisis in the sugar industry—people in industrialized countries are eating less sugar and the US government greatly reduced the Philippine sugar quota—there were only four months of work. Additionally, 250,000 workers were terminated. They had no work; they had no rice.

During late January 1986, I visited a hacienda where the workers had been on strike since early December. They had been getting $ .55 a day, and when they demanded the minimum wage, they were fired. However, the feudalistic relations with the planter is combined with paternalism: since the planter provides housing (of a minimal sort), losing your job means also losing your house and your community. The workers refused to leave the hacienda, even in the face of military harassment and continued their strike, even though there had been no work since the preceding May. (They were getting support from the NFSW and foreign visitors who would generally contribute to the strike fund when they visited.)

Their resistance scared the planter to the extent that he even tried to buy them off. One woman worked there eight years, making a *monthly* average of $5.76. She was offered separation pay of $23.03: after eight years! A male who had worked there also for eight years, making a monthly average way of $13.63, was offered $54.55. A 49-year-old man was offered extra separation money totaling $456.23 if he would leave immediately—he had lived on that hacienda since he was 10 years old—and warned that he would only get the legal minimum of $139.93 if he fought his firing. The people refused to give in: after a month-and-a-half on strike, 108 of the original 115 remained.

The National Federation of Sugar Workers is responding to these conditions by organizing sugar workers. Almost all of the workers on the haciendas belong to the NFSW.

(The NFSW only controls two of 18 sugar mills on the island. Philippine labor law prohibits workers from changing union affiliation while a collective bargaining agreement is in effect. TUCP-affiliated unions repeatedly have signed these agreements without their members' knowledge, keeping workers from joining KMU-affiliated unions.)

Besides organizing workers, NFSW is farming land that has been vacated by the planters. The presence of the New People's Army and the sugar crisis have resulted in geographically remote land being vacated. Additionally, the NFSW is asking planters to loan them land for food production, guaranteeing its return when the planters request it.

The NFSW sees the crisis in the sugar industry and that of the country as being caused primarily by US domination of the Philippines. They have joined BAYAN's efforts to end US domination.

For their efforts, the NFSW has suffered the brunt of repression on Negros. During 1985, 15 trade union organizers on Negros were "salvaged";[9] of these, 12 were from the NFSW. Four more organizers were salvaged during January 1986, right before I visited.

The worst case of repression occurred on September 20, 1985 in Escalante, Negros Occidental. Twenty-one unarmed peaceful protesters were killed on a picket line. They were shot at close range, while lying on the ground. Twenty-seven others were wounded, with two young children dying months later from the tear gas poisoning they received that day. Most of the protestors were members of the NFSW.

In face of this brutal repression, the NFSW membership has decided that their struggle must be non-violent. The most important reason for this, in addition to the moral principles of any individual, is the moral and political legitimacy it gives their efforts. It maintains the support of the Catholic Church, which is important in a country 85 percent Catholic, and which has played an important role in establishing and maintaining the union. It also does not allow the government to label the organization as "subversive terrorist." This would give the government the excuse to directly repress the union, stopping its threat to the sugar barons.

The members feel that keeping their struggle non-violent is the best way to fight for their rights and economic well-being. Besides, being a legal organization, despite the risks, gives the membership the greatest control over their organization.

The key to their adopting and maintaining a non-violent stance organizationally, from what I saw, is educating, involving and empowering the membership. The members must be clear on the goals of their organization. They must be given all information and be able to critically discuss it, and then be allowed to have final say on the direction chosen. In other words, democratic organization with power invested in the members, combined with broad education, is essential.

The repression is not enough to stop them. "We have to liberate ourselves," said NFSW General Secretary Serge Cherniguin. "We have no other choice."

The conditions for women workers in the Export Processing Zones, where most non-traditional export manufacturing/assembly takes place, is somewhat better than those for sugar workers on Negros. Still, the wages are incredibly low, in the range of $3 a day. Workers must put up with conditions such as severe eye strain for electronic workers, which forces them out of their jobs after a few years with permanent eye damage, and exposure to glues and chemicals used in production of shoes, or textile dust in garment assembly plants.

While I did not spend much time with workers in non-traditional export industries, I spent two days and a night with striking garment workers from the Intercontinental Garment Manufacturing Corporation (IGMC). The IGMC factory is located in the Bataan Export Processing Zone (BEPZ) on Luzon Island.

The IGMC Workers' Union[10] is one of the most respected in BEPZ. They have gone on strike several times to support victimized workers in other factories, leading Zone-wide general strikes during 1982 and 1983. The IGMC Workers' Union is not affiliated to any union center. However, along with the other unions in BEPZ, it is a member of the KMU-affiliated alliance, AMBA-BALA (Bataan Alliance of Labor Associations).

There are approximately 700 members in the IGMC union. Between 85–90 percent of the members are young women. All but one of the officers are women, and all work full time on the shop floor. (IGMC is a subsidiary of Britain's Telemac Corporation, itself a subsidiary of William Baird—assembles garments from foreign-manufactured materials imported from Hong Kong. These garments are shipped to the US, Australia and the UK for sale.)

Education of the union members is comprehensive. Not only do members take the PAMA and GTU courses, but they take a union-designed course on the relations of production within the factory. Why is the shop laid out the way it is? What is the company doing to control the union? What can the union do to counter the company's efforts? These are among the many issues looked at in this course.

Organizing workers within the factory for action is a very comprehensive process. Once an issue is decided upon by the members, an entire campaign is designed to win the struggle.

For example, the first step may entail a person who has a problem—perhaps with a foreman—going to the personnel manager with their union steward. If no satisfactory offer is received, then a petition will be circulated, signed and then taken to management. If still no satisfactory resolution, a "reverse work shirt" day will take place with everyone wearing their work shirt inside-out. After that, perhaps a mass visit to management, with everyone leaving their work stations to join in. If still nothing is settled, then perhaps a "noise barrage," with everyone banging tools on machines, etc., will be initiated for a short period. Noise barrages can be extended in duration and frequency—work obviously being stopped and the noise being very obnoxious to management. If still no response, there can be work stoppages.

By this time, workers are generally prepared to strike. Once this level of determination is reached, a "notice to strike" is filed with the Ministry of Labor and Employment in Manila. Two weeks' prior notice must be given to the government. During this time, preparations will be made for the strike, both within the union itself as well as educating and seeking support from other unions and workers throughout BEPZ.

Although strikes are illegal in BEPZ and all export processing zones—that is one of the attractions to multinational capital—unions abide by the law as much as possible. For example, the KMU has lawyers on staff to fight government repression in the courts. This is not an acceptance of the government's repressive labor laws, but a determination not to concede any arena of struggle to the government.

Should a strike ultimately be necessary, the workers are totally prepared for a long, hard battle. They know they can get no justice from the courts: one labor case, still active when I was in the Philippines, had been in the courts for 27 years! Workers know only their efforts, joined by workers and community people, will achieve victory.

This long involved process of organizing workers through a campaign is felt to be very necessary. Strikes, especially because of the threat—and often reality—of harassment by the military, are very dangerous. They are not entered into lightly. People must be prepared to not only stop production but resist extreme management pressure—including threats of job loss—and government/military intervention.

This "mobilization campaign" is designed to pressure management while building support and solidarity within the work force. Ideally, it will force management to act to solve the problem before there is a strike. Of course, should management not get the picture, the mobilization campaign will result in a most determined and firm organization of strikers.

The strike in effect during my visit was the first time the IGMC union had gone on strike for itself. Over 500 IGMC workers had been given termination notices for participating in a *welgang bayan* during June 1985.

The *welgang bayan* was a province-wide protest against a nuclear power plant that is being built by Westinghouse on both an active earthquake fault and on the side of an active volcano! The protest was described thusly:

> Several major protests have been launched against the plant. The largest was the three-day province-wide strike in June 1985. Eight towns were brought to a standstill. All banks, shops, schools, public transport, private businesses and

> government offices shut down. Even fishing boats in the local port refused to put out to sea. Workers from the industrial free trade zone [BEPZ-KS], where the factories of the multinationals are located, marched for two days to join the protests. Workers blockaded all roads to the nuclear plant and grappled with armoured cars sent to clear a way through.[11]

The company claimed the strike had violated the existing labor agreement. The union claimed that victimizing workers who had not taken industrial action against the company was illegal. It claimed those who had left work did so to participate in a political protest concerning a local Filipino issue. Accordingly, the union claimed the company was interfering in Filipino internal politics, a blatant act of foreign intervention.

After months of negotiating with the company, trying to resolve the dispute, the workers struck in late January 1986. The strikers turned the tables on a management that regularly searched workers as they left work, making sure no one stole any jackets: the strikers searched management as they left the building! The strikers wanted to make sure management did not remove garment patterns from the factory that would allow them to set up production elsewhere.

The strikers smuggled me into BEPZ, past armed guards. I found over 200 strikers on the picket line, most assembled in front of IGMC's building. The rest formed roving patrols that continuously circled the factory, keeping an eye out for management or security patrol activities.

The strikers had set up a number of cardboard shacks in front of the factory to provide shelter from the elements, places to sleep and a way to avoid the prying eyes of the security patrols. They had me stay in one of the shacks. Throughout the night, strikers would come in and we would talk about the strike and about our common lives as workers. A group of us finally laid down to sleep for a couple of hours. The strikers smuggled me out of the zone early next morning before the sun rose.

The organization and determination of the strikers finally prevailed. On March 14, the company gave in, rescinding all termination notices and conceding the right for workers to participate in *welgang bayans.*

Just as the KMU is more than a trade union, it is also more than just another political organization. Few political organizations can immobilize the economy whenever they decide to do so.

Earlier, it was noted that KMU is a part of BAYAN, a coalition of nationalist cause-oriented groups. What has been the role of KMU and BAYAN in political events during the past year and a half?

BAYAN boycotted the February 1986 presidential "snap election." They took this course because Marcos had totally rigged the election: I've seen reports he spent $450 million to ensure his re-election! Aquino[12] refused to incorporate BAYAN's 15 point platform—including demands for genuine land reform and the end of US bases after 1991—into her platform. Accordingly, BAYAN felt both candidates failed to address pressing national problems and, thus, the election was a sham.

After Marcos' efforts to steal the election fell apart and Aquino claimed victory, KMU leaders threatened to call a nation-wide general strike if Marcos refused to concede. Before this could happen, Enrile and Ramos staged their revolt, Cardinal Sin called people into the streets, and the US pulled Marcos out of the country. [No general strike was ever called-KS.]

Since Aquino took power, BAYAN has recognized her assumption of power because of her attaining it through the masses' direct action. BAYAN has decided to critically support her, and has worked to pull her further to the left.

President Aquino appointed Augusto Sanchez to be her government's Minister of Labor and Employment. Sanchez has recognized the legitimacy of the KMU, something the Marcos government refused to do. He has even made the KMU a member of the Ministry's Labor Advisory Consultative Council, which includes all the major labor centers, except the TUCP. (The TUCP withdrew in protest of some of the Aquino government's actions.) Sanchez has taken a lot of personal criticism for his recognition of the KMU but he refuses to accept it: "I support the KMU because they're the only ones who are honest." (After Enrile's attempted coup in November 1986, the military emerged with greater power. One of the "suggestions" to Aquino was that she fire Sanchez. The KMU threatened a nation-wide strike should she do so. Ultimately, Sanchez resigned his post. As of this writing—January 1, 1987—no replacement has been named.)

President Aquino addressed a huge labor rally on May Day (May 1, 1986). She promised major labor law reforms. The *Philippine Labor Alert* (1986a) reported:

> She urged many measures long sought by the KMU, including the repeal of some of the unpopular labor laws of the Marcos era, abolition of an unwanted "welfare projects" tax (3 percent) on workers' wages, and a redefinition of the minimum wage formula which would substantially raise wages for 70 percent of the Philippine workers.
>
> Aquino also revoked a law allowing employers to replace striking workers with scabs and ordered an end to military intervention on picket lines. She eased policies for qualifying for union elections and authorizing strikes (from a 2/3 vote to a simple majority), and gave private security guards and workers in government-owned companies the rights to have unions.

According to the KMU, Aquino has not put any of her May Day promises into law (*Philippine Labor Alert*, 1986b). Massive problems in industrial relations have resulted from her unwillingness to legalize these reforms.

A few weeks before her May Day speech, Aquino put forth a plan for a six-month strike moratorium as an effort to create an atmosphere attractive to foreign investors. The KMU leaders refused to accept this, demanding as prior events, a defined economic program and legalized industrial relations guidelines. This has not been done. However, the KMU endorsed a position of "maximum restraint," whereby it promised it would exhaust all forms of airing demands before striking.

During October 1986, the KMU joined with BAYAN and other left-wing nationalist organizations to form a new electoral party, *Partido ng Bayan* (PnB—People's Party). This is a coalition party, designed to unite all left-wing nationalist organizations to challenge the right in future elections, specifically those coming up in May 1987, which will elect the new parliament. The KMU's Chairman, Rolando Olalia, was elected President of PnB.

Also during October 1986, the 48-member Constitutional Commission put forth its new proposed Constitution. Hand-picked by Aquino, this fairly conservative group is proposing "free enterprise" and an export-led economic policy be enshrined into the national Constitution.

In November 1986, KMU Chairman Rolando Olalia was salvaged by right-wing elements. (His close friend and driver, Mr. Leonor Alayay, was murdered with him.) This was a very brutal murder, as Olalia's eyes were gouged out and he was stabbed and shot several times, after having his mouth stuffed with newspapers (Jackson, 1987).

Olalia's murder resulted in strikes throughout Manila. Over a million people turned out to protest his killing and to commemorate his life. Newspapers described it as the largest leftist mobilization since the February "revolution."

The murder of Rolando Olalia was obviously hoped to reduce the KMU's presence in opposing the right wing. Olalia was chairman of the KMU and BAYAN, and president of *Partido ng Bayan.*

During December 1986, the KMU held a national convention to elect a new chairperson to replace Olalia. Crispin Beltran, general secretary before his detention in 1982, subsequent escape and then resurfacing after Aquino took power, was chosen as KMU's chairman.

The convention also decided to campaign against the proposed new constitution that will be before the voters in February 1987. The KMU has been campaigning to have pro-people policies incorporated into the constitution. The KMU has been proposing a self-reliant and internally-focused economy, to protect the Philippines from exploitation by foreign capital, a non-aligned foreign policy and removal of US bases from the Philippines.[13] Olalia's assassination certainly didn't intimidate the KMU as his killers obviously hoped.

The emergence, development and continued growth of the KMU since May 1980, gives the Filipino struggle a much greater chance of success. Most national liberation struggles have developed with only one force—usually a revolutionary army leading the struggle. This has allowed the US and its ruling class allies to concentrate their power against this single opponent. The existence of the KMU has divided the reactionaries' efforts, forcing them to split their attention between the KMU on one hand and the Communist-led New People's Army on the other.

Yet the existence of the KMU also presents problems for the Communist Party of the Philippines. The KMU, a genuine trade union center, that is controlled by its members, that is class conscious and confident of its abilities, must be respected and treated as an equal. The Communist Party cannot dominate the KMU as other Communist organizations in other countries have traditionally been able to dominate the working class.

It is the key role being played by the KMU, both in the national struggle and in the class struggle, that makes the KMU a subject worthy of attention.

NOTES

1. This article was originally published as Scipes, 1987c. This is largely as written, with some changes, including additions, to the endnotes. This is a report of my 1986 trip to the country, which grounds the general overview as presented in Chapter 8. While I have cut out a section of this chapter that was previously reported in previous chapters, there still remains some repetition. This is because some of the reporting herein was used in subsequent writings, such as in my book (Scipes, 1996). Again, my apologies for any repetition.

2. While illegally visiting the Bataan Export Processing Zone during February 1986, I was told by workers that only 13,000 jobs remained from a high point of 26,000. In "Free Trade Zones: Putting Asian Women on Assembly Lines" (*Dollars and Sense*, 1985), hourly wages and fringe benefits of different Asian countries were compared: wages and fringes in the Philippines were $ .50 an hour (wages, $ .48); in Malaysia, they were $ .60 (wages, $ .48); and in Indonesia, there were $ .35 (wages, $ .19). These figures were from Fuentes and Ehrenreich (1983), and were current in February 1982.

3. This is conveyed well in the 1986 film, *The Global Assembly Line*.

4. For an overview of the entire labor movement of the Philippines, see Dejillas, 1994.

It is commonly claimed that the KMU is Communist-controlled. There are Communists among the members and, I'm sure, the leadership. The same can be said of anti-Communists and Christians. During my four week stay with the KMU (January

10–February 5, 1986), I specifically and critically researched this issue. I am confident that the KMU is controlled by its membership and not the Communist Party of the Philippines (CPP).

5. See Phil Bronstein and David Johnson, 1985. See also Tim Shorrock and Kathy Selvaggio, 1986; Enid Eckstein, 1986; and Scipes, 1986a. Altogether, according to *International Labour Reports* (1989), between 1983–1988, the TUCP was the largest trade union recipient of funds in the world from the so-called National Endowment for Democracy, channeled through AAFLI. Monies sent to the TUCP totaled approximately $6,000,000, far surpassing those sent to *Solidarnosc* in Poland, which totaled $3, 631,913. (Amounts reported on p. 11.)

In my 2010a book, I specifically put all of this into a historical context. I also have a section (pp. 48–56), based on my field research, where I discuss the KMU and report on the struggle at Atlas Mines in Cebu.

6. The *Philippine Labor Alert* was produced by John Witeck of the Philippine Workers Support Committee, headquartered in Honolulu, and gave invaluable reportage on labor affairs in the country while it was being published. Begun, I believe, in 1984, it continued until No. 40, dated December 1997–March 1998.

7. This section discussing KMU is reported in Chapters 8 and 10, and it was not felt necessary to repeat a third time.

8. I discuss alliances more completely in Chapter 10, herein.

9. The term “salvaging” refers to people being killed by extra-judicial means, and then their bodies are left unburied, often on the side of a road, so as to provide a warning to others. As far as I know, this practice began under Marcos.

10. As is generally the case in the Philippines, there is one union for each factory. Multi-site unions are fairly rare.

11. This account was from Watts and Jackson, 1986.

12. Corazon Aquino was the widow of political leader and Marcos opponent, Benigno Aquino, who was assassinated by forces under the control of Ferdinand Marcos on August 21, 1983. She also comes from one of the richest families in the country. The brave woman decided in late 1985 to run for president against Marcos in the snap election (for an important account, see Robinson, 1996). Eventually, after Marcos’ fraud was exposed, Archbishop Jaime Cardinal Sin of the Catholic Church called out his followers and they supported forces within Marcos’ military that had rebelled against Marcos, and the US counseled Marcos not to launch a military attack on the rebels. Marcos fled on February 25, 1986.

Corazon Aquino became the president of the Republic of the Philippines on February 25, 1986, and served until 1992. The human rights’ abuses under Aquino ultimately were seen as being worse than under Marcos. (For a good overview of her rule, see McCoy, 2009: 433–451. For an excellent interview with KMU Chair Crispin Beltran, detailing the change in Aquino’s positions and policies, see Butler, 1988.)

There are many books on “People’s Power,” the mobilization of ordinary people to support the military rebels which led to Aquino’s assumption of power (for one oral history/photographic account, see Mercado, 1986). However, the KMU’s (and much of the left’s) role in these developments is almost never mentioned or, if mentioned, downplayed; their role, in my opinion, was significant.

My book (Scipes, 1996) covers the KMU's development from 1980 to 1994, which includes the overthrow of Marcos and developments across the entire Aquino Administration and into the early years of the Ramos Administration. It's the only book that covers this period from the perspective of organized labor.

13. The Constitution was passed with about 80 percent acceptance. In May 1987, none of the seven left-wing nationalists were elected, although Ka Bel got the highest vote totals of the seven.

Particularly in the first year and a half of Aquino's administration, she was unbeatable in anything she did, no matter how cogent or detailed the argument was against her.

Chapter Ten

Learning from the KMU

Alliance Building

If North American activists are going to build a labor movement that is democratic, militant and class conscious, we need to study the experiences of other workers. American and Canadian workers in earlier times, such as those of the IWW or early days of the CIO, as well as those of workers in other industrialized countries, especially European labor movements after World War I and Poland's *Solidarnosc,* have much to teach us. And there are important lessons that we can learn from the dynamic trade union movements currently emerging in developing—often called "Third World"—countries. In fact, as I've discovered during my two trips to the Philippines, there is a lot the *Kilusang Mayo Uno* (KMU-May First Movement) can teach us about alliance building as part of building a new labor movement.[1]

The KMU is grounded on the principles of being "genuine" (class conscious), militant and nationalist. This means the KMU is democratically run by its members, and represents the interests of the working class; its leaders believe in militant, mass actions to political consciousness instead of backdoor deals; and the KMU acts for the benefit of Filipinos and not other nations or multinational capital. These principles are not rhetoric; they guide the practice of the KMU.

Because of its solid roots at the point of production and its nationalist politics, the KMU is a political power in the nation. It is fighting for national liberation and socialism.

Accordingly, it has suffered great repression throughout the years. During a 1982 effort to decapitate the organization, Ferdinand Marcos arrested 69 leaders, including its Chairman and Secretary General. In 1986, Chairman Roland Olalia was assassinated, along with his driver (see Jackson, 1987). And during 1987 alone, 498 KMU members were victims of repression, either through arrest (322), "massacre" (multiple killings at one time) (6), injury on a picket line (137), death on a picket line (5), "salvaging" (summary torture and then assassination (18) or disappearance (10).[2] These 1986–87 events occurred under the "liberal" Corazon Aquino regime.

Despite this repression, the KMU has not been stopped. It participated as a key force in an August 1987 nation-wide people's strike (*welgang bayan)* that immobilized about 95 percent of the economically-important cities and towns of the country, and it led a national general workers' strike during October of that year.

The power of the KMU comes from several sources: its leadership is decentralized; its members are extremely well-educated; and it has built strong ties to community organizations. These community ties are largely through membership in BAYAN ("people" or "country"), a 2.3-million member nationalist coalition of organizations, including those of the urban poor, women, students, and anti-nuclear and anti-militarist activists.

There is another component, one that joins organizationally all these approaches together, which makes the KMU so much more powerful than just a militant trade union organization: "alliances." Alliances are "horizontal" coalitions of workers from different workplaces and unions, organized on the basis of geography, industry or company ownership. The goal of each alliance is to unite worker for economic gain, provide self-defense from military harassment, win political demands outside of the workplace, and provide "genuine trade unionism" education for all workers.

(Geographical alliances are the most powerful, joining together all local unions in a chosen geographical area.. Industrial alliances consist of unions that are located in the same industry, such as health care or transportation. Conglomerate alliances unite unions in multi-site workplaces that are owned by the same capitalist. The latter two alliances are much more directed toward concerted activity around workplace issues, whereas geographical alliances tend to focus on larger political issues.)

The first geographical alliance was developed by the overwhelmingly female workforce in the Bataan Export Processing Zone (BEPZ) in response to military repression against strikers at the Inter-Asia Company during 1982.[3] The workers had gone on strike to protest intensification of their work; previously, each worker operated four machines in the textile plant; management increased that to six. The military intervened against the strikers, using fire trucks, truncheons and mass arrest in an effort to break the strike.

Although strikes in the Zone were illegal, other workers realized that if they allowed the military to break that strike, then the military could break any strike. Further, they realized that BEPZ was a key component of the IMF/World Bank/Marcos development strategy for the country, and thus union organization there would have a much larger importance than in less economically strategic areas.

The women organized clandestinely on the job, in the company-provided dormitories and in the community. Workers in every factory in the Zone were mobilized. On June 4, 1982, 26,000 workers walked out in support of the nine union organizers who had been fired by Inter-Asia, and the 54 arrested picketers that were confined by the military in a single jail cell designed for six to eight people. The union organizers were reinstated; the people in jail were freed; and the first alliance, AMBA-BALA (literally meaning "aim bullet"), was born.

AMBA-BALA is a geographical alliance that now includes over 12,000 of the 16,000 unionized workers throughout Bataan Province.[4] Other geographical alliances may cover an area as small as a district in a city, or they can be city-, region-, province-, island-, or even nation-wide.

There are two things unique about the geographical alliances. First, although initiated by unions that are members of KMU-affiliated federations,[5] they are open to all unions in the particular area, including those from other KMU federations and even those affiliated to competing labor centers. In fact, in some areas such as BEPZ, local unions affiliated to the KMU's arch-rival, the Trade Union Congress of the Philippines, are members of the KMU-led alliances. This, of course, presents a "united front," which keeps unions from scabbing on each other. It also allows the KMU alliances to give workers in competing unions the KMU education course on genuine trade unionism. This is an excellent program that includes the KMU's perspective on class conscious, democratic and militant unionism.[6]

Second, alliances have joined with local community groups to fight for political change. The key weapon is the *welgang bayan* (people's strike); in addition to a general workers' strike, public transportation is stopped, all shops and stores are closed, and community members set-up barricades to stop still-operating private vehicles or join workers on their picket lines. A *welgang bayan* took place during 1984 on the large southern island of Mindanao. In response to increased military operations and brutality on the island, people paralyzed most significant economic activity. Two more island-wide *welgang bayans* were launched during 1985, again protesting the militarization of the island. The third *welga* was so successful that the island's military commander asked the leaders to call it off after one day, and they refused. "We'll call it off when we reach our objectives," they replied. The *welgang bayan* lasted for three days.

Another significant *welgang bayan* took place in Bataan Province during 1985, when people opposed the construction of a nuclear power plant by Westinghouse. The plant was being built on the side of an active volcano in an active earthquake zone.

> Several major protests have been launched against the plant. The largest was the three-day province wide strike in June 1985. Eight towns were brought to a standstill. All banks, shops, schools, public transport, private businesses and government offices shut down. Even fishing boats in the local port refused to put out to sea. Workers from the industrial free trade zone [BEPZ], where the multinationals are located, marched for two days to join the protests. Workers blocked all roads to the nuclear plant, and grappled with armoured cars sent to clear a way through (Watts and Jackson, 1986).

The first nation-wide *welgang bayan* was launched during August 1987, in response to an oil price hike by the government. Although called off early in response to a military coup attempt, the effort had immobilized 95 percent of the country beforehand.

The power of *welgang bayan* depends upon unity and commitment within the alliances, as well as with the community organizations. While this requires substantial time to properly organize, once unleashed, it is a powerful weapon.

The increased capability to launch powerful political actions becomes more necessary as the repression increases. Things are getting worse: Crispin Beltran, KMU Chairman, says human rights abuses under Corazon Aquino "outstrip even the Marcos regime" (Butler, 1988).

One of the big differences between Marcos' time and Corazon Aquino's is the rise of vigilante organizations, which are death squads similar to those in El Salvador and Guatemala. Initiated on Mindanao during 1986, there are now over 200 vigilante organizations throughout the country. They are trained and armed by the military, inculcated often with bizarre forms of Christian ideology (e.g., labor organizers are "Satan," etc.), and turned loose.

The vigilantes have made KMU organizations key targets. During my April–May 1988 visit, every single trade union leader I met with on islands south of the northern island of Luzon, who worked above the shop floor level, was listed *by name* on a vigilante death list!

The situation at Atlas Mines on the island of Cebu demonstrates specifically the attack on the KMU. In 1985, a KMU-affiliated union, PAMA, won representation rights for the 10,000 workers. Since January 1987, five shop stewards have been killed, workers' houses have been set on fire, the union office has been shot into, and some workers feel so threatened that they live in, and commute from, Cebu City, which is three hours away. In August 1988, two vigilantes pulled guns on Tony Cuizon, PAMA's president, and fired; miraculously, both guns misfired! Cuizon has a 50,000 peso ($2,500) price on his head. The next union representation election will be held this December; obviously "someone" wants the KMU out of there.

The vigilantes do not work alone. The company gives some of them paid time off for "refresher military training." The major of the nearby town is the wife of the Executive Vice President of the mine, and is the regional chairperson of the extremely pro-vigilante People's Alliance Against Communism. The police will not protect the workers. The Trade Union Congress of the Philippines (TUCP) affiliate in the area—again, the TUCP is the arch-enemy of the KMU, and is an affiliate of the AFL-CIO's AAFLI (Asian-American Free Labor Institute)—broadcasts openly pro-vigilante propaganda on its radio station, while sponsoring anti-communist and "human rights" seminars for the workers to denounce the KMU and preaching the "Christian" values of the TUCP (Williamson, 1988).[7]

In short, the full-scale attack on the KMU is obviously part of a multi-pronged effort by the military, reactionary businessmen and their American allies to carry out their Low Intensity Conflict strategy to stop the political mobilization taking place throughout the country. The KMU's level of organization has so far derailed their efforts within the labor center.

Workers in developed, industrialized countries can learn from workers' struggles in developing countries. In fact, the KMU's alliance building strategy has a lot to teach us.

To a major extent, the US economy has been "deindustrialized" since 1973. Thousands of factories have been closed. Bluestone and Harrison (1982) estimated that between 32–38 million jobs were lost during the 1970s, and a US Bureau of Labor Statistics report documented 13.4 million jobs lost during the period 1979–84 due to deindustrialization.[8]

The overwhelming large numbers of those lost jobs were in industry. Companies shifted production overseas to exploit cheaper labor—a non-unionized electronics plant worker in the US will generally earn between $5–8 per hour, while her co-worker in BEPZ will earn $3 per day!—or they replaced workers through introducing automation, computers and/or robots here in the US. These efforts supplemented closure of their least efficient plants, a drastic management strategy designed to concentrate company resources to fend off competition from foreign-owned corporations.[9]

Unemployment is a structural requirement of capitalism. Capitalism cannot provide jobs for every person living in this society, as it cannot provide jobs for all the people around the world. Ultimately, American workers have no alternative but to join with workers around the world to build a liberated form of socialism (Scipes, 1987d).[10] Building a socialist labor movement would be an important contribution to the fight for this liberated society, and an alliance building strategy is one that could help build it.

An alliance-building strategy gives organizers a concrete goal: joining workers together in new organizations that enable them to fight and win. Such a strategy recognizes that industrial action by today's unions is not enough to defend workers' standards of living, nor can it lead the fight for a new society. [Even the UAW (United Auto Workers), in the relatively concentrated auto industry, has not been able to preserve jobs, wages or working conditions, much less improve the situation for non-unionized auto workers.] An alliance-building strategy recognizes that all industrial and service workers in a geographical area, both unionized and non-union, must unite among themselves to win their demands.

A geographical alliance would give workers the capability to stop production throughout an area. This would open the door to many potential victories; a chance to win union elections without outside interference; a chance to win strikes without the police breaking picket lines; and a chance to win political demands such as increased unemployment benefits.

As important, organizers of geographical alliances would encourage workers to unite with local community-based organizations to fight for contract demands: better schools and health care, employment, lower taxes, a halt to environmental destruction, and severe cut-backs to military spending. Obviously, the range for possible action grows with the enlargement of the geographical area organized.

This would give some real muscle to community organizations, a situation generally unfamiliar to them.[11] To ensure community support for their demands, workers would have to support community demands. Housing for the homeless, better pre-natal care for single mothers, and a raise in welfare payments are all issues that are generally outside of the workplace. They are the sorts of issues that a geographic alliance could choose to address.

The necessity of joining workers' organizations with those in the community is not just some pie-in-the-sky fantasy; it is required by the way the system functions. Employers generally break strikes through the use of the legal system and the police. To stop production during a strike, workers must occupy the plant and/or keep scabs out; and the only way the latter can be accomplished is by having community groups convince their members not to take strikers' jobs. To get them to do that, however, requires that workers' organizations fight with those in the community to address community problems, specifically including unemployment. Each worker's organization must convince community organizations through its actions that it is an important ally, deserving to be supported and that this support will be reciprocated.

There would be other benefits to implementing a strategy of geographical alliances. It would support militant unions while going around the labor reactionaries, and "pulling" progressive leaders along with the alliance. Should the reactionaries oppose the alliance, organizers would go directly to shop floor workers and enlist their support, both to join the alliance and to campaign within their union to win its support for the alliance.

Going around the reactionaries is not enough; obviously, they could try to "recapture" the membership by moving to the left as they did in the 1930s with the CIO (see Wetzel, 1988). To make the alliance system work requires thorough-going democracy among and between all worker and community organizations. This means class conscious education must be made available for everyone, all information must be shared with the members, and members must have the responsibility and the power to decide what course of action to take. Empowerment of the membership of all organizations, community as well as worker, is the essential requirement of this approach.

A commitment to democracy and member-empowerment would also have a positive influence on unions in the area. An alliance could serve as a model of how an organization should be run, and it would give progressive unionists support for fighting to make their unions run by the rank and file. Hopefully, this would result in more unions joining the alliance.

It is vital to understand that alliance-building is a long-term project—alliances cannot and should not be built overnight. Building an alliance requires building trust among the organizers and among the members; developing and providing class conscious education programs; and meeting numerous times to design structures that are democratic and allow for quick decision-making. And they require building trust among members who will directly control their own organizations.

Is this alliance-building strategy a panacea? Obviously not, because no magical cure-all exists for the labor movement. However, it does offer some real positive things to think about.

An alliance-building strategy offers several important possibilities. It offers a direction that goes beyond the limited strategy of "capturing" control of individual local unions. It gives us a relatively short term but important goal—to improve the lives and situations of people in our areas—while developing tools to fight for long-term, fundamental change in our society. It builds ties between workers and community organizations. And it provides class conscious education for all, couple with a democratic process and member self-empowerment.

If nothing else, alliance building creates intriguing possibilities. This approach deserves much further examination and discussion. It should also encourage us to build solidarity with the KMU, primarily to support their liberation struggle, and to find out more that might help us in ours.

NOTES

1. This chapter was initially published as Scipes, 1988b.

2. Source of 1987 figures: Commission on Trade Union and Human Rights (CTUHR) press statement on June 8, 1988. CTUHR, Rm. 703, Culmat Building, 127 E. Rodriquez Avenue, Quezon City, Philippines.

[CTUHR remains an important and vibrant organization, as I found out during my visits to the organization in 2016 and 2018. Its web site, which is excellent, is at http://ctuhr.org/. In meeting with its Executive Director, Daisy Arago, in 2016, although we did not recognize each other immediately, we realized we had met back in 1986!]

3. The story of the first alliance, AMBA-BALA in the Bataan Export Processing Zone, was told above in Chapter 8 on the KMU, as were a couple of others. Despite the repetition, I have decided to keep the integrity of the original article because it helps make this chapter even stronger. My apologies, nonetheless, for the repetition.

4. The drastic reduction in numbers between 1982 and 1986 was largely due to factories in the Zone being shut down and moved to lower-wage countries such as Malaysia and Singapore, where workers' organizations are considerably weaker. Flor Collantes, Political/ External Officer of AMBA-BALA during an interview on May 4, 1988, provided most of this information. Collantes also pointed out that the 1982 strike was the first general strike in any export processing zone in the world. For an excellent written account of the situation in BEPZ and workers' efforts to organize, see Jackson, 1985. [For a more in-depth account of workers' organizing in BEPZ and across the province, see Scipes, 1996: 159–180.]

5. The term "federation" is used differently in the Philippines than in the US; KMU federations are similar to national and international unions in North America.

6. Since Philippine labor law provides a 60-day "free period" at the expiration of each five-year long collective bargaining agreement (CBA)—during this time, competing unions can campaign among the workforce to represent them and negotiate their next CBA after being elected—this practice is helping to build the KMU over the long term.

7. Fortunately, despite the tremendous level of repression, in a Philippine government-certified Certification Election in March 1989, out of 7,395 valid votes, PAMA won 5,025 (68 percent). For an in-depth examination of the struggle at Atlas Mines, see Scipes, 1996: 116–125; see also Scipes, 2010a: 52–55.

8. This information was gathered by the Plant Closures Project of Oakland, CA. [I volunteered for six and a half years with the Project from 1983–89, and the Project disbanded in 1993.]

9. I have been researching episodically the changing global economic system and how that has been affecting American workers for over 35 years (see Scipes, 1984a). For the most inclusive understanding of this subject, with the cut-off period being the summer of 2007—before the Great Recession hit, so none of my findings can be attributed to it—see Scipes, 2009a. See also Greenhouse, 2008.

10. In this article, I argued, after placing this in a global context, that "There are three essential components to building a socialist labor movement in the United States: it must be internationalist, it must be democratic, and it must come out of

workers' experiences in [the United States]" (Scipes, 1987d: 3). Whether one wants to call something a "socialist" labor movement or not, I still think these components are essential for any revitalized labor movement, 30+ years after I first wrote them.

11. In addition to volunteering for over six and a half years with the Plant Closures Project in Oakland, California as mentioned above, I also served as the Executive Director of The Calumet Project in Northwestern Indiana between June 2001 and September 2002.

For an examination of labor-community coalitions, embedded in a review of Jeremy Brecher and Tim Costello's *Burning Bridges: The Emerging Grassroots Coalition of Labor and Community,* see Scipes, 1991b.

Part III

BUILDING GLOBAL LABOR SOLIDARITY

In Part II, a lot of ground—theoretically and empirically—was covered: most importantly, a theoretical basis for understanding social movement unionism was presented; it was argued that the ideological conceptualization chosen would determine organizational activities; and then, this argument was supported by an empirical study of the KMU which, to this author, serves as an exemplar of social movement unionism.

Now, we apply this knowledge. In Chapter 11, we see if the understanding that I developed in the early 1990s to theoretically understand the KMU is such that it can be generalized beyond the Philippines; in other words, is this simply something specific to KMU or can this version of SMU be successfully applied elsewhere, say to include a labor center in a country at a differing level of development, such as South Africa? In Chapter 12, we turn our attention to how the KMU works to develop international labor solidarity. While developing international labor solidarity has not been made a requirement for SMU, it has been at the center of KMU's work from quite early on—and the innovative program developed by KMU, alone in the world as far as can be determined, is one that every labor organization can learn from. And in Chapter 13, things discussed previously are brought together, as I try to disentangle the theoretical confusion that has developed over the years regarding social movement unionism.

Chapter Eleven

Social Movement Unionism in South Africa?

> From the vantage point of the workers themselves, the struggle to achieve freedom of combination has been waged not only to gain protection and improvement of the terms and conditions of labor, but also to attain social justice and full equality in civil society where, as individuals, workers could not adequately contend with the power of employers and the state (Bonnell, 1983: 3).

This statement by Victoria Bonnell in her study of pre-revolutionary Russian workers in St. Petersburg and Moscow captures the thrust of labor movements, at least in the period of emergence and challenge to the established social order. Labor movements around the world have gone through this period; some, particularly in developing countries, are still in these periods, while others, particularly in the so-called developed countries, have long-past left them.

We have learned from the experiences of the KMU and, from that, developed a conceptualization of social movement unionism (SMU) that was explicated in Chapter 6. The question needing to be asked, though, is this something just confined to the Philippines, or does this also extend to other labor centers?[1]

MOBILIZATION IN SOUTH AFRICA[2]

The mobilization of workers in South Africa—particularly in manufacturing—must be placed in a historicized context which, in this case, includes industrialization under a racial dictatorship.

However, when considering the impact of industrialization, we must be careful. Although some analysts of industrialization in the "developing" countries argue that industrialization in general—especially rapid industrialization—causes mobilization (e.g., Seidman, 1994), others argue that the type of industrialization can either inhibit or promote mobilization—thus whether the industrialization is oriented for export or domestic usage can affect mobilization (e.g., Deyo, 1989; cf. Hutchison, 1992; see also Gereffi, 1990). Based on my work in the Philippines (Scipes, 1996), I would also add that levels of industrialization affect mobilization, so that mobilization can be affected by whether a country is a NIC (newly industrializing country) or at a different level of development.[3] Therefore, I argue that both levels of industrialization and types of industrialization within levels can be seen as independent variables that have differential effects on mobilization. However, again, what structural models of mobilization cannot do is determine the type of mobilization that takes place when workers do decide to act (cf. Seidman, 1994; see Chapter 4, herein).

INDUSTRIALIZATION IN SOUTH AFRICA

Industrialization in South Africa generally began in the 1920s, as the government began what would later be known as an ISI (Import Substitution Industrialization) program. This started to create an economic base of light manufacturing, although this shifted to include heavy industry after World War II. This was an economic program of industrialization, but also a political program as well: ". . . the importance of the state to South Africa's industrial development in the postwar era should not be underestimated," and under this program, ". . . controlling black workers and supporting Afrikaans-speaking whites were at least as important to the National Party as economic growth." But regardless of its motives, "the South African state had, by the early 1960s, laid a basis for rapid industrial growth" (Seidman, 1994: 75).

In the 1960s, this industrial growth took off. This was largely based on foreign capital. As Seidman notes, ". . . the industrial boom of the 1960s, depending as it did on foreign technology and capital to expand into new sectors, was dominated by large firms, closely tied to international investors" (Seidman, 1994: 81). This caused rapid growth of the manufacturing sector and large new factories were erected (which would bring large numbers of workers together in increasingly larger units of production) (Bonner, 1987: 55). Between 1960 and 1970, the economy grew by 56 percent, "expanding at a rate matched only by Japan"; foreign direct investment doubled, growing from R (Rand) 1819 million to R3943 million (MacShane, Plaut and Ward, 1984: 20).

However, Gay Seidman discusses how contemporary industrialization has differed from the earlier industrialization experiences:

> Despite some similarities, industrialization in what are sometimes called "semi-peripheral" areas may not mirror the European and North American experiences; patterns of proletarianization, labor processes and political opportunities may be quite different from those that prevailed a century earlier. . . . patterns of industrialization in the late twentieth century have often involved reliance on imported technologies developed in core industrialized areas, as well as on infusions of foreign capital, and have depended on links to international markets. While de-skilling of artisans has occurred from place to place, the new technologies have frequently been put in place without many of the labor process conflicts that apparently marked earlier industrialization. Mass production processes using semi-skilled workers have been in place from the start of industrial growth . . . (Seidman, 1994: 6).[4]

In any case, we can see the extent of this growth from the following figures: in 1960, the manufacturing sector had a total output of R7.121 billion; by 1970, this reached R16.267 billion; by 1980, this reached R27.342 billion.[5] In fact, by 1980, the output value of manufacturing surpassed that of mining, which has traditionally been South Africa's leading economic producer (COSATU, 1992: 43).[6] Accordingly, employment in the manufacturing sector reached 28.8 percent of total employment by 1980 (COSATU, 1992: 45). By 1989, South Africa's Gross Domestic Product (GDP) had reached $80.370 million, and its GDP per person was $2,296 (COSATU, 1992: 7).[7]

Because of Apartheid, economic benefits were stratified by race. In 1972, average money wages of Africans working in manufacturing were only 17.12 percent of whites working in manufacturing (MacShane, Plaut and Ward, 1984: 51). However, change was in the air.

With the growth of the manufacturing sector,

> . . . black workers replaced whites: between 1960 and 1976, the ratio of black to white workers in manufacturing increased from 2.75:1 to 3.6:1, a shift that appears to have been associated with increased skill levels among black workers. Between 1969 and 1981, white semi-skilled and skilled workers declined from 173,150 to 154,896, while the number of semi-skilled and skilled African workers rose from 847,444 to 1,300,173 . . . (Seidman, 1994: 85).

Over a slightly different period, we can see that there were 300,000 jobs for unskilled workers in manufacturing in 1965, but only 200,000 jobs in 1985. At the same time, in 1965, most African male workers were unskilled, but by 1985, most African males were semi-skilled (COSATU, 1992: 46). This demand for skilled labor in manufacturing (as well as the increasing strength of the new unions who organized these workers) led to a relative increase in black wages: where average money earnings of blacks had been 17.12 percent of white workers in 1972, it was 31.60 percent by 1982 (MacShane, Plaut and Ward, 1984: 51).

However, in the 1980s, manufacturing sector growth all but stopped: between 1980 and 1990, the yearly growth rate was 0.1 percent. Manufacturing output, which was R 27.342 billion in 1980, totaled only R 27.596 billion in 1990 (COSATU, 1992: 48 and 49, Figure 51). The annual average growth rates for major sections of the manufacturing sector declined between 1981–1989: −8.9 percent for transport equipment, −4.93 percent for motor vehicles, −4.36 percent for machinery and equipment, −3.12 percent for wearing apparel, −2.53 percent for textiles, and −1.07 percent for industrial chemicals, while tobacco production increased 2.77 percent, beverages, 3.38 percent, non-ferrous metals, 3.38 percent, and paper, 4.20 percent (COSATU, 1992: 51). Relative employment also decreased in manufacturing, from providing 28.8 percent of all jobs in 1980 to providing only 26.6 percent of all jobs in 1989 (COSATU, 1992: 45, Figure 46).

APARTHEID

However, industrialization does not take place in a vacuum: it takes place within a specific social order, usually within a particular nation-state. This is especially important to recognize in considering developments among black workers in South Africa.

To a degree unmatched in the contemporary world, South Africa was a racial dictatorship:

> Apartheid was a system of separation, exploitation, and domination just short of slavery. . . . in its heyday, [it] meant not only racial segregation, but the formal designation of all individuals as either White, African, Indian or Coloured, and the determination of where they could live, whom they could marry, where their children went to school, what they were taught, whether they could be in a particular area (cities especially) without a pass, what swimming pool, library and restaurant they could use, and, of course, whether they could vote. Less formally, the situation was even worse: police brutality was legendary, civil rights in daily life virtually nonexistent, wage differentials immense, and women's household labor virtually domestic slavery (Marcuse, 1995: 39).

As one contemporary report characterized it, "In South Africa, a 4.5 million minority rules over a 21.5 million black majority. In order to perpetuate this system, the racist minority authorities have, through a series of enactments, established a system of untrammeled power which affects every aspect of human life" (ICFTU, 1984: 7).

> While the social brutality of apartheid was unparalleled, blacks had fought against racial oppression since its introduction into the country. To understand black workers' mobilization, we must place it within the context of the struggle against racial oppression, which developed particularly since the late 1940s, when the system of apartheid was introduced by the Nationalist Party (ICFTU, 1984: 7).

The increasing opposition to apartheid during the 1950s, the killing of 69 blacks at Sharpeville in 1960—during a protest against the passes that blacks were required by the state to carry—and the accompanying repression, resulted in the opposition movement choosing to go underground. It was only with the rise of the Black Consciousness movement (BC) in the late 1960s that opposition re-surfaced.

BC was an effort that developed initially among a small number of black university students, and was intended to help blacks overcome their psychological dependence on whites and the internalized oppression that accompanied it. Key to the rise of BC was the building of a group identity, of taking pride in their group membership that the apartheid state denigrated, and of stressing the positive nature of blackness (as opposed to being "non-white"): "The point was for blacks to define themselves as a group, rather than to accept a negative self-conception defined in terms of what they were not and referring only to their exclusion from the privileges of being white" (Marx, 1992: 45).

The BC conceptualization of "race" recognized that race was a social construct, not a biological reality, and the movement's leaders chose to define it in a way that challenged the government's definition. For example, they included Asians and "coloureds" in the category of black, specifically undercutting the government's efforts to separate the different groups through racial categorization. And while BC excluded whites from their movement, it was a situational response rather than a categorical one, as they saw that all racial categories would dissolve after "liberation."

The BC movement was ultimately a cultural project, seeking social change by reshaping values and attitudes.[0] However, when the material conditions of society changed, BC provided a way of interpreting the changes, and did so in a way that was grasped by the large number of blacks, and particularly poor, black, urban youth. "When a wider array of the oppressed were aroused by changing material conditions to join the opposition, the mood and language of Black Consciousness proved to be more pervasive than the breadth of formal BC affiliation had suggested. At least among urban youth, the days of bowing and scraping were long gone . . ." (Marx, 1992: 61).

By the mid-1970s, material changes were widely affecting the population. The economy was drastically slowing, with a concurrent downturn in employment: where 2,850 new manufacturing jobs for blacks had been created each month during 1974, "fewer than half as many new jobs were created in the subsequent eighteen months" (Marx, 1992: 61). The burden of apartheid on the state's resources—duplicated administration, additional military and policing expenditures, restrictions on growth of domestic economic markets and skilled labor by blacks, and investment too inefficient to overcome the oil and arms embargoes—limited the state's ability to respond to the economic slowdown (Marx, 1992: 61).

And, of course, it was the poor and those at the bottom of the social order that the crisis struck hardest. General living standards declined, as the black population doubled in the largest urban centers but housing only grew in these areas by 15 percent during the 1971–75 period. Black secondary school enrollment leaped by 160 percent between 1970–75; in the black township of Soweto, outside of Johannesburg, "there were over sixteen thousand families for every high school, as compared with thirteen hundred families per high school in white Johannesburg" (Marx, 1992: 62).

Black youth began building their own BC organization, the South African Student Movement (SASM) in late 1975–early 1976. SASM opposed the state's new effort in early 1976 to have mathematics taught in Afrikaans—the "language of the oppressor"—in the schools instead of English. The secretary of a SASM chapter in a high school was to be arrested by police in early June, but students fought the police, forcing them to retreat off campus. On June 13th, students called for a demonstration on June 16th to protest the state's attack. The police responded harshly to the students' efforts: 25 students were killed, and local workers were also attacked without provocation. ". . . the casualties of June 16, 1976, were only the start of a violent conflict, exacerbated by discontent over material conditions and assertiveness encouraged by BC rhetoric. . .," and "Six days after the initial uprising, one hundred and thirty people were officially listed as having been killed" (Marx, 1992: 68).

Ultimately, the mobilization inspired by the June 16th demonstrations ended by the end of 1977, as the BC movement had not built the organization necessary to advance its politics:

> . . . the BC movement was not well suited to move from inspiring an end of psychological submission to orchestrating a physical struggle for liberation, having long eschewed the forms of organization necessary for the latter. Other

> than scattered student groups, no local organizations had been established that could maintain discipline and oppositional momentum once state repression was heightened. Links with the workers had not been solidified by BC, and the workers themselves were not yet organized enough or otherwise ready to confront the state. Nor did the BC movement, particularly as it was expressed by the youth, present a concrete program for a transfer of power (Marx, 1992: 71–72).

But what the BC movement accomplished was to break the chains of mental subjugation that had kept large numbers of blacks politically immobilized, and this change was most obvious in the urban areas; areas in which most of industry was located.

MASS RESISTANCE INTENSIFIES

The 1976 students' uprising directly affected the emerging labor movement. "Following this, a new spirit of militancy and a younger generation of factory floor leaders schooled in this environment began to emerge" (Bonner, 1987: 58). Gay Seidman supports this: ". . . years later, workers on the East Rand attributed increased worker militance after 1976 to anger at repression and shame that students had taken the lead in resisting apartheid" (Seidman, 1994: 181).

The increase in political consciousness stimulated by the BC movement also resulted in a revitalization of the "Charterist" movement, the political mobilization headed by the African National Congress and motivated by the Freedom Charter. The concept of "national unity as a strategic necessity" began being adopted by a growing majority of the opposition movement after the uprising of 1976. "An ideological transition from a primary concern with values to a greater focus on mobilizing physical resistance was taking shape within the opposition, driven by the external pressures of state repression as these were assessed and interpreted" (Marx, 1992: 80).

The primary organizational form that this development took was the creation of the United Democratic Front (UDF) in 1983. Where the BC movement had been led by blacks and for blacks, the UDF coalition was a non-racial project that was intended to mobilize the greatest number of South Africans in the struggle against apartheid, and thus accepted anyone of any "race" that opposed apartheid. Its project was based on mass mobilization, and worked through community mobilization, publicity, and massive demonstrations.[9]

While the BC movement had been stymied by its lack of attention to organization building, the UDF was limited by its type of organization. Perhaps most importantly, as a political coalition, its multi-class membership was immobilized when facing class-related questions and, accordingly, on how to proceed in the struggle against apartheid—officially, it was reduced to a politics of "least common denominator" in efforts to maximize oppositional mobilization. However, in practice, local UDF-affiliates mobilized extensively in the townships and communities and acted quite militantly at the local level. The other limitation was that because it was based in the townships and communities, and dependent on publicity through the mass media, it was very susceptible to repression by the state. Yet the UDF was able to mobilize increasing numbers of people across the country in militant political opposition to the apartheid state (Marx, 1992: 106–146).

Beginning in late 1984, a massive revolt by blacks across the country shook the state. Stimulated by the development of the UDF and worsening economic conditions, mass organized revolt emerged and was met by heavy repression. Between August 1985 and the end of that year, between 650 and 879 people had been killed; 371 by police. In July 1985, a partial state of emergency was declared by the state. This failed to halt the upsurge, was withdrawn for a few months, and then surpassed as governmental leaders imposed a total state of emergency nationwide in June 1986. This hampered the opposition, and in February 1988, the UDF itself was banned (Marx, 1992: 147–188).

It was out of the unrest that COSATU was launched in November 1985 (Baskin, 1991: 87–90; see also *International Labour Reports,* 1985).

The range of oppositional politics—along with those of an "independent worker" bloc—were reflected within the labor movement. BC-inspired unions stayed in black (as differentiated from non-racial) labor centers such as CUSA (Council of Unions of South Africa) and AZACTU (Azanian Congress of Trade Unions), and these two labor centers merged in 1986 to form NACTU (National Council of Trade Unions). Although NACTU has co-operated with COSATU to a greater or lesser extent over the years, it has remained a separate labor center. Nonetheless, in November 1985, a number of regionally-based general unions—unions not limited to any particular industry—inspired by the ANC/UDF movements, joined with the independent industrial-based unions of FOSATU (Federation of South African Trade Unions) to create a new labor center, COSATU (Congress of South African Trade Unions). And interactions between these different political ideologies and traditions—which played out differently depending on the issue at hand (Baskin, 1991: 101–104; and, more generally, see Kraak, 1993: 180–205)—helped shape the internal politics of COSATU and its organizational development.

With some idea of the political-economic situation, it is now time to focus on worker mobilization during the period of industrialization. I focus here on the black, but non-racialist, trade unions in South Africa that eventually came together to form COSATU in 1985.

BLACK WORKER MOBILIZATION

Although there had been African unions since 1919, the black union movement had been basically wiped out by the mid-1960s. Although never banned as an organization, the non-racial unions of SACTU (South African Congress of Trade Unions) were devastated when their leadership was "decimated by arrests, detentions and bannings": "The capacity to organize workers inside South Africa had been destroyed" (MacShane, Plaut and Ward, 1984: 118; see also Maree, 1987: 2; Lambert, 1988). A listing of strikes between 1962–72 shows that only in one year, 1972, had more than 8,000 workers gone out on strike nationwide (MacShane, Plaut and Ward, 1984: 20).

However, after a dockworker strike at the end of the preceding year (see Cole, 2013), 2,000 black workers in Durban at the Coronation Brick and Tile Company went on strike in January 1973. This touched the nerve of other workers: within a month, over 30,000 workers were on strike in and around Durban—29 firms had been struck during January, and then strikes spread to Durban municipal workers—and strikes had begun to spread throughout the province of Natal (Institute for Industrial Education, 1979).[10] Within the first three months of 1973, over 61,000 workers had been on strike, which was more than the total for the previous eight years (Baskin, 1991: 17–18). By the end of the year, around 100,000 workers in the Durban area had struck (MacShane, Plaut and Ward, 1984: 21).

"The most significant immediate consequence of the [Durban] strike wave was that masses of militant African workers poured into newly founded working class organizations in Durban and Pietermaritzburg," writes Johann Maree. "This heralded the start of the resurgence of African trade unionism as a whole . . ." (Maree, 1987: 2).

In an article providing an overview of the emergence of the new trade unions between 1973–1984, Maree delineated three periods of development. Between 1973–1976, there was the "struggle for survival" where unions emerged and then, toward the last part of 1976—after the students' uprising—were almost destroyed. In fact, union operations were "completely ruptured" in the areas around Cape Town and Johannesburg. Between 1977 1979, the new unions went through a period of "reconstruction and consolidation," and in April 1979, FOSATU (Federation of South African Trade Unions)—further discussed below—was founded. Also, in 1979, the state decided to recognize African trade unions after the Wiehahn Commission's first report. And then, between 1980–1984, the new unions expanded rapidly (Maree, 1987: 1–7):

> During the four-year period from the end of 1979 to the end of 1983, signed-up membership of the emerging independent unions went up more than fourfold from about 70,000 to almost 300,000. . . . But the unions made their most impressive headway in gaining formal recognition from companies. This is indicated by the enormous increase in the number of signed recognition agreements: between 1979 and 1983, they increased from a mere five to no less than 406 with the FOSATU unions accounting for 285 or seventy percent of the agreements (Maree, 1987: 7).

As stated above, strikes in Durban were the first step in building the black trade unions nationwide: in 1972, there had been 13,381 work days lost to industrial action by black workers—in 1983, there were 390,314 work days lost (Marx, 1992: 194). But along with noting the great increase in striking, we need to keep in mind why workers were striking and some suggestive data is available from 1982. Out of 69 strikes in the metal industry that year, 36 (52.17 percent) were primarily over wages, and the number of strikes over wages were more than three times greater than the number of those over retrenchments, the next most significant issue. Of the 26 strikes in the motor (automobile) industry that year, 14 (53.85 percent) were primarily over wages, and there were more strikes over wages than over the next two issues—dismissals and retrenchments—combined (MacShane, Plaut and Ward, 1984: 60; percentages calculated by author).

But there were more to the strikes than just the identified "main demands." Gerald Kraak explains:

> Low wages were the root cause of the vast majority of industrial disputes in South Africa in the 1970s and 1980s. But in acting to redress low pay and poor working conditions, workers were confronted by the problem of getting employers to deal with genuinely representative structures, be they factory committees, elected representatives or unions. Organization around wages and conditions was transformed into a struggle for the legitimacy of trade unions (Kraak, 1993: 127).[11]

Phil Bonner supports this claim, noting that two things developed from the strike wave: "workers provisionally won a de facto right to strike" and "a large number of strikes centered on issues of management control and affronts to personal dignity" (Bonner, 1987: 60).

Central to the emergence and development of the new unions, and their increasing shopfloor and strike power, were early decisions by workers and their unions that the unions had to be internally democratic, and that rank-

and-file members had to be actively involved at the workplace and in the union. This meant that the members had control over union affairs and officials. And that the union organization on the shop floor had to be in-depth, "with shop stewards being given a key role" (Maree, 1987: 3). "The emphasis on strong, self-reliant shop steward committees" was what, ultimately, allowed the new unions to survive (Bonner, 1987: 57).

Some of the new unions, though, also began addressing "new" issues—new perhaps for the labor movement—such as those that particularly affected women workers; CCAWUSA was an early innovator. By discussing this union and some of its experiences, we can get some idea of how member-leader interaction resulted in a union taking on issues not historically considered as trade union issues.

CCAWUSA, the Commercial, Catering and Allied Workers' Union of South Africa, had been founded in 1975, under the leadership of a black woman, Emma Mashinini. She was joined by Vivian Mtwa, a black man. We can get a sense of the development of CCAWUSA—which merged into the South African Commercial, Catering and Allied Workers' Union (SACCAWU) in the late 1980s—by quickly looking at the development of the union and its shift to fight specifically for women's rights in their contracts, and then worked to eradicate the double shift between women and men among union members. Mtwa discussed the early years, suggesting some of the early problems they faced:

> Those early years were very frustrating—management did not want to speak to you, they weren't prepared to give to access to workers, and workers were afraid to talk with you because they feared victimization.
>
> There were many, many incidents of intimidation by management. For example, if I went into a shop and the boss saw me talking to a worker, the worker would just leave me and walk away. Then I would be left standing there, not knowing what to do. The next thing, the security guard would come and ask me what I was doing there. I would have to make some excuse and disappear fast because if they discovered that you were from the union, they called the police. Thank God I was quick, so I never got arrested! Management would then follow up on that worker and really intimidate him or her—so the next time you came, you had to get a new contact (quoted in SACCAWU, 1991: 6–7).

Yet through hard work, and innovative and determined efforts, CCAWUSA grew throughout the late 1970s. It had been founded in 1975 with 300 members, and grew to 4,000 in 1979. Its membership exploded in the early 1980s, after the 1979 Wiehahn agreement legitimized black unions and as a number of major strikes broke out in the Johannesburg area. The new union was not prepared; it simply didn't have the personnel nor the financial resources to lead all the strikes. The union had to adjust:

> But the new space to organize meant that union officials could speak to and organise workers. They used the opportunity to educate and inform workers of their rights. This brought a new confidence to workers on the shopfloor and they began to voice their demands.
>
> The union also used the space to bring in democratic shop-steward structures that led to the important principle of the union that is accountable to the members on the shopfloor (SACCAWU, 1991: 9).

It was through rank and file democracy and accountancy of leaders to members on the shop floor that resulted in the union's addressing women's specific issues. This approach, forced by women members, emerged during the 1983 strike against OK Bazaars, a major retail chain. A maternity agreement was made a major clause in the recognition agreement: pregnant women were guaranteed their jobs after enjoying a 12-month maternity leave.

While a major win, an unpaid maternity agreement, no matter how generous, did not mean much if the family were dependent on the woman's wages. In 1985, the union took on Metro Cash and Carry, another retail chain, and won another major advance: "Not only were women assured job security, but in addition, they were given seven months leave, paid at 33 percent of their salaries." However, the agreement went further than that:

> Also included in the agreement was time-off for women to go to the clinic to have check-ups before and after the baby was born. Women who were pregnant were protected from doing heavy work or other work that could harm the baby. The company also gave pregnant women R100.00 [approximately US $80.00 at the time—KS] to buy baby clothes and even agreed in principle to the possibility of negotiating childcare arrangements in the future (SACCAWU, 1991: 13).

A three day paid paternity leave was also incorporated into the agreement.

But this was not the end of efforts around these issues. CCAWUSA saw that these agreements, while beneficial to new mothers, were excluding men from childcare. They took their efforts on this issue to a higher level in the 1987 struggle against Pick n Pay, again another retail chain: ". . . the Pick n Pay agreement recognizes that pregnancy will always be an issue for women and that they should be protected, it also makes the point that both women and men should be involved in caring for and bringing up their children":

> The provisions of the agreement cover broad areas, ranging from health needs of pregnant women, caring for adoptive children, paid leave for mothers and fathers, providing for miscarriages, paid medical aid and advice on contraception. All female employees working for the company are entitled to 11 months leave, nine of which are paid. Three of the nine months are paid at 75 percent of the worker's wage and six of them at 30 percent. Couple who are both employed

by the company can share this leave. Parents are able to save leave for anytime until a child's fourth birthday.

The agreement makes provision for paternity leave—fathers are entitled to eight days paid leave at the time of the mother's confinement. Fathers also have time off to take their babies to the clinic. Also provided for in the agreement is leave for parents who adopt children (SACCWU, 1991: 18, 20).[12]

The struggle for parental rights in their collective bargaining agreements was most developed within CCAWUSA. But while I have tried to suggest the range of new approaches developed in the new unions, by discussing political developments around a single issue in this one union, it is time to return to the overall state of affairs.

In the middle of this upsurge of labor militancy, as well as to address the problem of increasing dependence on black labor, the South African state legalized the new unions "in the hope of creating a more disciplined and complacent 'labor aristocracy'" (Marx, 1992: 247–248).[13] This program failed to constrain the new unions; union organizers used the opportunity to expand and strengthen these unions.[14]

This was reflected in national-level strike activities (not including stoppages or lockouts). Between 1970 and 1979, the yearly number of strikes varied between a low of 69 (in 1971) and a high of 384 (1974), with the average over these 10 years being 179 strikes. The numbers of strikers for the same 10 years varied between a low of 4,146 (1970) and a high of 98,379 (1973); the average was 27,903 strikers per year. The number of working days lost varied from a low of 10,558 (1978) to a high of 229,281 (1973), with an average number of working days lost between 1972 (the year records first became available)—1979 being 51,373. However, between 1980 and 1987, comparable figures report a significant increase in worker militancy. Strikes fluctuated between 207 (1980) and 1,148 (1987), with an average of 510 over these eight years. The number of strikers ranged from a low of 61,785 (1980) to a high of 591,421 (1987), averaging 224,773 strikers. And the number of working days lost varied from 124,594 (1983) to 5,825,231 (1987), averaging 1,135,408 days lost due to strike activity (Data from Kraak, 1993: 129, Table 6.1, Computations by author).[15]

Table 11.1. Strikes, Number of Strikers, and Annual Working Days Lost in South Africa, 1970–1979 and 1980–1987

Years covered:	*Average annual number of strikes:*	*Average annual number of strikers:*	*Average annual number of working days lost:*
1970–1979	179	27,903	51,373
1980–1987	510	224,773	1,135,408

The April 1979 founding of FOSATU (Federation of South African Trade Unions), a non-racialist labor center with strong organization in the factories, was a key development in consolidating these new independent unions (MacShane, Plaut and Ward, 1984; Maree, ed., 1987; Marx, 1992: 194–198; Seidman, 1994: 183–193; Adler and Webster, 1995: 79–81). FOSATU was created by 12 unions that had 20,000 members (Baskin, 1991: 25). By November 1983, FOSATU-affiliated unions had organized over 106,000 workers in almost 500 factories (MacShane, Plaut and Ward, 1984: 38).

FOSATU's development is crucial to understand since it was the largest and most militant of the new labor centers,[16] and then it later played a key role in the development of COSATU, an even larger and more politically advanced labor center that was founded in November 1985. In 1985, FOSATU's paid-up membership reached 139,917, and its power came from its affiliates' position in the industrial economy. FOSATU unions "had become the majority unions in the motor, tyre and rubber industries, as well as in chemicals, metal and engineering, paper and printing, furniture, transport sectors and (outside the Western Cape) textiles" (Kraak, 1993: 185).

Jeremy Baskin writes:

> FOSATU was established as a tight federation with strongly centralized decision making, and policies binding on affiliates. It pioneered the principle of direct worker control in South Africa, with worker delegates constituting a majority in all structures of the federation. It also developed the system of union branch executive committees composed of delegates from every factory, rather than a branch executive that was elected at an annual general meeting. Other key FOSATU principles involved non-racialism, shopfloor organization, a stress on developing shop stewards, and worker independence from political organizations. It favoured intensive organizing, based on the targeting of key plants (Baskin, 1991: 26).

Glenn Adler and Eddie Webster also detailed FOSATU's approach to the strategic use of power: ". . . (1) democratic processes to win voluntary consent from members for mobilization and for restraint when necessary, and (2) tactical flexibility, which included a capacity to distinguish principles from tactics and to choose those tactics most likely to succeed, including negotiation and compromise" (Adler and Webster, 1995: 80).

Key to FOSATU's organizational development was the principle of members' controlling their unions. "FOSATU argued strongly that workers on the shopfloor should dominate all union structures and control union officials, and insisted on mandates, report-backs, and worker control" (Baskin, 1991: 31). According to Anthony Marx (1992: 195), "FOSATU was most clearly distinguished on building unions from a strong base of member participation and on pursuing its members' economic interests as workers."[17]

Politically, however, FOSATU limited itself. Because it prioritized the building of strong unions in workplaces, it generally refused to get involved in "community" issues that focused on issues outside of the workplace as it "concentrated on consolidating its industrial presence" (Kraak, 1993: 220).[18] This caused considerable tension, especially early in FOSATU's development, between community-based organizations and FOSATU unions. Part of this hesitation was from an understanding of SACTU's (South African Congress of Trade Unions) experiences in the 1950s–early 1960s where engagement in larger political campaigns brought on the direct enmity and repression of the state, which SACTU unions had generally been unable to withstand. But part of the hesitation was due to recognizing the diverse membership of FOSATU-affiliated unions, a considerable number who had no experience of community organization or political struggle, or who belonged to outside organizations such as Inkatha, which would oppose mobilization around community issues (Hindson, 1987; see also Seidman, 1994: 186). Thus, there was a real need to consolidate its members, and this took time.

> The perspectives of the FOSATU unions were gradually changed in the recognition battles and struggles against the Industrial Council system. Regional and cross-union co-operation brought a greater uniformity of perspective among its affiliates, and in February 1982, FOSATU led the stoppage to protest at the death in police detention of AFCWU organiser Neil Aggett. Until then, the stay-away had been the primary way in which workers had asserted political demands by withholding their labour power. The Aggett stoppage was a political gesture at the workplace and it widened the methods of struggle used by workers (Kraak, 1993: 220).

Despite the unwillingness to engage in community-based issues, FOSATU came to understand the importance of community issues, not only for its members for all members of black communities. Hindson (1987: 213) argues that the key force in this change was that union members "were becoming involved in community based action" and that there was a high degree of frustration "at the lack of union assistance in fighting township issues" (see also Seidman, 1994: 197–203; 227–254).[19]

FOSATU also came to recognize the validity of the community organizations' mobilizing abilities; the challenge was how to consolidate organization after successful mobilization. One development that had important ramifications for FOSTATU and the labor movement was the establishment in the early 1980s of local area-based shop stewards' councils. These brought together stewards from a township or an industrial area, and they began taking up more general issues, such as developing strike support for colleagues in neighboring factories, and stopping shack destruction in nearby communities (Baskin, 1991: 30–31). This ultimately led to a broader conceptualization of politics by the union center.

By FOSATU's second congress in April 1982, delegates took positions on a number of explicitly political issues:

- Supported democracy under the principles of one man [sic], one vote, and majority rule;
- Rejected the homeland policy of the South African government which had set up "Bantustans"—contrived "countries" to which black Africans were arbitrarily assigned, largely on the basis of language and culture, depriving them of their South African citizenship and turning them into foreigners in their own country;
- Argued that wealth should be democratically produced and equally distributed;
- Refused to affiliate to any party political organization;
- Planned to take part in campaigns establishing a more just society, but only after thorough discussion with FOSATU-affiliated union members at the grassroots level (ICFTU, 1984: 42–43).

The labor center also sought to join other unions with whom they could ally with, and indicated that it was willing to dissolve FOSATU to create a larger, more inclusive labor center.

At the same time that FOSATU unions were building strong organizations on the shop floor, "community unions" were emerging. These were unions that had been more directly inspired by community-bases struggles and then later, the UDF—they believed it was impossible to separate workers' demands in the factories from their township problems. These unions were more obviously political than the "workerist" unions in FOSATU, but not as well organized. These unions tended to organize widely across entire communities, but not very extensively within the factories: "their organizational structures were unequal to the task of maintaining a massive post-strike membership or the winning of effective economic gains" (Baskin, 1991: 29).

Members in the two wings of the labor movement—the "workerists" of FOSATU, and the "populists" of the various community unions—recognized the need to build a united labor movement. On the ground, these various unions formed an alliance with civic organizations and youth and student congresses, "actively participating in the series of general strikes and political organizations from late 1984" (Adler and Webster, 1995: 81).

The first mass mobilization was in November 1984, when "800,000 workers stayed away from work and 400,000 students boycotted classes." This was "the beginning of united mass action between organized labour, student and community organizations, with unions taking a central role" (Adler, Maller and Webster, 1992: 318).[20] Hindson points out the importance of this 1984 stayaway to political developments within the union movement: "What distinguished the action taken by the Transvaal unions in support of the students and residents in the townships was that the union and community organizations came together and forged a plan of joint action with specific objectives to take place over an agreed period of time" (Hindson, 1987: 217). "For the trade unions," write Adler, Maller and Webster (1992: 318), "it marked a decisive break with its previous strategy of remaining aloof from township struggles."

At the same time as these developments were taking place "on the ground," these unions engaged in a series of "unity meetings" between 1981 and late 1985. Finally, on the last weekend in November 1985, unions from five different traditions joined together to create the Congress of South African Trade Unions or COSATU (see Baskin, 1991: 49–50).[21] At the founding meeting in Durban, there were "760 delegates from 33 unions, representing over 460,000 organized workers" (Baskin, 1991: 53).[22]

The organizational ramifications of COSATU were fairly obvious; if nothing else, by the size and nation-wide geographic reach of the new labor center. However, the political ramifications of the emergence of COSATU were perhaps even more important: this merger between the industrial-based and community-based unions signaled ". . . a strategic compromise in which the integrity of the industrial unions was acknowledged while the new [center] committed itself to participation in the national democratic struggle under the leadership of the ANC" (Adler and Webster, 1995: 82). By February 1986, a resolution was put forward that discussed COSATU's position:

> The resolution noted that the political and economic crisis in the country had resulted in unemployment, starvation and degradation, as well as violent repression. This "repression, hardship and suffering" affected workers not only at their workplaces, but "in every other aspect of their lives and within the communities where they live." COSATU and the working class should thus play a major role in the political sphere and "not hesitate to take political action." The resolution also asserted the independence of COSATU, and spoke of the "independent political interests, position, action and leadership of the working class in the wider political struggle" (Baskin, 1991: 92).

This resolution was adopted a mere two months after the launching of COSATU. Anthony Marx relates that both economic and political goals had to be integrated in the labor movement's experience: "The experience of confronting both employers and the state in constructing unions had led them to appreciate how economic exploitation and political domination were linked and had to be confronted together." Further, they recognized that "an exclusive focus on short-term economic interests could result in complacency once concessions were granted, unless the workers had broader goals" (Marx, 1992: 204–205).

The importance of this type of trade unionism and its moving to the center of the liberation struggle simply cannot be over-emphasized. After the apartheid state enacted the State of Emergency in the country in June 1986, and then banned the UDF in 1988, it was COSATU that kept the anti-apartheid movement inside the country together, allowing it to survive (Baskin, 1991); in fact, "the labor movement emerged at the height of the state of emergency as the de facto leader of the internal democratic opposition" (Adler and Webster, 1995: 92).[23] Had COSATU been destroyed, it is all but certain that Nelson Mandela would still be residing in his cell on Robben Island—assuming he had remained alive—instead of being the former President of South Africa!

But COSATU was not destroyed, despite swimming in a maelstrom. Its paid-up membership grew from approximately 460,000 when launched in late 1985 to almost 1.5 million members in late 1990 (Baskin, 1991: 448). It helped create the political-economic conditions that forced the state to un-ban oppositional organizations (including the African National Congress, the Pan African Congress, and the South African Communist Party); free a number of political prisoners—most notably Mandela; and began dismantling apartheid between 1990 and 1992, all which led to free elections in 1994.[24] As of the middle of the decade, COSATU remained in the center of the post-apartheid transitions (Marcuse, 1995).

DISCUSSION

In this chapter, I have presented the context and development of the new trade union organizations in South Africa between 1973–1992. Although this paper has been primarily written to respond to labor-related issues, because I join both labor and social movement theory, my research provides data related to a number of theory-related issues. I report some of the more significant findings, moving from social movement theory concerns toward labor movement theory concerns, and simultaneously from the more macro-level level to the more meso- and micro-levels and then back to the more macro-level:

- Labor movements in their emergent stage can be understood similarly to other social movements, and so appropriate social movement theory is applicable to them at this stage of their development.

- We should be extremely reluctant to attribute social movement emergence to "structural" factors: cultural factors—in and of themselves and not as a result or reflection of structure factors—are important (see Laraña, Johnston and Gusfield, eds., 1994; Darnovsky, Epstein, and Flacks, eds., 1995; Johnston and Klandermanns, eds., 1995). Melucci's and Mueller's focus on cultural identity needs to receive more critical examination. Certainly the role of emotions must be added in considerations of development of collective identities (Goodwin, Jasper and Polletta, eds., 2001). This work needs to be considered in both "developing" country contexts as well as in "developed" countries.
- The concept of "political opportunity" creating space for social movement emergence seems of less and less importance. It certainly was not relevant in Durban in 1973, or for the founding of CCAWUSA in 1975, although political space was created by the Wiehahn reforms in 1979 that offered legitimacy to black unions that registered with the government. However, I argue that the reforms came after the state had tried but failed to repress the new unions. And just because the government and some "enlightened capitalists" were willing to accept unionization, it didn't mean that the unions would agree to such controls—in fact, there was strong debate over how to respond to the offer (Lewis, 1987)—or that every firm would accept unionization. To this day, for example, agriculture as a whole remains still remains all-but-unionized. Further, just because a researcher after the fact defines a situation as a "political opportunity," this does not mean that activists on the ground saw it, or even if they saw it, that they understood it at the time.[25]
- And finally, noting the dismemberment of the formal system of apartheid, unbanning of a number of political organizations, and the implementation of a presidential vote on the basis of one person-one vote, we have to make note that social movement mobilization can have qualitative effects on the political/institutional and cultural bases of an established social order (see Giugni, McAdam and Tilly, eds., 1999).

There are also meso- and micro-level findings immediately of interest:

- We should not treat a movement as a given, but rather focus on how it has been built: without an examination of the processes by which the non-racial, but black-led labor movement in South Africa developed, our findings would have remained at the most general and least important levels as far as validating theoretical approaches to social movements, and we simply could not describe how this labor movement had developed.
- Creation of a collective identity is a precursor for consciously collective action: without the efforts by the "Black Consciousness" movement, and

the diffusion of its ideology through particularly black students and then later black workers, we cannot explain the massive mobilization by blacks in South Africa. We also saw this in the example of CCAWUSA, the black Commercial, Catering and Allied Workers' Union: without efforts to consciously organize their union, these workers would not have been able to expand their conceptualization of what a union should be and, accordingly, would never have tackled such difficult issues among members as those related to women's rights or parental rights.

- That the status quo must be challenged at the cultural level in terms of legitimacy before mass collective action is feasible. Without challenging the legitimacy of the status quo, any imagining of the creation of alternative social forces, much less an alternative social order, will not be accepted by the broad masses of people even if they rationally "make sense."
- That the creation of collective identities is central to creating social action, although it is never enough in and of itself. While individuals can and do partake in "exemplary actions" that are dramatic and spark the imagination, unless efforts are collectivized, they are unsustainable. To do this, people must become united in groups and each group must create a collective identity that not only results in agreement to engage in certain actions but also results in an emotional commitment to the continuation and well-being of the group itself, and this must nurture and affect the self-identity of the individual group member.
- That conscious collective action is the product of widespread interaction, negotiation and conflict, and can continue only when actors are self-conscious about their efforts, and willing to develop continually evolving organizations with innovative strategies and tactics. Struggles motivated by Black Consciousness, important in and of themselves, were found nonetheless to be insufficient to the struggle for liberation; and critical actors recognized the need to surpass and transcend these limitations if they were to move the struggle forward: this led to the formation of non-racial unions and community-based organizations, and this led to mass struggles and eventually the development of COSATU.

With these issues now mentioned, there are three labor theory-related, macro-level issues on which I wish to comment: the first two—which support some of my earlier claims—I touch on only briefly; when discussing the third issue, concerning whether the new unions of COSATU can be conceptualized as "social movement" unions, I do so in greater detail.

To address the earlier claims that labor movements involve more than just workers and their organizations, and the central role of collective identities in labor mobilization, I refer to the work of Gay Seidman, who addresses both of these issues. She points out that the emerging labor movements, especially in Durban in 1973, included networks of students and intellectuals—who publicized low wages and legitimized workers' grievances to the public and other workers—as well as clandestine factory activists, although she does not know the extent of the latter (Seidman, 1994: 176). I would go farther and add that networks of women, unemployed workers, students and other groups—both on an individual basis and as mobilized members of community organizations—helped support the emerging unions. I think the point has been sufficiently established: *labor movements include more than just workers, and many, if not most, unions could not survive without this support, at least initially.*

Supporting my earlier claim of the centrality of collective identity to mobilization, Seidman focuses on the class identities of the workers: "Undoubtedly, the most striking features of the labor movements that emerged in Brazil and South Africa in the 1970s was the creation of working-class organizations and identities . . ." (Seidman, 1994: 149).

I also suggested, through discussing the efforts by the Commercial, Catering and Allied Workers' Union of South Africa (CCAWUSA) to win parental rights for their members, that "class" issues and "class" identity went beyond productionist-related issues or even broad community-development issues, and specifically included issues around procreation, birthing, care and development of children. Thus, when even limiting consideration to only "class" issues, we cannot limit this consideration to production-related or community-development issues.

Also, Seidman downplays the racial identities of the workers, ignoring that the overwhelming majority of workers who mobilized in the new unions in South Africa were *black* (including Asian and "coloured") workers—this was not an across-the-board class mobilization as the vast majority of white workers did not join the new unions. The point stands that *collective identity is crucial to labor mobilization;* I only disagree with Seidman on the importance of racial identity, to which I believe she fails to give sufficient attention.

Where she is correct is that it was only with the creation and development of black workers' identities as workers (i.e., their class identity) that these workers were able to build powerful labor organizations that (1) surpassed the efficacy of multi-class organizations such as the UDF in the struggle (see Marx, 1992), and (2) were able to withstand the repression of the apartheid state. This eventually forced the state to negotiate with the opposition movement, dismantle the apartheid state, and hold free elections in 1994 (Baskin, 1991; Kraak, 1993; Adler and Webster, 1995; Marcuse, 1995).

The key issue at hand, however, is whether the development of COSATU and its member organizations between 1972–92 fit my conceptualization of social movement unionism or not. Therefore, I return to my conceptualization, of which there are five basic components:

- Workers' struggles are seen as only one of many types of efforts to qualitatively change society, and therefore are neither the only site nor necessarily the primary site for political struggle and social change; their organizations ally with mutually-respecting social movements when possible;
- Trade unions and other labor organizations are controlled by the members, and not any external organization;
- Unions and other labor organizations fight exploitation and oppression within the workplace, as well as domination both external from and internal to the larger social order;
- Struggles for control over workers' daily work life, pay and conditions are consciously understood as being intimately connected with and inseparable from the national political-economic situation; and
- Unions and other labor organizations are autonomous from capital, the state and political parties, yet willing to interact with, and consider modifying their perspectives on the basis of negotiations with the movements that it is allied with and that it has equal relations.

Although I did not set any specific requirements for fitting his conceptualization of social movement unionism—are three out of five or four out of five conditions sufficient, or must a labor center or affiliated unions meet every condition?—I think it is safe to say that any labor organization that largely incorporates these components into the self-conceptualization on which it acts qualifies as implementing social movement unionism.

In this case, it seems unquestionable that the type of trade unionism created and carried out by COSATU and its affiliated unions qualifies as social movement unionism: they see trade unions as only one site of struggle, not necessarily the only one or even the pre-eminent site, although they would probably argue that the unions are the "most important" site, and they ally with other social movements when possible; they see the unions as being controlled by their members and not by any external organizations; they see conditions in the workplace as being intimately linked with the national political-economic situation; they fight exploitation and oppression in the workplace along with domination from within and without the larger social order; and they are autonomous from other political organizations.

This finding, however—that COSATU meets the criteria for social movement unionism—also testifies to the validity of the conceptualization. We now have findings that two of the three most dynamic labor movements in the world—KMU and COSATU—specifically meet the criteria of this conceptualization.[26]

This finding is even stronger when it is realized that these labor movements exist in two very different countries: South Africa is classified as a "newly industrializing country" (NIC), with extensive industrial development, while the Philippines is at a lower-level of economic development; the countries, both colonized at one time, have completely different colonial histories, which has affected subsequent "development"—South Africa was colonized by settlers from The Netherlands and then England, while the Philippines was colonized by Spain and the United States; South Africa's colonization was by settlers who established a racial dictatorship, while the Philippines was occupied by outsiders who intermarried and created a mestizo elite; and South Africa has incredible amounts of extractive natural resources, while the Philippines' has qualitatively less. While I'm sure that other useful comparisons could be made, it should be clear that a new type of trade unionism has been developed by specific labor centers in these countries, countries that differ qualitatively: this new type of trade unionism is not a product of similar material factors.

But out of these findings that are of immediate relevance to researchers, what has been learned that is of direct relevance to new emerging labor movements? I project four:

- The crucial role of cultural factors: establishing collective identity is key to mobilization, and offers the best chance to resist the inevitable repression that is unleashed in response, whether physical, ideological and/or legal. This collective identity can be established through conscious deliberation or participation in collective action;
- Central to establishing this collective identity must be a decision on the type of trade unionism the group wants to establish. This decision, which is not a one-time thing but must be consistently constructed over time, will affect strategy, tactics, and relationships with other social movements and people's organizations, as well as internal developments such as educational programs. Evidence from my study of the KMU and now this examination of the new unions in South Africa suggests that creating social movement unions provides workers with the best chance of being an independent political force for social change—however they define it—while maintaining internal democracy within their own organizations, at least through the emergent stage of development. More research is required to suggest the best way to proceed during subsequent stages.
- Key to organizational survival as a labor movement is to develop strong organization in each workplace, based on a network of educated, trained

and militant shop stewards who are determined to develop leadership capabilities among rank-and-file members and to ensure further organizational development by organizing members to act to solve their own problems. These stewards should be democratically elected by those whom they are supposed to represent, and the organizational principle should be to resolve issues as close to the grassroots as possible.
- Direct political involvement should be initiated only after the establishment of a strong organizational base in the workplace, and after the discussion and decision by a large proportion of members to do so.

CONCLUSION

Chapters 5 and 11 herein, when combined, has covered a lot of ground to reach its conclusion.

Starting with labor movement theory, I clarified a number of concepts that have been used in a myriad of different ways, seeking to encourage researchers/activists to use common understandings for similar concepts, and suggesting a fruitful way to examine labor movements. I then concluded that it was ideological conceptualizations of trade unionism—initially advanced by activists but necessarily ratified by rank and file workers—that was the most important factor in the development of labor movements, and not material factors.

I then turned to social movement theory, applying it to labor movements in their emergent stage, to explain how labor movements emerged. I particularly focused on the development of collective identity as being central to this process.

Turning to empirical data, I shifted to the mobilization processes in South Africa. I placed these processes within the context of industrialization in a racially stratified social order. I looked at the mobilization of blacks, beginning in the late 1960s, and suggested the impact of their conscienization on other mobilization processes.

And then I looked at the emergence and development of the new unions in South Africa. Based on their location within the social order's production, distribution and exchange processes, the new unions in COSATU built strong, shopfloor-based organizations that were able to withstand repression and united to become a political force for liberation in the country: specifically, they played an absolutely central role in the struggle to overthrow apartheid. I argued that these unions were of the social movement union type.

The mobilization efforts by the South Africans were all the more impressive in face of an economic system that was largely controlled by foreign investors, and under the domination of a repressive state that was bound and determined to maintain the racial hierarchy. While working and living conditions for African workers under this late industrialization process have been terrible, rather than to accede to their situation in a country that has an oversupply of labor, they organized one of the most dynamic labor movements in the world.

These workers' choice of social movement unionism as the type of trade unionism they wanted to develop is inspiring because they identified their interests as workers as part of those of the majority of the population and not separate from nor superior to the majority. This certainly was not predetermined for them. It might be more understandable had they chosen to monopolize a few positions and engaged in some type of economic unionism, but that would not have solved the problem of the racial hierarchy in the country. And while it is not known whether this conceptualization will take them beyond a "defensive" form of social movement unionism, it at least indicates their willingness to confront the larger issues faced by all people of color in South Africa.

A turn to political unionism, say in deference to the African National Congress for example, also would not be totally out of the realm of possibility. Certainly by sending a number of senior COSATU leaders to Parliament after the 1994 elections—that is, after the end of the emergence and challenging period—COSATU weakened itself, and has since been trying to get back on its feet (Adler and Webster, 1995). But COSATU has refused to just submit to ANC leaders, preferring to maintain an independent position and stance, and there has been some significant debate about its relationship with the ANC, as well as with its other formal alliance partner, the South African Communist Party, with some unions calling for COSATU to withdraw from their formal alliance that was established in 1990. Certainly in light of shared political ideologies, additional research must be done in the post-1992 period to see how these relationships have developed, and their effects upon workers.[27]

So how can we understand this selection of social movement unionism as the basis for COSATU's trade unionism, particularly in light of strong arguments that could have been made for engaging in either type of rival unionisms, economic or political unionism? This is where my discussion of social movement theory, with the detailed explanation of movement cultures, becomes so important. Basically, workers moved toward a social movement unionism type of labor movement as they maneuvered in a very difficult field of action. Nothing was predetermined. These workers were trying to figure things out, but from the standpoint of principally standing up for their rights both as economic actors and (potential) political citizens within the social order.

This chapter has found that COSATU and its member unions have been developing a type of trade unionism now known as social movement unionism. This type of trade unionism differs qualitatively from economic- and political-types of trade unionism. And by demonstrating its existence in South Africa, in addition to the Philippines, I have strengthened arguments for the validity of this conceptualization: after initially establishing the existence of SMU based on my research on the KMU, I have now established that my conceptualization of SMU now extends to labor centers beyond the KMU, and in fact, can apply to labor centers in countries at a qualitatively different level of economic development.

Based on all of these conclusions, I then suggested four findings of immediate interest to those who are involved in building new labor movements. The idea has been to learn from past experiences so as to help those who are following in the footsteps.

The effort to examine the emergence and developments of the new unions in South Africa has been a very fruitful one. Not only has it validated my version of social movement unionism in general, but also it has extended this concept to incorporate the new unions in COSATU along with the previous included unions in KMU. Further, this examination has allowed me to extract a number of important findings from the experiences in South Africa, which can now be utilized by subsequently emerging labor movements around the world. It is hoped that this will lead to the further development of other unions and labor centers as social movement-type labor organizations.

NOTES

1. It must be remembered that Rob Lambert and Eddie Webster (1988) claimed that COSATU and its member unions exemplified social movement unionism, and they developed their concept of SMU on that basis. However, my conceptualization (Scipes, 1992a, 1992b)—Chapter 6 herein—went beyond theirs. Now, I'm asking if COSATU fits under my conceptualization? Should it do so, then we can see that my conceptualization fits more than the KMU, and importantly, that it fits labor movements in countries at different levels of development than the Philippines.

2. This is the second part of an article that, to date, has only been published on the internet (Scipes, 2001). The first part was published herein as Chapter 5.

3. It must also be kept in mind that in many countries—perhaps all but the city-states, such as Singapore and Hong Kong—there are a number of regionally-based political economies. In my Philippine study, I focused on four regionally-based political economies: plantation agriculture (in Negros), capitalist agriculture (Mindanao), extractive mining (Cebu), and capitalist industry (Bataan Export Processing Zone). In each of these political economies, the mobilization process differed from the others (Scipes, 1996). Thus, a structural analysis is even more inadequate than I mentioned

in the body, as I discussed above, in Chapter 4. Further comment is beyond the scope of this chapter.

4. I do not agree with Seidman's implicit use of world systems theory, which I find inadequate (cf. Nederveen Pieterse, 1989: 29–45). Nonetheless, she well captures the processes going on within these industrializing countries.

5. South Africa's manufacturing sector has had fairly high rates of growth over a long period of time: from 1920–30, it averaged 4.5 percent per year; from 1930–40, 9.1 percent; from 1940–50, 6.8 percent; from 1950–60, 6.0 percent; from 1960–70, 8.6 percent; and from 1970–80, 5.3 percent (COSATU, 1992: 48). Thanks to Deanne Collins for providing me with a copy of COSATU, 1992.

6. All valuations used in COSATU (1992) are in Rands (R) and listed in constant 1985 values, unless otherwise indicated.

While I do not have comparative economic data for 1985, I have found some indicators for April 1984, which are suggestive: the exchange rate was 1R=US $.80 (one Rand was equal to 80 cents), the *monthly* minimum wage in the metal industry was equivalent to $215.00; and "Prices in the shops for food, clothes, leisure were about the same as Western Europe or North America" (MacShane, Plaut and Ward, 1984: 8).

7. South African Gross Domestic Product (GDP) figures and GDP/person in 1989 are placed in the context of other countries that same year for comparative purposes, with figures from all countries given in US dollar amounts: Japan's GDP was $2,818,520 million ($2.818 billion), and its GDP/person was $22,896; France's respective figures were $995,790 million and $17,007; South Korea's were $211,880 million and $4,997; South Africa's were $80,370 million and $2,296; and Zimbabwe's were $5,250 million and $553.00 (COSATU, 1992: 7). These comparative figures are in US dollar amounts, and must not be confused with values expressed in South African Rands.

8. But this "Black Consciousness" process must not be seen as only taking place in the political realm of society; it was also taking place within the black church (as well as elsewhere). On the changes taking place within the black church, see, for example, Goba, 1988; Kretzschmar, 1986; and Young, 1992. My thanks to Michael Montgomery for bringing these sources to my attention.

9. This is an incredibly truncated account of the changes taking place among the opposition in South Africa during these years—I limit myself to highlights, as I understand them, that had a direct impact on the development of the new unions that ended up in COSATU in the late 1980s.

There is much I simply do not begin to include. I do not discuss the Pan African Congress (PAC), or any of the organizations that emerged in the late 1970s or 1980s that continued in the "black consciousness" tradition, such as AZAPO (Azanian People's Organization), or the unions that developed from them. As important as they were, their importance to the opposition movement pales in comparison to organizations of the non-racial Charterist tradition, which includes the African National Congress (ANC), the United Democratic Front (UDF) and COSATU. For information on the black consciousness-inspired political organizations, see Marx, 1992; for information on black consciousness-inspired trade unions, see Kraak, 1993. I also do not discuss the important role of the South African Communist Party, which has long been allied with the Charterist organizations (see Pillay, 1990). I also do not discuss external efforts, whether by forces in exiles such as the ANC leadership or SACTU, or the global solidarity movement that emerged around the world in support of the peoples of South Africa.

10. This is an extract from a publication titled "The Durban Strikes," which was initially published in 1973. In the extract, not only is there a description of the spread of strikes, but a more in-depth examination and analysis of conditions, strikes, and developments in the textile industry is provided.

Seidman (1994: 174–175) presents evidence that there was some clandestine activity by activists linked to SACTU in the Durban strikes, although she is unable to determine to what extent or how extensively these activists were involved.

11. Kraak (1993) emphasizes "class" issues, which are certainly important; unfortunately, he tends to downplay racial issues. [Seidman (1994) takes a similar approach.] Trade unions had long-been recognized as legitimate for white workers—it was the efforts by black workers to extend this legitimacy to black workers that made these battles so intense and violent. See Baskin, 1991; Friedman, 1987; MacShane, Plaut and Ward, 1984; Maree, ed., 1987; Marx, 1992: 189–234.

12. I wonder how many US unions have won these levels of benefits around reproduction issues for their members . . .

Thanks to Jeremy Daphne for providing me with a copy of SACCWU, 1991.

13. For a discussion of the development of industrial law—which attempts to regulate labor relations—within the context of state regulation and control, see Maree and Budlender, 1987; for a discussion of the development of industrial law between 1979–1988, see Kraak, 1993: 113–125.

14. For a description of union organization in a number of industries—automobile, building and construction, chemical, longshoring (docks), food, insurance and clerical, metal and engineering, mining, municipal workers, print and paper, retail, textile and clothing, and transport—see MacShane, Plaut and Ward, 1984: 91–110.

15. Kraak (1993: 127–173) provides a wealth of information regarding workers' strikes between 1970–1987. He analyzes them chronologically as well as by the issues over which they were fought; for example, registration under industrial law and recognition; struggles against official bargaining machinery (including industrial councils by selected industries); and struggles against employer and government controls. He notes strikes against racism in the workplace, and struggles to improve women workers' situations including maternity (such as for 12 months unpaid maternity leave with guaranteed return to job) and parental leave. He analyzes strikes against retrenchments (lay-offs), for pensions, against disinvestment. And he reports new tactics and new trends in workers' fights, including company-wide strikes (beginning in 1983) and factory occupations (1985), as well as efforts to build unity through shopfloor activity, and efforts to build alliances between unions and community organizations.

16. Although not all unions were affiliated to a labor center—some remained independent—there were three major labor centers of new unions by 1984: FOSATU (Federation of South African Trade Unions), CUSA (Council of Unions of South Africa) and AZACTU (Azanian Congress of Trade Unions). Of these, only FOSATU

was organized on non-racial grounds; members, elected leaders and full-time staff could be of any racial background, including white. In 1984, FOSATU-affiliated unions had 122,302 paid-up members. CUSA-affiliated unions claimed 99,223 members in 1983/84, but these were only signed-up members and not the more accurate paid-up membership category. AZACTU-affiliated unions claimed 30,513 members in 1983–84, although only about half were paid-up (Kraak, 1993: 256–259).

These labor centers also differed by militancy. "In 1982, FOSATU-affiliated unions were involved in 145 strikes with 90,000 workers taking part. This compares with CUSA where 10,000 workers took part in 13 strikes, or SAAWU [South African Allied Workers Union, an unaffiliated black union-KS], which organized six strikes involving 2,600 workers" (MacShane, Plaut and Ward, 1984: 58).

17. For details on FOSATU's organization and structure—specifically addressing the key role of shop stewards, branches and locals, full-time officials, white organizers, recruitment, how unions are financed, communications, training and education—see MacShane, Plaut and Ward, 1984: 64–74.

18. MacShane, Plaut and Ward (1984: 126–129) discuss the political role of the black unions, comparing the position of the General Workers' Union (representing FOSATU's position), CUSA, and two UDF-affilliates, the Municipal and General Workers' Union and the General and Allied Workers' Union. They present the positions of these different organizations in their appendices.

19. Seidman tends to see developments in community organization and struggle as a product of class consciousness; that is, that political consciousness developed among workers in the factories, who then transmitted their analysis and understandings to community members who, in turn, adopted them as their own and acted accordingly. From my reading of the literature, I do not think this is an accurate description of what happened, nor do I think it is an accurate analysis of what did happen.

It is clear that some workers (as well as probably most community members) got politicized in community struggles (such as those against influx controls, or in those for adequate housing, schools, services, etc.) and took their new understandings into the factories. (This is a schematized version of what I understand happened, as workers are community members at the same time, as are their family members, friends, etc.) (Marx, 1992). In any case, I think a much more accurate analysis would see the interpenetration of race- and class-related understandings, with racial-consciousness being primary at some times and class-consciousness being primary at others. (I would also include gender-consciousness in this interpenetration as well—see, for example, SACCAWU, 1991.) Further discussion is beyond the scope of this chapter.

20. For details of labor's—and particularly COSATU's—involvement in mass mobilization, which was central to forcing the democratic transition that repudiated apartheid between 1985–1991, see Adler, Maller and Webster (1992). Adler and Webster (1995) place this labor mobilization in the context of "transition theory," arguing that "a mobilized civil society and powerful social movements—especially the labor movement—played a central and constructive role in creating the conditions for the transition, shaping its character, and indeed in legitimizing the transition process itself" in South Africa (Adler and Webster, 1995: 77), and thus need to be included in transition theory (pp. 99–100). I make a parallel argument in my study of the KMU

in the Philippines, especially in the transition from Marcos to Aquino (Scipes, 1996), but without the theoretical specificity of Adler and Webster.

21. For a contemporary discussion of the key issues facing COSATU at its founding, see Dropkin, 1985. See also *International Labour Reports,* 1985.

22. Baskin's 1991 book is the recognized standard on the emergence and development of COSATU during its first five years. His is an incomparable account from inside, at the highest levels of the organization.

Kraak (1993: 180–205) provides additional information on the new unions, including more on the unions that joined to create NACTU. Kraak also places the struggle to build the new unions in the context of the struggle against apartheid, despite underplaying it. Kraak presents data on workers' responses to calls for stay-aways and on-site stoppages between 1982–1987, by region and by specific call (Kraak, 1993: 232–233), as well as specific information on unions affiliated to COSATU and NACTU, and growth of union membership of the affiliated unions between 1980 and 1986 (Kraak, 1993: 252–259).

23. Key to COSATU's emerging power was the "stayaway," the joining of unions, community organizations and students to fight for demands, both in the industrial relations realm as well against state policies not directly related to the workplace. In November 1991, COSATU led a stayaway against state efforts to institute a Value Added Tax. The stayaway lasted two days, with estimates that 3.8 million people participated on the first day, and 3.4 million on the second (Adler, Maller and Webster, 1992: 332). For a discussion of the development of stayaways, from 1950 to 1991, see Adler, Maller and Webster, 1992: 312–337.

24. For a contemporary report of the situation and issues facing COSATU—and its allies, the African National Congress (ANC) and the South African Communist Party (SACP)—immediately after the unbanning of these organizations and the release of Nelson Mandela, see Pillay, 1990.

25. The concept of political opportunity was even less relevant to my study of the KMU in the Philippines. Despite helping to replace the dictator Marcos with the "elite" democrat Corazon Aquino—a situation I think most researchers who accept the concept would label as a "political opportunity"—the KMU suffered more repression (deaths, torture, physical assaults) under Aquino than under Marcos (Scipes, 1996).

26. Seidman (1994) makes a strong claim that the new unions in Brazil that joined in CUT developed similarly to those in South Africa. I think she is correct: evidence I've seen to date suggests that she is. However, she focuses on the collective identities developed out of the industrial processes and, particularly in South Africa, downplays collective identities developed in struggle against racial oppression. Anthony Marx (1998) certainly argues the case for more attention to racial issues in both Brazil and South Africa (and the United States).

Jeffrey Sluyter-Beltrão (2010: 4–8), using a truncated version of my conceptualization of SMU (see Sluyter-Beltrão, 2010: 6), specifically argues that the concept of social movement unionism applies to the CUT of Brazil.

Seidman (1994: 264–272) also suggests similar development among the new unions in South Korea. Initially, I had thought she was correct, although I argued that these unions, too, needed a stronger argument. However, after considering the very strong case made by Hagen Koo (2001) that the Korean workers and their organizations did *not* develop as social movement unions, I no longer consider them as exemplars of SMU.

Work to date, therefore, has confirmed that the CUT, KMU and COSATU each has developed a type of trade unionism that fits my conceptualization of SMU.

27. Peter Rachleff (2001) reports a case, at Volkswagen South Africa, that took place in early 2000, whereby insurgent workers refused to accept a deal negotiated by their union (NUMSA) and supported by leaders of both COSATU and the ANC, including Thabo Mbeki, the President of South Africa. Further research is needed to determine if this is an individual case or symptomatic of something much larger. But it raises the question for future investigation on the relationship between social movement unions and political movements they support.

For another paper, that I only found years after writing the article that served as the basis for this chapter, that largely supports my report, but then discusses further the shift of COSATU from social movement to another type of unionism (although not put in those terms), see Rachleff (2000). Further comment is beyond the scope of this chapter.

Chapter Twelve

Building International Labor Solidarity in the Face of Political-Economic Globalization Processes

The Case of the KMU Labor Center of the Philippines

The political-economic globalization processes that many sociologists have only just become aware of have actually been going on for an extremely long time. They reached qualitatively greater development levels in the 10th Century with the Crusades, in the 16th Century with the new global trade centered around northwestern Europe, in the 19th Century with the hegemony of the British Empire, and again in the mid-20th Century with US hegemony over the non-Soviet part of the world.[1]

Yet as the proponents of US imperialism proclaim victory over their recently disintegrated Soviet foes, the internal conflict within the US Empire—hidden in the face of Cold War imperatives—has become more obvious to many. First, there is increasing competition *between* the state-capital alliances of different countries. This is generally referred to as international competition between countries, such as the US and Japan, but in reality, it is competition between the different state-capital alliances. And second, there is increased conflict *within* each country, as the state-capital alliances try to expand their control and their ability to create profits.

The increased internal competition has meant greater attacks on working people. This is currently taking place in both the more economically developed countries and the less economically developed countries. Generally, these attacks have focused on the most vulnerable members of society, but as they have gained steam, these attacks have begun affecting institutions and processes that have served the interests of broad sectors within each social order.

Where democratic and progressive labor movements exist—and as we know, not all labor movements are democratic and progressive—they are among the greatest impediments to the plans of the state-capital alliance. But, besides being key targets in each country for "their" respective alliance, more importantly, these democratic and progressive labor movements are also key *actors* in the struggle for democracy and social development. One of the ways these labor movements are acting is by trying to unite with workers around the world; that is, through building international labor solidarity for the purposes of mutual support and encouragement to challenge both their respective state-capital alliances and their resulting social orders, and the global political-economic order in which their countries are enmeshed.[2]

In this chapter, attention is focused on the *Kilusang Mayo Uno* (KMU) Labor Center of the Philippines, and its efforts to build international labor solidarity.[3] The KMU sees building and communicating labor internationalism as a singular process that, in this case, allows one to discuss what is being developed and how this is being communicated at the same time. To put this into a theoretical perspective, the literature on both internationalism—and especially labor internationalism—and the literature of alternative communications, under which this discussion fits, must be discussed. Then the case of the KMU is presented, and the process by which it creates international labor solidarity is examined. Greatest attention is placed on KMU's yearly International Solidarity Affair, which, as far as can be discovered, is a unique effort within labor internationally. This chapter concludes by suggesting that if labor organizations around the world want to build international labor solidarity, then there is much they can learn from the practice of the KMU.

INTERNATIONALISM AND ALTERNATIVE COMMUNICATION THEORY

There has been a major revival in the practice and communication of international labor solidarity by workers and their allies in a number of countries of the world since 1984,[4] and theorization about this,[5] but there is very little known about the *process* by which international labor solidarity is actually created. To theoretically understand this process, one example of which is discussed below, we must examine relevant literature.

Labor Internationalism

Rather than trying to survey the field of labor internationalism, which has previously been done by Peter Waterman (see especially Waterman, 1988d, 1998), and because Waterman has made the most consistent and extensive efforts to theoretically and politically understand this issue, we start with his conceptualization. After reviewing this, a somewhat different approach is suggested, and then the implications for the KMU are discussed.

Waterman's Conceptualization

Waterman suggests that the understanding of labor internationalism must be placed in the larger context of *internationalisms* (plural), including "Third-World" solidarity movements, "Third-World" aid and development policy, feminism, environmentalism, etc.: "It is necessary today to talk of internationalisms in the plural and to recognize this plurality as essential to the meaning of a contemporary internationalism" (Waterman, 1988d: 64).

Waterman then defines labor internationalism as a general term including "workers at the shopfloor level, of working class communities, of trade unions and labour-oriented parties and of socialist intellectuals," and that labor internationalism takes place "where and in so far as labour rejects subordination to capital, statism and imperialism, and recognizes the interpenetration of its national and international interests" (Waterman, 1988d: 64–65).

The place where new forms of labor internationalism are being developed are overwhelmingly in "third world" countries. In a later article, Waterman (1990) discusses documents from South Africa, Latin America, South Korea and the Philippines that typify the new forms of labor internationalism. He critiques each of these documents. Noting especially that they ignore workers in the "second world" (i.e., the communist countries before the changes in Eastern Europe and the Soviet Union in 1989–90), Waterman discusses labor internationalism in regard to these workers. From out of this discussion, he develops 12 criteria for labor internationalism, although he fails to prioritize or discuss how they interact. He concludes with:

> Implicit in these propositions is the following understanding: that the development of a new internationalism requires contributions 1) from West, East and South, and a dialog between worker movements in each of these areas; 2) that a new internationalism requires contributions from many international movements (women, peace, ecological, etc.); 3) that whilst labour is not the privileged bearer of the new internationalism, it is essential to it (Waterman, 1990: 45).

But how is this to take place? Waterman suggests two major principles that he thinks are central for the development of labor internationalism: it must be "practical rather than ideological in nature" and that "it should be simultaneously addressed to the Third, First and Second Worlds"[6] (Waterman, 1990: 46). He explains:

> By suggesting it should be practical, I mean it should be drawn from worker practice rather than traditional socialist, nationalist or other theory. We have surely had enough of the ideological internationalisms, which ended as the internationalisms of ideologues. An internationalism based on workers' interests,

> capacities and aspirations will surely have more meaning and be longer lasting. Being non-ideological in origin does not mean that it will be without values—particularly those of democracy, equality and solidarity (to slightly update the secular trinity of the French Revolution). Nor does it mean that it will not result in a new *programme*—that is, in a set of proposals to guide social action and for further discussion. But "being practical rather than ideological" also means proposing activities that can be achieved rather than calling for an apocalyptical transformation ("Workers of the World Unite . . . ," etc.) that cannot be achieved in this lifetime, and that some will in any case reject.
>
> By suggesting that it be simultaneously addressed to the Third, First and Second Worlds, I mean it should incorporate an understanding of the increasing interpenetration of social processes and increasing identity, or similarity, of worker struggles. It does not mean ignoring or repressing Third World "interests, capacities and aspirations," but of seeing and expressing these in a way that maximises their relevance to workers elsewhere (Waterman, 1990: 46).

In short, labor internationalism cannot be limited to being only between workers of the first and third worlds, but can only be truly developed when it takes into consideration and includes workers everywhere in the world.

Discussion of Waterman's Conceptualization

Waterman's thinking is clear and has a sophistication lacking in most other accounts. He argues, in fact, that traditional labor and socialist internationalism might have been more developed around democratic and national issues than specifically proletarian ones, even at their peak. And conceptually, he suggests that to understand labor internationalism, we must include internationalist subjects, purposes, forms (spaces, strategy, direction and scope), organization and leadership.

But there is still something lacking. While these points are well-taken, they beg the issue that I think needs to be confronted: how can we evaluate the labor internationalism that takes place?

Rather than limit our understanding of labor internationalism to a "shopping list" of propositions—Waterman advances 12 propositions but implies that all are equally important, making them practically useless—it seems helpful to recognize that there are different levels of labor internationalism and they should be prioritized. By suggesting that some efforts are more developed (or even more desirable!) than others, I am not suggesting that those less desirable should be negated—as in saying, if they don't meet my standards, they're "reactionary," harmful or even worse—but rather it implies that they should be appreciated for what they accomplish, while suggesting more can be done.

With that understanding, I suggest there are three levels of labor internationalism. This can be conceptualized as a series of concentric bands, with the more encompassing surrounding those less so, merging together rather than remaining discrete, so that each successive band incorporates the previous one:

> Level One: Workers cooperate with each other across international boundaries: this can include everything from letter writing and donating funds up to and including taking direct action (sabotage, "hot cargoing"/black-listing of goods and equipment, strikes) in support of other workers' labor and democratic struggles.
>
> Level Two: Workers help people in the "target" country change their social order: thus workers supporting social movement unions that are specifically fighting to change their social order; workers supporting different social sectors such as women who are struggling to change the social order, as well as workers supporting liberation struggles as a whole, would be forms of this level of labor internationalism.
>
> Level Three: Workers in one country struggle to change their *own* social order so as to be able to both support peoples in other countries struggling to change their respective social orders, and to live in solidarity and on a more equitable level with people throughout the world.

Approaching labor internationalism in this manner recognizes the reality of imperialist (oppressor/oppressed; dominator/dominated) power relations in the world, and suggests that ending them is better than allowing them to continue to exist. And approaching labor internationalism in this manner validates the struggles by workers in an oppressed nation—in this case the Philippines—as being just as important as those by workers in an oppressor nation—such as the United States—when they struggle to change their respective social order: by challenging their social order, both internally as well as its external relations, workers confront dominative power that is ultimately the very basis for their own subjugation.

Implications for the KMU

With an understanding of these different levels of labor internationalism, the labor internationalism being practiced by the KMU is of the third level. However, especially in seeking international labor solidarity from workers in the more economically developed countries (MEDCs),[7] its efforts in seeking support would fit with the second aspect; that is, they are trying to get workers in the MEDCs to support them in their efforts to change their own social order.

Locating their efforts in the second level of labor internationalism includes worker-to-worker cooperation, but it specifically includes building support for KMU efforts in the face of harassment and intervention by the Philippine state, whether by legal or illegal forces.[8] This also allows supporters in the United States to challenge efforts by the US Government to send aid and give trading privileges to the Philippine government, giving opportunities for supporters to address issues through invoking campaigns about "labor rights"[9] which, in turn, allows other ways for international labor solidarity to be built. It also provides KMU supporters in the United States the opportunity to challenge the AFL-CIO's international operations in the Philippines. Furthermore, this aspect of labor internationalism also allows KMU supporters in every country to challenge international labor organizations, such as the International Union of Food and Allied Workers Organizations (IUF), when they attack the KMU (see Scipes, 1989b).[10]

Prioritizing different levels of international labor solidarity provides criteria by which solidarity work can be measured and suggests additional work that can be undertaken.

It is important to locate the KMU's efforts to build international labor solidarity within labor internationalism theory before going on to communications theory. But having done that, we can now proceed.

Alternative Communications Theory

Before evaluating the KMU's efforts as a form of internationalist labor communication, we must review relevant communications theory. Because the KMU's minimum project is to extend mass democracy throughout the entire social order, this specifically requires that we review media theory that addresses the role of building democracy within social conflicts.

In this section, I review two accounts of media involved in social struggle from less economically developed countries—one from South Africa (Tomaselli and Louw, 1989), and the other from Mexico (Stangelaar, 1986)—as well as refer to Peter Waterman's work in The Netherlands where he is trying to develop propositions supporting the development of internationalist communication (Waterman, 1988b). After reviewing each, I then discuss their respective perspectives and suggest what they might mean to this study of the KMU's efforts as a communications strategy.

However, the issue of communications goes beyond "simple" communication. As will be seen, the struggle to establish a "people's media"—media that is squarely on the side of the disempowered in the battle to change the social order—is, in reality, a struggle to democratize society. Thus the relevance of communications theory to the KMU extends far beyond "just" building international labor solidarity: it is crucial to its very vision of a new social order.

Several studies are addressed that run, in relation to my concerns, from the more general to the more specific.

Tomaselli and Louw

Keyan Tomaselli and Eric Louw are two activists/academic researchers in South Africa. Their article is an effort to reflect on their overall experiences with a media activist research unit at the University of Natal, and to try to share some of the issues and problems shared by "the movement" in the struggle to democratize South Africa. It is an effort to draw out lessons from their experiences and generalize them.

These authors state that there are two categories of media in South Africa that can be considered "progressive": these are "the social democratic independent, and the left-alternative presses" (Tomaselli and Louw, 1989: 204). Papers of both these categories have a different view of communications than do the traditional presses:

> For the "progressive presses" in particular, communications is a multidimensional grassroots process. Communication for them means facilitating the communication of their readers' experiences, and providing a centre of gravity for the development of a consultative and participatory production process. Communication is basically the articulation of social relations (Tomaselli and Louw, 1989: 209).

Central to this type of communication is participation by those who the media is writing about and establishing "a real two-way communication structure." And media that have been organized on this model have a role much larger than just reporting information: "Media thus generate democracy rather than only information" (Tomaselli and Louw, 1989: 213).

Thus, Tomaselli and Louw argue that in creating a media network to support social change, it should meet several principles. It should

a) help create and maintain grassroots participatory democracy;
b) militate against totalitarian-centralism;
c) provide structures small and accessible enough to allow mass democratic (two-way participation);
d) provide a learning experience that teaches useful technical and social skills as well as a respect for democracy itself; and
e) encourage an engagement with ideology (and awareness of the degradation of self-worth that occurs in the working class under capitalism) (Tomaselli and Louw, 1989: 214).

They also look at the role of theory in building a progressive press, suggest a number of issues that have garnered increasing attention among media workers in South Africa, and report how the Contemporary Cultural Studies Unit at the University of Natal has been contributing to the development of an "alternative" press in their country.

Stangelaar

For the best example of theory of alternative communications found to date, developed through his work on video in Latin America, we turn to the work of Fred Stangelaar, 1986. In this piece, Stangelaar defines what he means by "alternative communication":

> The concept of alternative communication (AC) in this outline is a political one. The adjective "alternative" does not, therefore, refer in the first place to alternative forms, contents or technologies of communication themselves. It refers explicitly to an alternative political tendency, which reflects the concrete daily-life struggles of the subaltern classes. [. . .]
>
> A definition of AC as "the organization, forms, contents and technologies of subaltern communication" would, however, be both too wide and too limited. But it would, above all, be too static. It would be too wide because subaltern or popular communication covers a more specific field of action—one relevant to its ultimate political cause. It would be too limited because it would exclude the communications practices of individuals or groups which do not themselves belong to the subaltern classes but who stimulate and develop subaltern political expression outside the dominant media structure and in a way that allows some control by the subaltern classes or their organizations. It would be, above all, too static because AC developed and continues to develop not only due to the sophistication of subaltern struggle during the various historical stages of capitalist and imperialist development but precisely as a result of the continuing sophistication of the dominant communications structure (Stangelaar, 1986: 11–12).

Within the field of political communication, Stangelaar identifies five different types. However, his distinctions are somewhat unclear so I turn to Peter Waterman's review of Stangelaar, which I think clarifies Stangelaar's murkiness on this particular issue:

> Stangelaar sees the major source for alternative communication in the practical resistance to international capitalism, this implying struggle against racism, sexism, the state and war. He wishes to distinguish four different types of non-dominant communication, [the last being] alternative communication (AC). The four fundamental and interdependent characteristics of the last are: a) a content, language, imagery and symbolism that comes direct from the people and confronts those of the oppressor; b) an orientation toward total social transforma-

> tion; c) a mobilising and organising role, surpassing both vertical and horizontal information flows with a "spiral" communications model; d) an active role in production and distribution by the relevant sector of the people and/or popular organizations (Waterman, 1988b: 24–5).

But the characteristic of alternative communication that makes it different from other types of communication is that "AC aims at a fundamental transformation of not only the dominant communications structure but of society as a whole" (Stangelaar, 1986: 13).[11]

Waterman

From this perspective, Peter Waterman has proposed "10 propositions on "'internationalist' communication." Waterman is interested in developing a concept of internationalist communication, which he defines as "the creation of transterritorial solidarity relations which enrich and empower popular and democratic communities or collectivities by exchanging, sharing, diversifying and synthesizing their ideas, skills and arts" (Waterman, 1988b: 26). In a proposition focusing on labor communication, he writes:

> There may be cases or practices that embody a number of the four fundamental and interdependent characteristics of AC listed earlier. But we can hardly expect such particular cases or practices to each confront the oppressor, be oriented toward a total social transformation and have the participatory, educational and critical characteristics required. The development of such a model therefore requires the identification and analysis of the whole range of international labour communication practices, whether of a non-dominant or a specifically alternative nature (Waterman, 1988b: 29–30).

And then Waterman presents and analyzes the Chasquihuasi radio news service of Santiago, Chile.

Discussion

The most immediate consideration is that all of these studies are related to the expansion of democracy, and of social struggle to create it, from the bottom up through the transformation of the various social orders. Therefore, each is of immediate relevance to this study concerning the KMU.

Tomaselli and Louw provide a clear idea on the interrelationship between the media, although they only address the print media, and developing democracy. They see the development of "progressive" media as being a key issue for the development of democracy and, although I didn't specifically refer to it, the maintenance of democracy once it is achieved; that is, in their work, they also specifically raise the question of "how organic intellectuals of the left can be prevented from becoming a new elite" (Tomaselli and Louw, 1989: 214). But while putting out some excellent thinking and a general "philosophy" of the role of progressive media in the midst of social struggle, and ideas on how this can best be operationalized, they do not provide theory regarding communication itself.

Stangelaar, on the other hand, theorizes different types of communication, and specifically provides some basic principles of alternative communication (AC). He firmly places AC in the social struggle, rather than being removed from it. His conception of communication is not limited to the print media and, in fact, although he writes of AC as a communications process, it seems quite plausible that his conceptualization can extend to include direct, interpersonal communication as well as that which is mediated.

Waterman puts forth 10 propositions on which the concept of "internationalist communication" can be developed. While these are interesting in general, his is the only effort that specifically mentions labor (as in labor movements) as a particular area in which to develop alternative communications.

To summarize, all three of these writings are interesting and useful to our evaluation of the KMU's efforts. Stangelaar in particular provides some clear guidelines from which to approach this communications work, although Tomaselli and Louw provide a context and general lessons from working within that context that are very important to our evaluation, and Waterman suggests the importance of evaluating labor movement efforts. With this background, it is now time to evaluate the KMU's efforts to build international labor solidarity as internationalist labor communication.

KILUSANG MAYO UNO: BUILDING INTERNATIONAL LABOR SOLIDARITY

The KMU was founded on May 1, 1980, during the dark days of the Marcos Dictatorship. Initially including 50,000 workers, it has expanded to include approximately 750,000 workers by the late 1980s–early 1990s.[12]

There were three reasons to found the KMU.[13] First, workplace conditions were terrible. Second, the traditional unions had sold out workers. And third, there was a clear need for a workers' organization that would organize against foreign domination; as long as the country remained subservient to foreign interests, it would be unable to develop and confront the problems that faced its people.[14]

There is something special about the KMU. After all, how did the KMU survive the repression of a dictator, including the arrest and detention of its chairperson, secretary general, and almost 100 top leaders? How could the organization continue after the assassination of its subsequent chairperson, facing massive human rights violations and almost total opposition from the military and the elite? Where did the KMU find the strength to be able to lead and win its second national general workers strike within nine years of its founding?

Part of the KMU's power to endure is related to its basic principles of being "genuine, militant and nationalist." A top leader interviewed in January 1986, who asked that his name not be used, explained what these principles mean to members of the KMU:

> By "genuine," we mean that the KMU is run by its members. The members are given all information and decide the policies which run the organization. By "militant," we mean that the KMU will never betray the interest of the working class, even at the risk of our own lives. The KMU believes workers become aware of their own dignity through collective mass action. By "nationalist," we believe the wealth of the Philippines belongs to the Filipino people and that national sovereignty must never be compromised. The KMU is against the presence of the US bases (quoted in Scipes, 1996: 10).

In other words, the KMU is class conscious, believes that workers learn more from mass struggles than from leaders cutting back room deals, and is determined that Filipinos should control the Philippines. The statement about never betraying the interests of the working class, even at risk of KMU leaders' own lives, is not hyperbole; many KMU organizers, leaders and members have been arrested or killed. The assassination of KMU Chairperson Rolando Olalia in November 1986 (see Jackson, 1987), demonstrated the risks involved in being a "genuine" trade unionist, even for those highest in the organization.

Further organizational strengths stem from the internal processes within KMU-affiliated organizations: the KMU is committed to union democracy and accountability to its membership. It requires sacrifices from leaders and fights internal corruption. It is controlled by its membership and not by any other organization, from either the left or the right.

The KMU is engaged in a project to transform the Philippine social order. But it is a non-violent struggle. As KMU Chairperson Crispin Beltran stated in an interview on May 2, 1990 in Manila, in which he differentiated the KMU's strategy from that of the Communist Party of the Philippines: "The most important consideration is the peaceful and parliamentary character of our struggle: we denounce the use of violence in order to achieve our goal" (Scipes, 1996: 184). Key to this is the full establishment of democracy. And while there are many within KMU who want to take this further, and counter pose socialism to capitalism, this has not been concretized and, in fact, the events in China, Eastern Europe and the former Soviet Union over the past few years have forced some within the KMU to re-evaluate their ideas.

The key to achieving this project of social transformation for the KMU leaders is the development of a strong, democratic labor movement that is based in workplaces throughout the society. This labor movement has built strong ties to other social movements in the Philippines, and has been and continues trying to do the same with labor movements around the world. Thus the concept of labor internationalism has been integral to their project from the beginning. Central to this has been the establishment of an International Department to coordinate this work. The International Department has developed a sophisticated communications strategy by which to carry out the project of building international labor solidarity. I review the overall communications strategy, and then focus specifically on the International Solidarity Affair.

KMU's Six-Part Communications Strategy

There are six aspects to the KMU's communications strategy that has been designed to build labor internationalism, both in general and specifically with the KMU itself. One aspect has been the development of periodicals to convey news and information about the KMU and its struggles, as well as to provide KMU's analysis of the situation in their country to others. Initially there was *KMU Correspondence* and *KMU International Bulletin*—with the *Bulletin* being limited to only a couple of times a year, albeit in greater depth, with *Correspondence* being generally a monthly magazine—but in 1988, KMU dropped the *Bulletin* and began producing an improved *Correspondence* monthly.[15] And while most of the news focuses on the Philippine situation, there is always news of labor and democratic struggles around the world included in *Correspondence*—and this has included news of labor struggles in the US, such as those against the Hormel, Greyhound and International Paper corporations.

Another publishing effort, which is tied into KMU's internal education program, is the publication and dissemination of their key trade union education manual, *GTU: Genuine Trade Unionism* (EILER, 1988). One edition of *GTU* is in English, allowing them to send it to labor organizations in different parts of the world. I have been told by a senior South Korean trade unionist that *GTU* was very useful in their efforts to develop their new democratic union movement, and KMU Chairperson Crispin Beltran has told me that the South Koreans have translated it into their language.

Another aspect of the KMU's communication strategy is encouraging groups in other countries to set up "solidarity" or "support" committees, which are designed to communicate updates on the situation in the Philippines and specifically KMU struggles to people and workers of other countries.[16] Thus, in the US, there are the Philippine Workers Support Committees, with chapters in several different cities; in Britain, there's the Trade Union Committee of the Philippine Solidarity Committee; in Australia, there's the Asian-Australian Solidarity Links committee; all which have done considerable work in building support with the KMU. Both PWSC in the United States and AASL in Australia have their own publications, while the TUC in Britain publishes news and reports in the journal of the Philippine Solidarity Committee. These solidarity groups also work to facilitate visits by KMU leaders in their respective countries, while serving as contact points and screens for people wanting to visit the KMU.

The fourth aspect is international travel by leaders. KMU leaders have carried out extensive international travel to communicate about and build support for their efforts, particularly focusing on various labor movements. While most of these trips have been to the more economically developed countries, where the labor movements are generally larger and have more financial resources, they have also traveled to various "third world" countries as well as to Eastern Europe and the former Soviet Union. One innovative effort was organizing a European Solidarity Conference in London during February 1986, which included labor leaders and representatives from a number of unions from throughout Europe.[17] KMU leaders have also participated in four conferences of labor organizations throughout the Indian and Pacific Oceans Area in Perth, Australia during 1990, 1992, 1994 and 1997.[18]

The fifth aspect is the development of "exposure" visits throughout the Philippines by foreigners. This takes place in its most formalized and developed sense during the International Solidarity Affair, but KMU coordinates visits throughout the country all through the year. This may be little more than just arranging for union leaders in different parts of the country to meet with the "exposurists" and update them on the situation in their area, or it may involve a very detailed "exposure" to a local area. In any case, it is another attempt to communicate the reality of Filipino workers to foreign guests. This work can often pay off to an even greater degree if and when the visitors report back to people in their own country, and even more so if the visitors get reports of the visit published or get interviewed in the alternative or mass media at home.[19]

And the sixth aspect of this communications strategy is the initiation and development of the International Solidarity Affair as a means to both communicate to worker-visitors the real situation of Filipino workers and to involve KMU members at all levels in this communications process. That this even takes place around International Workers' Day (May Day), which the KMU correctly recognizes as originating in workers' struggles in Chicago during 1886 around the eight-hour day,[20] reinforces the international solidarity focus on the event.

Three things are immediately observable concerning the KMU's communications strategy: (1) it takes place within a larger struggle for social change; (2) it is a multi-faceted approach; and (3) it is highly integrated into the KMU's strategy for social change. It is clear that the KMU takes its communications work extremely seriously.

And within this larger communications strategy, I now want to focus specifically on the ISA as one aspect. The ISA differs from the other aspects of the KMU's communications strategy in how it is carried out. The first four aspects are based on continuing work by a relatively small number of full-time staff or elected leaders, but exclude rank-and-file workers. The fifth is generally limited although it doesn't have to be and, in the case of specific exposure programs, is not. Nonetheless, for the purpose of this chapter, I will include the fifth with the previous four.

The point is that the ISA is a unique communications effort within the overall communications strategy of the KMU. But it is also, as far as I can discover, a unique effort within labor internationally: I can find no other example of a systematic, regular program that is designed to build international labor solidarity. Thus it deserves being analyzed independently.

The International Solidarity Affair (ISA)

Each year for the ISA, the KMU invites workers and labor leaders from around the world to travel to the Philippines for an extensive 10-day program revolving around the celebration of International Workers' Day (May 1). This is seen as a way to develop both international labor support for the struggles of the KMU, and to help build international labor solidarity between Filipino workers and workers from other lands; hence, it is more than a one-way process. During this program, "visitors"[21] are given an in-depth "exposure" to the day-to-day reality of Filipino workers. While the program includes formal ceremonies with national dignitaries and meetings with KMU leaders, its centerpiece is going out into the various regions of the Philippines and meeting workers and, at times, their families. This takes place at their workplaces, picket lines and sometimes in their homes. What follows is a report of my personal experiences in attending the 1988 ISA, so as to give an idea of what this program looks like in practice.

The 1988 ISA

While working as a printer and being a member of the Graphic Communications International Union, AFL-CIO, I participated in the 1988 ISA along with workers and labor leaders from Australia, Belgium, Canada, England,

France, Germany, New Zealand, Sweden and the United States. (There were also Japanese workers there but because of translation needs, they had a separate program.)

Preparation was extensive. Prior to traveling to the Philippines, visitors received an orientation program that acquainted them with the country and suggested what they would experience and what they might like to take with them. Preferences for where each person might like to travel or what they were specifically interested in seeing were solicited. In addition, visitors received information about how they should act while in workers' communities, what type of clothing was appropriate, and how they should donate money to an organization should they desire to do so.[22]

Once we were in the Philippines, we received a considerable amount of information.[23] The KMU had prepared "orientation packets" for each visitor, in which we were given an overview of the national situation and the KMU's position on specific national issues such as the US military bases, and specific information on the region that we would visit.

The importance the KMU placed on the International Solidarity Affair was obvious. There was an impressive opening ceremony in which some of the visitors actively participated. Senator Wigberto Tañada of the Philippine Senate gave the keynote address. Speeches were also given by KMU Chairperson Crispin Beltran and other leaders. The event was covered in the national media. And throughout the entire 10-day program, visitors had extensive access to high-level KMU leaders.

After the formal ceremonies, the visitors were informed where we would be visiting. The group was split up by destination and our guide gave us a "situationer" (situation report) for the area in which we would be traveling. I was traveling to Mindanao with Philip Statham, an Australian trade union official, and we were given a three-hour situationer by KMU-Mindanao Deputy Secretary General Joel Maglunsod, who had been flown in from Davao City to brief us and to serve as our guide.

Since building personal connections between each visitor and Filipino workers is seen as the key, and while visitors are treated with respect and given access to high level leaders throughout the KMU, the crucial point is to get the visitors out of Manila and into the provinces where they can see the real situation. Once in the provinces, besides introductory meetings with local area leaders, visitors are taken to meet with workers at various workplaces.

After reaching Davao City and having introductory meetings with a number of leaders of KMU-Mindanao, we were taken to meet hotel, dock and garment workers. At each stop, we got an overview and analysis of their situation, and an update on their current activities.

We were exposed to a number of issues facing workers in the Philippines. At a garment factory, we got to see firsthand the problems of "labor only" contracting, the illegal process where labor contractors offer temporary workers to replace regular workers. The dock workers were on strike, fighting for increased wages and better working conditions. The hotel workers explained to us how they organized themselves within the hotel, and what problems remained. We were encouraged to ask any questions we might have, and the union members shared their personal experiences and tried very hard to get us to understand.

But we also gave reports on the situation for workers in our respective countries, and talked about how our labor movements were confronting the problems in our societies. The workers asked us questions: why did we come to the Philippines, and particularly Davao City? They wanted to know why we were willing to take serious risks—the vigilante movement (i.e., death squads) was stronger in Davao City than anywhere else in the country, and quite obvious with numerous "check points" throughout the city—to come learn about their struggles. As we talked, we got a sense of each other and one could also see solidarity being created. One man even gave me the address and phone number of a sister in California and asked me to call her and tell her he was ok—I was pleased at how much this message meant to her when I later contacted her and delivered it.

After spending a couple of days in the more urban parts of the city, we went to a rural part to visit workers on a banana plantation. These workers had been waging an intense struggle to maintain their union, with Army units all around the area in this supposedly "rebel-infested" area. In fact, union officer Peter Alderite had been hacked to death by vigilantes using bolo knives right outside the union office on the plantation the year before. Other officers lived in the banana trees for months following the killing, although things had been a little quieter for a while.

We had an extensive program at the plantation. We received an in-depth briefing by the union president, who told us both about the union struggles and the labor process for growing bananas. We then spent hours walking around the plantation, talking to workers as they worked, who explained their tasks. We covered the whole range of the growing process, from planting to boxing the bananas for shipment, and the workers told us that 32 chemicals were used through growing, processing and shipping.

After spending the day in the workplace, we were invited by workers to visit their "community" and to eat with them. We met spouses and children, and visited their homes. We shared information about schooling in the different societies and various things from our lives. Although very poor, they shared what they had and related to us as equals—they conveyed their strong sense of self-assurance and confidence that comes from having stood up for themselves and their colleagues.

We then traveled to another part of the plantation and talked with Lisa and Philip Alderite, the widow and son of the slain union leader. It was a particularly intense conversation since we met on the first year anniversary of Peter's assassination. Afterwards, we returned to the community where people shared some coconut wine called "tuba." We spent the night on mats on the floor and had breakfast in the community before going to other parts of the plantation and meeting other workers.

We returned later to the urban center of Davao City, where we joined leaders of 40 local unions and KMU-Mindanao leaders for a press conference. Being trade unionists from foreign countries, we were interviewed by newspaper and radio reporters, and were asked for our impressions of the Philippines. We not only shared our impressions, but made statements condemning the vigilantes, feeling that perhaps as visitors who were soon to leave, we could say some things publicly that our hosts might not chose to publicize on their own. The KMU leaders were very appreciative of our efforts.[24]

After several days in Davao City, we returned to Manila where we rejoined the other visitors. On May Day, we marched with approximately 150,000 workers through the streets of the city to Luneta Park for a spirited rally and speeches. The day after, we spent time sharing each group of visitors' particular experiences, and hearing the details of an armed attack on marchers in Laguna Province on May Day. The ISA ended with a *dispedida* (departure) party. Among other things, we sang songs of struggle from our respective homelands. It seemed an excellent way to end the ISA.

Having a sense of what actually takes place during these visits allows one to see that there is a second part of this communications strategy: our presence signified to those workers that their lives, their struggles, their victories, their losses and their pain was important to workers in other parts of the world. And that we were willing to spend considerable amounts of money to travel to the Philippines and then take certain risks to show our concern and make these connections illustrated to them that this was a serious concern, not something taken lightly. It is from this second part that one can see the ISA as a *mutual* communications process, a spiral, in which we learned from each other; it surpasses a one-way flow of information.

Evaluating the ISA from a Communications Theory Perspective

But how do we evaluate this from a theoretical perspective? First of all, following Tomaselli and Louw, this communication process is multidimensional—as stated above, this is a spiral process. It definitely is a process to strengthen the grassroots democracy in the union and larger society.

Following Stangelaar, the ISA qualifies as alternative communication. It meets all of his criteria for AC: it is based on an orientation toward total social transformation; it has a language that comes directly from the people and confronts that of the oppressor; it has a mobilizing and organizing role, following a spiral communications model; and the people are directly involved.

And, following Waterman, it qualifies as internationalist communication. The ISA "aids in the creation of transterritorial solidarity relations which enrich and empower popular and democratic collectives by diversifying, exchanging and synthesizing their ideas . . ." (Waterman, 1988b: 12).

EFFECTING WORKERS GLOBALLY

The KMU's efforts to build international labor solidarity are having impacts on workers in other countries—and have the potential to do more so when workers from still other countries respond to KMU efforts—and they are affecting their own members.

Workers Outside the Philippines

The KMU's communications practices have placed the issue of international solidarity again at international labor's table: workers supporting workers is counterposed to the post-World War II traditions of labor movements in so-called developed countries either supporting their "own" state which may then act in support of workers overseas but also may act against them (as sometimes in the US, and throughout Western Europe and Japan), and/or attempting to dominate overseas labor movements (a favorite approach of the AFL-CIO) (for the latter, see Scipes, 2010a, 2010b, 2016a).

The KMU's practices differ from "traditional" efforts in another extremely significant way: they are not done behind the backs, and without the knowledge, of their members. To the contrary, especially during the ISA, the KMU involves its members, and generally tries to keep the membership well informed overall. Again, this directly contradicts the practices of the AFL-CIO, which tries to hide its international operations and, when forced to publicize them, usually lies, deceives and in other ways distorts the actual situation (see Scipes, 1987a; 2010a).

By inviting workers to the Philippines to experience much of the day-to-day reality of Filipino workers, the KMU takes the issue beyond being an "intellectual concept": spending the night with a worker's family immediately demonstrates the difference between workers' situations there and those in the developed countries. Yet at the same time, the pride of these workers shows immediately that they consider themselves second to none (in an assertive rather than an aggressive manner), despite their poverty and general lack of power. It also fills one with admiration for the level of organization and success achieved to date by these workers, oftentimes under horrible situations.

If nothing else, travel to partake in the ISA forces the visitor to re-evaluate her or his "knowledge" of developing countries. It brings home to the visitor the reality that there are working people in the "Third World"—as opposed to mass media images of victims always seeking handouts; that these workers are not the enemy, stealing jobs from developed country workers, but sisters and brothers in the struggle against domination and especially by Capital; and that there is a lot we can learn from these workers and their organizations. These factors can combine to get visitors to be willing to consider alternatives to their own trade union practices, as well as alternative views concerning their own social order. Additionally, experiences on this level also contribute to building a new global consciousness.

However, I think the most important impact of the KMU's international activities is that of providing an alternative view of what trade unionism can be. While certainly riskier than the economic type of trade unionism practiced today in the developed countries, social movement unionism as practiced by the KMU offers workers their own position of power in the struggle to determine the future course of development of their own society, and a means of uniting with social movements for maximum impact.

Workers in the Philippines

But what benefits accrue to KMU members from its efforts to build international labor solidarity? Obviously, financial aid, as well as moral and political support from workers overseas, are two benefits.

However, there are even more important benefits. Knowledge that developed country workers are coming to learn from them is extremely important; besides any other benefits, this contradicts the "message" given in Philippine schools and mass media that they are inferior to developed country workers, and it indirectly challenges the racism that "brown" people aren't as valuable or human as "whites." These visits also signify that Filipino workers are part of something larger, that they are part of the world-wide struggle against domination. Especially during hard-fought struggles where it is easy for workers to feel all alone and isolated, this becomes a significant factor.

But the solidarity visits also bring something of more immediate benefit: they are a concrete way by which Filipino workers learn that workers around the world know about their struggles, are concerned about them as human beings, and that visitors are willing to spend valuable time and money—and at times, take considerable risks—to come express their support and solidarity by the most real way possible. The impact of this on Filipino workers is something that simply cannot be underestimated.

Additionally, the communications practices discussed herein can serve as a basis for further extending democracy within their own unions and within the larger social order.

From my experiences with the KMU, I have seen that it is democratically run. Having participated in meetings at different levels of the organization, I've found debate to be lively, critical and open. It seems that issues can be put forth by the rank and file for discussion and debate, although I've only been present at meetings where issues have been presented by leaders. However, I've never seen any situation where I felt members were unable or reluctant to talk with their leaders—the situation is such where the organization could not survive if this type of situation emerged.

Yet I do wonder what the situation will be like should the pressure be taken off the KMU, and some type of real democracy institutionalized in the country. Will this mean a deterioration of the democracy in the organization as people "relax"? Will bureaucratization raise its ugly head? Obviously, no one knows, but as I pointed out previously (Scipes, 1996: 195–196), this issue needs to be confronted beforehand so as to be able to reduce any negative tendencies within the organization. Some of this communications theory suggests a way to try to nip this problem in the bud: establishing democratic forms of media at the grassroots level—not by staff or leaders but by rank and file members—would be a way to both counteract any anti-democratic tendencies in the organization and, more importantly, institutionalize additional democratic structures in the union, while helping to further develop democracy throughout the larger society.

CONCLUSION

In this chapter, I pointed out that workers around the world are targets of the political-economic globalization processes that are intensifying today, but also noted that progressive and democratic labor organizations are acting to challenge these processes; a key aspect to this challenge is the building of international labor solidarity.[25] I suggested that to understand this process, it is necessary to discuss literature focusing on both internationalism and communication theories, and particularly that which addresses the role of democracy building within social conflicts. Following that, I discussed the development of the *Kilusang Mayo Uno* (KMU) Labor Center of the Philippines, and focused on its efforts to build international labor solidarity. I showed that KMU's international work is sophisticated, with the International Solidarity Affair being that which is most developed. I've also suggested that this international work affects both workers outside and inside of the Philippines, and believe that it serves as a model for workers everywhere.

In short, while political-economic globalization is hitting workers hard, progressive and democratic labor organizations such as the KMU are creatively acting to respond to globalization's impact. While organized and politicized labor is not sufficient in and of itself to stop the ravages of globalization, especially on the most vulnerable members of our societies, it is a force to be reckoned with, and one that will become even more potent as other social movements ally in the struggle for justice, democracy and equality.

NOTES

1. This is based on the work of Jan Nederveen Pieterse (1989), whose work on imperialism is, in my opinion, the best done to date. Nederveen Pieterse's analysis is not based on, and in fact rejects, Wallerstein's World System Theory.

2. I am not ready to proclaim that success in building global labor solidarity will necessarily result in a changed international political-economic order that meets the goals of such labor centers as the KMU, although I do feel that this international order cannot be changed without the building of international labor solidarity.

3. Thanks to Peter Waterman of the Institute of Social Studies in The Hague, who has inspired and provoked much of my thinking on the subject of international labor solidarity and communications over the years. However, responsibility for what is written here is mine alone.

This chapter was written in 1996, although never published in a journal. Waterman uploaded it on his "Global Solidarity Dialogue" web page in early 2000 (Scipes, 2000a). It has been slightly revised since then.

4. For some of the more interesting accounts, see American Labor, 1984; Barry and Preusch, 1986; Brecher and Costello 1988, 1991a, 1991b; Cantor and Schor, 1987; Eckstein, 1986; Eisenhower, 1991; Fitz, 1990; Garver, 1989; Hirsch and Muir, 1987; Karmel, 1990; KMU, 1993; NILS 1986, 1987, 1988, 1989; SALB, 1991; Scipes 1985, 1986a, 1986b, 1987a, 1987b, 1988a, 1988b, 1989b, 1989c, 1990a, 1990b, 1990c, 1996; Shorrock and Selvaggio, 1986; Sims, 1992; Slaney, 1988; Southall (ed.), 1988; Spaulding 1988a, 1988b; Spooner, 1989, TIE, 1983, 1984; Waterman, 1991a, 1998; Waterman (ed.), 1984; Webster, 1984; Weinrub and Bollinger, 1987; West, 1991, 1997; Witt, 1990; and the journals *International Labour Reports* [which succumbed to inadequate funding in 1990], *Philippine Labor Alert* [Honolulu] and *Middle East Labor Bulletin* [San Francisco].

5. See particularly Waterman 1985, 1988a, 1988b, 1988c, 1988d, 1988e, 1990, 1993, 1998; and Haworth and Ramsay 1984, 1988; Munck, 1988; NILS 1986, 1988; and Scipes, 1989a, 1992a, 1992b.

For subsequent theorization, see Scipes, 2016b, 2016c.

6. Waterman wrote some of the articles that I refer to before the political earthquakes of 1989–90 that destroyed so much of the "second world" of state socialism, so references to the "second world" and the "East" seem very dated. Nevertheless, his point holds that labor internationalism has to be directed toward and developed with workers from all parts of the world.

7. While the KMU seeks to build international labor solidarity with workers in less economically developed countries (LEDCs) as well, most of its efforts are directed toward workers in the MEDCs. This is because the MEDCs have a vastly disproportionate impact on the Philippines, particularly through their international trade and finance policies and power in the international lending agencies such as the International Monetary Fund and the World Bank. This is especially true of the United States, the former colonial master of the Philippines.

Also, it is in the MEDCs that workers have the money to travel to the Philippines, and there are national labor organizations which can provide concrete, material support to the KMU in these countries: a number of Australian unions, for example, have been notably supportive. These situations do not exist in other LEDCs. Therefore, it makes sense that the KMU focuses its international efforts toward workers in the MEDCs.

Along with that, it is in the US that workers can—should they choose to—play a key role in stopping the AFL-CIO's foreign operations in the Philippines. These operations have been focused against the KMU, and have been extremely destructive despite their overall lack of success.

All that said, it must also be said that the KMU makes extensive efforts to join with unions from other LEDCs, and has specifically sought funding at different times to enable unionists from various LEDCs to visit the Philippines. Still, the potential for material support from unions in the MEDCs is qualitatively greater than that possibly available from unions in the LEDCs.

8. During the late 1980s, there was a systematic campaign of violence against the leadership of the KMU by forces aligned with, or spawned by, the state. I'm specifically referring to the rise of the vigilante (death squads) movement. By 1988, over 200 different vigilante organizations had been identified throughout the country (Lernoux, 1989; see also Bello, 1988; Collins, 1989; and Delacruz, Jordan and Emmanuel, eds., 1987). They not only focused on the leadership of the KMU, but on the leadership of all "people's organizations."

This was a very broad attack. For example, at Atlas Mines in Cebu, where a KMU-affiliated local union was seeking to continue representing the workers, this union was opposed by an alliance between the company management, the Philippine Constabulary (an armed police force), 12 competing unions, local government officials and a vigilante organization. Despite suffering great violence against its leaders, including the deaths of several union leaders and relatives of leaders, the KMU union won the certification election with 68 percent of the vote. This struggle is briefly reported in Scipes, 1989c and 2010a: 52–55, and extensively documented in Scipes, 1996: 116–125.

9. While I am personally very skeptical about pursuing a "labor rights" strategy, especially when it is presented as a chance to improve the economic conditions of US workers as it often is, it can be an important tool to give material support to workers in other countries when it is approached in consultation and coordination with these other workers' organizations. For a limited and general discussion of this approach that however suggests some ways this strategy can be supportive to unions such as the KMU, see Brecher and Costello, 1991b: 89–90.

10. While it might seem strange that "Western" labor organizations have attacked the KMU, and even more considering its important international role, unfortunately they have done this. There has been a virulent international campaign against the KMU, particularly by the AFL-CIO but to a lesser degree also by the IUF, where they have both claimed the KMU is nothing more than a front for the Communist Party of the Philippines (CPP). At the same time, however, neither organization has been able to present any substantial evidence to support their charges (see Scipes, 1987a).

I have examined this charge in as much detail as possible and reject it: the KMU is not, in my opinion, a front of the CPP or any other political organization, even though it does have members of probably every Philippine political organization existing (see Scipes, 1992a: 147–152; 1992b: 92–95; and in more detail, 1996: 183–192).

I believe the real problem in this case—especially for the AFL-CIO—is that the KMU refuses to confine itself to the imperialistic and largely economic trade unionism of the AFL-CIO and is, therefore, beyond its control. And the AFL-CIO doesn't like this.

11. It should be specifically pointed out that Stangelaar's definition of alternative communication differs considerably from that broadly used today by activists in the US, who focus much more on alternative forms and content.

12. These figures are not limited to just workers covered by collective bargaining agreements (CBAs), but include all those who will mobilize in support of KMU efforts. However, KMU's strength is due more to its location within the production-distribution-exchange system than its sheer numbers. For a history of the development of the KMU between 1980–1994, see Scipes, 1996: 22–70.

13. This following section has been conveyed above, but I decided to leave it in to maintain the consistency of the original article. My apologies for the repetition.

14. For the best source on how the KMU sees itself and presents itself to its members, see EILER, 1988. This is the educational program designed to reach all KMU members, not just leaders.

15. Financial limitations in late 1992–early 1993 forced the KMU to shift its publication schedule from monthly to bi-monthly. They later shifted to communicating electronically.

However, the KMU has not given the attention to electronic communications that I think they should have; by early 2020, they had lost their website to a business. They currently have a Facebook page at https://www.facebook.com/KMUinternational/, where one can get their latest information.

16. For one discussion of solidarity committees, with a particular focus on those involved with Philippine workers, see Waterman, 1990: 57–61.

Waterman published a very interesting book in 1998, titled *Globalization, Social Movements and the New Internationalisms* (Waterman, 1998), with a specific chapter on "Beyond Westocentrism: New World, New Unions, New Labour Internationalism?" In this chapter, he discusses many of the issues addressed within, largely as he incorporates some his previously-written articles into this chapter; for example, he discusses "Solidarity Committees" on pp. 132–136.

However, I disagree vehemently with many of his conclusions about KMU, and we have had many personal, and some quite heated discussions, about KMU. He dismisses the KMU as being "intimately associated with the 'national-democratic' project of the Maoist-inspired Communist Party of the Philippines" (Waterman, 1998: 125).

The frustration comes not from him disagreeing with me—I'm fine with that—but that he does that with much less experience and without even considering the substantial evidence and reasoning that I (and numerous others) have presented that opposes his position; I argue, up to April 1994 when I was last in the Philippines, that the KMU was not controlled by the CPP or any other organization, that it operated on its own dynamic, and its members would have never withstood the extensive violence they have withstood over the years had their organization been controlled by another organization (see Scipes, 1996). [After I returned to the Philippines in 2015 and published an article on the KMU's International Solidarity Affair (Scipes, 2015a), Waterman attacked me and my work, and I responded to him; for his attack and my response, see Scipes (2015b).]

I go into this to say that people need to understand his ideological approach to the KMU—unlike his other work—and to compare it to material written by myself and many others over the years before accepting his conclusions on the KMU.

17. After returning to London from Manila after my first (1986) visit to the Philippines, I attended this conference; I found it excellent. KMU Secretary General Roberto Ortaliz was brought in for the conference, and he provided up-to-date information.

18. This organization later renamed itself as SIGTUR (Southern Initiative on Globalization and Trade Union Rights). For details, see articles by Robert Lambert and Eddie Webster (2001), Bruno Dobrusin (2014), and the recent book on SIGTUR by Robert O'Brien (2019).

19. Visits to the Philippines by foreigners have resulted in extensive reporting on the KMU and its struggles. Besides the reports carried by the support/solidarity committees, and articles listed in this chapter, the KMU was extensively covered in the journal *International Labour Reports* before the latter's demise in 1990.

20. The KMU's name, *Kilusang Mayo Uno,* also honors US workers—it translates to "May First Movement" and refers specifically to the 1886 events in Chicago.

21. Although the KMU refers to these visitors as "delegates," because most are delegated representatives of their various labor organization, some are not delegated but attend on their own initiative. When I attended in 1988, for example, I was not delegated. Because of the different situations, I refer to all foreigners participating in the ISA as "visitors."

22. While these may seem to be "small" issues, building international labor solidarity on the basis of mutual respect and not on a patron-client relationship, despite

vast differences in personal and organizational wealth, demands that attention be paid to issues such as these.

23. The question could be raised as to whether this was not just one big propaganda effort by the KMU to get visitors to accept their distorted version of reality. The KMU presents its version of reality. But having compared what they say with what is in the Philippine mainstream media, having talked with opponents as well as supporters, and having traveled around the country—alone and with others—and talked with people during six trips in a nine-year period, I've found their information to be as accurate as any available. In short, the KMU's version is not distorted although, as they acknowledge, it does come from a certain perspective, that of a labor movement seeking radical change in the existing social order.

24. This got a little more intense later on than expected. Our guides dropped us off early at the airport for our flight to return to Manila, as they wanted to get home before sundown, when dangers from the vigilantes intensified. However, it turned out our flight to Manila had been canceled, due to lighting problems on the runway. While we were digesting this—and having no way to reconnect with our guides or KMU Mindanao leaders at the time—two truckloads of armed vigilantes arrived at the airport, apparently looking for "someone." Philip and I had some nervous moments before the vigilantes left the area.

We later convinced the Philippine Air Lines staff to put us up in a hotel, and they put us up in probably the finest hotel in Davao City, right on the just-raked beach. After getting to our room and finding cold San Miguel beers in the room's refrigerator, we took off our shoes, put our feet up on the beds, hoisted our beers, and took pictures of each other, each saying "All power to the international working class!"

To say we'd been in several different "worlds" in just one day would be an understatement!

25. In Scipes (2016b), I discuss "globalization," and argue it should properly understood as a bifurcated process, with two layers, one being a top-down version of globalization that I call "corporate/militaristic" globalization, which is designed to advance capitalism and destroy efforts against it, and a bottom-up globalization movement for economic and social justice . [This challenges the monolithic version of globalization that writers like Thomas Friedman (1999) have presented, and which have been so quickly adopted by political and economic elites.] Of the bottom-up version, building specifically on the work of Vandana Shiva (2005) and Amory Starr (2005), I write

> Globalization from below . . . is life-enhancing: it rejects domination in all its forms and seeks to build a new world based on equality, social and economic justice, and respect for all living beings and the planet. . . . The two worldviews, and the values on which they are based, could not be more opposed (Scipes, 2016b: 17).

I argue that the KMU and all progressive, internationalist-focused, projects are in the process of creating this bottom-up, global economic and social justice movement.

For my efforts to theorize global labor solidarity, see Scipes, 2016b.

Chapter Thirteen

Disentangling Confusion in Global Labor Drive

After the election of John Sweeney as President of the AFL-CIO (American Federation of Labor-Congress of Industrial Organizations) in October 1995—the result of the first democratic election for the presidency in the 40 years of the AFL-CIO—labor activists and supportive intellectuals in the United States began thinking about how to revitalize the almost moribund American labor movement (see Fletcher and Gapasin, 2008).[1] The resulting literature on labor revitalization is broad, and includes current issues as well as research on things US Labor may learn from a re-examination of some of its past. A key part of this literature revolves around the concept of "social movement unionism."[2]

The term "social movement unionism" has been attracting increasingly greater attention by labor theorists and writers focusing on unionism in North America since 1994 (among them, Devinatz, 2008; Paul Johnston, 1994; Moody, 1997; Nissen, 2003; Schiavone, 2004, 2007, 2008); as they have tried to describe the "new unionism" that has been emerging in particularly the US trade union movement.[3] Based on union member mobilization, social movement unionism is being projected positively and presented as the way that US Labor as a whole should develop in the early 21st Century. The term certainly seems to be resonating with activists, and is increasingly being used by researchers (see, among others, Fantasia and Voss, 2004; Lopez, 2004; Milkman, 2006; Milkman and Voss, eds., 2004; Nissen, 2003; Schiavone, 2004, 2007, 2008; Tattersall, 2009; see also Ross, 2008).

To support this understanding, some theorists (Johnston, 2001; Robinson, 2002; Nissen, 2003; Schiavone, 2008; and see Ross, 2008) have been trying to define more precisely the concept of "social movement unionism" (SMU) as developed in North America, and particularly in the United States. (See also Fairbrother, 2008; Fairbrother and Webster, 2008; and Waterman, 1993, 1999, 2004, 2008 for a more global focus.)

At the same time, a strong and vibrant section of the American Sociological Association (ASA) has developed since 1997, focusing attention on labor and labor movements. More and more of these labor researchers have been recognizing the global impact of labor, and how changes in the global economy have been affecting workers in North America and around the world. Thus, as interest in labor has expanded globally among sociologists—particularly through the International Sociological Association's research committee (RC) on labor, RC 44[4]—an increasing number of ASA members since 2006 have been participating in RC 44. As American (and other) sociologists make these international ties, and become increasingly aware of labor around the globe (see Burowoy, 2009) and join in international discussions and debates, the necessity to understand similarities and differences between efforts to revitalize the Canadian and particularly the US labor movement and innovative efforts in (particularly) developing countries becomes all the more important, as does theoretically understanding these differences.

This chapter focuses on changes in the US labor movement, and efforts to theoretically understand these changes, but *within the context of developments in three labor centers in developing countries* that have far surpassed American efforts, both in practice and in theory. Recognizing developments in these particular developing country labor centers, however, presents labor theorists around the world with a significant problem: *labor theorists are using the exact same term, social movement unionism, to describe two qualitatively different social phenomena.* To say that this has the potential to create considerable confusion and misunderstandings is an understatement.

The purpose of this chapter, therefore, is twofold. First, this paper recognizes that there are two qualitatively different social phenomena,[5] and argues that we need different terms to refer to each. Second, it suggests how we can understand these differences theoretically, providing guidance for future research and understanding.

The conceptualization of "social movement unionism" was based initially on empirical research and political involvement in and around specific labor centers in three "third world" countries in the 1970s and 1980s: CUT *(Central Única dos Trabalhadores*-Unified Workers' Central) of Brazil, KMU (*Kilusang Mayo Uno*-May First Movement) of the Philippines, and the Congress of South African Trade Unions (COSATU) of that country (although the phenomenon was not limited to them, nor even limited to just the "third world").[6] As discussed below, this type of trade unionism was and still is qualitatively different from the type found to date in North America.

However, current writings suggest most of the North American-focused theorists and writers are not aware of this earlier work and, if they are, that they have relied on a truncated interpretation of this. Accordingly, this discussion has become terribly confused,[7] and threatens to lose the considerable benefits of research to date; this chapter is an effort to untangle the considerable confusion around this concept and to preclude such losses.

At the same time, those who developed the earlier conceptualizations have shifted their foci from the subject at hand, leaving a vacuum in the discussion. Two sets of the key writers who initially worked to develop the concept of social movement unionism (SMU)—Peter Waterman and Rob Lambert/Eddie Webster—have traveled subsequently in different directions, but yet have remained close enough to their original positions so as to suggest that they are still writing consistently from where they began. This writer, Kim Scipes, having contributed to the debate in 1992 and published an internet-based article in 2001, nonetheless also has been focusing subsequently on other subjects—most importantly, the AFL-CIO's foreign policy program—and is only now returning to this discussion. The long and short of this is that there has been no long-term, internationally consistent development of this concept.

As a result, and as will be explicated below, there are currently three sets of writers who each use the rubric of social movement unionism in one way or the other: those writing on contemporary unionism in North America, especially those stimulated by the work of Kim Moody; those writing initially in regards to the new unions and labor organizations that emerged in the 1970s and 1980s in the Global South, and subsequent theorization based on experiences by certain "southern" organizations; and then subsequent writings by early theorists who have gone in different directions without explicitly noting their respective changes in direction.

This creates the basis for a great deal of confusion among labor theorists and writers, as well as trade unionists: people coming from different perspectives can use the exact same term to describe completely different things—and without even knowing it. This is not a firm basis from which to increase our knowledge about labor around the world, nor a viable means by which to build international labor solidarity, nor a grounded way to develop theory to understand these developments.[8]

Along with the practical ramifications of the lack of clarity, however, there are theoretical implications as well. "Social movement unionism" in North America—as well as "social unionism" (see Ross, 2008)—has not been placed within a global theoretical context, while the social movement unionism coming out of these developing countries has been so placed. Thus, by attributing the term "social movement unionism" to developments in labor in North America, theorists are, in fact, replacing a more theoretically developed conceptualization with one less so, and without even knowing this is being done.

All of these varied conceptualizations have been published in books and articles around the world, with many of the sources being unknown or undiscovered by subsequent researchers. Others have inappropriately "mixed and matched" research findings, leading to more uncertainty. Substantive contributions have been ignored. Simply put, the understandings created to date have created a "goulash" that is theoretically inchoate, and global diffusion of this "discussion" has also contributed to the confusion.

It is argued that this situation needs first to be recognized, and then to be disentangled and rectified. This chapter seeks to connect a number of issues that heretofore have been generally approached separately in an effort to untangle the confusion about social movement unionism. This is done through two steps, with the first one based on empirical studies, while the second is empirically-based but theoretically-focused.

First, an empirical-based discussion of "social movement unionism" is provided. This first step, in turn, is in divided into three parts. The first part provides a quick overview of the adoption and development of the term "social movement unionism" in North America in regard to North American (US and Canadian) trade unionism.[9] In the second part, readers are introduced to an international theoretical discussion and debate concerning the new unions (organized into labor centers) that emerged within several developing countries during the late 1970s–early 1990s. In the third part of the first step, the "social movement unionism" that emerged in three labor centers located in three different developing countries is shown to be qualitatively different from the type of unionism that currently exists in North America, and it is argued that these two qualitative different types of unionism should be distinguished by different terminology.

The second step advances a theoretical model that is intended to overcome the currently existing confusion, suggesting how theorists can address the problem. This is to untangle the concept and provide theoretical clarity from which further work can develop.

This theoretical model, based on *sets of practices,* suggests that there are two levels of trade unionism: *types* of unionism and then *forms* (or subsets of the types) of unionism.[10] It is argued that trade unionism around the world can be categorized into three *types:* economic, political, and social movement unionism. Further, it is suggested that each type of trade unionism can be subdivided into *forms,* although only forms of the economic type of trade unionism—what are called "business unionism" and "social justice unionism" —are addressed herein.

In order to illustrate the difference between the two forms of business and social justice unionism, and to better understand present-day North American trade unionism, a theoretical model that was developed in my Ph.D. dissertation (Scipes, 2003) is introduced, which was specifically designed to establish theoretically the concept of trade union "forms." I examine the different (and competing) forms of economic trade unionism that developed within Chicago's steel and meatpacking industries between 1933–1955, and argue that this comparison provides needed guidance. From consideration of this study, I argue that *social justice unionism* as developed by the United Packinghouse Workers of America (UPWA) and a few others is, in fact, the precedent for the current "social movement unionism" in North America.

This suggests ways to proceed. It suggests that *social movement unionism* be retained as a term to describe a specific type of trade unionism created by particular labor centers that so far have existed in only certain countries in the Global South.[11] Further, it suggests that the term "social movement unionism" (along with "social unionism") in regards to North American unionism be dropped, and be replaced with the term *social justice unionism*. This would allow researchers/theorists to recognize relatively recent developments in trade unionism in North America (and other developed countries) and to properly situate them theoretically, while no longer ignoring or confusing North American developments with the particular type of trade unionism found in specific labor centers in certain developing countries. Finally, by incorporating this dispersed literature into a single chapter, it is hoped that subsequent scholars may cover the field more accurately and completely. Accordingly, this chapter seeks to make a major contribution towards resolving both the practical and theoretical confusion that currently exists, whether it is recognized or not.

SOCIAL MOVEMENT UNIONISM: AN EMPIRICAL-BASED DISCUSSION

This section discusses the concept of social movement unionism in both North America, and among particular labor centers that have developed in the "Global South." It first discusses the definition of SMU in North America, notes how it developed, and how it has been applied subsequently. From there, focus is shifted to the initial theoretical work on SMU that emerged from studies of particular labor centers in the Global South. And through these processes, it shows the qualitative differences between these two social phenomena.

Based on these discussions, it shows that the same term has been applied to two qualitatively different social phenomena, and argues that a different terminology is needed to distinguish between each of the two phenomena.

Social Movement Unionism (SMU) in North America

Kim Moody, in his 1997 book *Workers in a Lean World,* was the first to popularize SMU in North America.[12] He offered "social movement unionism" as a positive alternative to the traditional "business unionism" that has for so long been dominant with the US labor movement. Moody defined SMU as:

> Social movement unionism is one that is deeply democratic, as that is the best way to mobilize the strength of numbers in order to apply maximum economic leverage. It is militant in collective bargaining in the belief that retreat anywhere only leads to more retreats—an injury to one is an injury to all. It seeks to craft bargaining demands that create more jobs and aid the whole class. It fights for power and organization in the workplace or on the job in the realization that it is there that the greatest leverage exists, when properly applied. It is political by acting independently of the retreating parties of liberalism and social democracy, whatever the relation of the unions with such parties. It multiplies the political and social power by reaching out to other sectors of the class, be they other unions, neighborhood-based organizations, or other social movements. It fights for all the oppressed and enhances its own power by doing so (Moody, 1997: 4–5).[13]

And Moody correctly—though in too limited a manner—attributes SMU to the new unions of Brazil and South Africa (Moody, 1997: 205).[14]

It is to the work on the unions of Brazil and South Africa that we must turn for the origins of this term. Moody, as he recounts (Moody, 1997: 208–212), relied for much of his knowledge about unions in these countries on the work of Gay Seidman (1994). Seidman, in a very innovative monograph, compared the development of labor centers CUT *(Central Única dos Trabalhadores)* in Brazil and COSATU (Congress of South African Trade Unions) within their common context of rapidly industrializing countries, providing the understanding of social movement unionism from which Moody developed his thinking.

According to Seidman, "Theoretically, social movement unionism is perhaps best defined as an effort to raise the living standards of the working class as a whole, rather than to protect individually defined interests of union members" (Seidman, 1994: 2). She amplifies a little further, but it can be summed up as seeing SMU as being more than just the workplace-focused and institutionally-defined forms of trade unionism that has been present among so much of the labor movement around the world. Seidman further notes, after writing about unions joining campaigns for community-based issues such as housing, health care and running water, that "These campaigns link factory-based unions and communities, and *they lead to challenges to states* as well as to individual employers" (emphasis added) (Seidman, 1994: 3).[15]

What does "challenges to states" mean in day-to-day reality? It means these unions were challenging the anti-democratic dominance of the state by the elites and their allies, and the *systematic* propagation of policies and operations that were intended to hinder if not attack the well-being of working people (including peasants, women, and the urban poor) of their respective countries. Key to this challenge was the establishment and development of member-run, popular democratic and militant trade unions and pro-people organizations. These organizations, in turn, focused resistance against employers, contractors, contractors and urban police, against the elite-based state itself and, at best, suggested radical alternatives to the current social order for the benefit of all working women and men.

Moody's definition of SMU, therefore, comes out of developing countries (specifically Brazil and South Africa) but already in an attenuated version: where Seidman specifically included "challenges to states" in her discussion, Moody did not.[16] Moody suggested good things, but challenging the state is clearly not in his definition. This is an important point, however: the trade unionism that emerged in labor centers in several developing countries in the 1970s and 1980s—and the KMU should be included in the mix as well (Scipes, 1992a, 1992b, 1996, 2001)—specifically and consciously challenged the existence of the state (specifically, the dictatorships that controlled each of these respective countries), the entire established social order of each country,[17] and the global political-economic-cultural networks in which their respective countries were enmeshed.[18]

Despite this attenuated version of SMU—an attenuation that most theorists and writers are not aware of—Moody's terminology has resonated in North America and has expanded greatly. A wide variety of authors have used the term, including (among others) Dreiling and Robinson, 1998; Eimer, 1999; Voss and Sherman, 2000;[19] Huber and Luce, 2001; Johnston, 2001; Turner and Hurd, 2001; Robinson, 2002; Wilton and Cranford, 2002; Clawson, 2003; Nissen, 2003; Lopez, 2004; Milkman and Voss, eds., 2004; Sharpe, 2004; Fantasia and Voss, 2004; Milkman, 2006; Schiavone, 2004, 2007, 2008; Devinatz, 2008; Ross, 2008; and Tattersall, 2009.

The best effort to date to pull together this entire "school" of thought is Bruce Nissen's 2003 article in *Labor Studies Journal*. Nissen, in comparing "social movement" to what he calls "value added" unionism, gives an excellent overview of the SMU "school"—including a thorough bibliography. He basically describes social movement unionism theorists as arguing for the need to champion the issues of those oppressed by the US economic system; to require an internal transformation of unions; and to advocate increased union member mobilization (Nissen, 2003: 140–143). In short, those promoting the concept of social movement unionism in North America argue for a democratic, rank and file-led unionism that mobilizes their members to address not only issues of the union's (institutionalized) self-interest, but also issues within unions themselves, as well as the interests of all poor and working people in general, but *without challenging the existence of the current social order.* And these writers argue that it would be extremely desirable for the US labor movement to move further and faster toward this approach.[20]

However, there is one more set of scholars who have been influenced by Moody and are writing, and who deserve to be mentioned at this time; these scholars are trying to think out developments in unionism and social movements within Western Europe (see Dunn, 2007; Mathers, 2007; Upchurch, Taylor and Mathers, 2009; Upchurch and Mathers, 2012).

Without going into details, and while their empirical work appears sound, there are considerable problems with their theoretical efforts regarding unions. They show no awareness of the early debate about the Southern labor centers, and thus adopt Moody's conceptualization. They approach unions in South Africa, the US, and several Western European countries as though they developed according to similar processes, which they did not.[21] They privilege "class" and Marxist analysis (Upchurch, Taylor and Mathers, 2009: 14–21; Upchurch and Mathers, 2012), even when they provide no empirical evidence to support this position (see especially Mathers, 2007). They tend to focus on theory over empirical examples (see especially Dunn, 2007), even though sometimes raising excellent points. They over-emphasize the state and its institutionalization of labor, while under-emphasizing dynamics internal to unions (Upchurch and Mathers, 2012). And they suggest the emergence of a new type of unionism "to the left" of traditional "social democratic trade unionism," which they call "radicalized political unionism," but which they never define (Upchurch, Taylor and Mathers, 2009: 168–174).[22]

With that understanding of the Moody-inspired version of social movement unionism, however, it is now time to consider the "other" version of social movement unionism, as it developed initially, *before* Moody, and as it has been developed subsequently.

Social Movement Unionism (SMU) by New Unions of the Global South

During the 1970s and 1980s, a new type of trade unionism emerged among particular labor centers in several developing countries. The most advanced versions were the CUT in Brazil, KMU in the Philippines and COSATU in South Africa.[23] In each of these countries, these new labor centers were challenging employers, their respective state, and the global political-economic-cultural networks in which their countries were enmeshed.[24]

The Initial Debate

In the late 1980s and early 1990s, an international debate took place among scholars concerned with or interested in the new labor movements that had emerged in these three countries (Scipes, 2000c; Von Holdt, 2002: 285–287; for the original arguments, see Waterman, 1988e, 1991b; Lambert and Webster, 1988; Scipes, 1992a, 1992b; and for an early discussion of them, see Munck, 1988. See also Lambert, 1990; Scipes, 1996).[25] Attempting to take advantage of the then-emerging developments in social movement theory (Waterman, 1988e), these scholars were trying to theoretically understand the new phenomenon, and therefore advanced the concept of "social movement unionism" to understand these new labor movements. Peter Waterman, a long-time labor scholar and writer who coined the term, wanted to ensure that this concept was theoretically developed so that it would be much more than merely a terminological substitute:

> I am concerned that the term be defined in such a way that it provides both a new theoretical tool and suggests a new political norm. In other words, that it be distinguished from both traditional terminologies and traditional practices (Waterman, 1988e: 1).

Not surprisingly, the occasion of a new conceptualization yielded different understandings of what was meant by "social movement unionism," and the debate was an effort to refine the conceptualization for possible further generalization. The intention of this effort was to try to learn from the examples of the "advanced" labor movements of the late 20th Century so as to inform subsequent efforts, so this already-existing knowledge could hopefully be used to assist later-developing movements. However, unstated at the time but implicit in the methodology, was that by clarifying the understanding of these new labor movements and the social phenomena they represented, theorists could then reflect back on understandings of previously-existing unionism around the globe and hopefully further develop these understandings as well.

Rob Lambert and Eddie Webster, both of whom had been actively engaged in efforts to build the new, non-racial unions in South Africa, developed an argument in response to Waterman (1988e), and presented a conceptualization of three types of trade unionism from their work on unions in South Africa: they called these "orthodox," "populist" and "political or social movement" types of trade unionism.[26] These types of unionism were conceptualized on the basis of sets of particular practices (Lambert and Webster, 1988: 20–21).

Then this author followed, attempting to refine the thinking of Waterman and Lambert/Webster in two articles that were published in 1992:[27] the *Kasarinlan* article, in which the discussion was drawn out in detail and to the greatest extent (Scipes, 1992a), and the *Critical Sociology* article, which differentiated social movement unionism from Leninist approaches (Scipes, 1992b). As an American shopfloor worker (printing press operator), labor activist and researcher/writer, I was not satisfied with the Lambert/Webster conceptualization, although I considered it better than Waterman's effort. Assessing Lambert and Webster's work, an alternative conceptualization that surpassed their's was advanced. In this alternative, again based on specific sets of practices, it was argued that there were three types of trade unionism in the world: economic, political, and social movement unionism.

Economic trade unionism was defined as:

> . . . unionism that accommodates itself to, and is absorbed by, the industrial relations system of its particular country; which engages in political activities within the dominant political system for the well-being of its members and its institutional self but generally limits itself to immediate interests . . . (Scipes, 1992a: 126).

Political unionism was defined as:

> . . . unionism that is dominated by or subordinated to a political party or state, to which the leaders give primary loyalty—and this includes both the Leninist and "radical nationalist" versions. This results in generally but not totally neglecting workplace issues for "larger" political issues (Scipes, 1992a: 127).

And then, after detailing the debate over "social movement unionism" (Scipes, 1992a: 127–133), I defined my version of social movement unionism as:

> . . . a model of trade unionism that differs from the traditional forms of both economic and political unionism. This model sees workers' struggles as merely one of many efforts to qualitatively change society, and not either the only site for political struggle and social change or even the primary site. Therefore, it seeks alliances with other social movements on an equal basis, and tries to join them in practice when possible, both within the country and internationally.
>
> Social movement unionism is trade unionism democratically controlled by the membership and not by any external organization, which recognizes that the struggles for control over workers' daily work life, pay and conditions is intimately connected with and cannot be separated from the national socio-political-economic situation. This requires that struggles to improve the situ-

> ation of workers confront the national situation—combining struggles against exploitation and oppression in the workplace with those confronting domination both external from and internal to the larger society—as well as any dominating relations within the unions themselves. Therefore, it is autonomous from capital, the state and political parties, setting its own agenda from its own particular perspective, yet willing to consider modifying its perspective on the basis of negotiations with the social movements [and political parties] with which it is allied with and which it has equal relations (Scipes, 1992a: 133).[28]

This theoretical work was followed with a monograph on the KMU that attempted to use this conceptualization to understand an empirical study (Scipes, 1996).

To my knowledge, however, there have not been any direct responses to these conceptualizations by the others in this initial debate, nor in whole by any other writers (Sluyter-Beltrão, 2010: 6, uses an attenuated version of my concept), although my work has been referenced, suggesting it is at least known by a number of writers who have tried to develop the concept. Neither Lambert nor Webster, together or individually, has responded directly to my conceptualization, positively or negatively, although Webster published an article discussing it in the newsletter of Research Committee 44 (Labor Movements) of the International Sociological Association (see Scipes, 2000c). Waterman (2004) *appears* to have responded to my conceptualization if one looks at the bibliography of this piece which, as Waterman notes (2004: 243), "includes items beyond those referred to in the text above." However, in the body of his paper, instead of confronting my conceptualization or accurately describing my work, Waterman accuses me (along with Lambert) of "identification with" the KMU.[29] My conceptualization of SMU, as can be seen, does not fit into either of Waterman's "Class/Popular-Community" or "Class + New Social Movement" understandings (Waterman, 2004: 217–220) from which Waterman builds his argument.

In short, by ignoring a serious contribution to the debate on social movement unionism instead of substantively addressing it, these theorists have, in turn, helped further confuse the debate.

And at the same time, these other authors have shifted their foci from the subject at hand, leaving a vacuum in the discussion, without substantially announcing their change in focus. Waterman shifted his writings from focusing on *sets of practices* of the new unions to reflecting on his experiences, joining this with his increased knowledge and learning from his previous theoretical work; thus, his work has shifted from focusing on sets of practices to *normative prescriptions* of how he thinks this new unionism *should* develop (see Waterman, 1993), and has subsequently tried to apply this globally in what he calls "new social unionism" (Waterman, 1999), and then later "new international social unionism" (Waterman, 2004, 2008).[30]

From writing an important article on social movement unionism together, Rob Lambert and Eddie Webster (1988) have shifted as well. Lambert (1990), in a strong article, applied the concept of social movement unionism to the KMU, but as far as is known, never did further research in the Philippines, and subsequently shifted to writing about SIGTUR (Southern Initiative on Globalization and Trade Union Rights) and global social movement unionism. Webster, along with Lambert, has been writing about SIGTUR (Lambert and Webster, 2001; see Lambert, 2002), and has written about strategic unionism with others (see Joffe, Maller and Webster, 1995; for an evaluation of this concept from a case study in South Africa, see Von Holdt, 2003). Webster and Lambert, along with Andries Bezuidenhout (2008), conducted an innovative three-country study on the "white goods" industry. Webster, most recently, has returned to the SMU debate (with Peter Fairbrother), but without addressing many of the developments since he last published on the subject in 1988 (see Lambert and Webster, 1988; Fairbrother and Webster, 2008).

For those who know of Lambert and Webster's involvement in the early debate, as well as Waterman's, but who have not gone back to read their earlier writings, there is a tendency to assume they have been on a consistent path to develop the concept of social movement unionism, when they clearly have not.

Subsequent Debate and Development of Social Movement Unionism in Regard to the Specific Labor Centers of the Global South (post 1992)

However, the general effort to develop the concept of social movement unionism in regards to this "new unionism" in the Global South has continued beyond the initial effort, particularly regarding unionism in South Africa, and has continued to be seen as a valid perspective by a number of labor researchers (for South Africa, see Hirschsohn, 1998, 2007; Von Holdt, 2002, 2003; and see Bramble, 2003; Wood, 2003; Pillay, 2006: 169–172; and Barchiesi, 2007; for South Korea, see Koo, 2001; Park, 2007; Gray, 2008; for Brazil, see Sluyter-Beltrão, 2010).[31]

In an article published in 1998, Philip Hirschsohn argues that COSATU (Congress of South African Trade Unions) exemplifies social movement unionism (Hirschsohn, 1998). Not surprisingly, but nonetheless, theoretically important, Hirschsohn builds on the earlier work on Brazil, the Philippines and South Africa.[32] His work adds to the conception of social movement unionism:

> The existing literature of SMU either explains how or why the phenomenon has emerged and what distinguishes it from economic and political unionism,

> but fails to explain its organizational development systematically. Furthermore, there has been limited effort to integrate the rich [social movement] literature into the analysis of SMU. I adopt the political process approach to SMs to explain the origins, emergence, and development of SMU in South Africa (Hirschsohn, 1998: 634).

Unaware of Hirschsohn's research, yet trying to further develop my conceptualization of social movement unionism—and to critically test my conceptualization to see if was applicable outside of the Philippines—I wrote a subsequent article that has only been published on the Internet, reducing its impact. In this article, it was argued that COSATU of South Africa also fit my conceptualization of social movement unionism—strengthening the validity of the conceptualization—at least up until 1992[33] (Scipes, 2001, republished herein as Chapter 11).

In other words, while not trying to put these labor movements into a theoretical straitjacket—I take an activist-centered, but not determined, approach—it is argued that the workers in these specific labor centers in these particular developing countries collectively see themselves as actively trying to change the social order in which they are located as well as the global political-economic-cultural networks in which their respective countries are enmeshed.

It seems that three criteria must be met before a labor center can be accurately described as embodying social movement unionism: (1) that this understanding of challenging the existing social order is at least the general understanding of workers and their leaders across the unions of the entire labor center; (2) that this understanding is developed and adopted through an interactive process between leaders, both formal and informal (i.e., activists), and worker-members; i.e., *that it is not imposed by the top-down by leaders on members;* and (3) that this understanding predominates within the unions that lead any particular labor center (Scipes, 2001—herein, Chapter 11). The level of understanding could go beyond that, and certainly any educational program developed from this perspective and carried out within the unions across the labor center would try to generalize this understanding among all members—the KMU, at least, has taken this approach in its educational program (see Scipes, 1986b, 1996).

In short, workers and leaders in unions that lead particular labor centers have come to a general understanding in which they see themselves as actively trying to change the social order in which they are located, as well as the global political-economic-cultural networks in which their respective countries are enmeshed. Thus, these workers see themselves and their unions as being social change agents, but agents on behalf of themselves and their allies, and therefore *not* agents for external groups, such as a political party or a political candidate. They have collectively organized to change their world, with the help of allies at home and abroad, and to engage in mutual solidarity and support.

The discussion of social movement unionism has continued, with Karl von Holdt examining the development of SMU inside of a steel complex in South Africa, Highveld Steel. Here, Hirschsohn's plea for "systematic organizational development" gets met. In a carefully constructed monograph based on a case study,[34] Von Holdt defines social movement unionism

> as a highly mobilized form of unionism based in a substantial expansion of semi-skilled manufacturing work, which emerged in opposition to authoritarian regimes and repressive workplaces in the developing world. Social movement unionism is fiercely independent, but establishes alliances with community and political organizations. It demonstrates a commitment to internal democratic practices and to the broader democratic and socialist transformation of authoritarian societies (Von Holdt, 2003: 9).[35]

Von Holdt shows the erosion of social movement unionism during the period of transition to a post-apartheid society as NUMSA (the national union to which the metal workers' union at Highveld is affiliated) and COSATU shift towards "strategic unionism" wherein the union participates and engages in relations with both the state and management (Von Holdt, 2003: 305; see also Bramble, 2003, as well as Joffe, Maller and Webster, 1995).

The discussion of SMU has been supported, at least in part, by Geoffrey Wood's (2003) article on shop floor democracy in South Africa, and Sakhela Buhlungu's edited collection (2006) on "trade unions and democracy"—see, in particular, Devan Pillay's piece, pp. 169–172—as well as Hirschsohn's work in South African auto and clothing plants to support his earlier claims (Hirschsohn, 2007).

These approaches differ still from the latest contributions by Peter Fairbrother, Peter Waterman and Edward Webster (Fairbrother and Webster, 2008; Fairbrother, 2008; Waterman, 2008). These three scholars, as part of an international scholarly forum, try to "think out" the concept of social movement unionism. Yet, while very much aware of struggles in the Global South, they make a mistake similar to that of Moody (1997), yet from the other side: they don't question the generalization of the concept to unions in both the Global North and South, nor do they distinguish between the different types of unionism in the Global South (see Collombat, 2011, for a comparative study that specifically addresses this). In other words, they think they can generalize the conceptualization, once the "true nature" of social movement unions is explicated, which they try to do.

Nonetheless, regardless of how well or how poorly they do, the fact remains that there are a range of scholars who see the concept of social movement unionism as a vibrant concept, and one with enough "meat on the bones" to fight over. This author agrees. That is why it is so important to understand it on all levels—and to distinguish between what it is and is not.

Synopsis

There are three important points that must be recognized here. First is the *qualitative difference* between the *practices* of these particular labor centers in these developing countries and the practices of unions in North America. Specifically, labor centers in these developing countries—again, CUT, KMU, and COSATU—developed a type of trade unionism that consciously seeks to change the social order in which they are located, and the relations of their respective country with others.[36] While nothing theoretically precludes any "developed country" union or labor center from consciously seeking to change the existing social order, the fact is that none of the contemporary unions in North America have been or are challenging the existing social order, nor are they challenging the global political-economic-cultural networks in which their countries are enmeshed. Some North American unions are, interestingly, beginning to challenge aspects of the neo-liberal regime—such as the Free Trade Agreement of the Americas (FTAA) and the shift of manufacturing to outside of the US—that directly affect them and their members,[37] but this is far from what has been developed by workers in these three specific labor centers. Thus, the qualitative differences in practices must be recognized, and terminology recognizing these qualitative differences must be adopted, so as to illuminate and distinguish between these different sets of practices.

Second, researchers on unions in the developing countries have continued to work from this social movement unionism framework when regarding these particular labor centers in these respective countries. Thus, this concept is established and remains useful theoretically, even if the proponents have not agreed upon one specific definition. Hopefully, my conceptualization of SMU will be seen as substantial, and that future scholars will use this in their work as they go forward.

And third, and following from the above, the different practices between these particular labor centers and progressive efforts in North America (and elsewhere) must be addressed on a theoretical level: it is not sufficient to understand them only at descriptive or analytical levels if we want to try to generalize findings from them to help guide developments of other labor centers and their affiliated unions. The trade union practices of social movement unionism-based labor centers are practices qualitatively different from other existing unions and labor centers, especially in the United States, and require a theoretical conceptualization that recognizes these differences.

OVERCOMING THEORETICAL CONFUSION

To overcome the theoretical confusion discussed above, it is useful to deploy a taxonomy of global trade unionism—encompassing economic, political, and social movement unions—which allows commentators to theoretically locate the unionism they are referring to by separate type (see particularly Scipes, 1992a, 2001, and Chapter 6, herein). Thus, once located, hopes, expectations, and challenges can be more realistically addressed for that particular type of unionism—one can focus on specificities, rather than simply on general union aims.

It is argued that the types of trade unionism can be distinguished by variations regarding which forces determine organizational dynamics, the relations to the established industrial relations system of the country, and relationship of the labor center to the social order of the country:

Table 13.1. Types of Trade Unionism (based on sets of practices)[1]:

	Economic	*Political*	*Social Movement*
Organizational dynamics determined by	Members	Subordinated to and/or subjugates itself to an "outside" political party	Members
Relationship to established industrial relations system of the county	Accommodates to established IR system	Challenges IR system until its political party gains political control, and then accommodates to it	Challenges IR system

	Economic	*Political*	*Social Movement*
Relationship to social order of the country	Accommodates to social order, although tries to improve situation of its members within such order	Challenges social order until its political party gains political control, and then accommodates to it—tries to improve situation of its members within such order	Challenges social order and international political-economic-social-cultural networks in which country is enmeshed. Builds counter-hegemonic political-economic-social-cultural power through location in production-distribution-exchange sphere of society; represents and fights for "larger" worker, urban poor and peasant interests; and demonstrates willingness to use such power to challenge established social order in conjunction with political allies, both domestic and internationally

1. Historical examples are used to illustrate his three types of trade unionism. From Selig Perlman's (1968/1928) comparative study of labor movements in Germany, Britain, the US and Russia in the 19th and early 20th centuries, I use Perlman's work on trade unionism in the US—which was described as "an economic institution," based on "job consciousness" that limits itself to "wage and job control" (Perlman, 1968/1928: 169)—to illustrate what I call "economic unionism." I use Victoria Bonnell's (1983) study of workers in St. Petersburg and Moscow between 1900–1914, whereby workers ultimately decided to subordinate themselves and their unions to a group of intellectuals' organization (Bolshevik Party) (Bonnell, 1983: 7–8), to illuminate what I call "political unionism." And I use my own study of the KMU (Scipes, 1996) to explicate what I advance as "social movement unionism" (Scipes, 2001: 5–6). This is presented in more detail herein in Chapter 6.

It seems, however, that delineating by type, while necessary, is not sufficient. Different sets of practices can be empirically distinguished between unionism types, but are there differences in union behavior *within* unionism types?

It is argued there *can* be qualitative differences in union behavior *within* union types, and to delineate behaviors within types, the concept trade union "form" has been advanced: forms are different sets of practices *within* a particular type of trade unionism (Scipes, 2003). Thus, there are two different *levels* of trade union conceptualizations—"types" and "forms"—with forms being *subsets* of types.

To return to the issue at hand: if *social movement unionism in North America* is not the same type as social movement unionism developed in these particular labor centers in certain developing countries, as established above, then what is it; how can it be understood? To understand these recent developments in North American unionism, it is time to consider a study specifically designed to establish theoretically the concept of trade union "forms."

STEEL AND PACKINGHOUSE UNIONISM IN THE CHICAGO AREA, 1933–1955

By examining the emergence and development of unions in the steel and packinghouse industries in the Chicago area between 1933–55 for my Ph.D. dissertation,[38] this author sought to discover if these unions differed in how they addressed racial oppression in the union, workplace and community and, if so, how this could be theoretically explained (Scipes, 2003).[39]

To do this in light of the discussion above, these unions had to be theoretically located. It was established that both unions were of the economic type: both accepted the industrial relations system of the particular country (the US), and both engaged in political activities within the dominant political system for the well-being of their members and their institutional selves—they did not challenge the established social order, nor did they challenge the legitimacy of the established industrial relations system. Neither union has been dominated by nor subjugated itself to an external organization (political unionism), nor did either try to challenge the dominant social order (social movement unionism). Accordingly, both unions were recognized as being representatives of the economic type of trade unions.

A historical-comparative, naturalistic study of two comparable trade unions was undertaken to see if two qualitatively different sets of practices (forms) could be delineated among these unions that exemplified the economic type of unionism. To do this, it looked at the development of two unions in fairly similar industries (regarding the process-nature of production) and with similarities in workplace conditions (long hours, low pay, dangerous conditions) in the same area (the greater Chicago area, including Northwest Indiana), at the same time (1933–55), and with workers drawn from the exact same labor pool (white ethnic groups from Eastern and Southern Europe, African Americans from the rural southern US, and a smaller group of Mexican workers). This also meant that the workers shared the same general demographics: similar immigration origins and histories, same ethnic and racial compositions, same religious backgrounds, same educational attainment, same cultures, etc. (Scipes, 2003: 45–50).

The initial focus of this research was on how each union addressed the issue of racial oppression, and a close examination showed that the packinghouse workers "aggressively tackled this social evil that had caused and was continuing to cause so much harm and hurt to its members, both workers of color and whites," while the steelworkers "either acquiesced to or actively collaborated in the continued existence of racial oppression" (Scipes, 2003: 343–344). However, it was found that the unions not only qualitatively differed in this, but they also differed qualitatively in the form of trade unionism that each had developed. And when the differences in regard to racial oppression were explained, it was found that the form of trade unionism developed determined whether or not each union would address racial oppression.

Different Conceptualizations of Trade Unionism

This study from Chicago focuses on both internal factors and processes by which a union is constructed, and the results it has achieved; accordingly

> . . . its explanation differs from those who argue that structural position determines development, and [differs] from those who focus on the results of leadership differentiation and political struggles around institutional issues. It is argued that it is the collective identity suggested by activists, when negotiated and finally adopted by rank and file members, that creates an organizational collective identity (see Melucci, 1995, 1996). [From] this organizational collective identity, [members] establish the form of trade unionism chosen and that, in turn—by mediating members' understandings and actions—effects trade union activities in regard to other relationships; in this case, it is argued that the different forms of unionism effect how a union approaches working people's oppression in general, and in this project, racial oppression in the union, the workplace and in the local community (Scipes, 2003: 28).

Close examination of these two unions' respective development reveals different ways of understanding unionism. The argument is that a union's willingness to address the issue of racial oppression—as well as other non-economistic caused oppression, such as gender oppression—depends on the organizational form of trade unionism that it has developed—whether its members have adopted what is known as "business" or "social justice" unionism.[40] These forms of trade unionism are based on different conceptualizations of trade unionism and the processes by which they are adopted, and are developed below.

While it is well known that, in general, members of the proletariat have different interests than do members of the bourgeoisie, and that these interests are antagonistic (Marx and Engels, 1978/1848), this does not necessarily hold in specific situations. Workers, as we know, can be opposed to their bosses; can ignore/disregard their bosses; can work with them; and/or a combination of these different approaches. And they can act in solidarity with other workers, ignore/disregard them, and work against them; and/or a combination of these different approaches. In short, we cannot assume that workers' general interest holds specifically, or at all times and all places (see Hodson, 1991).[41] Accordingly, by examining the social processes by which a group of workers construct their own organizations, we can see how they define their particular interests within specific situations.

This approach is supported on a theoretical level by Alberto Melucci's (1989, 1995) work on social movements. It is argued that Melucci provides guidance here for the establishment of trade unions and their amalgamated organizations, as he can, arguably, for any organization. Melucci critiques most research on social movements because it assumes any social movement is an empirical reality; he argues that to understand a social movement, one must understand the *constitutive* processes by which any social movement emerges and develops (Melucci, 1989). Similarly, this author argues that it is the constitutive processes that determine how an organization emerges, which will effect subsequent developments. Key to this in regard to the development of a trade union (or similar organizations) is the form of unionism chosen to guide subsequent development.

The form of trade unionism chosen is based on different conceptualizations of trade unionism. Both conceptualizations see unions as organizations based in the production sphere of society, but one sees the unions taking a *narrow* approach, limiting its concerns and operations to benefit those groupings that are dominant within the union, and even sometimes at the expense of other working people ("business unionism"), while the other takes a *broad* approach, working for the well-being of their members and working people in general throughout society ("social justice unionism").

As a result of my 2003 study, business unionism can be formally defined as:

> . . . one form of the economic type of trade unionism. While its internal decision-making processes can range from a top-down, results-oriented model to a bottom-up, process-oriented model, *its scope is narrow,* limiting its interests to those of the dominant members of the organization, and not necessarily to all members of the organization. These self-defined interests can be seen as separate from those of working people as a whole, and sometimes even opposed to this larger group interest. Because of this limited vision of trade unionism, business unionism depends on the ability of unions to win demands by themselves, or if they get the support of other organizations which adopt the business union's interests and goals as corresponding to their own, it is without the union making any commitment of reciprocation to its allies. It is a form of trade unionism ultimately based on individualism, albeit expressed in a collective manner (emphasis added) (Scipes, 2003: 373–374).

Social justice unionism can be formally defined as another

> . . . form of the economic type of trade unionism. While its internal decision-making processes can range from a top-down, results-oriented model to a bottom-up, process-oriented and democratic model, *its scope is broad,* seeing the necessity of addressing the needs and concerns of all its members, in the union, in the workplace and in the community. In short, these self-defined interests are

> integrated with those of working people as a whole. It builds support through solidarity with other people-focused organizations and projects, working in mutual efforts to improve the well-being of all concerned. It is a form of trade unionism ultimately based on collectivity and mutual respect (emphasis added) (Scipes, 2003: 375).[42]

The adoption of a particular conceptualization of unionism by any union at best is a product of a three-way interaction between members, activists (informal leaders) and formal leaders, although obviously, formal union leadership in some cases can promote or hinder membership or activist involvement in such choice. In other words, the form of trade unionism chosen is more than just a product of the presence or absence of activists and their particular politics: activists *are* important, but how they are facilitated or constrained by formal leaders is a factor, as is how the membership responds or does not respond to their ideas/activities/proposals, etc.

At the same time, this is a process critically affected by how collective decisions are made, whether inclusively from the bottom-upwards, or exclusively from the top-downwards: unions whose positions are based on inclusive rank-and-file participation and collective decision-making are more likely to have greater membership participation and maintain vibrant internal democracy than are unions that exclude rank-and-file members from decision-making processes (see Ross, 2008: 148–153). Further, support for any form of unionism based on inclusion and collective decision-making is much more likely to survive difficult times than those with exclusive decision-making.

While this process is developed in detail elsewhere (Scipes, 2003), it is important to recognize that the steel workers' union adopted a business union conceptualization of trade unionism early-on, while the packinghouse workers' union adopted a social justice conceptualization.

One final question remains: while these forms of trade unionism are obviously different, how can we make sure they are *qualitatively* different; that is, how can we be sure the differences are significant? To address this question, in addition to a very detailed historical examination of the development of the respective unions—which were unquestionably different—I developed a 30-point measurement scale to see if the differences were significant. The measurement scale used business unionism as the referent, and required a union to get a minimum of 20 points to be confirmed as a social justice union (Scipes, 2003: 412–415). The findings: "when measured across the years 1936–1954, the packinghouse workers' organizations in Chicago scored 29 out of a possible 30 points, while the steelworkers' organizations in the same region scored only two out of 30 points" (Scipes, 2003: 52).[43] The findings were deemed significant.

Accordingly, the argument herein is that the form of unionism based on a broad conceptualization of trade unionism (i.e., social justice unionism)—creates unions that are qualitatively more likely to address racial (and/or other) oppression than are unions based a narrow conceptualization of trade unionism (business unionism).

THE CORRECT PRECEDENT: UNITED PACKINGHOUSE WORKERS OF AMERICA (UPWA)

Despite not getting a lot of attention at least until 1997 within the genre of work that perhaps can be called collectively "CIO Studies," unionism in meatpacking—in both the Packinghouse Workers Organizing Committee between 1937 and 1943 and, after October 1943, the United Packinghouse Workers of America—developed further than almost any other union within the CIO. The union was by far the best on addressing racial oppression—by 1961, 100 percent of all UPWA collective bargaining agreements banned discrimination based on race, creed and national origin, either in employment applications or in employment—and one of the better unions in addressing gender oppression, although their work on gender was not as strong as on race. It was responsible for considerable economic gains, and definitely improved working conditions. Throughout its entire existence—until it was forced to join the Amalgamated Meat Cutters and Butcher Workmen in 1968 due to industry restructuring (the Amalgamated, in turn, was one of the founding members of the United Food & Commercial Workers' Union in 1979)—the United Packinghouse Workers of America (UPWA) was a democratically-run, rank and file-led, militant union that not only addressed issues in the workplace, but also in the union and the communities in which it was located (see Halpern, 1997; Horowitz, 1997; Halpern and Horowitz, eds., 1999; Scipes, 2003; and Street, 1993).

As suggested in the introduction to this chapter, the relatively recent "emergence" of a militant unionism that addresses issues in the workplace, union and community is, in reality, the re-emergence of the form of trade unionism developed by the United Packinghouse Workers of America and a few others—such as the United Electrical Workers and the International Longshore and Warehouse Union—in the 1930s and '40s.

Does this conceptualization—social justice unionism—better describe the forms of unionism currently re-emerging in North America than social movement unionism?

Discussion: Social Movement Unionism or Social Justice Unionism?

To answer this question, we must turn to the work of Kim Moody, the writer who popularized the term "social movement unionism" in North America, to see if he can provide guidance to resolve this question. Unfortunately, Moody's work does not give us the tools to resolve this issue, nor does the work of others who have built on Moody's conceptualization. His conceptualization of social movement unionism is quite limited, as is Seidman's on which Moody's is based: neither are theoretically located; they are presented only at an analytical level.

Nonetheless, there is another way to approach this issue. It is argued that using a theoretically-based model offers us a way forward to resolve this issue. The way to resolution is to remember that all unions can be theoretically categorized as one of three types of unions: economic, political, or social movement (Scipes, 1992a). As indicated above, these North American unions do not fit into either the social movement or political types of trade unionism, but do fit in the economic type.

However, within the economic type of trade unionism, where do they fit? This author has argued that there are two forms or subsets of the economic type of unionism: business and social justice unionism. Based on the analysis above, and learning from the experiences of the United Packinghouse Workers of America, it seems quite clear that they fit in the social justice form of economic trade unionism.

Thus, *social justice unionism* is the best term to describe the form of economic trade unionism currently developing. Accordingly, it is argued that now and in the foreseeable future, those writing on the "new" unionism of North America should replace the term "social movement unionism" with "social justice unionism," and that the term "social movement unionism" be reserved for those types of unionism that seek qualitative social, political and/or systemic economic change in their respective social order as well as in the global political-economic-cultural networks.

CONCLUSION

This chapter has argued that as North American labor writers and theorists have tried to develop "new" thinking about trade unionism that has emerged in Canada and the United States relatively recently, their chosen terminology has conflicted with previously-developed terminology, leading to the use of the same term to refer to two qualitatively different types of trade unionism, causing unnecessary confusion. This, it was argued, hinders our understanding of global trade unionism, and it was suggested that it should be reconsidered. At the same time, because "social movement unionism" in North America has not been placed within a global theoretical context, writers have been, in fact, overriding a theoretically developed model with one that has not been theoretically developed.

To untangle the problem of terminological confusion and to advance theoretical understanding, this work took four general steps. First, emergence of the "social movement unionism" school in North America was discussed (Nissen, 2003), with particular attention being paid to the work of Kim Moody (1997).

Much of this work, unfortunately, was conducted without knowledge of the already-existing theoretical work done using the term "social movement unionism," used to describe the "new unionism" that developed in three specific labor centers in three particular developing countries in the 1970s and 1980s (Scipes, 1992a, 1992b, 1996, 2001). Efforts to understand the unionism of these specific labor centers led to an initial theoretical debate that was discussed, as were subsequent efforts to refine the concept of social movement unionism. This, in turn, led to a theoretical understanding of global trade unionism.

After theoretically distinguishing between different types of trade unionism to help resolve the issue, the concept of trade union form was advanced. The development of two CIO unions was briefly considered, each an example of economic trade unionism, but exemplifying two qualitatively different forms of unionism: business unionism and social justice unionism (Scipes, 2003).

And finally, arguing that a theoretical model is the only orientation developed to date that is capable of giving us tools to resolve this issue, it was suggested that this theoretical model proposed herein be adopted to provide resolution on the issue: accordingly, the broad-scope form of trade unionism that is currently developing in North America should now be seen theoretically as a form of economic trade unionism properly titled "social justice unionism."

Thus, this author argues that labor writers and theorists should no longer use the term "social movement unionism" to describe union activities in North America, but rather replace that term with "social justice unionism."[44] This allows us to recognize the different practices among unions in a number of countries, and to theoretically understand the form of trade unionism currently developing among some unions in North America, while not ignoring or denigrating the accomplishments of workers elsewhere. Once the literature ceases to mis-identify global unionism as identical to that occurring in North America, linguistic precision will enhance the accuracy of these writers discussing global labor issues.

NOTES

1. For a set of reviews by an American labor activist that covers many of the struggles and much of the writings on US labor over the past 30 years—particularly by activists, but also some academic studies—and which particularly focuses on issues related to revitalization, see Early, 2009.

The broadest compilation of writings on the contemporary US labor movement (along with a fair collection on selected labor movements around the world) that this author is aware of, including books and articles, is my on-line "Contemporary Labor Issues Bibliography" at https://www.pnw.edu/faculty/kim-scipes-ph-d/publications/contemporary-labor-issues-bibliography/. While this does not claim to be complete, the listings cover a wide range of particular subject areas, are updated fairly regularly, and include writings by academics as well as labor activists. These references are also linked to Internet sources whenever possible.

It should be noted that, the Canadian labor movement has been facing many of the problems faced by those of us in the US, although they are not in quite as bad of shape (see Gindin, 1995). Nonetheless, other Canadian scholars—see, for example, Fairbrother and Yates, eds. (2003), Kumar and Murray (2006), Kumar and Schenk, eds. (2006), and Ross (2008)—have joined the discussion about labor movement revitalization, focusing primarily on the Canadian labor movement. As Ross' bibliography (2008: 153–157) indicates, however, this is in interaction with the relevant American literature as well as their own.

2. This chapter was published in 2014, and as of February 1, 2020, it has had over 2,700 full-text downloads from around the world. It was written after most of the other chapters—excepting Chapters 3 and the Epilogue, which were specifically written for this collection—and as an effort to end at least some of the confusion and lack of clarity that had developed over the years. Accordingly, it responds to initial articles and how they were subsequently reacted to, but tries to do so in a way that is coherent and makes sense to readers today.

3. There is growing interest in "social movement unionism" (SMU) in developed countries outside of North America—see in particular Vandenberg (2006) for Sweden; and Dunn, 2007; Mathers, 2007; Upchurch, Taylor and Mathers, 2009; and Upchurch and Mathers, 2012 for Western Europe in general—but Ince (2007) says it is mostly confined to the "Anglophone world." An important part of this is due to the popularization and dissemination of the concept by Kim Moody (1997), and the North American network in and around the English-language labor activist journal, *Labor Notes*. Discussion of social movement unionism herein, unless specifically identified otherwise, is confined to North America, but it is important to recognize that discussions on SMU in the developed countries are not just confined to Canada and the United States.

4. This author served as an elected board member of RC 44 from 2006–2010, being elected at the International Sociological Association's World Congress of Sociology in Durban, South Africa in 2006.

5. Thus, this chapter addresses the problem of applying the same term to qualitatively different social phenomena, and is not merely a focus on terminology, as one previous reviewer initially claimed.

6. Thus, it is the trade union *organization* that is the independent variable, not the country. As stated in previous chapters, any country could have two or three different types of trade unionism.

7. In a strong and thoughtful article that I found just as I was preparing this manuscript for publication in July 2013, Stephanie Ross discusses "social unionism" in Canada. In it, she notes, "There is a great deal of confusion about the definition of social unionism, and a wide variety of terms and practices are associated with it in both labor movement documents and academic literature. In particular, 'social unionism,' 'social movement unionism,' 'community unionism,' and the 'organizing model' are used interchangeably to refer to a common set of North American union orientations and revitalization strategies" (Ross, 2008: 131).

8. In another recently found article, Gay Seidman (2011) discusses some of the confusion around this term as well, although I don't think her analysis is as clear as we need.

9. While Mexico is geographically located in North America, it is not included in this discussion because of a number of distinct factors—including colonial history, social structure, political system, culture, dominant language, level of economic development, form of trade unionism, etc.—that qualitatively differ from the US and Canada, which are much more similar among themselves. This is not to imply that the social situations in the US and Canada are superior vis-à-vis Mexico—they are in some ways, but not in others—but for this discussion, Mexico is not included.

10. This is not to suggest that, in the future, additional types and/or forms could not be added to this theoretical approach. However, these would be limited to being based on identified sets of practices. The normative prescriptions suggested by Waterman (1993, 1999, 2004, 2008), ostensibly part of this discussion, might guide future trade union development, but until sets of practices of how this works in practical terms are identified, it is argued that these should not be included in this theoretical model.

11. To be clear: there is no theoretical reason that social movement unionism could not appear in the Global North; however, to date, it has not.

12. Paul Johnston (1994), in an excellent study that has not received the attention it deserves, was the first to use this term regarding unionism in North America as far as I can ascertain. Nonetheless, almost all references to this subject refer to Moody, 1997.

13. Schiavone (2007: 281), who is the first to analyze Moody's conceptualization of SMU in regard to actual trade union practices, uses the exact same quote from Moody to define Moody's conceptualization. Waterman (2004: 217–218), discussing Moody's concept theoretically, uses another quote from p. 276 of the same book (Moody, 1997), as does Fairbrother (2008: 214–215). Neither quotation, in this author's opinion, is a theoretical explanation of social movement unionism, despite suggestions otherwise.

14. For some unknown reason that he has apparently never publicly explained—and surprising in light of the considerable amount of published material available on the KMU before 1997, including a number of articles in *Labor Notes,* of which he was

a founding staffer, as well as Labor Notes having Leto Villar, KMU National Vice Chairman, speak at their November 1986 conference (I stood next to Villar while at the conference as he made a call to the Philippines during which he learned about the assassination of KMU Chairman Rolando Olalia)—Moody totally ignores the KMU (*Kilusang Mayo Uno* or May First Movement) Labor Center of the Philippines in his book on "Unions in the International Economy" (Moody, 1997; see Labor Notes, 1986a, 1986b; Scipes, 1986a). Even if the KMU did not fit his understanding, he nonetheless should have recognized its existence (see Lambert, 1990; Eckstein, 1986; Eisenhower, 1991; Scipes, 1986a, 1989b, 1996; also West, 1991, 1997).

15. In one of a number of conversations during 1993–94, when I was studying with her at the University of Wisconsin-Madison, Seidman told me—although I cannot date the conversation—that her use of SMU was stimulated by Eddie Webster at the University of the Witwatersrand in Johannesburg in the mid-1980s. Webster, as will be discussed below, later engaged in an international debate on different types of trade unionism, and especially on the new unions of the Global South. Seidman, although using Webster's terminology, was apparently unaware of this international debate, for she did not participate in it.

16. Writers who have used the concept of SMU in discussing labor organizations in the Global South, subsequent to the initial debate, have also focused recognized challenges to the state as being a key aspect of SMU. Philip Hirschsohn (1998: 634) specifically focuses on challenges to the state as part of his understanding of social movement unionism. Jeffrey Sluyter-Beltrão, in his study of the CUT, builds off my work (specifically, Scipes, 1992b), and defines SMU as having three "core commitments": participatory democracy, political autonomy, and societal transformation. He further amplifies: "Although western labor observers and organizers have often neglected SMU's commitments to societal transformation, that third basic dimension is *an equally essential characteristic*" (emphasis added) (Sluyter-Beltrão, 2010: 6–7).

Gay Seidman (2011: 96) herself, in a later piece, supports this broader understanding: ". . . industrial workers discovered they could use factory-based unions as a vehicle for political demands, their movements often became central to broad challenges to what Brazilian unionists often called the 'savage capitalism' of elitist, inegalitarian growth."

17. Although it had been previously suggested that this author was, in fact, referring to capitalism here, I disagree: while the economic base of these respective social orders was and is capitalist, it is incorrect to conflate the social order with capitalism. By larger social order, I mean the entire range of social relations within a stratified society, and while including the economic system, this definitely goes beyond it. However, there is a range of positions within these labor centers as to whether capitalism must be replaced or not. Further discussion is beyond the scope of this argument.

18. Writers who have been influenced by the work of Immanuel Wallerstein would refer to these global political-economic-cultural networks as the "world system" (Wallerstein, 1974). This conceptualization is rejected—I do not accept that there is a world "system"—hence, this particular terminology. For the best theoretical critique of Wallerstein's work, see Nederveen Pieterse, 1989, especially Chapter 2.

19. Voss and Sherman (2000), while not adopting this terminology specifically in this article are aware of it, refer a number of times to social movements, and this author thinks it would be fair to place them within this "school" of studies.

20. Beginning in 2008, SEIU (Service Employees International Union)—which has served for many writers as the epitome of North American "social movement unionism"—became involved in several conflicts, both internally and with other unions in the US and Puerto Rico, especially raising issues of union democracy and member control over their organization. There are several articles regarding this listed on Scipes' "Contemporary Labor Issues" Bibliography, and see in particular Early (2011). Despite knowing of some of these developments, I chose not to address them herein, as they are not relevant to this specific argument.

21. Gay Seidman discusses how this has differed from the earlier industrialization experiences:

> Despite some similarities, industrialization in what are sometimes called "semi-peripheral" areas may not mirror the European and North American experiences . . . patterns of industrialization in the late twentieth century have often involved reliance on imported technologies developed in core industrialized areas, as well as on infusions of foreign capital, and have depended on links to international markets. While de-skilling of artisans has occurred from place to place, the new technologies have frequently been put in place without many of the labor process conflicts that apparently marked earlier industrialization. Mass production processes using semi-skilled workers have been in place from the start of industrial growth . . . (Seidman, 1994: 6).

22. All of that being said, I think their work *is* important. This will make more sense after reading more of the article, but I would place what they have found as social justice unionism (SJU), a subset of the economic type of trade unionism. However, their findings suggest a need to differentiate between institutionalized SJU and non-institutionalized SJU, which would broaden and perhaps deepen our understanding of SJU, in itself, thereby making an important contribution to our collective theoretical project.

23. Again, it is the trade union *organization* that is the independent variable, not the country.

24. There are considerable writings on these new labor organizations. For some of the best books on development of the new unions in South Africa, see MacShane, Plaut and Ward (1984), Friedman (1987), Baskin (1991), Kraak (1993), Von Holdt (2003), and Buhlungu, ed. (2006), and for additional references, see Hirschsohn (1998, 2007), Scipes (2001—republished herein in Chapter 11), Bezuidenhout (2002), Von Holdt (2002), Bramble (2003), Wood (2003), Barchiesi (2007), and Pillay (2008). For books on the development of the new unions in the Philippines, see Scipes (1996) and West (1997); for a strong article on the development of the KMU between 1980–86, see Lambert (1990); for an in-depth look at the social context in which the KMU operates, which has been subject to—at that time—37 years of neoliberal economic policies, see Scipes (1999), republished herein in Chapter 7. Jeffrey Sluyter-Beltrão (2010) has published a book in English on the "new" unions in Brazil, filling a massive hole in the literature, although two excellent articles that focus on the

new unions in Brazil, at least in part, had been published before his monograph—see Beynon and Ramalho (2000), and Guidry (2003). Also, Thomas Collombat's (2011) innovative yet unpublished Ph.D. dissertation, compares Brazilian and Mexican unions, and their efforts to build international labor solidarity throughout the Americas, providing another perspective on Brazilian Labor.

25. While this early debate began with a consideration of "labor movements," it was quickly seen that there were competing "labor movements" within each of these countries, and thus the debate shifted to considering "labor centers." As mentioned above, in international labor terminology, the AFL-CIO, for example, is a labor center. An earlier article specifically discusses the relationship between labor movements and labor centers (Scipes, 2001:4), republished herein in Chapter 5.

The larger point here is that the initial debate was around how do we understand these newly emerging types of trade unionism at the labor center level. Subsequent theoretical development, as shown below, has been to try to discuss the emergence of this type of trade unionism at more specific (and "lower") levels, such as at the industry-wide level (see Hirschsohn, 2007) and at the individual firm level (Von Holdt, 2003); see also Barchiesi (2007) for a discussion of municipal-based unions. Developments at these levels have subsequently been used to try to reflect upon, if not refine, the type of unionism exemplified at the labor center level.

26. These were based on "workerist," "populist," and "popular-democratic" visions of trade unionism that had developed in South Africa. For a recent discussion of this, see Pillay, 2008: 282–284.

27. Waterman's and Lambert/Webster's conceptualizations are described and critiqued in my article (Scipes, 1992a: 124–134), the first half—where these arguments are covered—is republished herein in Chapter 6.

28. By "national socio-political-economic situation," I was not only referring to the national situation within the country, but to each country's specific position within global political-economic-military-cultural networks; that is, I was placing this within the global context. Perhaps not as clear as it should have been, I've added this at the urging of one of the anonymous reviewers, to which I thank for this suggestion.

Incidentally, I must disagree with Gay Seidman, who states, "But the concept [of social movement unionism-KS] was not never clearly defined; even those of us who used it freely weren't entirely sure of its meaning" (Seidman, 2011: 98). I have been and remain quite clear on my conceptualization.

29. This is an effort to discredit my position (as well as that of Rob Lambert) regarding this issue, instead of seriously addressing my arguments, which Waterman has never done, here or anywhere else. And interestingly, especially in light of Waterman's emphasis on "internationalism," Waterman does not include an article that specifically discusses the very innovative international program of the KMU, which Waterman placed on his very own "Global Solidarity Dialogue" web site (Scipes, 2000a), republished herein as Chapter 12.

30. This claim that Waterman's prescriptions are normative has also been made by Von Holdt, 2002: 285. Fairbrother and Webster (2008: 310) specifically point out that Waterman's 2008 contribution "is normative."

Although I have problems with Dunn's (2007) larger argument, he also challenges the theoretical basis of Waterman's positions.

31. The latest set of articles published on SMU (Fairbrother, 2008; Fairbrother and Webster, 2008; Waterman, 2008) does not really fit into this specific discussion on SMU; the first two articles generalize a global perspective, unifying the concept across both the North and South instead of discussing the actions within certain labor centers, while Waterman continues his foray into his prescriptive normativism, arguing how unions should develop around the globe.

32. When writers in other countries refer to the Philippines, they reference my work. I cannot remember seeing any references from outside the US to Lois West's 1997 monograph on the KMU.

33. Hirschsohn (1998: 635) also limits his consideration of COSATU, stopping at 1990. It may be possible to decide whether Hirschsohn or myself were more accurate or not on this point, but it is basically irrelevant for this discussion: the point is that both of us recognize that COSATU fit our respective conceptualization up to a certain point in time, and then things became unclear.

This raises an important point: one never achieves "social movement unionism-ness"; it is a process of construction that continues over time. Accordingly, even labor centers seen to be social movement union-type centers can revert back to economic or political types of unionism.

In fact, Sluyter-Beltrão's (2010) project is to try to understand what happened with the CUT in Brazil (which he argues no longer is a social movement-type center), so that people can try to prevent this "reversion" in the future.

34. Von Holdt (2002, 2003) has provided us with a truly excellent case study of the development and disintegration of social movement unionism within a single industrial organization. Key to his study is the *internal contestation* (i.e., within the union) over the understanding, meaning and activities of SMU within one organization. There is a tremendous amount to be learned by his carefully done study.

However, while agreeing with him that "national reality counts" (Von Holdt, 2002: 299)—arguing against general prescriptions such as put forth previously by Moody (1997) and Waterman (1993)—this author argues that Von Holdt overgeneralizes the results from his study: he assumes that things he found in the specific case of Highveld Steel (specifically intra-union violence) to be representative of social movement unionism overall, for which he provides little evidence to support, but which is contradicted by research findings from the Philippines (see Lambert, 1990; Scipes, 1996; West, 1997), where this was not found.

35. Von Holdt specifically includes the Philippines, along with Brazil and South Africa in his understanding of social movement unionism. However, although he knows of Lambert's 1990 study and my study (Scipes, 1992a), he does not really make use of either in his conceptualization: he refers to Munck (1988), Waterman (1993—after Waterman took his more normative approach), Seidman (1994) and—most surprisingly—Moody (1997) (Von Holdt, 2003: 24–25, FN #4).

Had Von Holdt been aware of my monograph (Scipes, 1996), he would have seen that at least in the Philippines, SMU emerged in sugar plantations, capitalist agriculture, and extractive mining in addition to semi-skilled manufacturing, therefore emerging in both colonial and post-colonial production systems. Accordingly, Von Holdt (hopefully) would not have confined his definition to "semi-unskilled manufacturing work."

36. Development of SMU has not been linear, nor continuous; in fact, it seems likely that the transition to democracy and some sort of accommodation between the labor-supported political parties that took political office and the respective labor center in Brazil and South Africa directly affected social movement unionism, "diluting" it and perhaps leading back to some form of economic unionism. Bramble (2003) and Barchiesi (2007) raise similar questions, as does Sluyter-Beltrão (2010). [Upchurch and Mather (2012: 11) argue that SMU theorists have not considered sufficiently the role of the state, and argue that the changing institutional context could have an important impact on subsequent development.]

The transition from the dictatorship of Ferdinand Marcos to the "democracy" led by Corazon Aquino in the Philippines really was only a resumption of "traditional elite democracy" (see Kerkvliet and Mojares, eds., 1991; McCoy, 2009: 433–451), which did not lead to substantial change and, in fact, led to continued—and, in fact, worsened—repression against the KMU (Scipes, 1996), precluding any political accommodation.

Theoretically, this suggests that social movement unionism can arise during periods of authoritarianism—it does not have to—but that does not guarantee that unions who adopt social movement unionism as their type of trade unionism will always keep it; it seems clear that they can change—for better or worse—when they see their particular situation requiring it (such as the imposition of popular democracy). However, any change of regime to democracy must be "in fact," not just a "name change," as the experiences of the Philippines warns.

37. Devinatz (2008) provides an overview of how "social movement unionism" (based on Moody's conceptualization) has been used by unions and community organizations in the United States.

38. Trying to get my dissertation published as a monograph is my next scholarly project. Given the choice between writing on current efforts to dominate labor around the world by the AFL-CIO foreign policy leadership or publishing an important but historical study, I chose the former for my previous work (Scipes, 2010a), and this instant study grew out of thinking of alternative ways to build international labor solidarity and go "around" the AFL-CIO's labor imperialism (Scipes, 2010b). Neither of these subsequent projects undercut the value of my dissertation. In fact, this dissertation is under consideration by an academic publisher in early 2020.

39. The study herein is limited to examining qualitative differences among economic types of trade unionism, and does not examine differences among political or social movement types of trade unionism.

40. The term "social justice unionism" (SJU) was first advanced in my study (Scipes, 2003), although Tait (2005) and Fletcher and Gapasin (2008) have subsequently adopted the term, each independently from me. I wanted a term that both differentiated a form of trade unionism distinct from business unionism, and specifically referred to struggles for social justice, as that is how the packinghouse workers saw their efforts (see especially Halpern and Horowitz, eds., 1999).

What I am now calling "social justice unionism" has long been known within North American labor studies as "social" unionism (see Horowitz, 1997; and see Ross, 2008). This, however, was superseded by Moody's version of SMU. And now, this author is suggesting that SMU in North America be replaced with SJU, which I suggest is a much more accurate term for this type of unionism than either social or social movement unionism, and differentiates progressive trade unionism in North America from the type of unionism practiced, at least initially, by CUT, KMU, and COSATU.

41. For an initial effort to theorize these different approaches, see Scipes, 2010a: 130–152.

42. Ross (2008) argues that not all social unions are democratically run and criticizes this; as shown, I incorporate her understanding into my conceptualization of social justice unionism.

My conceptualization anticipates her critique and recognizes that not all social justice unions are democratically run—for example, I would place the UAW (United Auto Workers) and the SEIU (Service Employees International Union) in this category, as well as, following Ross (2008: 134), the Canadian District of the United Steelworkers of America. However, I would place social justice unions as a whole not in a dichotomy between democratic/not democratic unionism, but on a continuum, with the UAW and SEIU toward the "not democratic" end, with CUPE (Canadian Union of Public Employees), CUPW (Canadian Union of Postal Workers), the UE (United Electrical Workers), the ILWU (International Longshore and Warehouse Union) and the late UPWA (United Packinghouse Workers of America) toward the more democratic end.

43. I commented specifically on this point. "I had initially given the union a score of 28/30. However, on January 27, 2001, in an interview with Les Orear—who had gone into the stockyards as a labor organizer in 1933, was one of the founding members of Local 347 in Armour, one of the founding of the [United Packinghouse Workers of America], and who after 1947 served on the international staff of the UPWA and later, after the merger, the Amalgamated Meat Cutters and Butcher Workmen of North America until he retired in 1977—I asked him to evaluate the [Packinghouse Workers Organizing Committee]/UPWA on the basis of my measurement scale. It turns out, in Orear's opinion, that I had been too conservative: he said the union should have gotten 29/30, not just 28. (I had not been sure that elections for top-level officers were recorded by roll call vote, which he assured me they had.) Accordingly, I changed my rating based on Orear's account. (The one place that the union failed was that the top officers did not reflect rank and file gender demographics.)" Scipes, 2003: 63, Note #46.

44. Accordingly, after recognizing the qualitative differences between SMU and SJU, it will be necessary to review the (now) SJU literature (from Moody onward) after "removing" the attributes included from the specific "southern" unions, and theoretically solidify the concept.

Likewise, the "cleansed" SMU literature needs to be clarified and theoretically solidified, based on sets of practices.

Epilogue

In this book, I have argued that we need to build global labor solidarity among workers of the world—both among and between workers in both the Global South and the Global North—and this book is intended to advance this project by sharing some experiences known only by a relatively few people around the world. In other words, I have not argued that global labor solidarity will emerge "automatically" or that it is "desirable" by all workers, but have argued that *if* we want it, here are some lessons we can learn from these earlier struggles that might help us in today's struggles.

In this book I have shown:

- we do not have to start from scratch, that there is a lot to learn from efforts to create international labor solidarity in period between 1978–2010;
- that one of the most important things we can learn from building international labor solidarity is that there are experiences beyond ours from which we can learn; arguably, the most important are from struggles to create a new type of trade unionism, "social movement unionism" (SMU), by workers in particular labor centers—*Central Única dos Trabalhadores* (CUT), *Kilusang Mayo Uno* (KMU), and the Congress of South African Trade Unions (COSATU)—in Brazil, the Philippines, and South Africa, respectively;
- that SMU transcends the weaknesses of traditional economic and political unionism, and thus would be an advance over trade unionism in particularly the more economic developed countries such as the United States;
- that the best theoretical conceptualization of SMU developed to date has been based on the *Kilusang Mayo Uno* (KMU) Labor Center of the Philippines;

- that KMU is an exemplary case of SMU and, thus, to argue there is much to learn from their experiences;
- that this conceptualization of SMU is not confined to the Philippines, but can be extended to explain the development of COSATU in South Africa, at least up to the early 1990s, meaning that it is possible to implement SMU in both the Newly Industrialized Countries (NICs) as well as the near-NICs;
- that the KMU has developed a unique program consciously to build international labor solidarity and has been implementing it annually since 1984; and finally,
- that all of this knowledge can be used to disentangle the incredible theoretical confusion among labor theorists and activists that has hobbled further theoretical and organizational development.

In short, I argue that building global labor solidarity requires the building of egalitarian, solidaristic relations with workers around the world—not seeing them as better or more advanced, but not behind anyone else, either—based on respect (see Scipes, 2014a, 2016b).

Thus, this collection has been intended to show to workers around the world that, collectively, we have a tremendous number of experiences that can be shared and used to learn from each other. In other words, as long as we do not confine ourselves to just our national situation, but combine each with knowledge and information from workers around the world, we can advance workers' struggles here in the United States and across the world, and improve working people's lives as we work for a better world for each of us.

References[1]

Adler, Glenn, Judy Maller and Eddie Webster. 1992. "Unions, Direct Action and Transition in South Africa" in Norman Etherington, ed., *Peace, Politics and Violence in the New South Africa.* London: Hans Zell Publishers: 306–343.
Adler, Glenn and Eddie Webster. 1995. "Challenging Transition Theory: The Labor Movement, Radical Reform, and Transition to Democracy in South Africa." *Politics and Society,* Vol. 23, No. 1, March: 75–106.
American Labor. 1984. "Face to Face: An Inside View of Labor in Nicaragua." *American Labor,* No. 24.
Angus, Ian. 2016. *Facing the Anthropocene: Fossil Capitalism and the Crisis of the Earth System.* New York: Monthly Review Press.
Arnesen, Eric. 1998. "Up From Exclusion: Black and White Worker, Race and the State of Labor History." *Reviews in American History,* March: 146–174.
Aronowitz, Stanley. 1973. *False Promises: The Shaping of American Working Class Consciousness.* New York: McGraw Hill Book Company.
Asian Labour Monitor. 1987. *Min-ju No-jo: South Korea's New Trade Unions.* Hong Kong: Asian Monitor Research Center.
Barchiesi, Franco. 2007. "Privatization and the Historical Trajectory of 'Social Movement Unionism': A Case Study of Municipal Workers in Johannesburg, South Africa." *International Labor and Working Class History,* No. 71, Spring: 50–69.
Barry, Tom and Deb Preusch. 1986. *AIFLD in Latin America: Agents as Organizers.* Albuquerque, NM: Inter-Hemispheric Resource Center.
Baskin, Jeremy. 1991. *Striking Back: A History of COSATU.* Johannesburg: Ravan Press.
Bass, George Nelson III. 2012. "Organized Labor and US Foreign Policy: The Solidarity Center in Historical Context." Unpublished Ph.D. Dissertation, Department of Political Science, Florida International University, Miami. On-line at http://digitalcommons.fiu.edu/etd/752.

Battista, Andrew. 2002. "Unions and Cold War Foreign Policy in the 1980s: The National Labor Committee, the AFL-CIO, and Central America." *Diplomatic History,* Vol. 26, No. 3 (Summer): 419–451.

Bello, Walden. 1988. "Counterinsurgency's Proving Ground: Low Intensity Warfare in the Philippines" in Michael T. Klare and Peter Kornbluh, eds., *Low Intensity Warfare: Counterinsurgency, Proinsurgency, and Antiterrorism in the Eighties.* New York: Pantheon Books. On-line at https://archive.org/details/lowintensity warf00klar.

Bello, Walden, David Kinley and Elaine Elinson. 1982. *Development Debacle: The World Bank in the Philippines.* San Francisco: Institute for Food and Development and Philippine Solidarity Network.

Bernhard, Michael H. 1993. *The Origins of Democratization in Poland: Workers, Intellectuals, and Oppositional Politics, 1976–1980.* New York: Columbia University Press.

Beynon, Huw and Jose Ramalho. 2000. "Democracy and Class Struggle in Brazil" in Leo Panitch and Colin Leys, eds., *Socialist Register, 2001.* London: Merlin Press: 219–237.

Bezuidenhout, Andries. 2002. "Toward Global Social Movement Unionism? Trade Union Responses to Globalization in South Africa" in Jose, ed.: 373–406.

Bieler, Andreas and Ingemar Lindberg, eds. 2011. *Global Restructuring, Labour and the Challenges for Transnational Solidarity.* London and New York: Routledge.

Bieler, Andreas, Ingemar Lindberg and Devan Pillay, eds. 2008. *Labour and the Challenges of Globalization: What Prospects for Transnational Solidarity?* London and Ann Arbor: Pluto Press.

Bloom, Jack M. 2014. *Seeing Through the Eyes of the POLISH Revolution: Solidarity and the Struggle Against Communism in Poland.* Chicago: Haymarket Press.

Blow, Charles M. 2010. "Suffer the Little Children." *New York Times,* December 24. On-line at www.nytimes.com/2010/12/25/opinion/25blow.html.

Bluestone, Barry and Bennett Harrison. 1982. *The Deindustrialization of America: Plant Closings, Community Abandonment, and the Dismantling of Basic Industry.* New York: Basic Books.

Bonnell, Victoria. 1983. *Roots of Rebellion: Workers' Politics and Organization in St. Petersburg and Moscow, 1900–1914.* Berkeley and Los Angeles: University of California Press.

Bonner, Phil. 1987. "Overview: Strikes and the Independent Trade Unions" in Maree, ed.: 55–61.

Boyce, James. 1993. *The Philippines: The Political Economy of Growth and Impoverishment in the Marcos Era.* Honolulu: University of Hawaii Press.

Bramble, T. 2003. "Social Movement Unionism Since the Fall of Apartheid: The Case of NUMSA on the East Rand" in T. Bramble and F. Barchiesi, eds., *Rethinking the Labour Movement in the New South Africa.* Aldershot: Ashgate: 187–204.

Brecher, Jeremy and Tim Costello. 1988. "Labor Internationalism." *Zeta Magazine* (later renamed Z), November: 98–104.

———. 1991a. "Labor Goes Global: I—Global Village vs. Global Pillage." *Z Magazine,* January: 90–97.

———. 1991b. "Labor Goes Global: II—A One World Strategy for Labor." *Z Magazine,* March: 88–97.

Brenner, Johanna. 1998. "On Gender and Class in US Labor History." *Monthly Review,* Vol. 50, No. 6, November.

Broad, Robin. 1988. *Unequal Alliance: The World Bank, the International Monetary Fund, and the Philippines.* Berkeley and Los Angeles: University of California Press.

Bronstein, Phil and David Johnson. 1985. "US Funding Anti-Left Fight in the Philippines." *San Francisco Examiner,* July 21: 1+.

Brooks, Marissa and Jaime K. McCallum. 2017. "The New Global Labour Studies: A Critical Review." *Global Labour Studies,* Vol. 8, No. 3: 201–218. On-line at https://mulpress.mcmaster.ca/globallabour/article/view/3000.

Buhle, Mari Jo and Paul Buhle, eds. 2011. *It Started in Wisconsin: Dispatches from the Front Lines of the New Labor Protest.* New York: W.W. Norton.

Buhle, Paul. 1999. *Taking Care of Business: Samuel Gompers, George Meany, Lane Kirkland, and the Tragedy of American Labor.* New York: Monthly Review Press.

Buhlungu, Sakhela, ed. 2006. *Trade Unions and Democracy: COSATU Workers' Political Attitudes in South Africa.* Cape Town: HSRC Press.

Bureau of Labor Statistics, US. 2019. "Report #1082: Labor Force Characteristics by Race and Ethnicity, 2018." On-line at https://www.bls.gov/opub/reports/race-and-ethnicity/2018/home.htm.

———. 2020. "News Release: "The Employment Situation: January 2020." On-line at https://www.bls.gov/news.release/empsit-2.pdf.

Burowoy, Michael. 2009. "The Global Turn: Lessons from Southern Labor Scholars and Their Labor Movement." *Work and Occupations,* Vol. 36, No. 2, May: 87–95.

Butler, Alice. 1988. "ILR interview with Crispin Beltran." *International Labour Reports,* No. 27–28, Summer: 18–19.

Cantor, Daniel and Juliet Schor. 1987. *Tunnel Vision: Labor, the World Economy and Central America.* Boston: South End Press.

Carew, Anthony. 2018. *American Labour's Cold War Abroad: From Deep Freeze to Détente, 1945–1970.* Edmonton, Alberta, Canada: AU Press, Athabasca University.

Cella, G. and T. Treu. 1987. "National Trade Union Movements" in R. Blanpain, ed., *Comparative Labor Law and Industrial Relations,* 3rd Ed. Deventer (Netherlands): Kluwer: 197–228.

Chau, Michelle, Kalyani Thampi, and Vanessa R. Wight. 2010. "Basic Facts About Low-income Children, 2009." National Center for Children in Poverty, Mailman School of Public Health, Columbia University, New York: October. On-line at www.nccp.org/publications/pub_975.html, accessed May 16, 2013.

Chhachhi, Amrita and Renee Pittin. 1991. "Multiple Identities, Multiple Strategies: Confronting State, Capital and Patriarchy." Paper given to the "International Workshop on Women Organizing in the Process of Industrialisation." The Hague: Institute of Social Studies, April 15–26.

Chun, Soonok. 2003. *They Are Not Machines: Korean Women Workers and Their Fight for Democratic Trade Unionism in the 1970s.* Aldershot, UK: Ashgate.

Ciccariello-Maher, George. 2013a. *We Created Chavez: A People's History of the Venezuelan Revolution.* Durham: Duke University Press.

———. 2013b. "Constituent Moments, Constitutional Processes, and the Latin American Left" in Ellner, ed.: 126–145.

———. 2014. "Constituent Moments, Constitutional Processes: Social Movements and the New Latin American Left" in Ellner, ed.: 227–248.

Clawson, Dan. 2003. *The Next Upsurge: Labor and the New Social Movements.* Ithaca and London: Cornell University Press.

Cole, Pater. 2013. "No Justice, No Ships Get Loaded: Political Boycotts on the Durban and San Francisco Bay Waterfronts." *International Journal of Social History,* Vol. 58, No. 2: 185–217.

———. 2018. *Dockworker Power: Race and Activism in Durban and the San Francisco Bay Area.* Urbana and Chicago: University of Illinois Press.

Cole, Peter, David Struthers and Kenyon Zimmer, eds. 2017. *Wobblies of the World: A Global History of the IWW.* London: Pluto.

Collins, Joseph. 1989. *The Philippines: Fire on the Rim.* San Francisco: Institute of Food and Development Policy.

Collombat, Thomas. 2011. "Several Souths: The Dynamics of the International Labor Movement in the Americas." Unpublished Ph.D. Dissertation, Political Science Department, Carleton University, Ottawa, Ontario, Canada. On-line at www.ieim.uqam.ca/IMG/pdf/these-Collombat-2010.pdf.

Conrad, Lee. 1985. "IBM Resistors." *International Labour Reports,* No. 8, March–April: 14–17.

COSATU. 1992. *Our Political Economy: Understanding the Problems.* Johannesburg: COSATU Education.

Daenekindt, Roger. 1996. *Exchange Notes on Philippine Labor.* Quezon City: Labor Service Center.

Darnovsky, Marcy, Barbara Epstein, and Richard Flacks, eds. 1995. *Cultural Politics and Social Movements.* Philadelphia: Temple University Press.

Dejillas, Leopoldo J. 1994. *Trade Union Behavior in the Philippines, 1946–1990.* Quezon City: Ateneo de Manila University Press.

Delacruz, Enrique, Aida Jordan and Jorge Emmanuel, eds. 1987. *Death Squads in the Philippines.* San Francisco: Alliance for Philippine Concerns.

DeNavas-Walt, Carmen, Bernadette D. Proctor and Jessica C. Smith. 2012. "Income, Poverty and Health Insurance Coverage in the United States: 2011." US Census Bureau, Current Population Reports, P60–243, September. Washington, DC: US Government Printing Office.

Devinatz, Victor G. 2008. "Social-Movement Unionism and U.S. Labor's Uncertain Future." *Journal of Collective Negotiations,* Vol. 32, No. 3: 203–213.

Deyo, Frederic. 1989. *Beneath the Miracle: Labor Subordination in the New Asian Industrialism.* Berkeley and Los Angeles: University of California Press.

Diokno, Ramon. 1946/1987. "Ramos Violates the Constitution" in Schirmer and Shalom, eds.: 90–94.

Dobrusin, Bruno. 2014. "South-South Labor Internationalism: SIGTUR and the Challenges to the Status Quo" in Scipes, ed., 2014: 155–167.

Dollars and Sense. 1985. "Free Trade Zones: Putting Asian Women on Assembly Lines." *Dollars and Sense,* March.

Dreiling, Michael and Ian Robinson. 1998. "Union Responses to NAFTA in the US and Canada: Explaining Intra- and International Variation." *Mobilization,* Vol. 3, No. 1, October: 163–184.

Dropkin, Greg. 1985. "The Making of the 'Superfed.'" *International Labour Reports,* No. 12, November–December: 18–21.

Dunn, Bill. 2007. "Problems of Social Movement Unionism" in Andrew Gamble, Steve Ludham, Andrew Taylor, and Stephen Wood, eds. *Labor, The State, Social Movements and the Challenge of Neo-liberalism.* Manchester: Manchester University Press: 131–146.

Early, Steve. 2009. *Embedded with Organized Labor: Journalistic Reflections on the Class War at Home.* New York: Monthly Review.

———. 2011. *The Civil Wars in US Labor: Birth of a New Workers' Movement or Death Throes of the Old?* Chicago: Haymarket Books.

Early, Steve and Rand Wilson. 1986. "Organizing High Tech: Unions and Their Future." *Labor Research Review,* Vol. 1, No. 8.

Eckstein, Enid. 1986. "What is the AFL-CIO Doing in the Philippines?" *Labor Notes,* July: 5.

EILER. 1988. *GTU: Course on Genuine Trade Unionism.* Quezon City, Metro Manila: Ecumenical Institute for Labor Education and Research.

Eimer, Stuart. 1999. "From 'Business Unionism' to 'Social Movement Unionism': The Case of the AFL-CIO Milwaukee County Labor Council." *Labor Studies Journal,* Vol. 24, No. 2, Summer: 63–81.

Eisenhower, Kay. 1991. "AFL-CIO Agency Offers Cash to Filipino Union Leader for Vote on US Bases Treaty." *Labor Notes,* November: 1, 6.

Ellner, Steve. 2008. *Rethinking Venezuelan Politics: Class, Conflict and the Chavez Phenomenon.* Boulder, CO: Lynne Rienner.

———. 2013. "Social and Political Diversity and the Democratic Road to Change in Venezuela" in Ellner, ed.: 63–82.

———. 2014. "Social and Political Diversity and the Democratic Road to Change in Venezuela" in Ellner, ed.: 79–102.

———, ed. 2013. "Latin America's Radical Left in Power: Complexities and Challenges in the Twenty-first Century." *Latin American Perspectives,* Vol. 40, No. 3, May.

———, ed. 2014. *Latin America's Radical Left: Challenges and Complexities of Political Power in the Twenty-first Century.* Lanham, MD: Rowman and Littlefield.

Emma, Caitlin. 2020. "Federal Deficit to Top $1 Trillion Under Trump." *Politico,* January 28. On-line at https://www.politico.com/news/2020/01/28/federal-deficit-one-trillion-trump-107901.

Fairbrother, Peter. 2008. "Social Movement Unionism or Trade Unions as Social Movements." *Employee Responsibilities and Rights Journal,* Vol. 20: 213–220.

Fairbrother, Peter and Edward Webster. 2008. "Social Movement Unionism: Questions and Possibilities." *Employee Responsibilities and Rights Journal,* Vol. 20: 309–313.

Fairbrother, Peter and Charlotte Yates, eds. 2003. *Trade Unions in Renewal: A Comparative Study.* London: Continuum.

Fantasia, Rick. 1988. *Cultures of Solidarity: Consciousness, Action and Contemporary American Workers.* Berkeley and Los Angeles: University of California Press.

Fantasia, Rick and Kim Voss. 2004. *Hard Work: Remaking the American Labor Movement.* Berkeley and Los Angeles: University of California Press.

Fitz, Don. 1987. "The Scottish Caterpillar Sit-down of 1987." *Workers' Democracy,* Spring: 1–8.

———. 1988. "Solidarity Protects Spanish Dockers from Attack by Shipping Companies." *Labor Notes,* April: 11.

———. 1990. *"La Coordinadora:* A Union Without Bureaucrats" in Don Fitz and David Roediger, eds., *Within the Shell of the Old: Essays on Workers' Self-Organization.* Chicago: Charles H. Kerr: 88–96.

Fletcher, Bill, Jr., and Fernando Gapasin. 2008. *Solidarity Divided: The Crisis in Organized Labor and a New Path Toward Social Justice.* Berkeley and Los Angeles: University of California Press.

Fox-Hodess, Katy. 2017. "(Re-) Locating the Local and National in the Global: Multi-Scalar Political Alignment in Transnational European Dockers' Union Campaigns." *British Journal of Industrial Relations,* Vol. 55, No. 3: 626–647.

———. 2018. "Dockworkers of the World Unite: Transnational Class Formation and the New Internationalism." Unpublished Ph.D. Dissertation, Department of Sociology, University of California-Berkeley.

———. 2019. "Worker Power, Trade Union Strategy, and International Connections: Dockworker Unionism in Colombia and Chile." *Latin American Politics and Society.* Vol. 61, No. 3, August: 29–54.

———. 2020. "Building Labor Internationalism 'From Below': Lessons from the International Dockworkers' Council's European Working Group." *Employment and Society*, January 23. On-line at https://doi.org/10.1177/0950017019862969.

Freeman, Richard B. and James L. Medoff. 1984. *What Do Unions Do?* New York: Basic Books.

Freire, Paulo. 1984. *Pedagogy of the Oppressed.* New York: Continuum.

Friedman, Steven. 1987. *Building Tomorrow Today: African Workers in Trade Unions, 1970–1985.* Johannesburg: Ravan Press.

Friedman, Thomas L. 1999. *The Lexus and the Olive Tree: Understanding Globalization.* New York: Picador.

Fuentes, Annette and Barbara Ehrenreich. 1983. *Women in the Global Factory.* Boston: South End Press.

Garton Ash, Timothy. 1983. *The Polish Revolution: Solidarity 1980–82.* London: Jonathan Cape Ltd.

Garver, Paul. 1989. "Beyond the Cold War." *Labor Research Review,* No. 13, Spring: 61–71.

Gereffi, Gary. 1990. "Paths to Industrialization: An Overview" in Gary Gereffi and Donald L. Wyman, *Manufacturing Miracles: Paths of Industrialization in Latin America and East Asia.* Princeton: Princeton University Press: 3–31.

Gindin, Sam. 1995. *The Canadian Auto Workers: The Birth and Transformation of a Union.* Toronto: Lorimer.

Giugni, Marco, Doug McAdam and Charles Tilly, eds. 1999. *How Social Movements Matter.* Minneapolis and London: University of Minnesota Press.
Goba, Bonganjalo. 1988. *An Agenda for Black Theology: Hermeneutics for Social Change*. Johannesburg: Skotaville Publishing.
Golden, Miriam. 1988. *Labor Divided: Austerity and Working-Class Politics in Contemporary Italy.* Ithaca: Cornell University Press.
Goodwin, Jeff, James M. Jasper, and Francesca Polletta, eds. 2001. *Passionate Politics: Emotions and Social Movements.* Chicago and London: University of Chicago Press.
Gray, Kevin. 2008. *Korean Workers and Neoliberal Globalization.* London and New York: Routledge.
Greenhouse, Steven. 2008. *The Big Squeeze: Tough Times for the American Worker.* New York: Alfred A. Knopf.
Guidry, John A. 2003. "Not Just Another Labor Party: The Workers' Party and Democracy in Brazil." *Labor Studies Journal,* Vol. 28, No. 1, Spring: 83–108.
Hale, Angela and Jane Wills. 2007. "Women Working Worldwide: Transnational Networks, Corporate Social Responsibility and Action Research." *Global Networks,* Vol. 7, No. 4: 453–476.
Halle, David. 1984. *America's Working Man: Work, Home and Politics Among Blue-Collar Property Owners.* Chicago and London: University of Chicago Press.
Halpern, Rick. 1997. *Down on the Killing Floor: Black and White Workers in Chicago's Packinghouses, 1904–54.* Urbana and Chicago: University of Illinois Press.
Halpern, Rick and Roger Horowitz, eds. 1999. *Meatpackers: An Oral History of Black Packinghouse Workers and Their Struggle for Racial and Economic Equality.* New York: Monthly Review.
Haworth, Nigel and Harvie Ramsay. 1984. "Grasping the Nettle: Problems with the Theory of International Trade Union Solidarity" in Peter Waterman, ed., 1984: 60–85.
———. 1988. "Workers of the World Untied: International Capital and Some Dilemmas in Industrial Democracy" in Roger Southall, ed.: 306–331.
Hedges, Chris and Joe Sacco. 2012. *Days of Destruction, Days of Revolt.* New York: Nation Books.
Herod, Andrew. 2003. "Geographies of Labor Internationalism." *Social Science History,* Vol. 27, No. 4, Winter: 501–523.
Hindson, Doug. 1987. "Overview: Trade Unions and Politics" in Maree, ed.: 208–217.
Hirsch, Fred and Virginia Muir. 1987. "A Plumber Gets Curious About Exporting McCarthyism" in Ann Fagan Ginger and David Christiano, eds., *The Cold War Against Labor.* Berkeley: Meiklejohn Civil Liberties Institute: 723–768.
Hirschsohn, Philip. 1998. "From Grassroots Democracy to National Mobilization: COSATU as a Model of Social Movement Unionism." *Economic and Industrial Democracy,* Vol. 19: 633–666.
———. 2007. "Union Democracy and Shopfloor Mobilization: Social Movement Unionism in South African Auto and Clothing Plants." *Economic and Industrial Democracy,* Vol. 28: 6–48.
Hodson, Randy. 1991. "The Active Worker: Compliance and Autonomy at the Workplace." *Journal of Contemporary Ethnography,* Vol. 20, No. 1, April: 47–78.

Hopkins, Terence K. and Immanuel Wallerstein. 1970. “The Comparative Study of National Societies” in Amitai Etzioni and Fredric Dubow, eds., *Comparative Perspectives: Theory and Methods.* Boston: Little, Brown: 183–204.

Horowitz, Roger. 1997. *Negro and White, “Unite and Fight!” A Social History of Industrial Unionism in Meatpacking, 1930–90.* Urbana and Chicago: University of Illinois Press.

Howard, Stuart. 1985. “In Our Name: American Workers Challenge AFL-CIO Foreign Policy and Operations.” *International Labour Reports,* No. 12, November–December: 11–14.

Huber, Sonia and Stephanie Luce. 2001. “Building Social Movement Unionism: Jobs with Justice at 14.” *Labor Notes,* October.

Hunt, Scott A., Robert D. Benford and David A. Snow. 1994. “Identity Fields: Framing Processes and the Social Construction of Movement Identities” in Laraña, Johnston and Gusfield, eds.: 185–208.

Hutchison, Jane. 1992. “Women in the Philippines Garments Exports Industry.” *Journal of Contemporary Asia,* Vol. 22, No. 4: 471–489.

ICFTU. 1984. *African Workers Under Apartheid.* Brussels: International Confederation of Free Trade Unions.

Ince, Anthony. 2007. “Beyond ‘Social Movement Unionism’? Understanding and Assessing New Wave Labour Movement Organizing.” Paper presented at conference on *Networked Politics: Rethinking Political Organisation in an Era of Movements and Networking,* June 3–5. Berlin: Rosa Luxemburg Foundation. (Thanks to Peter Waterman for this item.)

Institute for Industrial Education. 1979. “The Durban Strikes: South Africa 1973” in Robin Cohen, Peter C.W. Gutkind, and Phyllis Brazier, eds. *Peasants and Proletarians: The Struggles of Third World Workers.* New York: Monthly Review Press: 401–417.

International Labour Reports. 1985. “South Africa: Unity—A New Era for Independent Unions.” *International Labour Reports,* No. 12, November–December: 17–27.

———. 1986. “ILR Interview: Ron Todd, Chairperson, British TUC International Committee.” *International Labour Reports,* No. 14, March–April: 16–18.

———. 1987. “ILR Interview: Dan Gallin: Not East or West but Below.” *International Labour Reports,* No. 20, March–April: 11–13.

———. 1989. “The National Endowment for Democracy: Winning Friends?” *International Labour Reports,* No. 33, May–June: 7–13.

Jackson, Henry. 1985. “We Can Fight.” *International Labour Reports,* No. 10, September–October: 13–17.

———. 1987. “‘Murdered,’ regarding the assassination of Rolando Olalia, Chair of KMU, and his driver, Leonor Alay-ay.” *International Labour Reports,* No. 19, January–February: 7–8.

Jaffee, David. 1990. *Levels of Socio-economic Development Theory.* New York: Praeger.

Jaffee, Sarah. 2016. *Necessary Trouble: Americans in Revolt.* New York: Nation Books.

Joffe, Avril, Judy Maller and Eddie Webster. 1995. "South Africa's Industrialisation in the Challenge Facing Labour" in S. Frenkel and J. Harrod, eds. *Changing Labor Relations in Industrializing Countries.* Ithaca: Cornell University Press: 88–109.

Johnston, Hank, Enrique Laraña and Joseph Gusfield. 1994. "Identities, Grievances, and New Social Movements" in Laraña, Johnston and Gusfield, eds.: 3–35.

Johnston, Hank and Bert Klandermanns. 1995. "The Cultural Analysis of Social Movements" in Johnston and Klandermanns, eds.: 3–24.

Johnston, Hank and Bert Klandermanns, eds. 1995. *Social Movements and Culture.* Minneapolis: University of Minnesota Press.

Johnston, Paul. 1994. *Success While Others Fail: Social Movement Unionism and the Public Workforce.* Ithaca: ILR Press.

———. 2001. "Organize for What? The Resurgence of Labor as a Citizenship Movement" in Turner, Katz and Hurd, eds.: 27–58.

Jose, A.V., ed. 2002. *Organized Labour in the 21st Century.* Geneva: International Institute for Labour Studies.

Karmel, Rachel. 1990. *The Global Factory: Analysis and Action for a New Economic Era.* Philadelphia: Americana Friends Service Committee.

Katsiaficas, George. 1987. *The Imagination of the New Left: A Global Analysis of 1968.* Boston: South End Press.

Kerkvliet, Benedict J. 1977. *The Huk Rebellion: A Study of Peasant Revolt in the Philippines.* Berkeley and Los Angeles: University of California Press.

Kerkvliet, Benedict J. and Resil B. Mojares, eds. 1991. *From Marcos to Aquino: Local Perspectives on Political Transition in the Philippines.* Manila: Ateneo de Manila University Press and Honolulu: University of Hawaii Press.

Klein, Naomi. 2015. *This Changes Everything: Capitalism vs. The Climate.* New York: Simon and Schuster.

KMU. 1993. "The ICFTU: Tainted with Blood and Bribery." *South African Labour Bulletin,* Vol. 17, No. 5, September–October: 60–65.

Kohn, Melvin L. 1987. "Cross-National Research as an Analytic Strategy." *American Sociological Review,* Vol. 52, No. 6, December: 713–731.

Koo, Hagen. 2001. *Korean Workers: The Culture and Politics of Class Formation.* Ithaca and London: Cornell University Press.

Kraak, Gerald. 1993. *Breaking the Chains: Labour in South Africa in the 1970s and 1980s.* London and Boulder, CO: Zed Press.

Kretzschmar, Louise. 1986. *The Voice of Black Theology in South Africa.* Johannesburg: Ravan Press.

Krugman, Paul. 2008. "Poverty is Poison." *New York Times,* February 18. On-line at www.nytimes.com/2008/02/18/opinion/18krugman.html.

Kumar, Pradeep and Gregor Murray. 2006. "Innovation in Canadian Unions: Patterns, Causes and Consequences" in Kumar and Schenck, eds., 2006.

Kumar, Pardeep and Chris Schenk, eds. 2006. *Paths to Union Renewal: Canadian Experiences.* Peterborough, Ontario: Boradview.

Labor Notes. 1986a. "International Solidarity Highlights Labor Notes Conference." *Labor Notes,* December: 8–9.

———. 1986b. "Philippine Union Leader Murdered, Military Blamed." *Labor Notes,* December: 9.

Laclau, Ernesto and Chantal Mouffe. 1981. "Socialist Strategy: What Next?" *Marxism Today,* Vol. 25, No. 1, January: 17–22.

Lambert, Rob. 1988. "Political Unionism in South Africa: The South African Congress of Trade Unions, 1955–65." Ph.D. Thesis, University of the Witwatersrand, Johannesburg.

———. 1989. "Social Movement Unionism: The Urgent Task of Definition. Comments on Peter Waterman's 'Brief Note on Social Movement Unionism.'" Unpublished paper. Perth: University of Western Australia.

———. 1990. "*Kilusang Mayo Uno* and the Rise of Social Movement Unionism in the Philippines." *Labour and Industry,* Vol. 3, No. 2 & 3, June–October: 258–280.

———. 2002. "Labor Movement Renewal in the Era of Globalization: Union Responses in the South" in Jeffrey Harrod and Robert O'Brien, eds. *Global Unions? Theory and Strategies of Organized Labour in the Global Political Economy.* London and New York: Routledge: 185–203.

Lambert, Rob and Eddie Webster. 1988. "The Re-emergence of Political Unionism in Contemporary South Africa?" in William Cobbett and Robin Cohen, eds., *Popular Struggles in South Africa.* London: James Currey: 20–41.

———. 2001. "Southern Unionism and the New Labor Internationalism." *Antipode,* Vol. 33, No. 3: 337–362.

Laraña, Enrique, Hank Johnston and Joseph Gusfield, eds. 1994. *New Social Movements: From Ideology to Identity.* Philadelphia: Temple University Press.

Larson, Simeon and Bruce Nissen, eds. 1987. *Theories of the Labor Movement.* Detroit: Wayne State University.

Lenin, V.I. 1953. "What Is To Be Done?" in V.I. Lenin, *Selected Works in Two Volumes,* Vol. 1, Part 1. London: Lawrence and Wishart Ltd.: 200–409.

Leonhardt, David. 2010. "In the Rearview, A Year that Fizzled," *New York Times,* December 29: B-1.

Lernoux, Penny. 1989. "Brute Force a Key to 'People Power' in the Philippines." *San Francisco Chronicle,* March 29: Briefing, 2.

Lewis, Jon. 1987. "Overview: The Registration Debate and Industrial Councils" in Maree, ed.: 170–175.

Lewis, Penny. 2013. *Hardhats, Hippies and Hawks: The Vietnam Anti-war Movement as Myth and Memory.* Ithaca and New York: ILR Press.

Lopez, Steven Henry. 2004. *Reorganizing the Rust Belt: An Inside Study of the American Labor Movement.* Berkeley and Los Angeles: University of California Press.

Luce, Stephanie. 2014. *Labour Movements: Global Perspectives.* Cambridge and Malden, MA: Polity Press.

Lydersen, Kari. 2009. "Forging International Labor Solidarity in Wartime No Easy Task." *Working In These Times.* Available on line at www.inthesetimes.com/working/entry/5271/international_unionists_and_war.

MacDonald, Oliver. 1981. *The Polish August: Documents from the Beginnings of the Polish Workers' Rebellion, Gdansk, August 1980.* (Much of this published by *Labour Focus on Eastern Europe,* Vol. 4, Nos. 1–3.) San Francisco: Ztangi Press.

MacShane, Denis, Martin Plaut and David Ward. 1984. *Power! Black Workers, Their Unions, and the Struggle for Freedom in South Africa.* Boston: South End Press.
Marcuse, Peter. 1995. "Transitions in South Africa: To What?" *Monthly Review,* November: 38–52.
Maree, Johann. 1987. "Overview: Emergence of the Independent Trade Union Movement" in Maree, ed.: 1–11.
Maree, Johann and Debbie Budlender. 1987. "Overview: State Policy and Labour Legislation" in Maree, ed.: 116–123.
Maree, Johann, ed. 1987. *The Independent Trade Unions, 1974–1984: Ten Years of the South African Labour Bulletin.* Johannesburg: Ravan Press.
Marx, Anthony W. 1992. *Lessons of Struggle: South African Internal Opposition, 1960–1990.* New York and Oxford: Oxford University Press.
———. 1998. *Making Race and Nation: A Comparison of the United States, South Africa and Brazil.* Cambridge: Cambridge University Press.
Marx, Karl. 1967/1867. *Capital,* Volume 1. New York: International Publishers.
Marx, Karl and Friedrich Engels. 1978/1848. "Manifesto of the Communist Party" in Robert C. Tucker, ed., *The Marx-Engels Reader,* 2nd Edition. New York and London: W.W. Norton & Company: 469–500.
Mason, Paul. 2012. *Why It's Kicking Off Everywhere: The New Global Revolutions.* London and New York: Verso.
Mathers, Andy. 2007. *Struggling for a Social Europe: Neoliberal Globalization and the Birth of a European Social Movement.* Aldershot, Hampshire: Ashgate.
McAdam, Doug. 1982. *Political Process and the Development of Black Insurgency, 1930–1970.* Chicago and London: University of Chicago Press.
———. 1989. "The Biographical Consequences of Activism." *American Sociological Review,* Vol. 54, No. 5, October: 744–760.
———. 1994. "Culture and Social Movements" in Laraña, Johnston and Gusfield, eds.: 36–57.
———. 1996. "The Framing Function of Movement Tactics: Strategic Dramaturgy in the American Civil Rights Movement" in McAdam, McCarthy and Zald: 338–355.
McAdam, Doug, John D. McCarthy and Mayer N. Zald. 1996. "Introduction: Opportunities, Mobilizing Structures, and Framing Processes—Toward a Synthetic, Comparative Perspective on Social Movements" in McAdam, Doug, John D. McCarthy and Mayer N. Zald, eds.: 1–20.
McAdam, Doug, John D. McCarthy and Mayer N. Zald, eds. 1996. *Comparative Perspectives on Social Movements: Political Opportunities, Mobilizing Structures, and Cultural Framings.* Cambridge: Cambridge University Press.
McAdam, Doug and David A. Snow. 1997. "Introduction—Social Movements: Conceptual and Theoretical Issues" in *Social Movements: Readings on Their Emergence, Mobilization, and Dynamics.* Los Angeles: Roxbury Publishing Company: xviii–xxvi.
McAdam, Doug and David A. Snow, eds. 1997. *Social Movements: Readings on Their Emergence, Mobilization, and Dynamics.* Los Angeles: Roxbury Publishing Company.

McCoy, Alfred W. 2009. *Policing America's Empire: The United States, the Philippines, and the Rise of the Surveillance State.* Madison: Center of Southeast Asian Studies, University of Wisconsin Press: 433–451.

———. 2017. *In the Shadows of the American Century: The Rise and Decline of US Global Power.* Chicago: Haymarket Press.

McCoy, Alfred W. and Ed. C. de Jesus, eds. 1982. *Philippine Social History: Global Trade and Local Transformations.* Quezon City: Ateneo de Manila University Press.

McMahon, Tim. 2020. "Current U-6 Unemployment Rate." February 7. On-line at https://unemploymentdata.com/current-u6-unemployment-rate/.

McMichael, Philip. 2012. *Development and Social Change: A Global Perspective,* 5th Ed. Thousand Oaks, CA: Sage.

Melucci, Alberto. 1989. *Nomads of the Present: Social Movements and Individual Needs in Contemporary Society.* London: Hutchinson Radius.

———. 1994. "A Strange Kind of Newness: What's 'New' in New Social Movements?" in Laraña, Johnston and Gusfield, eds.: 101–130.

———. 1995. "The Process of Collective Identity" in Johnston and Klandermanns, eds.: 41–63.

———. 1996. *Challenging Codes: Collective Action in the Information Age.* Cambridge: Cambridge University Press.

Mercado, Monina Allarey. 1986. *An Eyewitness History: People Power—The Philippine Revolution of 1986.* Manila: The James B. Reuter, S.J., Foundation.

Meyer, David S. and Suzanne Staggenborg. 1996. "Movements, Countermovements, and the Structure of Political Opportunity." *American Journal of Sociology,* Vol. 101, No. 6, May: 1628–1660.

Milkman, Ruth. 2006. *L.A. Story: Immigrant Workers and the Future of the U.S. Labor Movement.* New York: Russell Sage Foundation.

Milkman, Ruth and Kim Voss. 2004. "Introduction" in Ruth Milkman and Kim Voss, eds. *Rebuilding Labor: Organizing and Organizers in the New Union Movement.* Ithaca and London: Cornell University Press: 1–16.

Moghadam, Valentine M. 2020. *Globalization and Social Movements: The Populist Challenge and Democratic Alternatives*, 3rd ed. Lanham, MD: Rowman & Littlefield.

Moody, Kim. 1988. "*Min-ju no-jo* Tells Story of South Korea's New Trade Unions." *Labor Notes,* April: 10.

———. 1997. *Workers in a Lean World: Unions in the International Economy.* London and New York: Verso.

Mueller, Carol. 1994. "Conflict Networks and the Origins of Women's Liberation" in Laraña, Johnston, and Gusfield, eds.: 234–263.

Munck, Ronaldo. 1988. *The New International Labour Studies: An Introduction.* London and Atlantic Highlands, NJ: Zed Books.

———. 2010. "Globalization and the Labour Movement: Challenges and Responses." *Global Labour Journal,* Vol. 1, No. 2. On-line at https://escarpmentpress.org/globallabour/issue/view/123.

Nastovski, Katherine. 2014. "Workers Confront Apartheid: Comparing Canadian Labor Solidarity Campaigns Against South African and Israeli Apartheid" in Scipes, ed. 2014: 211–237.

———. 2016a. "Worker-to-Worker: A Transformative Model of Solidarity—Lessons from Grassroots International Labor Solidarity in Canada in the 1970s and 1980s" in Kim Scipes, ed.: 49–77.

———. 2016b. "Towards Transformative Solidarities: Wars of Position in the Making of Labour Internationalism in Canada." Unpublished PhD dissertation. Toronto: York University. Link: https://yorkspace.library.yorku.ca/xmlui/bitstream/handle/10315/33340/Nastovski_Katherine_2016_Phd.pdf?sequence=2&isAllowed=y.

Nederveen Pieterse, Jan. 1989. *Empire and Emancipation: Power and Liberation on a World Scale.* New York: Praeger.

———. 2015. *Globalization and Culture: Global Mélange,* 3rd Ed. Lanham, MD: Rowman and Littlefield.

Needleman, Ruth. 2003. *Black Freedom Fighters in Steel: The Struggle for Democratic Unionism.* Ithaca and London: Cornell University Press.

Nelson, Bruce. 2001. *Divided We Stand: American Workers and the Struggle for Black Equality.* Princeton: Princeton University Press.

Ness, Immanuel. 2016. *Southern Insurgency: The Coming of the Global Working Class.* London: Pluto Press.

New York Times. 2013. "Highlights of the July Unemployment Report." August 3: A-3.

Nichols, John. 2012. *Uprising: How Wisconsin Renewed the Politics of Protest, from Madison to Wall Street*. New York: Nation Books.

NILS. (Edited by Peter Waterman.) 1986. "Internationalisation and Internationalism." *Newsletter of International Labour Studies,* Nos. 30–31.

———. 1987. "Solidarnosc and International Labor Solidarity." *Newsletter of International Labour Studies,* Nos. 35–36.

———. 1988. "The New Internationalism and the New International Labour Studies." *Newsletter of International Labour Studies,* No. 39.

———. 1989. "USA: Beyond Trade Union Imperialism." *Newsletter of International Labour Studies,* Nos. 40–41.

Nissen, Bruce. 2003. "Alternative Strategic Directions for the US Labor Movement: Recent Scholarship." *Labor Studies Journal,* Vol. 28, No. 1: 133–155.

Nissen, Bruce, ed. 2002. *Unions in a Global Environment: Changing Borders, Organizational Boundaries, and Social Roles.* Armonk, NY and London: M.E. Sharpe.

O'Brien, Robert. 2019. *Labour Internationalism in the Global South: The SIGTUR Initiative.* Cambridge: Cambridge University Press.

Oliver, Pamela E. and Hank Johnston. 2000. "What a Good Idea! Ideologies and Frames in Social Movement Research." *Mobilization,* Vol. 5, No. 1, Spring: 37–51.

Olson, Mancur. 1965. *The Logic of Collective Action.* New York: Schocken.

Oxfam. 2020. "Poverty in the USA." On-line at https://policy-practice.oxfamamerica.org/work/poverty-in-the-us/.

Park, Mi. 2007. "South Korean Trade Union Movement at the Crossroads: A Critique of 'Social-Movement' Unionism." *Critical Sociology,* Vol. 33: 311–344.

Payer, Cheryl. 1974. *The Debt Trap: The International Monetary Fund and the Third World.* New York: Monthly Review Press.

Payumo, Felicito C. 1994. "Year-end Review and Prospects: A View from Congress." *Kasarinlan,* Vol. 10, No. 2, 4th Qtr.: 25–46.

Peijnenburg, Jeroen. 1984. "Workers in Transnational Corporations: Meeting the Corporate Challenge" in Peter Waterman, ed.: 107–117.

Perlman, Selig. 1968/1928. *A Theory of the Labor Movement.* New York: Augustus M. Kelley, Publishers.

Philippine Labor Alert. 1986a. "KMU Leads Huge May Day Rallies!" *Philippine Labor Alert,* No. 8, April–July: 1–2.

———. 1986b. "KMU Pushes for Promised Reforms." *Philippine Labor Alert,* No. 9, August–October: 4.

———. 1986c. "TUCP in Decline: Chickens Come Home to Roost." *Philippine Labor Alert,* No. 9, August–October: 5.

———. 1993. "KMU Moves Ahead Despite Split and Threatened Disaffiliations." *Philippine Labour Alert,* No. 29, September–December: 1–5.

Pillay, Devan. 1990. "COSATU: Driving Out Apartheid." *International Labour Reports,* No. 39, May–June: 7–10.

———. 2006. "COSATU, Alliances and Working-Class Politics" in Buhlungu, ed.: 167–198.

———. 2008. "Holding the Centre: Workers and 'Popular-Democratic' Politics in South Africa." *Journal of Asian and African Studies,* Vol. 3, No. 3: 279–305.

Pinto-Duschinsky, Michael. 1991. "Foreign Political Aid: The German Foundations and their US Counterparts." *International Affairs,* Vol. 67, No. 1: 33–63.

Piven, Frances Fox and Richard A. Cloward. 1979. *Poor People's Movements: Why They Succeed, How They Fail.* New York: Vintage Books.

Powell, Michael and Sewell Chan. 2011. "Slow Job Growth Dims Expectation of Early Revival: Unemployment rate is 9.4%—Recovery Could Require Another 4 or 5 Years, Fed's Chief Says." *New York Times,* January 18: A-1.

Rachleff, Peter. 2000. "'On the Ground' with the South African Labor Movement." *Macalester International,* Vol. 9, December 31. On-line at https://www.academia.edu/26130940/_On_the_Ground_with_the_South_African_Labor_Movement.

———. 2001. "The Current Crisis of the South African Labor Movement." *Labour/Le Travail,* Vol. 47, Spring: 151–169.

———. 2015. "From Racism to International Solidarity: The Journey of UAW Local 879, 1980–1995." *Working USA,* Vol. 18, No. 1, March: 127–135.

Radosh, Ronald. 1969. *American Labor and United States Foreign Policy.* New York: Random House.

Ragin, Charles C. 1987. *The Comparative Method: Moving Beyond Qualitative and Quantitative Strategies.* Berkeley and Los Angeles: University of California Press.

Reinsborough, Patrick and Doyle Canning. 2010. *Re-Imaging Change: How to Use Story-based Strategy, to Win Campaigns, Build Movements and Change the World.* Oakland: PM Press.

Rivera, Temario C. 1994. *Landlords and Capitalists: Class, Family, and State in Philippine Manufacturing.* Quezon City: Center for Integrative and Development Studies and University of the Philippines Press.

Robinson, Ian. 2002. “Does Neoliberal Restructuring Promote Social Movement Unionism? U.S. Developments in Comparative Perspective” in Nissen, ed.: 189–235.

Robinson, William I. 1996. *Promoting Polyarchy: Globalization, US Intervention, and Hegemony.* Cambridge: Cambridge University Press.

Robnett, Belinda. 1996. “African-American Women in the Civil Rights Movement, 1954–1965: Gender, Leadership, and Micromobilization.” *American Journal of Sociology,* Vol. 101, No. 6, May: 1661–1693.

Romm, Joseph. 2016. *Climate Change: What Everyone Needs to Know.* New York: Oxford University Press.

Ross, Stephanie. 2008. “Social Unionism and Membership Participation: What Role for Union Democracy?” *Studies in Political Economy,* No.81, Spring: 129–157.

Rueschemeyer, Dietrich. 1991. “Different Methods Contradictory Results? Research On Development and Democracy.” *International Journal of Comparative Sociology,* Vol. 32, No. 1–2: 9–38.

SACCAWU. 1991. *Sharing the Load: The Struggle for Gender Equality, Parental Rights and Childcare.* Johannesburg: South African Commercial, Catering and Allied Workers Union.

SALB. 1991. “Toward a New Labour Internationalism.” *South African Labour Bulletin,* Vol. 15, No. 7: 12–43.

Salgado, Pedro V. 1987. *The Philippine Economy: History and Analysis.* Quezon City: R.P. Garcia.

Schiavone, Michael. 2004. “Social Movement Unionism in North America: An Evaluation of Kim Moody’s Account.” Unpublished Ph.D. Dissertation, School of Social Sciences, Australian National University, Canberra.

———. 2007. “Moody’s Account of Social Movement Unionism: An Analysis.” *Critical Sociology,* Vol. 33: 279–309.

———. 2008. *Unions in Crisis? The Future of Organized Labor in America.* Westport, CT: Greenwood.

Schirmer, Daniel B. and Stephen Rosskamm Shalom, eds. 1987. *The Philippines Reader: A History of Colonialism, Neocolonialism, Dictatorship and Resistance.* Boston: South End Press.

Scipes, Kim. 1984a. “Industrial Policy: Can It Lead the US Out of Its Economic Malaise?” *New Labor Review* [Labor Studies Program, San Francisco State University], No. 6, Spring: 27–54. Updated and republished in pamphlet form (December). Pamphlet on-line at https://yumpu.com/en/document/read/35435605/industrial-policy-can-it-lead-the-us-out-of-its-economic-malaise .

———. 1984b. “The Reagan Toll.” *International Labour Reports,* No. 6, November–December: 9–10.

———. 1985. “San Francisco Longshoremen: ‘When that ship came in, we were ready.’” *International Labour Reports,* No. 9, May–June: 12–13. (Republished herein as Chapter 1.)

———. 1986a. “The Labor Movement in the Philippines.” *Labor Notes,* April: 8–9, 13.

———. 1986b. “Trade Union Education in the Philippines: Its Role in the National Liberation Struggle.” *Trade Union Studies Journal* [London, England], No. 13, Summer: 18–19.

———. 1987a. "AFL-CIO's *International Bulletin* is Sophisticated Misinformation." *Labor Notes,* January: 15.
———. 1987b. "Putting Movement Back in the Labor Movement." *International Labour Reports,* No. 20, March–April: 5.
———. 1987c. "KMU: Building Rank and File Unionism in the Philippines." *ideas and action,* Spring: 12–15.
———. 1987d. "Building a Socialist Labor Movement in the United States." *Workers' Democracy*, No. 25, Fall: 3–7.
———. 1988a. "Building the New Shop Floor Internationalism." *Workers' Democracy,* No. 26: 8–15. (Reprinted herein as Chapter 2.)
———. 1988b. "Learning from the KMU: Alliance Building." *Workers' Democracy,* No. 28 (Conference on WSO, Second Issue.) Reprinted in Don Fitz and David Roediger, eds., *Within the Shell of the Old: Essays on Workers' Self-Organization.* Chicago: Charles H. Kerr Publishing Company, 1990: 80–87. (Reprinted herein as Chapter 10.)
———. 1989a. "Trade Union Imperialism in the US Yesterday: Business Unionism, Samuel Gompers and AFL Foreign Policy." *Newsletter of International Labour Studies,* No. 40–41 (January–April): 4–20. [Subsequently updated and published as Chapter 1 in Scipes, 2010a.]
———. 1989b. "International Union of Food Workers Expels Philippine Affiliate." *Labor Notes,* April: 12.
———. 1989c. "The AFL-CIO Meddles in the Philippines." *The Progressive,* November: 33.
———. 1990a. "Aquino's Total War and the KMU." *Z Magazine,* January: 116–121.
———. 1990b. "Interview with Cleofe Zapanta, Secretary General of the KMK [women workers' organization] of the Philippines." *Z Magazine,* May: 105–107.
———. 1990c. "Three Weeks with the KMU of the Philippines." *Workers' Democracy,* No. 36, September–October: 1–7.
———. 1991a. "Social Movement Unionism in the Struggle to Build an Ecologically-sound Society in the United States." Unpublished MA Paper. The Hague: Institute of Social Studies.
———. 1991b. "Labor-Community Coalitions: Not All They're Cracked Up to Be." *Monthly Review,* Vol. 43, No. 7, December: 34–46. [A review of *Building Bridges: The Emerging Grassroots Coalition of Labor and Community,* edited by Jeremy Brecher and Tim Costello].
———. 1992a. "Social Movement Unionism and the Kilusang Mayo Uno." *Kasarinlan* [Third World Studies Center, University of the Philippines], Vol. 7, Nos. 2 & 3 (4th Qtr. 1991–1st Qtr. 1992): 121–162. (Reprinted herein, split into two chapters; as Chapters 6 and 8.) On-line at on-line at https://journals.upd.edu.ph/index.php/%20kasarinlan/article/view/1393/pdf_38.
———. 1992b. "Understanding the New Labor Movements in the 'Third World': The Emergence of Social Movement Unionism." *Critical Sociology,* Vol. 19, No. 2: 81–101. On-line at https://archiv.labournet.de/diskussion/gewerkschaft/smu/The_New_Unions_Crit_Soc.htm.

———. 1993. "Radical Labor in the Time of Marcos and Aquino: The Development of the *Kilusang Mayo Uno* (KMU)." *Solidarity* [Manila], No. 139–140, July–December: 35–68.
———. 1996. *KMU: Building Genuine Trade Unionism in the Philippines, 1980–1994.* Quezon City, Metro Manila: New Day Publishers.
———. 1999. "Global Economic Crisis, Neoliberal Solutions, and the Philippines." *Monthly Review,* Vol. 51, No. 7, December: 1–14. (Republished herein as Chapter 7.) On-line at http://monthlyreview.org/1999/12/01/global-economic-crisis-neoliberal-solutions-and-the-philippines/. [This article, with minimal editing, was republished as "Detrimental Development: The Global Economic Crisis and the Philippines." *Indicator South Africa: The Barometer of Social Trends* [University of Natal, Durban], Vol. 17, No. 1, March 2000: 87–90.]
———. 2000a. "Communicating Labor Internationalism: The KMU's 'International Solidarity Affair.'" January 3. On-line at http://globalsolidarity.antenna.nl/scipes.html. (Republished herein as Chapter 12.)
———. 2000b. It's Time to Come Clean: Open the AFL-CIO Archives on International Labor Operations." *Labor Studies Journal,* Vol. 25, No. 2, Summer: 4–25. [Posted on-line in English by LabourNet Germany at http://labournet.de/diskussion/gewerkschaft/scipes2.html.]
———. 2000c. "Social Movement Unionism: A Call for Theoretical Clarification." Comparative Labour Movements Research Committee (RC44) *Newsletter* [Johannesburg], International Sociological Association, December: 6.
———. 2001. "Social Movement Unionism: Can We Apply the Theoretical Conceptualization to the New Unions in South Africa—And Beyond?" Posted on-line in English on LabourNet Germany at https://archiv.labournet.de/diskussion/gewerkschaft/smuandsa.html [Incorrectly dated as 2003.] (Split in half, and republished herein as Chapters 5 and 11.)
———. 2003. "Trade Union Development and Racial Oppression in Chicago's Steel and Meatpacking Industries, 1933–1955." Unpublished Ph.D. Dissertation, Department of Sociology, University of Illinois at Chicago. (Available under my full name, Steven R. "Kim" Scipes.)
———. 2007. "Neo-Liberal Economic Policies in the United States: The Impact on American Workers." *Z Net,* February 2. On-line at https://zcomm.org/znetarticle/neo-liberal-economic-policies-in-the-united-states-by-kim-scipes.
———. 2009a. "Neoliberal Economic Policies in the United States: The Impact of Globalization on a 'Northern' Country." *Indian Journal of Politics and International Relations,* Vol. 2, No. 1, January–June: 12–47. On-line at https://zcomm.org/znetarticle/neo-liberal-economic-policies-in-the-united-states-by-kim-scipes-1/.
———. 2009b. "It's Time for a Deep Green Vision for the United States—and the World." *Synthesis/Regeneration: A Magazine of Green Social Thought,* No. 48, Winter: 8–11. On-line at http://www.greens.org/s-r/48/48-04.html.
———. 2010a. *AFL-CIO's Secret War against Developing Country Workers: Solidarity or Sabotage?* Lanham, MD: Lexington Books. (Published in paperback in 2011.)

———. 2010b. "Why Labor Imperialism? AFL-CIO Foreign Policy Leaders and the Developing World." *Working USA: The Journal of Labor and Society,* Vol. 13, No. 4, December: 465–479.

———. 2012a. "Globalization from Below: Labor Activists Challenging the AFL-CIO Foreign Policy Program." *Critical Sociology,* Vol. 38, No. 2: 303–323. On-line at https://www.researchgate.net/publication/254084376_globalization_from_below.

———. 2012b. "A Look Back at the Wisconsin Uprising: A Review Essay of *It Started in Wisconsin: Dispatches from the Front Lines of the New Labor Protest,* ed. by Mari Jo Buhle and Paul Buhle; *Uprising: How Wisconsin Renewed the Politics of Protest, from Madison to Wall Street* by John Nichols; and *Wisconsin Uprising: Labor Fights Back,* ed. by Michael D. Yates." *Z Net,* July 18. [Republished February 16, 2017, and on-line at www.substancenews.net/articles.php?page=6674.

———. 2013. "The Logic of Needed Social Change: US Empire, US Capitalism and Global Climate Change." *Z Net,* February 26. On-line at https://zcomm.org/znet article/three-legs-of-needed-social-change-us-empire-us-capitalism-and-global-climate-change-by-kim-scipes/.

———. 2014a. "Theoretical Reflections on the Emergence of *Global* Labor Solidarity." *Working USA: The Journal of Labor and Society,* Vol. 17, No. 2, June: 145–154.

———. 2014b. "Building Global Labor Solidarity Today: Learning from the KMU of the Philippines." *Class, Race and Corporate Power,* Vol. 2, No. 2 (July). Also published in Scipes, ed., 2016: 139–152. On-line at http://digitalcommons.fiu.edu/classracecorporatepower/vol2/iss2/2.

———. 2014c. "Social Movement Unionism or Social Justice Unionism? Disentangling Theoretical Confusion within the Global Labor Movement." *Class, Race and Corporate Power.* Vol. 2: Iss. 3, Article 9 (December). On-line at http://digitalcommons.fiu.edu/classracecorporatepower/vol2/iss3/9. Published herein as Chapter 13.

———. 2015a. "Celebrating May Day, KMU Style." *Countercurrents.org,* October 8. On-line at https://www.countercurrents.org/scipes121115.htm.

———. 2015b. "Peter Waterman's Recent Attack on the KMU of the Philippines, and My Work, Is Scurrilous: Kim Scipes Responds to Unprincipled and Inaccurate Attack." *Countercurrents.org.* November 15. On-line at https://www.countercurrents.org/scipes121115.htm.

———. 2016a. "Labour Imperialism" in Immanuel Ness and Zak Cope, eds. *The Palgrave Encyclopedia or Imperialism and Anti-Imperialism.* London: Palgrave Macmillan: 1294–1304.

———. 2016b. "Introduction" to Kim Scipes, ed.: 1–21. On-line at https://www.academia.edu/25374866/INTRODUCTION_to_Scipes_ed_Building_Global_Labor_Solidarity.

———. 2016c. "Multiple Fragments—Strengths or Weakness? Theorizing Global Labor Solidarity" in Kim Scipes, ed.: 23–48. (Available for downloading at https://www.researchgate.net/publication/315617986_Multiple_Fragments--Strengths_or_Weaknesses_Theorizing_Global_Labor_Solidarity.

———. 2017a. "Addressing Seriously the Environmental Crisis: A Bold, 'Outside the Box' Suggestion for Addressing Climate Change and other Forms of Environmental Destruction." *Class, Race and Corporate Power,* Vol. 5, Issue 1, Article 2 (April). On-line at http://digitalcommons.fiu.edu/classracccorporatepower/vol5/iss1/2.

———. 2017b. "The Epic Failure of Labor Leadership in the United States, 1980–2017 and Continuing." *Class, Race and Corporate Power,* Vol. 5, Issue 2, Article 5 (October). On-line at https://digitalcommons.fiu.edu/classracecorporatepower/vol5/iss2/5/.

———. 2018a. "I Read the News Today, Oh Boy! Observations from a Week in the Philippines." *Counterpunch,* August 6. On-line at https://www.counterpunch.org/2018/08/06/i-read-the-news-today-oh-boy-observations-from-a-week-in-the-philippines/.

———. 2018b. "Another Type of Trade Unionism *IS* Possible: The KMU Labor Center of the Philippines and Social Movement Unionism." *The Journal of Labor and Society,* Vol. 21, No. 3, September: 349–367. On-line at https://www.researchgate.net/publication/327472612_Another_type_of_trade_unionism_IS_possible_The_KMU_Labor_Center_of_the_Philippines_and_social_movement_unionism.

———. 2019. "*Labour Internationalism in the Global South: The SIGTUR Initiative* by Robert O'Brien: A Review Essay by Kim Scipes." *Labor and Society,* Vol. 22, No. 4: 920–925.

———. 2020a. "Is It Time for a New Labor Center in the United States? New Thinking on the Crisis of Labor." *Z Net,* February 19. On-line at https://zcomm.org/znetarticle/is-it-time-for-a-new-labor-center-in-the-united-states/.

———. 2020b. "Innovations in Labor Studies—Incorporating Global Perspectives: From Exhortation to Making It Real." *Class, Race and Corporate Power*, Vol. 8, No. 1, Article 1. On-line at https://digitalcommons.fiu.edu/classracecorporatepower/vol8/iss1/1/.

Scipes, Kim, ed. 2014. "Global Labor Solidarity." A special thematic issue of *Working USA: The Journal of Labor and Society,* Vol. 17, No. 2, June: 141–288.

———. 2016. *Building Global Labor Solidarity in a Time of Accelerating Globalization.* Chicago: Haymarket Books.

Seidman, Gay W. 1994. *Manufacturing Militance: Workers' Movements in Brazil and South Africa, 1970–1985.* Berkeley and Los Angeles: University of California Press.

———. 2011. "Social Movement Unionism: From Description to Exhortation." *South African Review of Sociology,* Vol. 42, No. 3: 94–102.

Shalom, Stephen Rosskamm. 1981. *The United States and the Philippines: A Study of Neocolonialism.* Philadelphia: Institute for the Study of Human Issues, Inc.

Sharpe, Teresa. 2004. "Union Democracy and Successful Campaigns: The Dynamics of Staff Authority and Worker Participation in an Organizing Union" in Milkman and Voss, eds.: 62–87.

Shiva, Vandana. 2005. *Earth Democracy: Justice, Sustainability and Peace.* Cambridge, MA: South End Press.

Shorrock, Tim and Kathy Selvaggio. 1986. "Which Side Are You On, AAFLI?" *The Nation,* February 15: 170–173.

Sims, Beth. 1992. *Workers of the World Undermined: American Labor's Role in US Foreign Policy.* Boston: South End Press.

Skocpol, Theda and Margaret Somers. 1980. "The Uses of Comparative History in Macrosocial Inquiry." *Comparative Studies in Society and History,* Vol. 22: 174–197.

Slaney, Dave. 1988. "Solidarity and Self-Interest." *NACLA Report,* Vol. 22, No. 3: 28–36

Slaughter, Jane. 1988. "Auto Workers Find Companies' Drive for Flexibility and Teamwork is International." *Labor Notes,* April: 7, 11.

Sluyter-Beltrão, Jeffrey. 2010. *Rise and Decline of Brazil's New Unionism: The Politics of the Central Única dos Trabalhadores.* Bern: Peter Lang.

Smith, Joseph B. 1981. *Portrait of a Cold Warrior: Second Thoughts of a Top CIA Agent.* New York: Ballantine Books.

Snow, David A., E. Burke Rochford, Jr., Steven K. Worden and Robert D. Benford. 1997/1986. "Frame Alignment Processes, Micromobilization, and Movement Participation" in McAdam and Snow, eds.: 235–251.

Song, Ho Keun. 2002. "Labour Unions in the Republic of Korea: Challenge and Choice" in Jose, ed.: 199–237.

Southall, Roger, ed. 1988. *Trade Unions and the New Industrialization of the Third World.* London: Zed Press.

Spaulding, Hobart. 1988a. "AIFLD Amok." *NACLA Report,* Vol. 22, No. 3: 20–27.

———. 1988b. "US Labour Intervention in Latin America: The Case of the American Institute for Free Labour Development" in Roger Southall, ed.: 259–286.

Spooner, Dave. 1989. *Partners or Predators: International Trade Unionism and Asia.* Hong Kong: Asia Labour Monitor.

Stangelaar, Fred. 1986. "An Outline of Basic Principles of Alternative Communication" in Peter Waterman, ed.: 11–22.

Starr, Amory. 2005. *Global Revolt: A Guide to Movements Against Globalization.* London and New York: Zed.

Street, Paul. 1993. "Working in the Yards: A History of Class Relations in Chicago's Meatpacking Industry, 1886–1960." Unpublished Ph.D. Dissertation, Department of History, SUNY at Binghamton.

Tait, Vanessa. 2005. *Poor Workers' Unions: Rebuilding Labor From Below.* Cambridge, MA: South End Press.

Tattersall, Amanda. 2009. "A Little Help from Our Friends: Exploring and Understanding When Labor-Community Coalitions Are Likely to Form." *Labor Studies Journal,* Vol. 34, No. 4, December: 485–506.

Thomson, Don and Rodney Larson. 1978. *Where Were You, Brother? An Account of Trade Union Imperialism.* London: War on Want.

TIE (Transnational Information Exchange). 1983. "Left-Hand Drive: Shopfloor Internationalism and the Auto Industry." *Transnationals Information Exchange-Europe,* No. 16, September.

———. 1984. "Brazil—The New Militancy: Trade Unions and Transnational Corporations." *TIE Report,* No. 17.

Tilly, Charles. 1984. *Big Structures, Large Processes, Huge Comparisons.* New York: Russell Sage Foundation.

Tomaselli, Keyan G. and P. Eric Louw. 1989. "Alternative Press and Practice: The South African Struggle" in Marc Raboy and Peter A. Bruck, eds., *Communication For and Against Democracy.* Montreal and New York: Black Rose Books: 203–220.

Turner, Lowell and Richard W. Hurd. 2001. "Building Social Movement Unionism: The Transformation of the American Labor Movement" in Turner, Katz and Hurd, eds.: 9–26.

Turner, Lowell, Harry C. Katz and Richard W. Hurd, eds. 2001. *Rekindling the Movement: Labor's Quest for Relevance in the 21st Century.* Ithaca and London: Cornell University Press.

Upchurch, Martin and Andy Mathers. 2012. "Neoliberal Globalization and Trade Unionism: Toward Radical Political Unionism?" *Critical Sociology,* Vol. 38, No. 2, March: 265–280.

Upchurch, Martin, Graham Taylor and Andrew Mathers. 2009. *The Crisis of Social Democratic Trade Unionism in Western Europe: The Search for Alternatives.* Farnham, Surry: Ashgate.

US Bureau of Labor Statistics, Employment Situation News Release, The Employment Situation, January 2013.

US Department of Health and Human Services. 2013. Annual Update of the HSS Poverty Guidelines, January 24. On-line at https://www.federalregister.gov/articles /2013/01/24/2013-01422/annual-update-of-the-hhs-poverty-guidelines.

Vandenberg, Arthur. 2006. "Social-movement Unionism in Theory and in Sweden." *Social Movement Studies,* Vol. 5, No. 2, September: 171–191.

Von Holdt, Karl. 2002. "Social Movement Unionism: The Case of South Africa." *Work, Employment and Society,* Vol. 16, No. 2, June: 283–304.

———. 2003. *Transition from Below: Forging Trade Unionism and Workplace Change in South Africa.* Pietermaritzburg (South Africa): University of Natal Press.

Voss, Kim and Rachel Sherman. 2000. "Breaking the Iron Law of Oligarchy: Union Revitalization in the American Labor Movement." *American Journal of Sociology,* Vol. 106, No. 2: 303–349.

Wallerstein, Immanuel. 1974. *The Modern World System.* New York: Academic Press.

Waterman, Peter. 1985. "Communicating Labour Internationalism: A Review of Relevant Literature and Resources." The Hague: Institute of Social Studies *Working Paper,* No. 28, September.

———. 1986. "WFTU: Money for Love?" *International Labor Reports,* No. 15, May–June: 22.

———. 1988a. "Needed: A New Communications Model for a New Working-Class Internationalism" in Roger Southall, ed.: 351–378.

———. 1988b. "From 'Global Information' to 'Internationalist Communication': Reconceptualizing the Democratization of International Communication." The Hague: Institute of Social Studies, *Working Paper,* No. 39, May.

———. 1988c. "The New Internationalisms: A More Real Thing Than Big, Big Coke?" *Review* [Fernand Braudel Center, Binghamton University], Vol. 11, No. 3, Summer: 289–328.

———. 1988d. "For the Liberation of Internationalism: A Long March Through the Literatures." The Hague, Institute of Social Studies, *Working Paper,* No. 42, September.

———. 1988e. "Social Movement Unionism: A Brief Note." Unpublished paper. The Hague: Institute of Social Studies.

———. 1990. "One, Two, Three, Many New Internationalisms! On a New Third World Labor Internationalism and Its Relationship to Those of the West and East." The Hague: Institute of Social Studies, *Working Paper,* No. 76, March.

———. 1991a. "A New Internationalism: What Content and What Form?" *South African Labour Bulletin,* Vol. 16, No. 2, October–November: 69–75.

———. 1991b. "'Social Movement Unionism': Beyond 'Economic' and 'Political' Unionism." *Working Paper,* No. 19. Amsterdam: International Institute for Research and Education.

———. 1993. "Social Movement Unionism: A New Model for a New World." *Review,* Vol. 16, No. 3: 245–278.

———. 1998. *Globalization, Social Movements and the New Internationalisms.* London and Herndon, VA: Mansell Publishing.

———. 1999. "The New Social Unionism: A New Union Model for a New World" in Ronaldo Munck and Peter Waterman, eds. 1999. *Labour Worldwide in the Era of Globalization.* London: Palgrave Macmillan: 247–264.

———. 2004. "Adventures of Emancipatory Labour Strategy as the New Global Movement Challenges International Unionism." *Journal of World Systems Research,* Vol. 10, No. 1, Winter: 217–253.

———. 2008. "Social Movement Unionism in Question: Contribution to a Symposium." *Employee Responsibilities and Right Journal,* Vol. 20: 303–308.

Waterman, Peter, ed. 1984. *For a New Labour Internationalism.* The Hague, Netherlands: ILERI Foundation.

———. 1986. *The Comintercomdoc Papers.* The Hague: ILERI Foundation.

Waterman, Peter and Jane Wills. 2001. "Space, Place and the New Labor Internationalisms? Beyond the Fragments? *Antipode,* Vol. 33, No. 3, July.

Watts, Simon and Henry Jackson. 1986. "Morong: Closed by People's Strike." *International Labour Reports,* No. 16, July–August: 17.

Webster, Eddie. 1984. "The International Metalworkers' Federation in South Africa (1974–1980)" in Peter Waterman, ed.: 213–230. (Originally appeared in *South African Labour Bulletin,* Vol. 9, No. 6: 72–94.)

———. 1987. "The Rise of Social Movement Unionism—The Two Faces of the Black Trade Union Movement in South Africa." Sociology Department, University of the Witwatersrand, Johannesburg.

Webster, Eddie, Rob Lambert and Andries Bezuidenhout. 2008. *Grounding Globalization: Labor in the Age of Insecurity*. Oxford: Blackwell.

Weinrub, Al and William Bollinger. 1987. *The AFL-CIO in Central America: A Look at the American Institute for Free Labor Development.* Oakland, CA: Labor Network on Central America.

Weir, Stan. 1987. "Dockers Fight for Control of Hiring: Spain and the US." *Workers' Democracy,* Winter: 1–10.

——— 2004. "Unions With Leaders Who Stay on the Job," in Stan Weir, *Singlejack Solidarity*, ed. by George Lipsitz. Minneapolis and London: University of Minnesota Press: 109–148.

West, Lois. 1991. "US Foreign Labor Policy and the Case of Militant Political Unionism in the Philippines." *Labor Studies Journal,* Vol. 16, No. 4, Winter: 48–75.

———. 1997. *Militant Labor in the Philippines.* Philadelphia: Temple University Press.

Wetzel, Tom. 1988. "When Bureaucrats 'Move Left': The Case of the CIO." *Ideas and action,* Fall: 15.

Williamson, Hugh. 1988. "Brand New Repression." *International Labour Reports,* Summer: 20–21.

Wilpert, Greg. 2007. *Changing Venezuela by Taking Power: The History and Politics of the Chavez Government.* London and New York: Verso.

Wilton, Robert D. and Cynthia Cranford. 2002. "Toward an Understanding of the Spatiality of Social Movements: Labor Organizing at a Private University in Los Angeles." *Social Problems,* Vol. 49, No. 3, August: 374–394.

Witt, Matt. 1990. "Mexico Must Be a Priority of US Labor Activists." *Labor Notes,* March: 10.

Wood, Geoffrey. 2003. "Solidarity, Representatively and Accountability: The Origins, State and Implication of Shopfloor Democracy within the Congress of South African Trade Unions." *Journal of Industrial Relations,* Vol. 45, No. 3, September: 326–343.

Yates, Michael D., ed. 2012. *Wisconsin Uprising: Labor Fights Back*. New York: Monthly Review Press.

Young, Josiah Ulysses, III. 1992. *A Pan-African Theology: Providence and the Legacies of the Ancestors*. Trenton, NJ: Africa World Press, Inc.

Zald, Mayer N. 2000. "Ideologically Structured Action: An Enlarged Agenda for Social Movement Research." *Mobilization,* Vol. 5, No. 1, Spring: 1–16.

Zweig, Michael. 2005. "Iraq and the Labor Movement: The Remarkable Story of USLAW." *New Labor Forum,* Vol. 14, No. 3: 61–67.

———. 2014. "Working for Global Justice in the New Labor Movement." *Working USA: The Journal of Labor and Society,* Vol. 17, No. 2, June: 261–281.

NOTE

1. URLs have been provided herein to facilitate access to materials on which this author has drawn. However, in the publishing process, many of the URLs have been broken, so it cannot be assumed that they will link properly when copied into a browser. At very least, check to see if spaces have been inserted when copied, and remove them. Also, if that does not help, copy the title of the item in quotes and place into Google—often times this approach will be successful. Along with that, of course, please remember that one problem with on-line resources is that they can be removed for moved from their present "site" at any time. Every effort has been made to make sure they are accurate at time of publication.

Index

About the Author

Kim Scipes, Ph.D., is a Professor of Sociology at Purdue University Northwest (PNW) in Westville, Indiana, where he has been teaching courses on Race and Ethnic Diversity; Developing Countries in a Globalizing World; Environment and Social Justice; Power, Social Control and the Media; and People's Movements and Social Power, as well as Introduction to Sociology, since August 2004. He has served as the founding editor (2000–2002) of *In Critical Solidarity,* the section newsletter of the Labor and Labor Movements Section of the American Sociological Association, and as an elected member of the Board (2006–2010) of Research Committee 44 (Labor) of the International Sociological Association.

Dr. Scipes has had a multifaceted career. He enlisted for four years in the U.S. Marine Corps (1969–73), eventually attaining the rank of Sergeant and an Honorable Discharge, while "turning around" against the US invasion of, and war in, Vietnam while on active duty; fortunately, he stayed in the United States for all four years. After leaving the military, he obtained his Bachelor's Degree *cum laude* at Florida State University (1975). Subsequently, he worked as a printer, inner city high school teacher, and office worker. Returning to academia in 1990, he attended and received a Master's Degree in [third world] Development Studies at the Institute of Social Studies in The Hague, The Netherlands (1991). He began his Ph.D. work in Sociology at the University of Wisconsin at Madison, and then transferred to the University of Illinois at Chicago, where he was awarded the Ph.D. in Sociology in 2003.

Dr. Scipes is the author of two previous books: *KMU: Building Genuine Trade Unionism in the Philippines, 1980–1994* (1996), and *AFL-CIO's Secret War against Developing Country Workers: Solidarity or Sabotage?* (2010). He also edited a collection in a volume titled *Building Global Labor Solidarity in a Time of Accelerating Globalization* (2016), and has published over 230 articles and book reviews since 1984. In addition to being published widely across the United States, Dr. Scipes's work has been published in 10 other countries around the world—in hard copy, on web sites, and both. Dr. Scipes has spoken at conferences around the world, and has given opening night and plenary speeches in Canada, Germany, South Africa and Vietnam. He taught courses on "Qualitative Research Methods" and "Sociology of Labor" at Ton Duc Thang University in Ho Chi Minh City, Vietnam during the summers of 2017 and 2018.

A long-time labor activist, he served as the North American representative of the British journal, *International Labour Reports,* from 1984–89. Dr. Scipes has also sat on the editorial board of *Labor Studies Journal,* and currently serves on the editorial boards of *The Journal of Labor and Society* as well as *Class, Race and Corporate Power* (both peer-reviewed), and is the Labor/Economics topic editor for the community-based journal, *Green Social Thought.*

Dr. Scipes has previously been a member of the Graphic Communications International Union, AFL-CIO; the American Federation of Teachers, AFL-CIO; and the National Education Association. He currently is a member of the National Writers Union, United Auto Workers #1981, AFL-CIO, and was elected as Chair of the Chicago chapter for two terms (2011–2015) and, accordingly, was a member of the National Executive Board of the union.

Dr. Scipes lives in Michigan City, Indiana, where he's a proud member of OUR MC, Organized and United Residents of Michigan City.

Dr. Scipes' publications are listed, with links to many original articles, at https://www.pnw.edu/faculty/kim-scipes-ph-d/publications/.

www.ingramcontent.com/pod-product-compliance
Ingram Content Group UK Ltd.
Pitfield, Milton Keynes, MK11 3LW, UK
UKHW041841031026
15587UKWH00002B/927

9 781793 631503